Boy Culture

Boy Culture

An Encyclopedia

Volume 1

Shirley R. Steinberg, Michael Kehler, and
Lindsay Cornish, Editors

GREENWOOD

AN IMPRINT OF ABC-CLIO, LLC
Santa Barbara, California • Denver, Colorado • Oxford, England

Library of Congress Cataloging-in-Publication Data

Boy culture : an encyclopedia / Shirley R. Steinberg, Michael Kehler, and Lindsay Cornish, editors.
      p. cm.
   Includes bibliographical references and index.
   ISBN 978-0-313-35080-1 (hard copy : alk. paper) — ISBN 978-0-313-35081-8 (e-book)
   1. Masculinity. 2. Stereotypes (Social psychology) I. Steinberg, Shirley R., 1952- II. Kehler, Michael. III. Cornish, Lindsay, 1979-
   BF692.5.B69 2010
   305.23081—dc22   2010021148

ISBN: 978-0-313-35080-1
EISBN: 978-0-313-35081-8

14 13 12 11 10   1 2 3 4 5

This book is also available on the World Wide Web as an eBook.
Visit www.abc-clio.com for details.

Greenwood
An Imprint of ABC-CLIO, LLC

ABC-CLIO, LLC
130 Cremona Drive, P.O. Box 1911
Santa Barbara, California 93116-1911

This book is printed on acid-free paper ∞
Manufactured in the United States of America

To our boys,

Ian, Chaim, Ryan, Cohen, Tobias, Seth, Milo Joe: as you grow, please keep your grossness, junior high jokes, and sense of transgression ever-present, keeping the spirit of little Jodie alive.

Shirley

To all boys and to girls who know those boys, Matthew, Claire, Justin, Nathan, Duncan and Arden.

Michael

Mike Trainor, Chris Cornish, Kevin Hurtubise, Chuck Hurtubise, and Mark Hurtubise, who will always be my boys.

Lindsay

Contents

Introduction:
Why Boy Culture?

Complex Boys in a Complex Cultural Landscape

To answer the question, why a book on boy culture, one need only look at the complex, rich, and sometimes troubling ways boys and boy culture manifests itself in North America. The reality of boys' lives and boy culture has not been well understood until more recent research began addressing the complexities of boys and boy culture within the area of masculinities research. (See, e.g., Brod and Kaufman, 1994; Connell, 1995, 2000; Kehler, 2000; Lesko, 2000; Mac an Ghaill, 1994; Martino and Pallotta-Chiarolla, 2005; Messner, 1997; Pascoe, 2007; Willis, 1977.) The emergence of men's studies and masculinities research comes out of feminist studies and gender research. Study after study has sought to examine the ways boys and masculine identities emerge within particular contexts.

Most significant perhaps is the work of Paul Willis, who in 1977 published *Learning to Labour.* In its time his work provided a major shift in the way male youth identities were examined and understood, uncovering and teasing out the complex relations that shaped the world of disaffected working class English males and their views of schooling and its relation to their anticipated adult lives. Later studies (Mac an Ghaill, 1994; Connell, 1995; Kehler, 2004; Pascoe, 2007; Skelton, 2001) continued to examine the nuanced and complicated ways masculinities emerged within specific contexts. In his 1994 work, *Making of Men,* Mac an Ghaill, for example, explored the interplay of schooling, sexuality, and masculinity. His work centered on inferring meanings by understanding the context and through participation in the life of the students and teachers. This kind of inquiry allowed him to understand in a deeper and richer vein the cultural production of different versions of masculinity. Connell's work, entitled *Masculinities,* highlighted the constant struggle for dominance in which certain types of masculine groups engage, and, conversely, the versions of masculinity that are oppressed in this struggle. Theoretically, Connell's work moved beyond naming groups of people and instead raised important questions for how patterns of gender and sexuality practices were examined and recorded. She provided a useful conceptual development by unsettling past rigid and linear notions of gender and sexualities and in there place pointed to relationships between bodies and social practice in a way that compelled researchers and ethnographers in particular to acknowledge the historicity of gender and the fundamental way masculinities were processes or what she referred to as *gender projects* located in particular times and places.

Individuals and the groups to which they belong are shaped by multiple and at times competing cultural influences. We may need to think of culture and specifically boy culture more as a performance or production constituted by discourses, practices, materials, and meanings that can be likened to sources of knowledge upon which individuals may draw to shape their identity.

This Encyclopedia

Hearn and Collinson (1994) acknowledge the difficulties in speaking of men and masculinity as a singular and monolithic entity. It is important to remind ourselves that categories are ever-changing and thus the very construction and invocation of categories must be interrogated. Hearn and Collinson note the importance of locating the discussion in a way that questions power and power relations. And while *Boy Culture: An Encyclopedia* is intended to be largely informative, it may at the same time serve as a springboard for raising broader questions about how cultural understandings, practices, and events are connected to particular ways of being boys and men. It may, moreover, lead to consideration of how particular masculinities are named and positioned in society. In this encyclopedia, the practices of masculinity or ways in which boys express various versions of masculinity are captured in the 167 entries, written by 116 knowledgeable experts and students of boy culture, and divided among these twelve broad sections:

- Becoming a Boy, Becoming a Man
- Differences and Boys
- Boys and Looks
- Boys and the Physical
- Boys in Mind, Boys in Relationships
- "Bad" Boys
- Boys on Screen
- Boys in Print
- Boys and Tunes
- Boys Play, Boys Learn
- Boys and Technology
- Boys and School

The range of topics across these sections reveal the multiple contexts in which boys and young men perform masculinities and, moreover, the way in which masculine identities are fluid, never stable, always changing. The practical everyday lives of young men and boys are at the core of this encyclopedia. The topics included are not exhaustive but rather suggestive of the many particular locations, contexts, and medium through which masculinities emerge. The entries range from, but are not limited to, cultural icons; the styles, the fashions, the struggles of boyhood; boys in print; boys and toys; boys on screen; and boys in music, but we do so not to suggest that these are the *only* places boys and boyhood are located, but rather to reflect that these are *some* of the places, representations, models, means, and mediums through which masculinity—and what it means to be a boy and be a man in North American culture—proliferates. In many cases the authors examine an aspect of culture that is largely but not exclusively masculine.

Almost every entry concludes with listings for useful further reading, and a general bibliography appears at the end of the encyclopedia.

The privileged status of masculinity and the power arrangements implicitly associated with being particular kinds of boys, as demonstrated in the host of entries included in this encyclopedia, are not questioned, but instead we, as the editors, note its existence through these entries. The landscape of boy culture is varied and problematic. Who is included and who is excluded, what is representative and what is not of the dailiness of being a boy, is an important if not central starting point for thinking about the range and possibilities for engaging with this book. We hope that this text is a useful reference as well as a rich and exciting entry point for probing further about how boy culture is defined and on what basis we define boy culture.

The Challenges of Being a Man

Assumptions underlying the routine discourse of masculinity suggest that there is but one way of being a man. One need only look in local bookstores at popular mainstream authors' books—such as Christina Hoff Sommers' *The War Against Boys* (2000), or Michael Gurian's *Saving Our Sons from Falling Behind in School and Life,* or Steven Biddulph's *Raising Boys: Why Boys Are Different and How to Help Them Become Happy and Well-balanced*—to see how concerns about boys and boy culture have taken hold in the public discourse. The problem however is that these books, primarily of a self-help nature, provide a limited and narrow conception of particular issues such as masculinity, achievement, and schooling. The range of issues addressing boys and masculinity that are currently scattered in book stores attempt to provide quick-fix and self-help advice for parents struggling to *understand* how they can help boys and young men. These authors suggest that boys, often defined in absolute terms, act and behave one way because they are *hard wired* as males. Contextually and culturally these authors provide little if anything about the popular culture of boys and young men and more about prescriptive ways to *help* or *save* boys. The suggestion is often times that boys need to be rescued from other forces that deny or prevent boys from fulfilling an inner, deeper masculine self. The assumption underlying much of the mainstream response to *help boys* is that there is one way to be a boy and schools and society more broadly are not allowing boys to be boys. The argument relies on a bio-determinist position by arguing that boys are more aggressive, more assertive, and more rational than girls, for example, because of biology. In short, this argument follows that boys are naturally one way while girls are the opposite. This dichotomous and essentialist framing of gender simplifies the complex negotiation of cultural practices that inform how and what boys and girls understand about appropriate forms of masculine and feminine identities. This position stands in stark contrast with masculinities and men's studies research in which boys routinely acknowledge the kinds of surveillance and policing of masculinities and clear codes of masculinities that guide and define masculine behavior.

The boy culture to which we refer to in this encyclopedia reflects a messy and ever changing repertoire of masculinities that are routinely negotiated in and between various contexts of some boys' everyday lives. We are not attempting to refute the biological arguments of these previous authors but rather want to suggest, through the collection of entries, that boy culture is complicated and varied. We need only look to the wealth of studies examining boys in school, for example, to understand the struggles among and between boys (see, e.g., Gilbert and Gilbert, 1998; Kehler, 2000; Lesko, 2000; Martino and Meyenn, 2001; Martino and Pallotta-Chiarolli, 2003; Pascoe, 2007). Messner reminds us that as a group, "men tend to pay heavy costs for their adherence to narrow definitions of masculinity. Because there are such vast differences and inequalities among men, it's impossible even to talk honestly about men *as* a coherent group" (1997, p. 8). As such, identity in the postmodern world needs to be considered as a multilayered, often contradictory construct formed at intersections in particular times and spaces. It is rarely permanent, stable, or uniform within any individual or group of individuals, but rather a construct that points to the fluidity and multiplicity of identities.

The difficulties of being a man and *doing* masculinity in what are determined to be appropriately masculine ways are complicated by the practices and cultural processes legitimated and valued in a cultural context. Kimmel (1994) aptly notes that masculinity is "a constantly changing collection of meanings that we construct through our relationships with ourselves, with each other, and with our world. . . . Manhood is neither static nor timeless; it is historical. Manhood does not bubble up to consciousness from our biological makeup; it is created in culture. Manhood means different things at different times to different people" (p. 120). It is difficult to capture, isolate, and clearly delineate boy culture because of its ever-changing nature and because of its historicity. In North America the everyday exchanges among boys and men are guided by a set of understandings about being men. These understandings are further bolstered by a dominant discourse of masculinity that suggests masculine identity is biologically determined and in short "boys will be boys." The struggle for most men is actually living up to the standard of masculinity, which is impossible for most but nonetheless revered by many. The strong, controlling, competitive, aggressive man typically associated with being a *real man* is repeatedly constructed and reconstructed in the marketplace.

There is a public face and public definition to masculinity. Connell (1987) describes this prevailing and dominant masculinity as "hegemonic masculinity." It is these very definitions and qualities of manhood that remain deep seated in cultural practices of masculinity. Manhood is tested and challenged in routine practices and through various representational tools such as the media not strictly to name what is masculine but also to name what is not masculine. Boys strive to distance themselves from anything that is remotely feminine. Kimmel (1994) explains that the cultural definition of masculinity is several stories. Men seek to accumulate those cultural symbols that denote manhood. Men also seek to have differential access to resources that exclude women and some men and through which cultural resources then are equated with a highly valued manhood. It is also about the power of definitions of manhood and the weight they carry over women and other men. Boyhood and boy culture is differently experienced by boys with uneven access to resources, boys with different positions of power, and boys with competing subjectivities. Not all boys know, engage with, or are similarly positioned within the same boy culture. For some, boy culture and boyhood look vastly different from what is captured in this volume of topics.

There is no one complete compendium of boy culture. Kaufman (1994), among others, describes this positioning of boys among boys and men among men within society and across cultural practices and institutions reserved for men and boys as a means for some men to affirm themselves and find common ground with other men (p. 151). The tension between men and boys is the unspoken yet clearly understood rules that guide them through the masculine maze so that they may prove they are men and, moreover, that they can demonstrate their masculinity in a convincing form. Mills (2001) describes the activities of risk and challenge typically witnessed and exercised by boys and men as a kind of "litmus test by which masculinities can be measured against each other and by which they can be contrasted with femininities" (p. 56). Peer groups are central as a context for proving oneself as a man. Boys seek and often times gain the approval of their male peers for what they know and can demonstrate. Routine conversations are ripe for demonstrating among boys what they know about such things as sport scores, cars, athletic events, physical abilities, and sex. The inability to share a familiarity or public signs of investment in boy culture is potentially damaging for these boys and men. They fail to measure up to the "mantle of masculinity" and run the real risk of harassment by their male peers (see, e.g., Mills, 2001). At the other end of the spectrum are young men and boys who both understand and invest in normative masculinity, and who, not surprisingly, are privileged because of the kind of cultural capital they possess among other boys.

The topics or entries we include in this volume are strictly that—topics and entries—and ought not be any indication of the endless ways in which boys engage with masculinity or masculinized practices. Images of masculinity are ever present and constantly shifting, yet the stranglehold of the media is considerable. "Media images of strong, muscular, athletic and active men are just one example of how hegemonic masculinity is stylized and inserted into the public realm . . . and although more than one kind of masculinity can be found within a cultural setting, hegemonic masculinity prevails, coercing society and thus young children to attain this type of 'normal' and desirable way of being" (Blaise, 2005, p. 58). Just as categories of men and types of boys are restrictive and potentially limiting in understanding masculinities, so too are topics that suggest they are more than a material, social, cultural point of entry to what is considered to be *masculine*. This is both a practical and conceptual note of caution then to our readers to fully acknowledge that the entries and topics are in and of themselves *created* just as the challenges to being a *real* man are created on the basis of unrealistic expectations and assumptions about masculinity.

The theorizing of masculinity is admittedly and intentionally less pedantic and hopefully less labored in this encyclopedia than one might find in, for example, academic texts aimed at deconstructing boy culture. We have purposefully developed a reference source intended to be accessible to a broad audience of readers. We do not subscribe to the position that there is one way of being a boy or a man. We reject the argument that being masculine is a biological determinant and fixed, just as we believe it is not so for being feminine. We are therefore advisedly cautious in preparing a volume about boy culture as a reference point but rather as an entry point for beginning a conversation and further examining some of the ways boy culture exists in North American society. There is nothing natural or unproblematic about the struggles, the icons, the boy toys, the illnesses, the media, and the music portrayals of boys and boyhood. One of the many aims in preparing this volume is to capture a broad array of flash points for examining, elaborating, extending, and questioning boy culture and perhaps debating the ways categories operate to define and restrict masculinity. The collective entries are not intended to end discussion with definitive answers to what is boy culture, but rather open discussion and provide informative insight to specific moments, places, acts, people, and medium through which we come to understand boy culture. This encyclopedia thus is not the end to a search, but rather a point to extend an exploration of boy culture and masculinity.

One Culture, One Boyhood?

As discussed above, boy culture is not easily defined or delineated from other cultural (re)presentations. Engaging or disengaging what has come to be understood as boy culture and therefore masculine involves acknowledging and accepting that masculinity is historically located. In short, the items, practices, and associations made at any one time are specific to the time, place, and raced, classed, gendered individuals for whom they hold significance. Not all items or practices of masculinity are equally relevant or significant for *all* boys. Each item and practice is imbued with a particular context in which and through which boys define themselves and others. Masculinities are produced and reproduced and as such are open to being negotiated and renegotiated among boys. Similarly masculinities are open to cultural variability and thus allowing for what it means to participate in boy culture or to *know* boy culture might vary between and within societies. There is a shift and slippage in North American culture that makes the definition of what is and will be boy culture relatively unstable. The instability and fluidity of masculinity is not a weakness but rather a strength in a deepening and broadening discourse about masculinities.

The power for many is how boy culture and the practices of being a boy are accepted and/or rejected. Martino and Pallotta-Chiarolli (2005) vividly and powerfully capture the impact gender normalization has on boys' and girls' school experiences. They highlight the troubling and problematic ways in which "the rhetoric informing many of the populist debates about the boys . . . [relies on] viewing boys through a normative and normalising lens, without differentiating hierarchical versions of masculinity" (p. 79). The ability to transgress normative masculinity is constrained by more powerful structural requirements of, for example, school culture. Butler (1999) describes the "unity of gender [as] the effect of a regulatory practice that seeks to render gender identity uniform through a compulsory heterosexuality." She further argues that "the force of this practice is, through an exclusionary apparatus of production, to restrict the relative meanings of 'heterosexuality,' 'homosexuality,' and 'bisexuality' as well as the subversive sites of their convergences and resignification" (p. 42). Butler extends her position arguing that if repetition is a mechanism of the cultural reproduction of identities, then it is crucial that we examine and more fully understand "What kind of subversive repetition might call into question the regulatory practice of identity itself?" (p. 42). Codes of masculinity and rules for expressing appropriate masculinity are two means through which masculinities simultaneously emerge and submerge. The prevalence of homophobia as a regulatory practice within boy culture operates then to demarcate boundaries of normative and transgressive masculinity. (See Martino & Pallotta-Chiarolla, 2005.) Within any one culture then there are a range of practices at work to maintain and perpetuate fundamental and core understandings of masculinity.

The Slippery Signs of Masculinity

In their discussion of the contemporary key debates addressing gender and achievement, Francis and Skelton (2005) go to great lengths to show the slippery signs of masculinity revealed in a raft of studies. While their book primarily addresses connections made between achievement levels and gender, they nonetheless offer a rich understanding of the many ways boys present themselves as boys. The negotiation of masculinities among and across groups of boys is unquestioned. The representation of masculinities as they are manifest in everyday interactions among boys are evidence of the powerful and damning effect constructions of masculinity, particularly those based in aggression, physical violence, intimidation, and derision, have on many of the people around them (Francis & Skelton, 2005). There is a wealth of research to indicate that being a boy and participating within boy culture involves a degree of impression management through which boys routinely maintain an identity that conforms to normative masculinity and rejects anything remotely feminine.

The entries contained in this encyclopedia reflect cultural understandings of boyhood. The selection of entries are not intended to reflect a core being of masculinity, but rather a set of sociocultural experiences that for some are quite common while for others they appear to be unfamiliar or remote. In short, not all boys will identify with or see themselves, their stories, their routines, or their ways of being a boy reflected in these entries. Connell (1995) reminds us that in addition to recognizing a diversity of masculinities, "we must also recognize the relations between the different kinds of masculinity: relations of alliance, dominance and subordination" (p. 37). She describes the differences among and between boys as a "gender politics within masculinity" based on "relationships [that] are constructed through practices that exclude and include, that intimidate, exploit and so on" (p. 37). The configurations of masculinity one witnesses on a daily basis are in part connected to the behaviors, attitudes, and actions deemed to be appropriately masculine in particular contexts. In short, this collection reveals the slipperiness or possible messiness in trying to name and identify boy culture as coherent and unified. The messiness of being a boy and attempting to at least define boy culture does not, of course, preclude us from considering how and to what extent boy culture is likely to be defined in concrete terms and by whom. We acknowledge the dangers in oversimplifying identities as a collection of cultural practices without examining how these practices are informed, why they are negotiated similarly and differently among boys, and what it means to hold some of these practices, icons, and historical moments of boy culture as more exalted than others.

In her introduction to *Slow Motion: Changing Masculinities, Changing Men*, Lynne Segal (1990) highlights her effort to look to the *differences* between men that are located in "the force and power of dominant ideals of masculinity" (p. x). Segal continues noting that the differences "do not derive from any intrinsic characteristic of individuals but from the social meanings which accrue to these ideals from their supposed superiority to that which they are not" (p. x). Her argument pivots around ever-changing political, social, and economic structures. There is then a level of uncertainty underscoring each of these structures; but it is because of the uncertainty and instability of these structures that change is bound to come forth in the various relations between men and women as well as between men among men. This sense of change, though slow in coming, is arguably captured in the efforts of profeminist men to be subversive by challenging and disrupting categories of sexual and gender identity. Gutterman (1994) describes this slipperiness of masculinity as it applies to profeminist men's efforts to work beside other men in a way that "dismantles the system from positions of power by challenging the very standards of identity that afford them normative status in the culture" (p. 229). In doing so, Gutterman notes the difficult and challenging work for boys and young men who seek to create change in relations not only with women but also with men among men. Change among men will not come about by repeatedly legitimating and empowering practices of masculinity that dominate and oppress others.

Boy Culture: An Encyclopedia serves as a resource for those interested in developing a broader picture of these practices and complex identities captured in a particular *boy culture* that, in varying degrees, has come to be understood as a representation of times, places, practices, and people among boys. We have produced what we consider to be a broad-reaching though admittedly incomplete set of entries to define boy culture. What we anticipate is that this encyclopedia prompts the discussion and the debate necessary to reconsider and possibly reconfigure our understandings of masculinity and boy culture in particular. To this end we offer this book as a powerful tool and as a vehicle for better knowing what is and what is not boy culture, what has been and what might be boy culture, and, moreover, to see between the gaps and silences in this text to begin redefining boy culture.

References

Biddulph, S. (1998). *Raising boys: Why boys are different—and how to help them become happy and well-balanced men.* Berkeley, CA: Celestial Arts.

Blaise, M. (2005). *Playing it straight: Uncovering gender discourses in the early childhood classroom.* New York: Routledge.

Brod, H., and Kaufman, M. (1994). *Theorizing masculinities.* Thousand Oakes, CA: Sage.

Butler, J. (1990). *Gender trouble: Feminism and the subversion of identity.* New York: Routledge.

Connell, R. W. (1987). *Gender and power.* Berkeley, CA: University of California Press.

Connell, R. W. (1989). Cool guys, swots and wimps: The interplay of masculinity and education. *Oxford Rev Educ, 15*(3), 291–303.

Connell, R. W. (1995). *Masculinities.* Berkeley, CA: University of California Press.

Connell, R. W. (2000). *The men and the boys.* Berkeley, CA: University of California Press.

Francis, B., and Skelton, C. (2005). *Reassessing gender and achievement: Questioning contemporary key debates.* Abingdon, UK: Routledge.

Gilbert, R., and Gilbert, P. (1998). *Masculinity goes to school.* London: Routledge.

Gurian, M. (2005). *The minds of boys: Saving our sons from falling behind in school and life.* San Francisco: Jossey Bass.

Gurian, M. (2001). *Boys and girls learn differently: A guide for teachers and parents.* San Francisco: Jossey-Bass.

Gutterman, D. (1994). Postmodernism and the interrogation of masculinity. In H. Brod and M. Kaufman (Eds.), *Theorizing masculinities* (pp. 219–238). Thousand Oaks: Sage.

Hearn, J., and Collinson, D. (1994). Theorizing unities and differences between men and between masculinities. In H. Brod and M. Kaufman (Eds.), *Theorizing masculinities* (pp. 97–118). Thousand Oaks, CA: Sage.

Kaufman, M. (1994). Men, feminism, and men's contradictory experiences of power. In H. Brod and M. Kaufman (Eds.), *Theorizing masculinities* (pp. 142–163). Thousand Oakes, CA: Sage.

Kehler, M. D. (2000). High school masculinity and gender politics: Submerged voices, emerging choices. Unpublished doctoral dissertation, Michigan State University, East Lansing, MI.

Kehler, M. D. (2004). Masculinities and resistance: High school boys (un)doing boy. *Taboo, 8*(1), 97–113.

Kehler, M. D., and Martino, W. (2007). Questioning masculinities: Interrogating boys' capacities for self-problematization in schools. *Canadian J Educ, 30*(1), 90–112.

Kimmel, M. (1994). Masculinity as homophobia: Fear, shame, and silence in the construction of gender identity. In H. Brod and M. Kaufman (Eds.), *Theorizing masculinities* (pp. 119–141). Los Angeles: Sage.

Lesko, N. (Ed.). (2000). *Masculinities at school.* Thousand Oakes, CA: Sage.

Mac an Ghaill, M. (1994). *The making of men: Masculinities, sexualities and schooling.* Buckingham, UK: Open University Press.

Martino, W., and Meyenn, B. (2001). *What about the boys? Issues of masculinity in schools.* Buckingham, UK: Open University Press.

Martino, W., and Pallotta-Chiarolli, M. (2003). *So what's a boy? Addressing issues of masculinity and schooling.* Buckingham, UK: Open University Press.

Martino, W., and Pallotta-Chiarolli, M. (2005). *"Being normal is the only way to be": Adolescent perspectives on gender and school.* Sydney, AU: University of New South Wales Press.

Messner, M. (1997). *Politics of masculinities: Men in movements.* Thousand Oaks, CA: Sage.

Mills, M. (2001). *Challenging violence in schools: An issue of masculinities.* Buckingham, UK: Open University Press.

Pascoe, C. J. (2007). *Dude you're a fag: Masculinity and sexuality in high school.* Berkeley, CA: University of California Press.

Pollack, W. S. (1998). *Real boys: Rescuing our boys from the myths of boyhood.* New York: Henry Holt.

Segal, L. (1990). *Slow motion: Changing masculinities, changing men.* New Brunswick, NJ: Rutgers University Press.

Skelton, C. (2001). *Schooling the boys: Masculinities and primary education.* Buckingham, UK: Open University Press.

Sommers, C. H. (2000). *The war against boys: How misguided feminism is harming our young men.* New York: Touchstone.

Willis, P. (1977). *Learning to labour: How working class kids get working class jobs.* New York: Columbia University Press.

Michael Kehler

PART I

What Makes a Boy a Boy?

SECTION 1

Becoming a Boy, Becoming a Man

Blue for Boys

What does the phrase *all boy* actually mean in our society? Many may know the research on gender stereotypes and try to ignore them, but often the stereotypes appear when a baby boy is born. The gifts he is given, the things people say to him, how people act toward him, how they expect him to act, and so forth, all abide by what our society has deemed as *masculine*.

Clothes and Toys

Often the gifts come pouring in before a baby boy (or girl) is even born. One constant theme remains consistent: blue = boy. Clothes, blankets, and bibs are blue—bright blue, baby blue, pastel blue, navy blue, and so forth. Additionally, items like the highchair, bouncer, swing, and tummy time mat are blue, as well. Often, no green, yellow, orange, purple, red, or certainly pink is anywhere to be found. The message becomes clear and a question is asked: Will *not* using blue make a boy less of a boy by society's standards and thus less masculine?

After an infant boy begins to grow in a typical North American home, the house will become full of *boy* toys: dinosaur toys, Spiderman toys, a rocking horse, a riding zebra, lots of Blue's Clues toys, Go Diego Go toys, stuffed Sesame Street characters and puppy dogs, and so forth. None of the toys will be pink or any shade of pink, none of the stuffed animals will wear dresses, and there will be no Dora the Explorer toys and no frilly *girly* toys.

North American consumer society has determined definite boundaries for boys, and those boundaries include blue and *tough* toys. It is amazing that even in the twenty-first century a walk through a toy store will feature scores of toys which are gendered, and often sexist. Many toy stores are huge manufacturing havens where gender is sold, and consumers are educated about what it means to be a little boy or a little girl. There are several main sections to any local toy store: the newborn/baby section, the girls' section, the boys' section, and the videogame section.

The newborn/baby section is where one can find unisex toys, as well as boy toys and girl toys—both signified by a specific color and specific animals. The boy toys are blue with animals such as puppies on them, whereas the girl toys are pink with kittens on them.

The girls' section in many toy stores has pink signs hanging from the ceiling over the department, whereas the boys' section has blue signs. The girls' section is full of toys that are fluffy, frilly, cuddly, cutesy, and pink. For Susie Homemaker, one will find such toys as kitchen sets, washers and dryers, baby buggies, cradles, tea sets, plastic foods, and so forth. And for many, there is the epitome of all things *girly*—Barbie.

In the boys' section, though, one finds quite the opposite types of toys. Their toys are not frilly and cutesy; instead they are *hard*. They tend to be more about destruction and killing rather than preserving and aiding. There are scary looking dinosaurs with blood dripping from their mouths, guns of all shapes and sizes with real sounding ammunition, remote-controlled cars, balls of all sports, and balls filled with slime, to name a few. Just as the girls have Barbie as their icon of all that is feminine, boys have their icon of all that is masculine—action figures. Although Barbie and the action figure are both dolls, one cannot call the action figure a *doll* and expect parents to purchase it for their sons, as that would go against society's apparent rules and norms.

The last section in the toy store may be the videogame section, which is separated into three main sections of its own: boys, girls, and unisex. The boys' games are just like the toys, consisting of sports, shooting/killing, and adventure, with titles such as *Madden NFL 08, Metroid Prime 3: Corruption, The Legend of Zelda: Twilight Princess,* and *Resident Evil 4.* The girls' games consist of fairy princesses and other pretty characters who do not engage in sports or kill anyone, with titles such as *Barbie Island Princess, Hannah Montana: Spotlight World Tour, My Little Pony: Pinkie Pie's Party Parade*, and *Disney Princess: Enchanted Journey.* The unisex games are knowledge-based, such as *Big Brain Academy* or what are termed party games, where there are various mini games that can be played, such as *Super Monkey Ball: Banana Blitz.*

Appropriate Behaviors

According to the gendered toys discussed, boys are to be athletic superheroes. Many North Americans agree with the stereotypes. It is assumed that boys are to be molded into masculine beings, which by definition means the polar opposite of the feminine. Crying out of pain or fear is considered feminine, so many encourage young boys to suppress these emotional behaviors. Boys are often taught that it is shameful to cry or express any emotion other than that of anger, which is often a key emotion that girls are supposed to suppress (because it is too masculine). Some boys may also learn at an early age that they should feel ashamed of themselves if they want to spend time with their mothers, instead of with their fathers. Many experts claim that a mother must "cut the apron ties" by the time her son begins school. Other researchers state that by "cutting the apron ties," boys are set up for a lifetime of confusion and insecurity, with some belief that such boys may have a difficult time being their true selves, and may be more apt to become depressed and develop other psychological and physical ailments.

Photographs of Children

Our society has set restrictions and rules not only upon appropriate activities and behaviors for boys and girls, but also as to how boy children and girl children are photographed. During the first year of a baby's life, new parents are apt to get a lot of experience with photographers, since the expectation in North America suggests having a child professionally photographed every 3 months: 3 months, 6 months, 9 months, and 12 months. Some recommend that children should be professionally photographed again at 18 months, 24 months, and every year thereafter.

Props in the studio are different according to the gender of the child—even at a young age. For boys there are such props as: navy blue leather back chairs, rocking horses, blocks, soccer balls, footballs, and baseballs. One studio even had a little toddler motorcycle. For girls the props are: bunny rabbits, pastel pink fabric chairs, satin pillows with frilly pink bows, and baskets with flowers. Notice the chairs are gendered—navy blue leather for boys and pastel pink fabric for girls.

Societal Influences Prevail

Society has a great impact upon what individuals learn. We learn from individuals around us, such as our parents when we are young; and as we grow our web of people who educate us grows, too. We come into contact with friends, enemies, teachers, and coaches. We interact with people of differing ages, genders, races, ethnicities, and languages. We also learn from the media, through billboard advertisements, magazines, commercials, television shows, movies, Internet, music, and so forth. Little boys are gendered before they are even born, and societal expectations tend to push them into being the blue-wearing, action-toy-playing tough guys that are created by media, toy manufacturers, and stereotypes.

Further Reading

Kindlon, Dan and Michael Thompson. *Raising Cain: Protecting the Emotional Life of Boys.* New York: Ballantine Books, 2000.
Pollack, William. *Real Boys: Rescuing Our Sons from the Myths of Boyhood.* New York: Henry Holt and Company, LLC, 1998.

Ruthann Mayes-Elma

Boi

The most popular use of the term *boi* is to describe women who are masculine, or boyish. Some think of themselves as women who were tomboys and have maintained and embraced their boyishness as they became adults. Some think of themselves as male, and have changed their female bodies to fit with their conception of themselves through hormones and/or surgery. Some consider themselves to be transgender or transsexual, whether or not they alter their bodies through medical procedures. While boi corresponds more closely with one's expression of gender rather than sexuality, those using the term nearly always identify as lesbian, bisexual, or gay as well. In addition, boi is occasionally used by gay men to describe another gay man who is youthful or boyish. The term has been popularized in English-speaking nations such as Australia, Canada, the United Kingdom, and the United States.

It is difficult to precisely designate which traits or actions qualify as masculine, but many possibilities are offered by psychologists, sociologists, the general public, and bois themselves: wearing male clothing (any garment located in the boys' or men's sections of a clothing store) and accessories (e.g., wallets, long key chains, baseball caps, and retro fashions such as suspenders and flat caps), styling one's hair in a traditional barber cut, engaging in male-dominated activities such as competitive sports (e.g., basketball, football, rugby, baseball) or entertainment (e.g., skateboarding, motorcycling, surfing, pool), using a male name, shaping one's female body into a male body by binding breasts or packing a bulge at the crotch, or even having one's stride or strut appear to be like a masculine boy's or man's movements to onlookers. Symbols of masculinity are not static, and change across many social locations; for example, what may seem masculine in an urban environment may appear as normal women's wear in a rural setting. Class, race, ethnicity, region, and nationality hold tremendous influence over which clothing and accessories are counted as masculine or feminine in a given context. The perspectives of others are often significant factors in recognizing bois. However, the most important element in determining whether or not someone is a boi is if the person self-identifies as a boi. If you feel that you are a boi, that this identity seems most natural to you, that it captures best how you walk in the world, then you probably are a boi. The list of traits and characteristics are possible styles and descriptions, but are secondary to your sense of self.

While bois may dress in fancy male attire for special events, or even perform as drag kings, it is important to note that bois generally find their masculinity to be a natural state rather than a performance. They are not mimicking boys and men; they are simply another kind of masculine being in the world reflecting and creating masculinity alongside these male counterparts. Masculinity is not a superficial role that these women can easily remove. Even if they are pressured by family or peers to wear more feminine clothing, their masculine bodies and gestures remain. Though boyish clothing for girls and women has become more socially acceptable since the mid-twentieth century, enforcement of femininity in women persists. Masculine girls and women continue to face taunts and insults (e.g., they won't ever find a man; they're dykes; they're freaks). Perhaps the character of Pat from *Saturday Night Live* in the 1990s is a good illustration of the position of masculine women in contemporary U.S. culture. Pat is not necessarily physically threatened, but s/he provokes obsessive fascination by others; s/he is weird, dorky, laughed at, and the embodiment of a joke, but the joke is partly on the people around Pat, who are unhappy that they cannot tell what gender s/he is and cannot bring themselves to ask Pat directly. Given such unwelcome treatment, the ability for bois to wear the masculine clothing that feels good and comfortable and conduct themselves as masculine women and transgender individuals in the world reveals genuine strength and resilience.

Boi is a relatively new term for masculine expression in women's bodies. It is a name embraced primarily by those currently in their teens, twenties, and early thirties. It can be not only a personal identity, but also a lifestyle—a carefree, Peter Pan sensibility: not wanting to grow up, going out to parties and bars, using hip slang, having multiple sexual partners, and avoiding serious responsibilities in work or relationships. Given that these descriptions are often ascribed to youth of any kind (males in particular), it is impossible to separate which characteristics are specific to bois, which are embraced by bois themselves, and which are observations by an older lesbian community that does not fully understand boi aesthetics. Certainly not everyone using the term desires a blithe existence; some possess familial and career commitments. But it's safe to say that most are young, masculine, and queer (not heterosexual). While there are contemporary trends in fashion and ideology that are components of this identity, female masculinity has existed across communities, nations, and history.

If Joan of Arc (1412–1431) had lived today, she might have called herself a boi. She was a strong, rebellious teenager who wore her hair in a man's cut, and refused to wear female clothing, preferring male attire and armour. She led the fight to forge the modern nation of France, only to be burned alive shortly after for refusing to wear female clothing. Her female masculine identity was more important to her than her life. Nzinga might have been a boi as well, wearing male clothing and ruling as the King of Angola from 1624 to 1653. There were also the thousands of Mexican revolutionary soldiers who cross-dressed for battle nearly a hundred years. Even Disney has offered young tomboys, such as the Chinese heroine Mulan, who wore boy's clothing to save her family's honor and take up the sword in battle. In addition, there is a long history of masculine females who have served as sacred or holy members of their communities: among the Lugbara in Africa, the Inuit in the Arctic, the figure of the mudang in Korea, and in particular in any society across the world with matrilineal roots. Masculine females have always existed, living as wives, nuns, reporters, police, midwives, nurses, mechanics, professors, farmers, doctors, cooks, teachers, couriers, hairstylists, and business(wo)men within numerous professions. The possibilities for their professions, however, are often limited by responses to their bodies, and patriarchal social structures that do not afford women, even masculine women, the same benefits as men.

Responses to female masculinity have ranged from worship to hatred. Transgender historian Leslie Feinberg finds that colonization, capitalism, and patriarchy have had devastating effects on the masculine female's (or feminine male's) position within a society. Indigenous cultures which had previously revered masculine females radically changed their perspective after colonization. Colonialism has relied upon the practice of dividing different kinds of people into categories and distributing resources on the basis of these categories. While fluctuating somewhat through centuries, countries, and degrees, in general, men have been valued more than women; light skin has been valued over darker skin; the wealthy have been more valued than the poor; the urban valued over the rural; and heterosexuals over lesbians, gays, and bisexuals. Masculine females do not fall easily into any kind of category and have thus faced confusion, fear, and hostility. They have been perceived as attempting to usurp male privilege, and all the financial and social resources it encompasses, for themselves. If they are identified as lesbian or bisexual, they face the additional hardship of not being part of the more valued social group of heterosexuals. The presence of lesbians is disruptive to legal and social traditions that have regarded women as the property of men; if a woman does not want or need men, and prefers other women, then men may lose control over her. Therefore, the wearing of male clothing by women as well as lesbian sexuality have often been designated as crimes. It was only in 2003 that the U.S. Supreme Court decriminalized homosexuality for all 50 states, and ordinances against cross-dressing (women wearing men's clothing) have been fought by queer activists and repealed region by region in the late twentieth century.

Sexologists and the psychological profession emerging in the late 1800s began to define both lesbianism and female masculinity as an illness or abnormality. Richard von Krafft-Ebing, Havelock Ellis, and Sigmund Freud identified female masculinity or male femininity as *inversion*, which coincided with homosexual desire. On the one hand, this knowledge offered masculine females the legitimacy of scientific study and definition, rather than blame. On the other hand, the condition of female masculinity was considered abnormal and a failure of proper development. Creating knowledge—a field of social science—which deems some people normal and others abnormal is yet another way to create social divisions and limit who should and should not have access to resources (e.g., the right to family and community financial and emotional support, the right to adopt children, the right to be protected from physical harm in schools).

In her 1928 novel *The Well of Loneliness*, Radclyffe Hall offers the protagonist Stephen Gordon as the embodiment of a sexual invert. She wears men's clothing, prefers male activities such as hunting, and desires women as a man would. While she proudly assumes her male identity, her social isolation and inability to be accepted by a heterosexual world leads to a fairly torturous existence. The book asked its early audience for acceptance of inversion, but was met instead with charges of obscenity upon its publication. Nevertheless, the novel and the trial that condemned it made female masculinity visible across English-speaking nations. In subsequent decades, it was the only book about lesbianism that people had heard of and might be able to locate. When butch-femme relationships became popular in the 1940s, 1950s, and 1960s, many lesbian readers were still turning to *The Well of Loneliness* for connection and understanding.

Butch is a term describing a masculine woman who is lesbian. It is the word most closely related to *boi,* and often referred to by bois when they are distinguishing the subtle differences of their contemporary identity. "Femme" is a feminine lesbian, and in butch-femme relationships she is the lover and partner of the butch. In the 1940s, 1950s, and 1960s, butch-femme relationships were an enforced norm in lesbian communities, as opposed to butch-butch or femme-femme partnering. However, in the 1970s, butch-femme relationships and butch and femme gender expression were attacked in feminist and lesbian circles as emulating patriarchy and heterosexuality. Butchness, masculinity in women, became despised both inside and outside of lesbian communities, compounding feelings of exclusion and isolation for many butch women. *Butch* is still a term embraced by many masculine lesbians, often as a badge of pride. This expression of gender announces that they cannot or will not hide away their masculine appearance, even as it provokes insults, violence, and limited employment opportunities. Butches, by virtue of their nonconforming masculine appearance, are extremely attractive to some, while repulsive to others.

It is from these historical foundations that boi emerges. The self-proclaimed casualness of bois about their masculine gender expression and lifestyle follows butch and invert identities loaded with personal and political conflict. Bois are post-civil rights babies empowered by laws that already protect their rights. Their voices resonate with those contemporaries who do not identify as feminists because there is a sense that this work is no longer needed. For many young people, words such as *butch* and *feminist* are not only identities from the past, but they also evoke images of the serious, inflexible, and perhaps ugly. In addition, while butches sometimes make sexist comments about femmes, some bois do so using derogatory terms like *bitches* and *hos*, unapologetically and seemingly unaware of a feminist movement. The fact that many masculine women literally look more like boys than men could be another draw to the term *boi*, as opposed to *butch*, which carries a connotation and promise of manliness. Bois also have more liberty in their choice of lovers, desiring femmes, butches, men, transgender men and/or women (depending on the boi), whereas butches have often been aligned exclusively with femmes. It is unclear how much bois actually worry about their safety and opportunities as masculine women. Perhaps they simply enjoy a freedom that their predecessors did not have. Or their devotion to a life of pleasure could be yet another kind of resistance to families, communities, and nations that continue to disparage them.

Further Reading

Feinberg, Leslie. *Stone Butch Blues.* Los Angeles: Alyson Books, 2004.

Feinberg, Leslie. *Transgender Warriors: Making History from Joan of Arc to Dennis Rodman.* Boston: Beacon Press, 1997.

Halberstam, Judith. *Female Masculinity.* Durham, NC: Duke University Press, 1998.

Levy, Ariel. "Where the Bois Are." *New York Magazine,* January 5, 2004.

Noble, Jean Bobby. *Masculinities without Men: Female Masculinity in Twentieth-Century Fictions.* Vancouver, BC: UBC Press, 2005.

Karleen Pendleton Jiménez

Boy

Boy is a versatile word. It has been used as an indication of difference in social status (for slaves and servants of any age in colonial times), as a term of endearment (*our boys* for soldiers), in referring to a common past (*old boys*), onward to pets (dogs), and for household appliances and devices (*Game Boy*). In the Middle Ages the word generally referred to low social standing. Sources from the thirteenth and fourteenth centuries show it could mean anything from servant, gate ward, herdsman, to soldier, and was often used out of angry abuse and ridicule. In America the word was also used to mean *slave* and well into the twentieth century it functioned as racist slur in reference to African Americans. Such name-calling was to *remind* people of their low social status, which could entail ethnic, racial, civil, or class status (often at the same time). Being called *boy* eventually and simply meant being belittled, but before abolishment of slavery it gave a language to not being granted the right to vote or marry as one pleases, and more generally to not being thought of as able to think or act in a mature or rational (i.e., white) way. In a 2006 legal case, however, it was ruled that *boy* alone could not be accepted as evidence of discrimination. As was argued, its meaning may depend on various factors including context, inflection, tone of voice, local custom, and historical usage.

What made a *man* out of a *boy* indeed varied throughout history. In America cowboys were initially so-called because of their life stage (early teens and twenties), but also because of the low wages and social status of the job. One study of the Irish peasantry notes that sons were called *boys* until the day their father surrendered the farm to one of them, even if they themselves were middle-aged adults. Legal texts may not answer this question; contemporarily they only define legal *majority,* not *adulthood* or *manhood.* Marriage has often been taken as a decisive moment. At least from the early fifteenth century *boy* meant anything from unborn baby to unmarried youth. Even today *boy*friend refers to lovers before engagement or marriage. Research suggests that the age when young males stop preferring to be called *boy* changed even over a decade's period. In the mid-1990s only 15 percent of American 17- to 20-year-olds still preferred calling oneself *boy,* while nobody did in the 1980s; 75 percent of this age group preferred *guy* (Bebout, 1995). According to 17- to 50-year-olds questioned during the 1980s, the perceived upper age limits for legitimately calling anybody a *boy* were said to be lower than those for calling young females *girls* (Bebout, 1984). There was little agreement, however: *older child,* according to 28 percent; *young adolescent,* 39 percent; *mid-adolescent,* 33 percent. This type of research is, of course, very dependent on who is calling whom a *boy,* and in what situations. For instance, a 1989 American study reported that in tennis and basketball, women athletes were regularly called *girls* by TV commentators, while men athletes were never called *boys.* What this says about American spectator sports, the profession of sports commentatorship, or the nature of boyhood is difficult to answer.

In popular culture, however, the word is often used as an indication not of maturity or age but of pride; *underdog mentality;* and a way of expressing bonds, common origins, and cultural resilience. Accordingly, in rap music words such as *homeboy* and *b-boy* (from *break* or *beat*) and creative spellings such as *boyz* have become entirely commonplace. Popular 1990s films such as *Boyz n the Hood* (1991) and the 1990s fad of the *boy band* show the word suits young unmarried males well across ethnic lines.

Further Reading

Bebout, Linda. (1984). Asymmetries in Male-Female Word Pairs. *American Speech, 59*(1), 13–30.

Bebout, Linda. (1995). Asymmetries in Male/Female Word Pairs: A Decade of Change. *American Speech, 70*(2), 163–185.

Harris, Keith. *Boys, Boyz, Bois: An Ethic of Black Masculinity in Film and Popular Media.* New York: Routledge, 2006.

Diederik F. Janssen

Gay Boys

Gay youth are coming out at younger ages, expressing more satisfaction with their identities, and becoming politically active at numbers unprecedented in recent history. This sea of change in youth sexual identities has likely been fed by the increasing number of people who no longer see homosexuality as a sin or a sickness. In fact, a 2006 Gallup Poll found that 54 percent of people found homosexuality acceptable, compared with 38 percent in 1992. This change in attitude is especially prevalent among young people, who are much more likely to espouse liberal attitudes about same-sex relationships than their elders. Gay youth report feeling better about themselves than at any point in history. While role models are still scarce, gay adults are increasingly visible in the public eye—on TV, in politics, and as other public figures.

In spite of this radical social change, contemporary boyhood is a tough place for boys who are different—too short, too fat, too quiet, too tall, too skinny, too smart, too dumb. Gay boys perhaps suffer the most for their difference. In other words, at the same time that social attitudes toward homosexuality are liberalizing, elementary, middle, and high schools are still, for the most part, inhospitable places for gay youth. However, because Western cultures look toward childhood sexuality with ambivalence, we know little about the experiences of gay youth. This entry speaks to that silence, sketching a portrait of gay boyhood, their experiences, their challenges and their possible futures.

Who Is Gay?

Simply experiencing attraction to or engaging in sexual encounters with another boy or man does not render a boy gay. Identifying as gay is a process that has as much to do with the culture in which a boy finds himself as his interpretations of his desires and practices. In multiple (usually non-Western) societies boys can engage in same sex practices that would often be seen as gay in the West, but do not take on that same meaning. This is especially true in societies where men and women as well as girls and boys remain separated throughout much of social life. For example, in India it is not uncommon for young men to dance together. Similarly, in Turkey it is not unusual for men to hold hands. In these sorts of gender-segregated societies boys might also have their first sexual experience with another boy, though it would mean little in terms of their sexual identity as gay or straight. In other societies, such as tribal groups in Papau New Guinea, boys enter into manhood through ritualized sexual contacts with older men. Even in the West, boys might have same-sex physical interactions in childhood and on into puberty without identifying as gay as a fixed sexual identity; just like gay boys might have opposite sex contact, but not identify as straight later in life. In fact, as many as one-third of adult men engage in same-sex erotic behaviors at some point in their lives. However, not all of these men identify as or are identified by others as gay, or organize their lives around the fact that they are sexually attracted to other men. In the West, boys are only likely to be recognized and to label themselves as gay when same-sex desire becomes their dominant erotic orientation.

Growing Up Gay

Gay boys' experiences of their burgeoning sexuality are by no means uniform. Their experiences vary depending on where they live, what sort of family they have, and who their friends are. Teens growing up in nonurban, conservative areas and those with nonaccepting parents report having the hardest time confronting their own sexuality. Many adult gay men remember the onset of same-sex desire or fantasies during their preadolescent and early adolescent years, even though they may not have identified explicitly as gay at that point. These men often feel that being gay is a natural part of who they are and they recall same-sex attraction in their earliest childhood experiences. Because of their desires and fantasies, some gay boys feel different than their friends and peers. Gay boys sometimes feel alienated from the sex talk, the flirting, and the pornographic pictures surreptitiously passed in elementary and middle school. By the time gay boys are in high school, they have usually experienced some sort of sexual contact with another boy. That said, many gay boys are attracted to girls during their adolescent years and often date girls for a time at least. Occasionally gay boys hope that their same-sex desires are a phase out of which they will grow.

The social worlds of gay boys vary, with some engaging in hypermasculine pursuits and others surrounding themselves with more artistic peers. A minority of gay boys find that they are affectively more suited to friendship circles constituted by girls. These types of boys tend to feel ill at ease with sports and be drawn to books and artistic endeavors. Surrounding oneself with girls can also be a strategic move to shield oneself from the homophobic teasing so prevalent in high school. Other gay boys, however, feel more at home in traditionally masculine environments and exhibit a desire to be around other boys who identify as strongly masculine (such as athletes). Contrary to stereotypical beliefs about gay men and sports, gay boys who participate in and enjoy sports do not find that it is incongruent with their sexual desires and emerging sexual identities. Commonly, boys who begin to identify as gay keep this identification to themselves or share it with a select few in their friendship group until they leave high school or discontinue living with family of origin.

"Mom, Dad, I'm Gay"

Homes can be places of refuge for gay boys as well as sites of struggle. How parents deal with their child's revelation deeply affects their child. If a boy tells his parents that he identifies as gay, they might be supportive, taking steps to protect their son from harassment at school or joining groups like PFLAG, Parents and Friends of Lesbians and Gays. However, other parents have less welcoming responses ranging from mild disapproval, such as "we love you in spite of the fact you are gay," to hostility, such as kicking their child out of their home. This latter reaction has devastating effects. A disproportionate amount of homeless youth identify as gay, a likely result of hostile parents. Still other parents try to *fix* their children by sending them to therapists or programs designed to cure homosexuality. A 16-year-old named Zach who identified as gay was sent to a program called Love in Action that promised to cure his homosexuality. Dismayed at being sent to this treatment facility, Zach wrote about his experience on his MySpace account and received support from people across the globe. While no major mental health organizations in the United States view same-sex desire as a mental health issue that needs fixing, young gay boys are frequently diagnosed with gender identity disorder. This diagnosis applies to boys who do not conform to stereotypically masculine forms of play, dress, and talk. Because some parents are fearful that if their child doesn't conform to gender norms he will be gay, they use this "disorder" to justify psychological treatment of their child's *abnormality*.

School Days

Most contemporary youth spend a large part of their waking hours at school. Schools are organizers of sexual practices, identities, and meanings, encouraging heterosexuality and discouraging homosexuality through rituals, pedagogical practices, and disciplinary procedures. As a result, for gay boys schools can be a place of profound discomfort and alienation. The heterosexualizing process starts early, in elementary school, and intensifies through high school. School curriculum frequently marginalizes gay boys. Even seemingly benign school lessons about grammar or mathematics might use metaphors of a heterosexual married couple to illustrate important concepts. To the extent that youth receive sex education, it is typically based on a heterosexual model and abstinence is frequently taught as the only safe practice. This leaves gay boys at a loss for how to navigate their sexual decisions about safer sex practices, partners, and sexual identity as they receive little information about sex in general and about being a sexual minority in particular.

High schools are especially hard places for gay teens, because by adolescence heterosexuality is the foundation of most school rituals, rules, and interactions. Proms, senior superlatives, dances, homecomings, and big man on campuses are all based on heterosexual models. As a result school events such as dances or assemblies are often places of intensified homophobic harassment. Sporting events and sports practices might be especially hostile environments as coaches often use homophobic slurs to bait opponents and punish team members. Many schools will not allow gay boys to go to a dance together, dance together once they are there, or engage in public affection during lunch or passing periods. Some school administrations have seen fit to report boys' same-sex behavior or relationships to their parents, effectively outing them into a possibly dangerous situation. Sometimes boys cannot go to the guidance office or school counselor for support and understanding because of fears around confidentiality. Homophobic teasing characterizes masculinity in adolescence and early adulthood. Teenage boys widely report that *gay* or *fag* are the ultimate insults one could hurl at another boy. Homophobic insults and attitudes, both serious and joking, are central to masculinity in school settings. By high school, boys understand that the best way to defend oneself against being labeled a *fag* or *gay* is to deflect the label onto someone else. Thus, much of boys' joking relationship is made up of joking about unmasculine men by calling them *gay* or *fag*. This sort of joking is rampant in schools. The Gay/Straight Alliance network documents that 53 percent of youth hear homophobic slurs as many as 10 times or more per day at school.

As a result of this teasing and the rampant interactional homophobia, the teenage years can be tough ones for gay boys. Gay teens are the most likely victims of harassment in high school. The bullying often leads to poor self-esteem, which then has ramifications on the other parts of the teen's life—school work, friends, family. Some boys are harassed enough that it impedes their education progress. This sort of daily harassment likely contributes to the fact that gay teens are more likely to contemplate suicide than straight teens, though not more likely to kill themselves. Gay teens are, however, more anxious and depressed than straight teens. Additionally, this sort of verbal harassment can escalate into physical violence. For example, Lawrence King, a middle school student in southern California, was murdered by a classmate in 2008 because he identified as gay, and the classmate claimed he had been harassed by King. Not surprisingly, given these threats to their safety, many boys (gay and straight) take pains to ensure that other boys do not think they are gay. Boys vigilantly police most signs of same-sex intimacy or desire. Boys can be teased for being gay, being too nice, dancing, smiling, caring too much about their clothing, or expressing too much or the wrong kind of interest in another guy. In order to avoided being the butt of homophobic jokes, boys will often avoid touching in any way except for an aggressive way. Clearly, very little of this has to do with actual sexual desire or identity. Gay boys specifically often adopt several strategies to avoid the teasing and harassment. Some boys purposefully date girls, though they identify as gay. Others engage in gender stereotypical behavior, such as strutting, lifting weights, playing aggressive sports, or exhibiting general aggression. Some gay boys surround themselves with a social circle of girls to avoid the harassment endemic to groups of teenage boys. Others vary their routes home from school and walk with eyes downcast so as not to start a fight. The result of this constant policing of intimate and public behaviors for gay and straight boys is that many boys miss out on intimate, though not necessarily sexual, relationships with other boys and eventually men.

Creating Community

While schools are often incredibly difficult places, gay boys create community both in school, often in the form of Gay-Straight Alliances (GSAs), and out of school, often by using the internet and new media to connect with other teens similar to themselves. Gay boys can start clubs such as GSAs. Teens have formed GSAs in every state in the country, with the exception of North Dakota. The GSA Network reports that there are more than 3,000 active GSAs. These clubs are having an immeasurable impact on school cultures and knowledge about gay youth. GSAs provide a safe space for gay boys in school—spaces free from teasing, harassment, and violence. GSAs are both social groups, where teens can meet others like them and put on social events such as the gay prom and movie night, and educational groups, where they can learn about gay history and gay rights.

Gay boys have also been increasingly creating community by using the internet. The internet and new media have given a great gift to gay boys in terms of their ability to find a community of youth like themselves. Because there often are not enough out gay boys at a given school to form a community, gay boys use social network sites to link to other teenagers like themselves who might not attend their school. In this way teens both expand their friendship circle and their potential dating pool. For gay teens, finding a boyfriend might be the biggest challenge. Because new media widens their social circle beyond the school peer group, gay boys are now being able to engage in the same sort of dating and romance rituals that straight teens allocate so much of their free time to.

Making Things Better

While harassment of gay teens may have intensified over the past several decades, so have the resources available to gay boys. Organizations, individuals, and professionals from a range of disciplines have been mobilizing around issues of harassment, bullying, sexism, and homophobia in schools over the last decade. Places such as the GSA Network and Gay, Lesbian and Straight Education Network (GLSEN) have initiated large-scale trainings of educators, parents, and teens themselves to help them understand the needs of their gay teens. However, stronger legal protections need to be in place to shield gay boys from the sort of harassment they currently endure. The state of California passed a groundbreaking law, the School Safety and Violence

Prevention Act, which protects gay youth from harassment and discrimination in schools. The District of Columbia, Maine, Minnesota, New Jersey, Connecticut, Massachusetts, Vermont, Washington, and Wisconsin have passed similar laws. However, as illustrated by the murder of Lawrence King, a law alone is not enough. Educators and parents need to understand and enforce these sorts of laws. Schools themselves need to modify homophobic and sexist social environments. Similarly, because of the large number of homeless gay youth, shelters need to address gay teens and their unique needs, much like Ruth's House in Detroit and the Ark House in Refuge in San Francisco have done.

Youth are leading the way in terms of social change for gay boys. Gay boys are coming out earlier, starting GSAs, and experiencing less conflict about their identities than their forbearers.

Further Reading

Gay, Lesbian and Straight Education Network. http://www.glsen.org/.
Gay-Straight Alliance Network. http://www.gsanetwork.org/.
Pascoe, C. J. *Dude, You're a Fag.* Berkeley, CA: University of California Press. 2007.
Savin-Williams, Ritch. *The New Gay Teenager.* Cambridge, MA: Harvard University Press. 2006.

C. J. Pascoe

Gender

Gender issues touch everyone's lives directly—after all, people grow up as girls, boys, or transsexuals. Some people assume that females and males are simply born with particular characteristics, and that as a result of biological factors little boys will inevitably want to bash one another over the head with pretend swords, while little girls will cuddle their baby dolls in the kitchen corner of the preschool. Others are equally convinced that biology has nothing to do with it, and that children are molded and shaped by how they are treated by their parents, as well as by imitating what they see in society around them. Probably any introductory child development textbook will make the point that there is nothing like nature versus nurture dichotomy, and that biological and socialization forces interact to shape children's development as a female or a male. Gender is both a cultural and an individual concept. A society's or group's culture shapes the people within it according to their biological sex. The resultant concepts of gender associated with males are called *masculine,* and those with females, *feminine.* A culture includes beliefs, social practices, and institutions, such as child-rearing practices, family, school, economic structures, and employment structures. In that these vary, different cultures shape biological males in different ways and biological females in different ways. Different cultures accordingly espouse different concepts of gender. Human gender characteristics are thus not just given, but rather socially constructed.

Biological Beginnings

"It's a girl!" "It's a boy!" When an infant is born, the gender assessment is usually based on a baby's genitals, assuming that a baby with a penis and scrotum is a male and that one with a clitoris and vagina is a female. Yet the birth of an infant with recognizably male or female genitals is only one milestone in an extended process of development as a girl or a boy. Several events have occurred much earlier in prenatal development that will eventually result in the birth of a boy or a girl baby. These events include the conception of an infant with male or female sex chromosomes and the development of a female or male system of internal reproductive organs, that is, testes in males and ovaries in females. The testes and ovaries also produce sex hormones in varying amounts that affect the developing fetus. The infant's biological sex involves all these factors—chromosomes, sex hormone levels, reproductive organs, and the external genitals.

Chromosomal Sex

One measure of biological sex is determined when the baby is first conceived. Humans have 23 pairs of chromosomes in each cell, with one of these pairs being the sex chromosomes. In females this pair consists of two X chromosomes (XX), while in males it is composed of an X and Y (XY). The egg and sperm cells are exceptions to the 23-pairs-per-cell rule; if they were like other cells in the body, the fertilized egg would have 46 pairs, twice the necessary number, and would not survive. Thus, the egg and sperm each have only 23 individual chromosomes, yielding 23 pairs when they combine at conception. Because the egg and sperm cells each have only half the necessary genetic information, it is only when their chromosomes are combined that the sex of the offspring is determined. The father's sperm cells can contain either X or Y chromosomes, while the mother's egg cells contain only X chromosomes Thus, if an X sperm fertilizes the egg, the baby will be a girl (X from the mother, X from the father), while if a Y sperm fertilizes the egg, the baby will be a boy (X from the mother, Y from the father).

Gender—Role Acquisition

As young children grow, certain behaviors come to be expected from them. Among these behaviors are those expected because of the child's gender. The acquisition of these behaviors that are expected of males and females within a particular society usually include dress and appearance, work and leisure activities, obligations within the family, skills, and social behavior. This acquisition provides an example of the interaction between the child's cognitive development and his or her culture, which determines which behaviors are deemed appropriate for each gender. These behaviours constitute what is known as a gender role. That is, how boys learn to be boys, and girls to be girls.

Gender roles are very often still socially determined and gender role expectations for children are still strong. Boys are expected to dress in pants and shirts, play outdoors, ride bikes, get dirty, find their way when they get lost, and hold back their tears when they fall off their bikes. Girls are expected to dress in skirts (at least sometimes), play close to home, stay neat and tidy, be nice to other children, and to be pretty.

Determining how children learn gender roles requires a theoretical understanding of gender role identification, which is the degree to which a child adopts the sex role of a particular model. Gender identity is the sense of being male or female, whether or not one follows the rules of sex typing.

Gender role differences affect so much of life that every major theory of child development has proposed explanations of how they develop in children. Psychoanalytic, social learning, and cognitive theories have all addressed this question. Each predicts that the parent's gender role—related behavior—should have a striking effect on the child's developing sexual identity, even though each theory views the development of gender role identification differently.

Psychoanalytic Theory

This theory emphasizes the child's identification with the same-sex parent. As a result of the crisis of the oedipal conflict, the child assumes the behavior and values of that parent. According to the Freudian view, boys and girls develop similarly during infancy and toddlerhood. But as they approach the end of early childhood and confront competition with their same-sex parent for the attention and affection of their opposite-sex parent, the genders diverge. According to this theory, boys identify with their father and reject the earlier intimate bond they felt with their mother. Girls become disappointed with their biological status as females; they feel disappointed with their mother and envious of their father's power and status. They therefore adopt the female gender role as a strategy to gain their father's interest.

Social Learning Theory

In this view, children's behaviors are reinforced or punished based on what parents and society deem appropriate for the child's gender. According to this theory, parents, peers, television, and society as a whole shape the acquisition of gender roles through observational learning. This approach assumes that children learn to be male or female just as they learn any other social lesson. Children see girls playing with dolls and women caring for babies, and they see boys pretending to be superheroes and men fixing cars. Moreover, they see that all of these people are positively reinforced with praise and support for behaving in the ways that boys and girls are supposed to behave; whereas, rewards may be withheld or punishments applied for behaviors that do not conform to what is expected. For example, a boy may be criticized for "crying like a girl," and a girl may be warned that "girls are not supposed to be so pushy." As a result of such observations and direct experiences, children tend to learn the gender roles and stereotypes that are held by the people around them. So, gender development may result from the combined effects of imitation and reinforcement.

Cognitive Theory

In the tradition of Piaget, cognitive explanations of gender development emphasize changes in children's active construction of knowledge, in this case, about gender. According to this view, after children realize that they have a self, they come to understand that they are either female or male, and this cognitive realization then guides the children to change their behavior to match what society deems appropriate for their gender. In this view, the time when children first become aware of their gender and its meaning is an important consideration. Young children must figure out the essential elements of gender identity, and they do so in several distinct phases. As toddlers, for example, boys and girls do not understand that gender actually stays constant. They think that they can change sex if they want to. Over the next several years, though, they gradually realize that gender doesn't change, although they need several more years to discover the basis for classifying individuals into one sex or the other. The cognitive theory predicts that gender-role acquisition will not begin until the child has the concept that he is a boy or that she is a girl.

The Development of Gender Understanding

Children appear to develop a gender understanding—that is, to comprehend that they are boys or girls—by about the age of 3 years. Although a 2-year-old child may tell you she is a girl, she may have trouble understanding who else is a girl, or, for that matter, why she is called a girl, and who is a boy and why. Also, 3-year-old children, whose cognitive processing is limited, generally fail to understand gender constancy, which usually develops in children by the age of 6 or 7 years. Gender constancy is the realization that one's sex is determined by constant criteria and is unaffected by one's behavior or activities. A child is demonstrating a grasp of gender constancy when she understands that just because a girl plays football, she does not turn into a boy—she is still a girl.

Gender Constancy and Cognitive Theory

Cognitive theory predicts that children should not show gender-role acquisition to any significant degree until they have a cognitive grasp of what it means to be a boy or a girl; but it is not what happens. According to John P. Dworetzky, children engage in stereotypical gender role behaviors well before they are cognitively conscious of their gender or its constancy. As early as 26 months of age, children are usually aware of the different things that constitute masculine and feminine dress and behavior—they already know that men often wear shirts and suits and shave their chins, and that women often wear blouses and dresses and makeup.

Gender Schema Theory

Gender schema theory, developed by Sandra Bem, explains how cognitive advances help the child to organize and integrate the information that he or she has learned about his or her sex. The gender schema theory explains the intertwining of cognitive and social learning theories. In her view, as children develop, they reach a point when they are able to integrate cognitively all the different gender-specific behaviors they have acquired through social learning and conditioning. This cognitive integration helps to constitute their attitudes and beliefs about gender roles, and gives guidance to them to establish their own decisions about what is gender-role appropriate. Bem's view explains how children can show gender-specific behaviors long before they have gender constancy. The theory also explains how, step by step, cognitive advances can help the children to organize and integrate all the information they have acquired about gender roles, so that their attitudes and beliefs can be influenced by their changing cognitive development. Femininity and masculinity are not opposite ends of a continuum. Many men are nurturing and compassionate (traditional qualities of the *feminine* woman), and many women are independent and assertive (traditional qualities of *masculine* man). Bem used the term androgynous to describe people who have both masculine and feminine qualities. Not all men are predominantly masculine; not all women are exclusively feminine; and not all children become traditionally sex-typed.

Further Reading

Askew, Sue, and Carol Ross. *Boys Don't Cry: Boys and Sexism in Education.* Buckingham: Oxford University Press, 1990.

Beal, Carole. *Boys and Girls: The Development of Gender Roles.* McGraw-Hill, Inc., 1994.

Butler, Judith. *Gender Trouble.* New York: Routledge, 2006.

Dworetzky, John. *Psychology.* New York: West Publishing Company, 1988.

Julia German

Growing Up Male

Most boys would rather live in a society with less restrictive rules of what it means to be a boy/man, rather than to behave in misogynistic, stereotyped *bad boy* behaviors. It is usual for teachers to expect their boys to play sports, to behave like jocks, and to act like men defined by previous boy codes. Adults frequently feel more comfortable when boys follow boy stereotypes, rather than nontraditional and alternative ways of growing up male. In this case educators need to examine their own definitions of what it means to be growing up male and to challenge their own beliefs and to open new doors for their young adolescent/teen boys to develop.

Growing Up Male and the Impact of Language

Derogatory misogynistic language can be found in music and entertainment media and in everyday youth culture. Some of the language is demeaning to women and other is demeaning to men; both are equally disturbing. When adults say "girls can't be doctors, boys can't be nurses, you throw a ball like a girl, you run like a girl, and boys don't cry," they are using language with limits. Sometimes when boys call women *bitch* or *ho*, they think it is okay or cute; and when some girls are called misogynistic names, they may think of it as a term of endearment. Name-calling, especially if prolonged and ongoing, leads to hostile behaviors, which may contribute to ridicule and gender-based violence to young adolescents who are nonconformists, especially those of gender nonconformity. The Columbine High School shooting incident in Colorado resulting in 15 deaths in 1999, where the killers were reportedly called homophobic names before the killings, provides one example; as does the death of Lawrence King, an openly gay eighth grade boy, who was shot and killed at school in 2008 in California by a classmate who felt threatened by King's sexual orientation.

How Boys and Men View the Meaning of Growing Up Male

In a random sampling (2009) for responses from North American boys and men asked what growing up male means, here are some responses:

- Growing up male means that we need to live in a caring supportive environment.
- Growing up male means that our role models do not need to be defined by gender rather defined by individuals with character and integrity that instill pride and confidence in all they surround, especially children.
- Growing up male means that I was the leader in my group of classmates and friends.
- Growing up male means different things based on social economics and ethnicity.
- Growing up male means having adults put external expectations on us to do things we do not want to do or to live up to.
- Growing up male challenges us to maintain our male friendships while developing romantic relationships.
- Growing up male means I have to play sports even though I don't want to.
- Growing up male means having to chose between right and wrong.
- Growing up a male means being like a fish in water and not having to examine my surroundings and worrying about power, agency and privilege.
- Growing up male means I have a possibility of getting into some kind of legal problem. Growing up male means the possibility of going to jail.
- Growing up male means for some boys believing that some forms of violence are OK.
- Growing up male means expecting to make more money than women.
- Growing up male means doing well in school.
- Growing up male means not doing well in school.
- Growing up male means thinking we have greater career options.
- Growing up male means expecting to pay for dates.
- Growing up male means expecting to be responsible for the family.
- Growing up male means being afraid of being picked on or being called names, especially names of fag, homo or gay.

- Growing up male means trying to survive growing up.
- Growing up male means being vulnerable to expectations based on gender codes and media images.
- Growing up male means feeling helpless based on society gender expectations.
- Growing up male can mean being challenged by social economic influences.
- Growing up male means wanting to pursue my own interests rather than imposed interests.
- Growing up male possibly means being made fun of since I am in the arts and not playing sports.
- Growing up male means being defined by the community one is raised—urban, suburban, and rural.
- Growing up male means possibly identifying with religious and spiritual ideologies that impose expectations.
- Growing up male means having a range of emotions, some I am allowed to express while others I have to hold back.
- Growing up male means growing up differently than females because of societal, cultural, and peer expectations.
- Growing up male means that at a young age developing an understanding of having to work in the future compared to women who may think of work as an option.
- Growing up male means abiding by the cultural responsibilities of the community we grow up in.
- Growing up male means for some being homophobic.
- Growing up male means believing that men are suppose to rescue, save, and support their wives and children.
- Growing up male means being entitled.
- Growing up male means that girls are treated nicer in schools.
- Growing up male means, for most, wanting to be liked by their peers and for others to be popular at all costs and doing whatever it takes to so do.
- Growing up male means believing that I am forced to grow up too fast and to act as an adult too soon.
- Growing up male means—I don't know what it's like to grow up any other way.
- Growing up male is a very complicated process and cannot be viewed by a singular lens.

How Girls and Women View Growing Up Male

Some responses from girls and women when asked what they think it is like growing up male:

- Growing up male means power and freedom.
- Growing up male means not having to worry about appearance as much as girls and women.
- Growing up male means my brother and I shared the same birthday cake because his birthday was two days earlier.

- Growing up male made me jealous of my brother because he could do more, go cool places, get cars and motorcycles.
- Growing up male means that men think women should stay at home, clean house, and take care of kids.
- Growing up male means being privileged and holding keys to a community where women and girls are not welcomed.
- Growing up male means boys don't have periods or PMS.
- Growing up male means they don't have to worry about getting pregnant.

Educators and Families Can Nurture Growing Up Male

No matter how a family is constructed, those who have studied the problems with gender stereotyping believe it is important to consider that a boy needs to be allowed to be himself and have his own voice. The best way to support growing up male is to provide a safe home and safe, successful school experiences. Parents of boys and educators need to accept and understand when growing up male that not all boys want to be athletes or act macho or believe in traditional male practices. Parents need to be assured it is acceptable that their boys do not have to buy into stereotyped boy code behaviors. Families and educators must advocate to the entertainment media in order to provide a range of boy and men images.

Researchers who are concerned about gender equality say that teachers need to know how each of their individual students learns and not to expect that all students learn alike. Not all boys learn alike, nor do all girls learn alike. Not all students from upper, middle, or lower income levels learn alike. Not all students from the same culture learn alike. When growing up male, each boy learns by what he brings into the classroom, his personal experiences, his family influences, his media influences, and, most important, his individual interests. Basic recommendations that educators can use to make growing up male a safe experience is to examine how language is used in and outside the classroom; to use and discuss everyday gender stereotyped experiences and behaviors; to provide opportunities for students to learn how to distinguish myth from reality in the media; to teach media literacy and critical viewing skills; and to examine the hidden messages in textbooks, movies, and novels. Teacher preparation programs need to address concepts of diverse learning and prepare their students to be teachers who advocate and advance equity in education and differentiation instruction in a student-centered curriculum.

Further Reading

Elkind, David. *The Hurried Child*. New York: Addison Wesley Publishing, 1981.

Forbes, David. *Boyz 2 Buddha Counseling Urban High School Male Athletes in the Zone*. New York: Peter Lang, 2004.

Katz, Jackson, and Jeremy Earp. *Tough Guise: Violence, Media, and the Crisis in Masculinity*. Produced by Sut Jhally, Media Education Foundation, 1999.

Pollack, William. *Real Boys: Rescuing Our Sons from the Myths of Boyhood*. New York: Henry Holt and Company 1999.

Cynthia S. Mee

Homophobia

Homophobia means hatred or fear of gay men and lesbians, often including bisexuals and transgendered people. Sometimes people, including children and teens, show scorn at the mere idea of sexual desire between two men or two women. There are individual expressions of homophobia including hurtful comments such as "Fag!" and there are institutional expressions of homophobia such as laws prohibiting gay men and lesbians from getting married. The most extreme feelings of homophobia have fueled physical attacks against gay men and lesbians resulting in injury and sometimes death. However, for nearly 50 years, activists of all kinds have worked publicly to combat homophobia, and have made considerable gains for broader social acceptance of same-sex desire and love. Every time the expression "That's so gay!" is used, one encounters homophobia. Some argue that they are talking about the poor quality of a book, or song, or piece of clothing when they use those words, and that it has nothing at all to do with same-sex desire. While individuals may have had no intention of insulting gay men and lesbians, constant references to disliked objects as gay reinforce the idea that gay individuals are also disliked or deficient. Both subtle and direct expressions of homophobia are present nearly everywhere in our lives, and so it is not surprising that people experience homophobia in reaction to same-sex desire. However, this social conditioning should not be confused with nature. There is nothing natural about being homophobic; it is a learned behavior. We know this because homophobia is not a shared trait across history, region, or culture.

Over 2,000 years ago the philosopher Plato believed that love between two males was superior to love between men and women. In hundreds of native cultures across the Americas, same-sex sexuality has been a common expression of desire; two-spirited individuals (those considered to have both male and female spirits) have often been partners in same-sex relationships as well as holding respected positions in their communities. Many children growing up with gay and lesbian parents today, having witnessed the love between their parents as the most natural thing in the world, cannot comprehend homophobia. In these examples, homophobia was not taught and therefore not a problem. However, they are exceptions to a world currently dominated by homophobia.

There are many possible causes for homophobia, but no definite answers. Some believe it is a religious right to express homophobia, especially since literal interpretations of the bible condemn gay men. However, literalists seem to have less problem disregarding biblical rules against eating shell fish, or working on the Sabbath, or adultery, or dishonest trade, or improper sacrifice, or the love of money, or many others. Choosing to believe only in the abomination against same-sex sexuality is in itself a type of homophobia. Some people believe that the rise of psychology, a social science which classified same-sex desire as an illness, popularized homophobia. Same-sex-desire dating from the late nineteenth century until 1973 was considered an aberration or mental disorder that needed to be treated and cured. While other scientists such as biologist Alfred Kinsey proved in the 1940s how common same-sex sexuality was, hoping to relieve the secret shame of those who thought same-sex desire was abnormal and wrong.

Pressure from the gay and lesbian movement in the early 1970s pushed for the removal of same-sex sexuality from the *Diagnostic and Statistical Manual, Mental Disorders* published by the American Psychiatric Association. However, many gay men and lesbians who are feminine men or masculine women can still be diagnosed as possessing a new mental illness defined as Gender Identity Disorder. While gender and sexuality are two different aspects of our bodies, there are a large number of feminine men and masculine women who are also gay or lesbian. Homophobic comments are often hurled at feminine boys and masculine girls regardless of their sexual orientation. Even though attempts at controlling gender do not alter someone's sexual desire, homophobia is often associated with maintaining distinct boundaries between two genders. Some believe the lack of protection and outright violence against gay men and lesbians by legal authorities also promote homophobia. It was only in 2003 that the United States decriminalized same-sex sexuality. Over 80 countries still consider same-sex acts between adults a crime (Ottosson, 1997). Punishments range from imprisonment to the death penalty. In addition, in countries where same-sex sexuality is legal, police might not punish those who attack gay men and lesbians, and may indeed attack them as well. When those in positions of authority such as priests, doctors, police, and judges promote homophobia, it gives others license to devalue the lives of gay men and lesbians.

The term homophobia was coined in the 1972 book *Society and the Healthy Homosexuality*, where psychologist George Weinberg defined it as "the dread of being in close quarters with homosexuals." Identifying homophobia as an irrational response has produced mixed results for those combating homophobia. On one hand it says that this is a condition that deviates from normal behavior, not something to aspire to. Finally it is the homophobe (one who is homophobic) who is the problem, and not the gay man or lesbian. On the other hand, though Weinberg seems to acknowledge that homophobia is an extreme reaction, he follows up with the idea that it is not a medical disorder because it is a feeling shared by the masses (of 1972). What is most disturbing is how a medical condition has been used subsequently to help in the defense of those who have attacked gay men and lesbians. In 1978, Dan White assassinated Harvey Milk, the first openly gay city official, and San Francisco mayor George Moscone. While his motivation was unclear, White claimed that his eating junk food right before the attack (known as the "twinkie defense") caused his attack, and he was found guilty of the lesser crime of manslaughter. In the trial of Russell Henderson and Aaron McKinney for the 1998 murder of 21-year-old Matthew Shepard, they claimed that they killed him because they panicked due to his gay sexual advances. However, they were not successful with this defense. Many accused of homophobic assault have claimed that they only meant to rob someone, or the injury or death was accidental because irrational fear of gay men overtook them. What emerges is the notion that men panic and injure or murder gay men, whether or not homophobia is ever named as motivation for the crime. Homophobia is unlike other phobias (e.g., height, or the outdoors, or spiders, etc.) where one's fear does not endanger other lives. Homophobia puts other lives directly in danger. How much understanding should be offered to someone who hurts others based on fear? How can someone rid themselves of their homophobic feelings and learn not to hate?

One's childhood home is a strong influence on perceptions of homophobia. If respected family members make homophobic comments or engage in homophobic violence, then an individual may have no idea that such behavior is hurtful. Sometimes parents believe they are protecting their children by warning them that gay men or lesbians could attempt to molest them, even though research indicates that less than 1 percent of child molesters are gay men or lesbians (Janoff, 2005).

Familial homophobia can be particularly hurtful for individuals with same-sex desire. Theorist Gloria Anzaldua offered an alternative definition of homophobia as "the fear of going home." If you realize that you are gay or lesbian, revealing your identity to your family can be terrifying. Your family may or may not accept you. If they accept you, this love can restore the confidence and power you need to resist homophobia encountered outside the home. If your family responds to you with homophobia, then you might feel that there is no safe place to go. If you are economically dependent upon your family, it may feel like you cannot survive. However, there now exist many groups, shelters, programs, phone help-lines, and sometimes schools to support LGBT (lesbian, gay, bisexual, transgender) youth through such difficulties. In addition, as lesbian writer Cherrie Moraga notes, LGBT people have a tremendous capacity for "making familia from scratch," creating new families with friends.

Schools are another powerful place of socialization. A 2007 student survey conducted in Iowa revealed that over 90 percent of LGBT students reported that they frequently heard homophobic remarks, and over a third had been physically harassed on campus. Such dismal results are common, though organizations such as GSA (Gay-Straight Alliance) and supportive teachers can make a big difference.

If teachers are willing to stop students when they make homophobic comments and open discussions in order to educate about the dangers of such hatred, they can create safer school climates. For many, school might be the only place where they hear that homophobia is hurtful. If teachers and administrators fail to educate on issues of homophobia, the consequences can be deadly. In the early 1990s, Jamie Nabozny faced repeated verbal and physical harassment in his Wisconsin school, only to be told by administrators that nothing could be done to protect him. He fought for his rights, however, and in 1996 a federal court found that LGBT students have a right to safe school climates. While this landmark decision has not translated into comprehensive anti-homophobia education (as evidenced by the previous example), it provides crucial legal support for those educators willing to protect their students.

Popular culture offers a broad-based medium for combating homophobia. In 2008 LGBT Caribbean Canadians insisted that two Jamaican bands, who sing violent, homophobic lyrics, be denied performance venues in Canada in what became known as Stop Murder Music. The community rallied together, held teach-ins, created spaces for dialogue about the implications of homophobia, and stopped the concerts. Other singers like Melissa Etheridge, Rufus Wainwright, Pink, and Madonna perform songs that speak explicitly about the acceptance of same-sex desire. Films such as *Philadelphia* and *Brokeback Mountain* and television shows such as *Queer as Folk, The L Word, Ellen,* and *Will and Grace* have brought gay men and lesbians into the lives and homes of the general public. PRIDE festivals bring LGBT and heterosexual community members to the streets for public celebrations, concerts, readings, theatre, and information about LGBT experience. Novels such as *A Boy's Own Story* by Edmund White, *Oranges Aren't the Only Fruit* by Jeanette Winterson, *Funny Boy* by Shyam Selvadurai, *Fun Home* by Alison Bechdel, and *Stone Butch Blues* by Leslie Feinberg provide intimate portraits of the lives of LGBT people. Learning about gay men and lesbians as whole, complicated human beings through these popular representations can significantly alter previously held homophobic stereotypes.

Today there remains difficult work in combating homophobia, particularly within the culture of boys and men. Research in Canada from 1990 to 2004 has shown that the majority of homophobic crimes are committed by men and boys who are attacking other men and boys. Less than 10 percent of assaults and less than 3 percent of murders involved female victims (Janoff, 2005). In addition, over 40 percent included at least one teenage basher (Janoff, 2005). Gay bashers tend to fall into two categories, men who carry a hateful obsession against gay men throughout their lives, and teenage boys who are looking for trouble and find gay-bashing a convenient sport to prove their masculinity. Why are boys and men destroying each other? What does masculinity have to do with hatred?

Sexism and misogyny play a role in homophobia against gay men. In this understanding of homophobia, men want the power to gaze upon women as an object of sexual desire. Straight men cannot be the object of another man's gaze, these types of homophobes think, or they feel that they have been made into a woman. Some version of the line "I'm ok with gays as long as they don't look at me" is often spoken. It's interesting to consider why many boys and men feel that it would be so horrible to be looked upon like a woman. Do they imagine that their own gaze upon women is a type of humiliating crime against women? For most women, if not a humiliating crime, the gaze is unwelcomed and unsettling. Even more devastating for some men is the fear of another man penetrating them. The penetrated lover would be viewed as the woman. It has often been surmised that gay-bashers are more likely than nonbashers to be latently gay or bisexual, or to have serious questions about their own sexuality. Women are held in such low esteem that to be perceived as a woman would be the worst accusation in the world for these men. Coincidentally, many consider a connection between men who abuse women and who are homophobic. Gay male theorists, such as Raul Coronado, have critiqued the sexism and homophobia in traditional masculinity and call for a stronger, more loving masculinity. They, as well as others, wonder why the pride of becoming and being a man should depend upon the denigration of women and gay men. Is manhood not worth something on its own?

Further Reading

Janoff, Douglas Victor. *Pink Blood: Homophobic Violence in Canada.* Toronto: University of Toronto Press, 2005.

Kaufman, Moisés. *The Laramie Project.* New York: Vintage Books, 2001.

Moraga, Cherríe, and Gloria Anzaldua. *This Bridge Called My Back: Writings by Radical Women of Color.* New York: Kitchen Table: Women of Color Press, 1983.

Ottosson, Daniel. State Sponsored Homophobia: A World Survey of Laws Prohibiting Same Sex Activity between Consenting Adults: An ILGA Report (International Lesbian and Gay Association). Retrieved March 13, 2009, from www.ilga.org/statehomophobia/State_sponsored_homophobia_ILGA_07.pdf.

Karleen Pendleton Jiménez

Queer Boys in Popular Culture

Queer boys provide us with one important way to critically examine the categories of sex, gender, and sexuality and how these intersect in complex and contradictory ways. Queer boys also draw attention to another important category: transgender.

Sex is often understood as a biological concept. The mainstream assumption is that biology creates two mutually exclusive sexes: male and female. From this perspective, human beings exist in one or the other category; they cannot belong to both of these categories simultaneously. If an infant is born with ambiguous genitalia, a doctor will typically intervene surgically so that the infant's genitals mark the infant as recognizably male or female. Because doctors in some cases determine the sex of an infant, this suggests that sex could be understood as a social construct, not just a biological concept.

Gender is a term used to describe socially prescribed behaviors and modes of comportment that are assumed appropriate for each sex. In other words, gender can be understood as the ways in which different cultures have constructed the categories of masculinity and femininity and have linked each to one of the sexes: masculinity to males, femininity to females. As with biological sex, it is assumed there are only two genders, and they are seen as mutually exclusive. In Western cultures such as the United States, sex and gender are made to be linked: males are masculine and females are feminine.

Sexuality, also, is constructed in mutually exclusive terms: one is said to be either heterosexual or homosexual, but never both. Furthermore, many societies have constructed heterosexuality as the norm; that is, heterosexuality is constructed as the right form of sexuality and identity and often linked to the imperative of reproductive heterosexuality. In many cultures, sex, gender, and sexuality are lined up as an inevitable trajectory: for example, males must be masculine and must sexually desire the opposite gender. Many institutions reinforce this idea through coercive and noncoercive means. Such institutions include government, the legal system, religion, the media, family, educational establishments, business and workplace environments, and the medical community. With so many institutions constructing and reinforcing a heterosexual understanding about biological sex, gender, and sexuality, it can be said that these categories are highly regulated and, thus, political.

The term *transgender* was coined in the 1980s. It was originally used by individuals who did not wish to undergo sex reassignment surgery but who also felt that the term *cross-dresser* did not accurately characterize their ongoing commitment to gender bending. Transgender is now used as an umbrella term to designate a broad range of gender-ambiguous identities and practices. From this perspective, queer boys can be seen as a gender-ambiguous category characterized by a reworking of the meanings of *boy* in ways that challenge the presumed naturalness of, stability in, and inevitable link between male, masculinity, and heterosexual desire.

Queer Boys and Queer Theory

As a gender-ambiguous category, the adjective *queer* in the phrase *queer boys* takes on a particular meaning. While the etymology of the term *queer* is unknown, its meanings have varied over time. Today, for example, *queer* is still used by some as an offensive term meaning gay. It is also used as an umbrella category, a catchall phrase, for gay, lesbian, bisexual, and transgender. In addition, *queer* can be used as a verb, as in to queer something. In many institutions of higher learning, *queer*, as a verb, has been deployed to queer our assumptions about the naturalness of the categories of heterosexuality and homosexuality. In this way, heterosexuality and homosexuality have been denaturalized—that is, revealed to be historically and socially constructed categories. This process of queering—of denaturalizing the assumed naturalness of, and links between, categories such as male/female, man/woman, and straight/gay—coupled with showing how these categories are not mutually exclusive but rather overlap in many complex and contradictory ways, highlights some of the critical work being done in the field of study known as *queer theory*, which developed in academia in the early 1990s. Taken in this context, the term *queer* in the phrase *queer boys* takes on a particular meaning and political significance as a form of gender and sexual politics. That is, wittingly and unwittingly queer boys queer/denaturalize our assumptions that sex, gender, and sexuality are fixed, coherent, and natural. They do this by living out their gender identity in ways that mix up and thereby highlight the socially constructed dominant heterosexual trajectory of male to masculinity to heterosexual desire. The story of Ludovic Fabre provides a case in point.

Ludovic Fabre: A Queer Boy, Girl-Boy
Ma Vie En Rose (My Life in Pink)

Winner (among many other awards) of the Golden Globe for Best Foreign Language Film at the 55th Golden Globe Awards in 1998, *Ma Vie En Rose* (English translation: *My Life in Pink*) was Belgian director Alain Berliner's feature film debut. In the United States, the film was rated R by the MPAA (Motion Picture Association of America). This rating caused some controversy because the film contains minimal sexual content and violence. Many believed the R rating was the result of transphobia—discrimination against transgender people.

The story centers on seven-year-old Ludovic Fabre, a biological male whose gender identity is female. The controversy about his queer boy identity begins to escalate early in the film when he and Jerome, the son of his father's boss, are caught pretending to get married. While several of the other characters view Ludovic's desire to marry Jerome as an expression of Ludovic's homosexual identity, Ludovic by contrast seems to understand his attraction to Jerome as indicative of his heterosexuality—for example, when Ludovic's mother tells him that boys don't marry other boys, Ludovic assures her that he understands that. This scene provides us with a glimpse of how queer boys, even unwittingly, queer or denaturalize the mainstream heterosexual assumption that one's sexual orientation is based on the relationship between biological sex and the gender of one's object-choice. For example, within a dominant heterosexual worldview, if one is biologically male and attracted to another male, then that person's sexual orientation is considered homosexual. However, for Ludovic, his sexual orientation is based on the relationship between his gender identity (female) and the gender of his object-choice (male), so in Ludovic's mind he is straight.

As a transgender child in a heterosexual world, Ludovic struggles to make sense for himself, as well as explain to those around him, his queer boy identity. For example, after receiving a short biology lesson from his teenage sister on how babies are made, Ludovic concludes that God intended for Ludovic to be a girl. Indeed, he imagines God casting from Heaven two Xs and a Y toward Ludovic's chimney. One of his X's, however, accidentally bypasses the chimney and ends up in the outdoor garbage can. Ludovic concludes this must be some kind of scientific error, and shortly thereafter he pronounces to Jerome and his parents that he is a girl-boy. Such a declaration causes alarm, anger, and confusion, especially with his father, because in a heterosexually dominant world, male/female and masculinity/femininity are constructed as mutually exclusive categories; to be sure, such categories are seen as discrete and self-contained.

Although Ludovic can be seen as someone who thinks of his gender identity as female, his own positioning of his identity, however temporary, as a girl-boy situates Ludovic in one of the most queer of possible identity spaces: that of a border zone dweller who lives at the intersection of multiple overlapping identity categories (i.e., girl-boy). In this way, Ludovic is indeed a queer boy, an individual who queers—that is, expands—the meaning of the category of boy by blending it with the category of girl.

Further Reading

Somerville, Siobhan. "Queer." In Bruce Burgett and Glenn Hendler (Eds.), *Keywords for American Cultural Studies*. New York: New York University Press, 2007, pp. 187–191.

Sullivan, Nikki. *A Critical Introduction to Queer Theory*. New York: New York University Press, 2003.

Tauches, Kimberly. "Transgendering: Challenging the 'Normal.'" In Steven Seidman, Nancy Fischer, and Chet Meeks (Eds.), *Introducing the New Sexuality Studies: Original Essays and Interviews*. London and New York: Routledge, 2006, pp. 173–179.

Nelson M. Rodriguez

Raising Boys

All infants, including baby boys, are vulnerable and open, desirous of loving contact, and very clear about expressing their feelings. The way boys are raised—from the touch they receive to the tone of voice they hear from those around them, from their playthings to the messages they receive about life—affects how these early qualities manifest in the men they will become. The role played by families, schools, religious groups, and community organizations in raising boys is crucial. All children grow up with culturally based gender expectations for their sex. For boys this means having to somehow *prove their masculinity,* which can be very challenging since what gets defined as masculine is not always the same in every situation, nor is it always in the best interest of boys themselves. As popular culture and changes in social structures increasingly indicate, boys growing up today will live in a world of greater equality between the sexes. Thus, raising boys means helping them see there are many ways of being masculine.

While biological differences between boys and girls do exist, cultural stereotypes about how males are *supposed to be* can be even more powerful than genes and hormones in affecting their lives as children and adults. Consciously or not, parents, teachers, and other caregivers raise boys so they will have the personality and behavior patterns considered necessary to be a successful male in their society. In Western cultures, this has traditionally meant that males should be aggressive, unemotionally rational, and competitive, given the expectation that such males will be more economically successful, and thus able to support a family in the role of husband and father. It's not just the caring adults in boys' lives who promote these values. Boys are exposed throughout their childhoods to cultural messages through television shows and commercials, popular music, video games, and films that promote a supercharged view of being male—tough, athletic, sexually aggressive, and even violent. Parents may struggle to find clothes, toys, and books for their sons that do not reinforce these stereotypes.

Possibilities for girls and women in the United States and around the world have increased in the last 40 years so that now they can also be economically successful and able to support themselves and their children. Despite these changes, expectations of males have not shifted as much. Girls with a wide range of gendered behavior are accepted—from athletes to violinists, from girls who want to become stay-at-home mothers to those who want to have careers—while boys may still be expected to act tough, win at all costs, and never show any feelings that would make them seem vulnerable.

The reality is that, discounting effects of culture and socialization, boys and girls are actually much more alike than they are different; not all boys are alike, nor are girls. Some boys are timid and shy while some girls are bold and aggressive. Biological differences exist between boys, as well as between girls. For example, both girls and boys have testosterone, even though, on the average, prepubertal boys have slightly higher levels than do girls. Also, even though some people look at boys playing rough, even to the point of meanness, and do not intervene—thinking "that's just how boys are"—the effect of testosterone on behavior remains unclear. Some studies have shown that aggressive behavior leads to higher levels of testosterone, rather than vice versa. Even having one's team win a competition can result in higher levels of testosterone among fans of the winning team, as compared to the fans of the team that lost. So testosterone itself does not explain how boys are. And, of course, not all boys even enjoy competitive athletics, aggressiveness, or playing rough. Some do; some do not.

Whatever the cause and effect of hormones, the reality is that boys need the same kind of supportive nurturance as girls in order to grow to be fully functioning adults in an increasingly egalitarian society. Yet studies have shown that both mothers and fathers hold and cuddle boys less, and respond to them more harshly than they do girls. They also talk less to boys, as infants, toddlers, and at school age, which shows up as boys having more limited verbal skills and vocabulary than girls. The words boys use and even their sentences are shorter; for example, "That was fun!" as opposed to "I really loved being with you!" Particularly lacking are words for communication of feelings or intimacy. Encouraging boys to have friendships that are emotionally close, with both boys and girls if they wish, can help them learn relationship skills needed in adult life.

The sense that "boys will be boys," as if it was biologically determined, can keep parents, teachers, and other caregivers from responding to boys in ways that will aid their emotional development. As with all children, what works best is clear expectations for behavior, with limits set and enforced, but not harshly. Children learn what they live; so hitting a boy for hitting another boy only leads to more of the same. In part due to expectations that boys and men need to be "on top of the heap," boys may be especially sensitive to being shamed. Their embarrassment about being yelled at or hit by a parent or someone else with power over them can lead to anger that is taken out on other children, especially other boys they see as somehow less powerful than themselves. Those who are smaller and/or less traditionally masculine are particularly vulnerable to getting picked on and beat up by other boys.

What about raising boys for whom traditional masculinity is just not their thing? This may be subtle, such as a boy whose interest in ballet or reading is much more compelling than playing sports. Parents and teachers can encourage this child to develop his strengths, and although he may be vulnerable to being picked on by other boys who see such activities as *girlish,* parents and teachers can help him understand that harassment by other boys is just a form of bullying that may be based on homophobia.

Homophobia—the fear or disdain for those who are perceived to be homosexual—serves to keep people entrenched in narrow gender roles. This is because of the confusion between ways of expressing one's gender and one's sexual orientation. They are not the same. Males who have feminine characteristics may be either heterosexual or gay, as may males who are more traditionally masculine. Education emphasizing the message that ways of being male can exist across a spectrum of possibilities will serve this boy well, and also those bullies whose masculinity may be threatened by his.

While there is increasing societal awareness of intersex or transgender children, parents and caregivers may feel confused and alone when a child who was labeled female at birth says she wants to be a boy, or when a boy wants to wear dresses to school. Having a supportive and not overly reactive response to children making such requests honors the idea of individual variability in gender presentation. Those around this child may need to be educated about his/her needs in order to support the child's development and safety.

Raising children to both survive and thrive given their own particular way of being a gendered person is an important task for all involved. Because gender expectations for males have been slower to change than for females, boys and those who love them face particular challenges. Those raising boys can help them develop their emotional intelligence and communication skills, and encourage them to find and appreciate their own way of being masculine.

Further Reading

Kindlon, Dan and Michael Thompson. *Raising Cain: Protecting the Emotional Life of Boys.* New York: Ballantine Books, 2000.

Nokoff, Natalie and Anne Fausto-Sterling. Raising Gender: Children Developing Millisecond by Millisecond [Online February 2008], *American Sexuality Magazine* Web site <http://nsrc.sfsu.edu/MagArticle.cfm?Article=821&PageID=0>.

Pollack, William. *Real Boys: Rescuing Our Sons from the Myths of Boyhood.* New York: Macmillan, 1999.

Betsy Crane

"Real Men"

"Why don't you be a *real man?*" "Man up!" "Grow some balls!" "Stop being a [fill in the blank with any label that tends to emasculate—*bitch, punk, sissy, fag, pussy, wuss*]!" These are just a few of the expressions that may be used today when challenging the male gender to be a *real man* in traditional *and* contemporary American society. What images or names come to mind when envisioning a *real man?* Some may conjure up images of the Marlboro Man or the Brawny paper towel mascot, or famous males such as Humphrey Bogart, Bruce Willis, John Wayne, Dean Martin, George Clooney, Sylvester Stallone, Bruce Springsteen, or John F. Kennedy. What are some of the characteristics that these *real men* have in common? They are charismatic, charming and confident, masculine and strong, cool and stylish, leaders and protectors, intelligent and powerful, brave and loyal (especially to their male friends), appealing to both men and women, garner respect from both sexes, and they tend to be white.

Where do these expectations of being a *real man* come from? Historically to present day, males have been the aggressive, hunter-gatherers whose job is to protect and provide for their families. *Real men* are supposed to be physically strong and aggressive, to shed no tears, and to be in control at the workplace and at home. Some heterosexual men believe they should dominate their women. It is not uncommon to hear such men make such statements as, "she should know her place." As boys grow into men, they internalize this belief and act accordingly; however, they often encounter personal conflicts and struggles when balancing the dual roles of being a *real man*—one who must act as protector and defend to death the honor of his woman and defend his own manhood, and yet still be sensitive, caring, romantic, expressive emotionally, and supportive of female needs and desires.

To understand this conflict, other avenues in which gender roles are constructed should be explored. Gender identity is psychologically constructed through interpersonal relationships influenced by family, peer groups, society, culture, and religion. However, biology also plays a role in the development of identity.

Biological features, such as physical makeup, internal reproductive organs, external genitalia, and functions of the brain, determine one's sex and gender. Biology, however, does not *determine* behavior or personality; it simply *influences* behavior. For example, research has suggested that due to higher levels of testosterone found in the male brain, males tend to act in more aggressive behaviors (a major characteristic that defines the *real man*). These behaviors are elaborated upon and shaped by outside influences as the male child moves from boyhood to manhood. Research also suggests that greater development of the left side of the male brain aides in linear and logical thinking—elements that may contribute to beliefs that characterize the male as being the *reasonable and rational* gender over the *emotional and illogical* female gender.

Psychological theories also determine gender development, including social learning, cognitive, and cultural theories. These theories focus on how interpersonal and social relationships and expectations influence gender-specific behaviors and personality traits. The process of socialization is a powerful mechanism that teaches children how to act and behave. One theory of how socialization works is through *social learning theory* developed by Albert Bandura. Peer groups, family members, mass media, and schools are highly influential in teaching children gender-specific behaviors, among other things, very early on in age. Children learn behaviors through observation, imitation, and reactions from others. Moreover, children learn quickly to repeat behaviors that elicit positive responses and rewards. For example, little boys receive rewards for not crying, thus perpetuating masculine behavior. They may receive positive reinforcement—"You're such a tough boy" or "Boys don't cry"—for holding in their tears and toughing it out regardless of how painful their injury or sadness may be. The positive reinforcement or rewards received for toughing it out or manning up teaches them how boys are supposed to act and behave, thus causing them to internalize the behavior and repeat it in the future.

Cognitive development theorists such as Jean Piaget, Lawrence Kohlberg, and Carol Gilligan argue that as children progress through several stages of development, they play active roles in developing their own gender identity and can identify behaviors that exhibit either masculine or feminine traits by the age of five or six. In the early stages (birth to approximately 30 months), children seek signs or labels from others to determine their gender ("I am a boy/girl"). They then mimic behaviors and seek approval from same-sex role models. As a result, children gain a sense of gender stability and gender constancy in which they understand they will always be a boy [or girl] and eventually grow up to be a man [or woman]. Same-sex models become extremely influential as children learn attitudes, feelings, and patterns of behaviors to emulate as they progress through childhood and adolescence.

Finally, cultural theorists explaining gender development contend that both males and females can enact similar characteristic traits such as showing aggressiveness or expressing emotions. However, it is the culture in which they live that determines the *rules* for appropriate or inappropriate behavior based on gender roles. Family, peer groups, mass media, and schools all play a role in cultivating or shaping gender identity. For example, research suggests that by the second and third grades, boys are highly influenced by their peer groups. Sex-segregation begins in the lunchroom and playground; boys assert their independence from teachers and place more importance on their male peer group; and boys openly challenge teacher authority. A powerful male culture may emerge with a sense of entitlement and privilege.

Boys who are excluded or rejected from the dominant male peer group are often times labeled as *sissies* for not fitting in or failing to exhibit masculine characteristics. These excluded boys often experience an increasingly high number of social, emotional, and academic problems as they progress through the elementary grade levels.

By the middle school years, gender roles are even more pervasive. Boys repress exhibiting artistic skills in music and art classes for fear of being called a *fag*. The male peer group becomes competitive and hierarchal with one or two leaders emerging from the pack. Play is rough and aggressive to show strength and toughness. Boys tend to misbehave and disrupt classroom instruction and as a result account for the majority of disciplinary actions, including suspensions, placement into special education tracks, and failure to advance to the next grade level. This pattern continues throughout the high school years resulting in an increasing number of boys dropping out of school. Research also reveals that boys place greater importance on sports, athletic prowess, physical appearance, and popularity over academics.

In addition to peer groups impacting gender roles, mass media play a significant role in shaping gender identity as well. Historically to present-day, various mediums in mass media have always stressed distinct differences in defining masculinity in opposition to femininity. Persistent images of masculinity have been constructed and sustained in the form of advertisements, film, television, popular music, male magazines, and sports, particularly professional wrestling.

Some common elements found in these various mediums is that masculinity is equated to physical strength, power, aggression, confidence, control, and even violence, especially prevalent in the movie and music industries, professional wrestling, sports culture, and children's toys and cartoons. The messages elicited from these images are portrayed as natural and normal, yet they are insidious and harmful if careful analysis and critique are absent.

Rejection from peer groups in schools, insidious messages from mass media, and conflicting gender expectations from family, schools, and community may all serve as strong indicators for future problems as boys enter the gates of manhood. Social and emotional problems such as depression, isolation, repression of feelings, drug or alcohol abuse, anger and frustration, and in severe cases violence and suicide have been reported.

Families, schools, communities, and media outlets can help alleviate and prevent potential problems resulting from gender stereotyping by first and foremost addressing it. Parents and schools could provide safe, shame-free zones in which boys can freely express their fears and emotions without feeling shame in doing so. School curricula should address gender bias and stereotyping across disciplines as well as begin to recognize and validate diverse male figures who exhibit caring, loving, and nurturing characteristics. Schools could also implement media literacy programs or entertainment assessment tools in hopes of creating media savvy consumers who are conscious of media influence, gender stereotyping, and dominant gender ideology. Media should follow suit by portraying males in a variety of roles in which they are shown expressing a wide range of emotions. Few images should not dominate, standardize, or narrowly define male gender roles. Employing these strategies will help lay the foundation of studying, understanding, and accepting how gender identity is shaped and formed, thus carving a safe space for alternative gender ideologies to enter the mainstream. Boys are then free to make independent and comfortable choices as to the role(s) they wish to identify with.

Further Reading

Holtzman, Linda. *Media Messages.* Armonk, NY: M. E. Sharpe, Inc., 2000.
Wood, Julia T. *Gendered Lives: Communication, Gender and Culture.* Belmont, CA: Wadsworth, 1994.

Priya Parmar

Rites of Passage

Ceremonies that are said to facilitate social development are variably called *rites of passage* and *initiation rituals*. Anthropologists distinguish such ceremonies from festivities in which major life accomplishments are celebrated or publically announced (e.g., graduation), and from occasions at which legal rights are recognized and exercised for the first time (e.g., acquiring a driver's license). The notion *coming of age* can variably refer to these events, but usually has a personal, psychological, and often psychosexual connotation. Whether life course ceremonialism for boys facilitates or recognizes either the beginnings of or transition to manhood often depends on sociological, anthropological, and individual interpretation. This is especially so where, as in the United States, legal definitions of majority, birthdays, high school graduations, first pay cheques, and "having done it for the first time" say nothing definite about maturity or masculinity.

The various forms of life course ceremonialism in the contemporary United States are mainly associated with world religions, ethnic minorities and community initiatives, the educational system (universities), and other state institutes (armed forces). Varying widely in their formalization, such ceremonies commonly introduce young men not to adulthood but variably to married life (*bachelor parties*), campus life (*fraternity initiations*), student life (*white coat ceremonies* for freshman medical students), gang life (*blood-in*, or the requirement for a murder to be allowed membership in urban gangs, and *jump-in:* veteran gang members beat an initiate to determine if he is *man* enough to be a member of the gang), athletic teams, or male-dominated professions (*wetting-down*, involving tossing a new Navy officer into the sea, and *Neptune's Day*, commemorating a sailor's first crossing of the equator).

Some native ceremonies, such as the *vision quest* and First Salmon (or *first kill*) Ceremony, encountered across a range of American Indian contexts may have been held on American soil long before it was called *American*. Other ceremonies have been imported by immigrant populations, such as the Jewish *bar mitzvah*. Still others have been invented to tackle what are perceived to be specifically American twentieth- and twenty-first-century problems with the male life course.

Whether life course ceremonies are to be held exclusively for boys, and, if so, whether they "make a man out of a boy" is often debated. For example, *bar mitzvah* among Jews is traditionally held only for boys at age 13 as they are called up to read from the Torah (part of the Hebrew Bible) for the first time. The traditional reason for this age is peculiar: The rabbis (teachers) of the Talmud (ancient Jewish law text) assume that a congregation would be dishonored if a *child* were to read from the Torah because people might assume that none of the adults present were competent to read! Rituals for girls, *bat mitzvah*, have historical precursors in the nineteenth century, but were not held in America until 1922 (more than a hundred years after its being instituted in Berlin) and variably at ages 12 or 13. Furthermore, how these boy and girl ceremonies overlap in meaning and practice is subject to controversy across Jewish denominations—some twentieth-century Orthodox (strict) authorities considered rituals for girls nonsense.

By contrast, in Christianity the life course rituals called *sacraments*, including *confirmation*, are not exclusive to boys; the age of the participants has varied from "the age of reason" (7) to 16. The Latina *quinceañera* or "sweet fifteen" (originally an Aztec rite) and also "sweet sixteen" parties are traditionally not held for boys. Other customs for boys, including Amerindian *vision quests*, were not always restricted to males of all ages, and usually only the first quest arguably had initiatory significance.

Comparably, the Amish *rumspringa* is not an initiation ritual in the technical sense, rather a custom that is to provide adolescents with the option of choice in determining what to do with their future. After age 16, Amish youth will venture outside the secluded life of Amish childhood and taste the outside English world, which in Amish views constitutes "the devil's playground," before they make the choice whether to be baptized in the order of the Amish church and thus settle down. Here, also, the custom is not restricted to boys, although boys may experience aspects differently than girls. Driving a car and drinking alcohol, which the Amish reject, are the outstanding attractions for boys.

Controversy exists over the role of male initiation in contemporary American society. On the one hand, the thesis of *ritual deprivation* maintains that Western adolescents, specifically boys, lack cultural practices that recognize, announce, and celebrate a necessary and fundamental transition between young and mature, between child and adult. Such would present a problem in money-driven economies, such as the United States, in which spiritual dimensions were often lost to men. Accordingly the psychological *storm* or *crisis* of adolescence, and specifically its male excesses (theorists have called these *rebellion, acting out*), would be the psychological *alternative* to formal rituals, or at least the *result* of their absence. In the 1990s proponents of the American and European *men's movement* started to organize workshops and weekends for grown-up men focused on male bonding and a tapping into what was identified as "the deep masculine self." It was argued that American society had stopped providing to boys a clear sense and unambiguously positive narratives of maturity and masculinity. Workshops were theorized as initiating men into proper masculine adulthood. Models were used of myths with heroes fulfilling a challenging quest. In urban contexts across the English-speaking world, specific initiation programs for boys began to be designed, often inspired (however loosely) by rituals known from the mythological and ethnographical record the world over. They may include elements of camping, hunting, and survival, as well as travel away from home, male mentors, trials and contests, victory speeches, decorations, and return home. They provide a context for strengthening self esteem, father-son bonds and an opportunity for promoting responsible (e.g., girl-friendly) forms of masculinity.

A somewhat related popular hypothesis maintains that lacking universally recognized initiations, boys will invent their own markers and events of proclaiming maturity which could include anything from binge drinking, joy riding, extreme sports, drug use, or gang rape. Such *kind-of, sort-of* initiations have been considered ritualistic by sociologists and psychologists arguing they would cater to a felt deep, pressing need for masculine/mature activities that necessarily take on demonstrative forms. This line of argument maintains that initiations need not be widely approved, traditional, dramatized, or organized to be effective; in fact, their recognition as transformative could be limited, even strictly personal, and perhaps only looking back on events.

A contrary interpretation of above notions of ritual maintains that they merely promote or provide a stage for traditional masculine values and do too little to prevent antisexist outcome. It is argued that male initiations are commonly occasions for violent behavior, destructive hazing, bravado, unacceptable levels of risk-taking, health endangerment, and a cultivation of anti-feminine attitudes. Initiations, accordingly, are not only unnecessary but also damaging to boys, especially in their (future) relating to girls and women, and thus to society at large. This perspective is certainly gaining popularity outside America, for instance, in cases where indigenous South African initiations are known to have been accompanied by botched circumcisions, kidnapping, extreme malnutrition, sexual abuse, and various degrees of anti-school rhetoric. Likewise, fraternity and gang initiations are regularly associated in popular media with sexual transgression, hospitalizations, and occasionally death.

However, even apart from the acute dangers of limit- and risk-seeking behavior, it can be argued that the thesis of American or wider Western lack of initiation rituals is hard to substantiate. Clearly, what psychologists call *adolescence* cannot be reduced to the themes of male initiation, man-making, or indeed to male developmental psychology. Likewise, the complex social and cultural practices of what anthropologists call *initiation rituals* cannot be reduced to the American notion of *adolescence* or, again, to psychological theories. Boys worldwide will adhere to or else invent many ways of proving, showing, or confirming their masculinity and maturity, often at the same time, and will continue to feel the need to periodically reaffirm their acquired status.

Further Reading

Johnson, Jay, and Margery Holman. (Eds.). *Making the Team: Inside the World of Sport Initiations and Hazing.* Toronto: Canadian Scholars' Press, 2004.

Mahdi, Louise, Nancy Geyer Christopher, and Michael Meade. (Eds.). *Crossroads: The Quest for Contemporary Rites of Passage.* Chicago: Open Court, 1996.

Nuwer, Hank. (Ed.). *The Hazing Reader.* Bloomington, IN: Indiana University Press, 2004.

Raphael, Ray. *The Men from the Boys: Rites of Passage in Male America.* Lincoln, NE: University of Nebraska Press, 1988.

Diederik F. Janssen

Sissies

"People make fun of me because I lisp. Really! Such a fuss over a few extra S's!" These famous words, replete with *S's*, were spoken by the recurring fictional character Buddy Cole, a gay socialite played by Scott Thompson in the 1980s Canadian comedy show *Kids in the Hall*. The show ran from 1989 to 1995 on the Canadian Broadcasting Corporation (CBC) and was also broadcast on CBS and HBO in the United States. In reruns and on his blog (http://mrbuddycole.blogspot.com/), Buddy presents himself as a feminine, flamboyant, and perfectly coiffed man. He holds a martini in one hand and speaks directly into the camera at the viewers. Buddy Cole *holds court*, meaning that all eyes are on him while he tells his tales of lust and love among the cultural elite. He is not *on* a baseball team, but instead designs their outfits. He emphasizes his *S's*, evidently with no shame. Buddy Cole is a stereotypical sissy.

As his famous line would suggest, sissies are generally reviled. They are often the source of ridicule and mockery in Hollywood films such as *Beverly Hills Cop*, as portrayed by Eddie Murphy. Sissies are perceived as different from other boys because of their gender-based mannerisms and interests that are usually classified within the purview of girls instead of boys. To be labeled a sissy among peers in school, or even within one's family, is to be the recipient of social ostracization and bullying. The implication is that sissies are not *real* boys at all, but inferior versions. Sissies are scorned for being timid, quiet, and preferring to play with girls. School cultures typically reward masculine boys with attention and elite places on sports teams, but are hostile environments for boys who are not competitive and aggressive.

Socially, sissies straddle an uneasy line between boy (and the requisite interests and characteristics usually considered to be masculine) and girl (and those considered to be feminine). Sissies are perceived as threatening to other boys, that somehow they will infect them with (what are perceived as) their feminine afflictions. To maintain masculinity of other boys, sissies must be rejected or expunged through bullying, ostracization, and violence.

In 2008 such panic took a deadly turn when 15-year-old Lawrence King was shot to death in Oxnard, California, by a male peer because Lawrence liked feminine jewelry, clothing, and makeup. He also happened to be gay; however, not all sissies are gay. Sissies are thus not included in boy cultures, but rather are rejected from them. Their being rejected signifies to all other boys what will happen to them if they do not live up to the social expectations of what it means to act like a boy. Successful boys require the presence of unsuccessful boys as a yardstick with which to measure their masculine progress and prowess. In short, malicious treatment toward sissies maintains gender boundaries and highlights how normalcy is constructed and regulated.

Boys who are labeled as sissies are usually instilled with shame. For most parents, feminine behavior and girlish interests of their sons raise the fear that they will grow up to be homosexual. Being a sissy is equated with being weak, which does not fit into ideas of masculinity, boyhood, and manhood. Accepting some cross-cultural variation, masculine attributes such as strength, emotional distance, individuality, and competitiveness are strongly rewarded. Enforcing masculinity among boys is tyrannical rather than natural. In spite of strong social sanction for gender nonconformity, being a sissy does not have to be viewed as a condition that persists, such as psoriasis or heartburn.

A more supportive view is to understand that there are not only two types of gender, and humans are a variety of different expressions. It is widely assumed, even among medical practitioners, that gender is a simple matter: either one is a boy (they should be masculine) or one is a girl (they should be feminine). Such notions do not allow room to consider that gender represents a myriad of expressions and identities. Generally, however, and in Western societies at least, such social conditioning to the expectations of gender begins at birth. Boys receive blue blankets, girls receive pink ones. A pink blanket being given to a boy would be treated as a mistake, as misguided, perhaps even as abuse.

The fact that some boys are stigmatized for being sissies indicates that children are encouraged to *perform* (Butler, 1990) gender in particular, socially acceptable ways, and shamed when such performances do not conform to social expectations. To characterize gender as a *performance* suggests that *doing* gender is intentional and chosen. Through habit and social conditioning, many people unconsciously demonstrate in public that they are typical boys/men or girls/women with relative ease, but doing so does not mean that gender is somehow biological or genetic. Such linkages are common, yet spurious. Examining the ways in which gender is enforced and regulated in society becomes highly evident in cases of gender atypicality, such as that of sissies. Daily conditioning results in the appearance of gender as natural and normal when in fact it is constructed and highly regulated.

Rather than being looked at as a condition or syndrome in need of medical or psychiatric intervention, or as mistakes that must be corrected, or even as character weakness, sissies can (and should) be looked at through an alternative set of lenses, ones that recognize gender variance and diversity. In schools, Rofes (1995) suggests that sissy boys should be given options for activities apart from those that are attributed to normative boys, and should be recognized for achievements beyond masculine domains such as team sports. In schools and out, sissies can and should be supported rather than ostracized. They need not feel shame or inferiority because of their gender-based performances and interests. In the TV show *Will and Grace* (1998–2006), for instance, Jack McFarlane (played by Sean Hayes) exemplifies *sissy pride* by holding his head up high as he prances throughout New York, as does Emmett Honeycutt (played by Peter Paige) throughout Pittsburgh in the U.S. version of *Queer as Folk* (2000–2005). Although men rather than boys, the characters of Jack and Emmett potentially serve as positive role models for boys who do not fit within mainstream notions of what it means to be a boy. Apart from fictitious characters, the Radical Faeries (http://www.radfae.org/) also celebrate and express their femininities.

For young boys, two picture books in particular provide the message that sissy boys are fine just the way they are. In *Oliver Button Is a Sissy* (dePaola, 1979) and *The Sissy Duckling* (Fierstein and Cole, 2002), the protagonists are males (human and duck, respectively) who enjoy activities that are mostly associated with girls, such as skipping, drama, dancing, and baking. In these two books, gender is constructed not as a natural outcome of human biology, but rather as ideology that hierarchically organizes the social world. In each of these stories, men and boys reject and harm Oliver and Elmer because both fail to meet the standards within their social worlds of what it means to be a boy. They are negatively perceived as different from the rest of their peers. Eventually, the fathers learn to accept their sons' gender difference, regardless of negative and prejudiced public opinion. Oliver and Elmer eventually embrace with pride their gender nonconformity. Films such as *Ma Vie en Rose* (1997) and *Running with Scissors* (2006) depict sissy boys with dignity and sensitivity. The ABC news program 20/20 in their documentary called *My Secret Life* (Gutman, 2007) did likewise in interviews conducted by Barbara Walters of transgendered children, some of whom had been vilified as sissies, and their families.

People who are marginalized (such as those of color, and gays and lesbians) know the tenacity of social oppression, prejudice, and hate. It is doubtful that sissyphobia (to use Bergling's 2001 term) will weaken any time soon. Meanwhile, sissy boys will have to resort to the usual tactics in order to survive schooling—such as refusing the label by taking on a *tough guise* (Jhully, 1999), pretending to be sick to avoid going to school, and running from tormentors. But even if only in secret, some sissy boys can instead retain their self esteem in the face of constant disavowal from those around them, even their loved ones. Those boys have little choice but to find commonalities with fictitious characters such as Buddy Cole. A lucky few may be able to enhance their *S's* in school and home environments where they will not be shamed from doing so.

Further Reading

Butler, Judith. *Gender Trouble: Feminism and the Subversion of Identity.* New York: Routledge, 1990.

dePaola, Tomie. *Oliver Button Is a Sissy.* San Diego, CA: Voyager, 1979.

Fierstein, Harvey, and Henry Cole. *The Sissy Duckling.* New York: Simon & Schuster, 2002.

Green, Richard. *The "Sissy Boy Syndrome" and the Development of Homosexuality.* New Haven, CT: Yale, 1987.

Gutman, Heidi (Producer, *My Secret Life*). (April 26, 2007). *20/20* [Television broadcast]. (http://abcnews.go.com/2020/story?id=3072518). Accessed 19 March 2008.

Jhully, S. Director. Tough Guise: Violence, Media, and the Crisis of Masculinity. Amhurst, MASS: Media Education Foundation, 1999.

Rofes, Eric. "Making Our Schools Safe for Sissies." In Gerald Unks (Ed.), *The Gay Teen: Educational Practice and Theory for Lesbian, Gay and Bisexual Adolescents.* New York: Routledge, 1995, pp. 79–84.

Gerald Walton

SECTION 2

Differences and Boys

Aboriginal/Native Boys

There are certain historical and cultural facts a person needs to know and understand while discussing aboriginal/Native boys. First, there is no such thing as a generic aboriginal/Native. There are over 500 Native American tribes in North America today (approximately 2.3 million members) (Babco, 2005). Each tribe sees itself as unique and different.

Native people must contend with negative stereotypes from the movies and children's literature. When people think of aboriginals/Natives, most of the time they think of Indians in war bonnets galloping around on horses while living in tepees. This stereotype represents the Natives of the Plains years ago, but it does not include the majority of other tribes. Most Native people are sensitive about these stereotypes and the grouping of all Native people together.

Overview

Each of the tribes has a different language, culture, and history. Today, most aboriginal/Native boys are urban Indians living in cities (approximately 1 million) while the remainder are reservation Indians living on trust land. The U. S. government has worked hard to acculturate (adapt to another culture) and assimilate (absorbed into another culture) Native peoples through government policies and education. These policies have had a destructive effect on the aboriginal/Native boy.

Since the first white man landed on the shores of North America, there was a thirst for aboriginal/Native lands and resources. Some settlers wanted to make friends with the Native people while others did not consider Natives as human beings. This confusion continued throughout Native history. The U.S. government really wanted the aboriginal/Native problem to just go away. General Phillip Sheridan in 1869 after the Civil War said, "The only good Indian is a dead Indian," which pretty much summed up the overall attitude of many powerful people from that time.

Church people in the late 1800s saved Native people from sure extinction by proposing educational programs. The U.S. government was anxious to do this because the Sioux had just defeated General Custer and they feared an uprising. Children, especially the children of chiefs, were taken from their homes and placed in boarding schools far away from their families. Many Native children were sent to Carlisle, Pennsylvania, to Captain Richard Henry Pratt's famous Indian school, the Carlisle Indian Industrial School, which operated between 1879 and 1918. Children were given inferior care and they were not allowed to practice their culture or speak their language. Many children ran away or died and were buried in the cemetery at Carlisle. In the end, the boarding school experience devastated the families and social fabric of the tribes. Most aboriginal/Native boys have relatives who were schooled at a boarding school. Jim Thorpe, the outstanding football player and Olympic gold medalist (1888–1953), attended Carlisle. The school was a model to other federal government boarding schools for young American Indian boys and girls.

Other government policies were equally devastating and unsuccessful. The Dawes Act in 1887 gave some Indians allotments of land to farm, but the underlying effect was that many Native people lost their land to taxes and unscrupulous settlers. Another policy was relocation, which is how so many Natives ended up in the cities. Indian families in the 1950s were offered the opportunity to move to a city of their choice with financial support from the federal government for a limited time. This is the history that has shaped the present social, political, and economic conditions in which Native boys live today.

There are about 50,000 Indian children attending school on their reservations and about 480,000 attending schools off the reservation. Most aboriginal/Native boys attend schools where the Native population makes up a small percentage of the overall school population with their school probably located in an urban area. About 60 percent of Native Americans live in urban areas while approximately 538,000 Native people live on reservations. It is interesting to note that 25 percent of the Native population lives in the states of California and Oklahoma (Cultural Marketing Communications, 2005). In the 1990s, tribes operated 170 elementary and secondary schools on their reservations while 1,244 public schools had Native population of at least 25 percent. In public schools with high and low populations of Natives, 91 percent of the students graduated from high school. On the other hand, only 86 percent graduated from Bureau of Indian Affairs (BIA)/tribal schools (Pavel, Curtin, and Whitener, 1997). Many Native boys will join the military because of the economic benefits and the fulfillment of their warrior spirit. It is estimated that there were over 163,000 Native American veterans living in the United States between 2005 and 2007 (U.S. Census Bureau, 2007). In fact, Menominees have the highest enlistment on a per capita basis of young people after high school graduation in the United States (O'Connor and Crowe, 2008).

Profiles of Aboriginal/Native Boys

Following are three profiles of three different young men that provide a three-dimensional view of aboriginal/Native boys and their families. These boys represent different tribes and living situations of Native people: one lives on the Menominee Indian Reservation in Wisconsin; another lives in the Pine Ridge Reservation in South Dakota; and the third lives in Buffalo, New York. They face different triumphs and different struggles: life on a reservation can be difficult because of the limited economic opportunities, but it can also be difficult in urban areas as Native people try to maintain their culture and traditions while trying to function in the dominant culture.

•

In my language, my name means "Little Thunder." The day I was born we were having a terrible rainstorm with thunder and lightning making a racket. When I have a son of my own, I will have his grandfather give him that name, too.

I am 16 years old and a junior in high school. We go to public high school on the Menominee Indian Reservation. My favorite food is pizza, but I like it when the cooks at school treat us with Indian tacos.

My favorite sport is basketball and I play as often as possible at Slam City. I also play football and baseball, but only to keep in shape for basketball. My mom works at the Headstart program with the little ones and my Dad works in the woods. We live in federal housing, but not in a project area with a lot of other houses. It's in a scattered site close to one of our lakes. I like this because I can fish all spring and summer and ice fish in the winter. I also like to hunt during the fall deer season. And we can hunt year around, but we never hunt in the spring and summer. Once we see the fireflies in late August, we know that the deer are waiting to provide food for our people. I killed my first deer when I was eleven years old and my parents had a big honoring feast for me.

I will be graduating from high school in another year and I would like to attend our local college. First I plan to join the Marine Corps, which is a family tradition. I come from a family of warriors and we all know that it is our duty to serve the people by offering protection to them. It is a scary thought to join the Marines, but it's something I am looking forward to.

•

I am 16 years old. My parents were killed in a car accident when I was about nine years old. I live with my grandparents in the Wounded Knee District located on the Pine Ridge Indian Reservation.

My reservation is huge and covers over two million acres of land in South Dakota. They say our reservation is as big as the state of Connecticut, but I don't know if that's true because I have not been there. The closest city is Rapid City, but we don't travel there very often because it is so far away.

My grandparents are lucky because we own a ranch and house. We raise hemp and buffalo, which is a lot of work. I like it because I can ride my horse. Most of my friends live in Manderson in public housing and many people live in their houses. The houses are pretty run down and some of them have mold in them that make the babies sick.

My high school is about 40 miles from my house. I have to get up early to catch the school bus and make it to school on time. Some of my friends stay at the dormitories there because they live so far away. I stayed in the dorms my freshman year.

I am an okay student and my grandparents expect me to do well in school. I would like to finish high school. This is a big deal because some of my friends are having a tough time making it through high school. Some of them have problems and so they miss a lot of school. I had a friend who committed suicide last year. It was sad. I am an exceptional basketball and football player because I am so tall and fast. It's one of the things I look forward to at school.

I still don't know what I will do if I graduate from high school. I will either go to college at the Oglala Tribal College or I might join the army. We don't have a lot of options here because there aren't many jobs around here.

•

My dad calls me Jose in honor of my grandfather from Mexico, even though that's not really my name. My mother is from the Seneca territory and my grandmother is traditional longhouse. We live in the nearby city in an apartment where my dad can get work. We have an interesting house. During the week my mother makes fried bread and beans for dinner and when my dad is home on weekends he makes tortillas for us.

I come from a large family and we are considered city Indians. Most of my older brothers and sisters never finished high school. They're smart but they don't like school. We all like to read. We are just not into school stuff. We are kind of a tough family and we don't take anything from anybody. Everyone knows not to mess with us unless they want a fight.

I am in junior high school, but I don't like school. The school has many students from different cultures and it is easy to get lost in it. My main interests are the computer and playing lacrosse. I am a good player and we play in the summer and spring.

My grandmother is proud of me because lacrosse is a traditional game in our culture. She wants us to know where we come from so she is always making us listen to her stories about our tribe. She has a house and land on the reservation. We go out to visit whenever we can. Sometimes she will take us to the longhouse. It's often hard trying to fit in. City people tell us to go back to the reservation and the reservation people tell us to go back to the city.

I don't know what I want to do when I am older. My brothers all joined the army, so I might do that. My mother says I should go to work at the casino our tribe runs. The pay is good, but I will have to finish high school to get a job there.

Further Reading

Adams, David Wallace. *Education for Extinction*. Lawrence, KS: University Press of Kansas, 1995.

Babco, E. L. *The Status of Native Americans in Science and Engineering*. Washington, DC: National Academy of Engineering, 2005.

Brown, Dee. *Bury My Heart at Wounded Knee*. New York: Henry Holt and Company, LLC, 1970.

Cultural Marketing Communications. Fact Sheet: First Nations/Native Americans in the United States (2005). Retrieved January 7, 2009, from www .culturalmarketingcommunications.com/FactSheet_nativeamericans.pdf.

Davis, Britton. *The Truth about Geronimo.* Lincoln, NE: University of Nebraska Press, 1929.

O'Connor, Philip, and Crowe, Kevin. Where to Find New Soldiers: Military Commitment Runs Strong in Menominee Tribe. *LaCrosse Tribune,* July 6.

Pavel, D. M., Curtin, T. R., and Whitener, S. Characteristics of American Indians and Alaska Native Education: Results from the 1990–91 and 1993–94 Schools and Staffing Surveys. U.S. Department of Education Web site. Retrieved January 4, 2009, from nces.ed.gov/Pubsearch/pubsinfo.asp?pubid=97451-21k.

Sugden, John. *Tecumseh's Last Stand.* Norman, OK: University of Oklahoma Press, 1985.

U.S. Census Bureau. 2005–2007 American Community Survey 3-Year Estimates. U.S. Census Bureau FactFinder Web site. Retrieved March 2, 2009, from http://factfinder.census.gov/servlet/DatasetMainPageServlet?_program=ACS.

Wheeler, Robert. *Jim Thorpe.* Norman, OK: University of Oklahoma Press, 1975.

Lisa S. Waukau and Lauren "Candy" Waukau-Villagomez

African American Boys and Stereotypes

Gangsta, pimp, buffoon . . . these images or representations of Black males are depicted regularly in the music videos, TV, and movies of contemporary popular culture. Our sense of what it means to be Black has thus been socially constructed, given a meaning that often works to create our beliefs about who African Americans are. Those contemporary notions of the Gangsta rapper or playboy/dog have long historical roots. Even prior to slavery, European's first encounters with Africans led to the image of them as uncivilized, oversexed savages. Those skewed ideas underwent a transformation during the Peculiar Institution of slavery in the United States. To the raced representations of what it meant to be Black were added gendered ideas, establishing society's views of Black women and men.

Black males were seen as Bucks—strong and physical—and as the Savage—uneducated, not fully human, and needing to be controlled. Later, as slavery gave way to reconstruction and an increasingly industrialized and urbanized United States, the social notions of the African American male morphed again. The new, but not so new, ideas of the Black man began to include the Coon—the Black man who wanted to be like whites, but who was not able to do so and became comical in the attempt with misspoken words, loud dress, and poor manner. To the Coon was added Step 'n Fetchit—the lazy shiftless Black male; the Uncle—reflecting the servile nature of Blacks; and the Brute savage—more interested in fighting, drinking, and gambling than anything else.

Using popular culture to spread these images, the caricatures of the Black male appeared on cookie jars, lawn ornaments, music sheet covers, and minstrel shows. They became the most common ways we thought of Black men, superceding the actual lives of Blacks being lived out around us. A film still considered a classic of early movie making, *Birth of a Nation* is a perfect example of the power of these constructions. Released in 1915, the film was seen as an account of our *history* as a nation. It showed happy slaves who reverted to savagery in the face of freedom. It depicted Black-elected government officials in session eating watermelon and chicken while shooting dice. And what some argue is one of the most potent images, it showed Black men obsessed with raping white women and the KKK as the heroes who came to the rescue. Though not solely responsible for it, the film's message, and other socially generated ideas of who Blacks were, made the establishing of Jim Crow laws seem necessary and the lynching of Black men justified.

These images and their power are not simply historical, through time they have remained, repeated over and over in media depictions, cultural stereotypes, and social messages. The Buck and Savage became the Brute savage and eventually today's idea of the Gangsta—strong, violent, and criminal; the image is not much changed from its historical roots. Similarly, today's depictions of the over-the-top comedic buffoon appears to find its roots in the Coon and Step 'n Fetchit of years gone by.

It is clear that part of the work these ideas produce are the impacts they have on how our society views African American men, but that is only part of the story. These images, representations, and social constructs are not simply seen by non-Blacks; all of us take them in. Once these messages are believed and internalized, they skew not only others' views of Blacks, but also their views of themselves. Some researchers argue that in response to these projected images and their potential internalizing work, Black men operate with a mask, trying to put on or emulate the images about them.

In an attempt to understand how all of this works in the minds of children, a study was conducted of fifth-, sixth-, and seventh-grade African American children in an after-school community program near a large, urban midwestern city. Like most boys, when initially asked what it means to be male, they said typical things such as "rough" and "tough." In their descriptions, maleness was centered on the body, strength, and athleticism. Not only was it physical, but it appeared as something one could earn. It was so external that some boys could lose it, as with the ones who were described as "fags" or "the kind of boys that girls don't like." Similarly, it could be attained by girls, as with a young woman who was good at fighting and basketball and was called "a boy," by the boys in the fifth-grade room.

Given those findings and existing research on Black maleness, a description of hypermaleness was expected when asked what masculinity meant. Instead, the boys described a caring and socially oriented maleness. One young man said masculinity was "be[ing] strong . . . like help a lady, like a old lady if she had heavy bags you'd . . . help her carry [them] across the street"; and another said, "fight less, work harder at education, be nicer"; and yet another, "being someone others could talk to."

This same theme arose again when the boys were asked what they wished their teachers knew of them. One young man said, "[T]hat I'm more kind . . . than they saw"; another, "that I am smart and that I do put my mind to things and that I have a funny side to me"; still another stated, "nice to other people

. . . kind . . . helpful . . . I'm a nice guy some of the time"; and one fifth-grader said, "my heart I guess."

In their words, it appears that young men think boyhood is marked by the constructions of maleness in society, yet masculinity, or mature maleness, is the ability to live beyond them. Masculinity was not merely being older, but having grown beyond a simplistic externally derived status and living instead in an emotive, relational sense of self and connection to others. These were not young versions of the males of gangsta rap videos or the drug dealers or pimps from movies, these were boys desiring for others to see them and their hearts.

Many Black boys will resist the notion of heart. Often when asked about what it means to be Black, children will reveal how much they are actually aware of the ways Blacks are stereotypically viewed in society and how important it is to work against those ideas. A sixth-grader said that being Black meant "be[ing] strong . . . just to know that you have accomplished something that no one else did, or you accomplished something that was very hard to do, you did something good, even if it's not that much . . . that's what really, like, enlightens me about being Black, that's why I love to be Black, cause it's like, we, sometimes we get more opportunities, sometimes we don't, but we still keep working hard." Another stated, "You have to be able to put up with things, like certain things, like being Black." The boys see the limited images of Blacks and see themselves as needing to fight to become triumphant over them.

Given those thoughts, the findings from the questionnaire were surprising. The questionnaire asked the children to write down the first words that came to mind when they saw the words "girls," "boys," "Black girls," and "Black boys." The boys' answers to the word "girls" were largely centered on appearance (pretty, makeup, hair, etc.), but in commenting on "Black girls" their answers became sexualized. One young man who said "booty" about girls wrote "booty call" for Black girls. Another answered "nice" for girls, but said "nice butts" about Black girls. Words such as "friendly" and "talks a lot," which boys said about girls, became "girls that talk stuff" and "crazy ghetto" when referencing Black girls. The boys appeared to be using a social construction of Blackness. In stark contrast to their interview answers on what it means to be Black, here they were employing images that came straight from music videos, movies, and TV. On the questionnaires, the boys seemed to speak not from the voice of their lived experience, as they had prior, but with the ideas that swirl around them in popular culture.

That finding was confirmed when the boys were interviewed and asked what Black women were like. The most common answer was "strong." When asked what kind of strength, they responded with "all kinds"—physically, mentally, and socially. They loved and admired the women in their lives, yet also had the stereotypical ideas of Black women surrounding them as well. That contrast seems to reflect the complexity, power, and implications of these constructions.

This study revealed African American boys' views of the raced and gendered constructs that surround them as well as their desire to live outside of them. The boys articulated a desire to become caring men whom others look up to, respect, and admire and the kind of African Americans that overcome society's image of Blacks. They want the power to be themselves and it is up to us to equip and support them in living beyond the constructions.

Further Reading

Majors, Richard, and Billson, Janet Mancini. *Cool Pose: The Dilemmas of Black Manhood in America.* New York: Lexington Books, 1992.

Takaki, Ronald, ed. *From Different Shores: Perspectives on Race and Ethnicity in America.* New York: Oxford University Press, 1994.

Tatum, Beverly Daniel. *Why Are All of the Black Kids Sitting Together in the Cafeteria? And other Conversations about Race.* New York: Basic Books, 1999.

Thorne, Barrie. *Gender Play: Girls and Boys in School.* New Brunswick, NJ: Rutgers University Press, 1993.

West, Cornel. *Race Matters.* Boston: Beacon Press, 1993.

Denise A. Isom

African American Boys and the Hip Hop World

Hip hop music and culture have touched the lives of many young people, both in the United States and abroad. The role of hip hop music in the lives of African American boys is evident through observation of the selected tunes on iPods, sounds coming out of speakers in cars, or a survey of African American boys in many urban schools. Recent conversations with a group of high school-aged African American boys revealed a diverse taste in hip hop music—Young Jeezy, Jay Z, Tupac, Mos Def, and Talib Kweli. While these are the artists often cited by many African American boys, the messages portrayed by *some* of the artists do not lead many to see a positive impact on African American boys. Certainly, some parts of hip hop do not positively affect the behaviors and attitudes of African American boys. However, there is evidence of positive impacts of hip hop music on African American boys.

An understanding of hip hop as music *only* is superficial and limiting; moreover, many people have a false understanding of both hip hop as music and hip hop as a culture. With this in mind, it is imperative to explore a definition of hip hop.

What exactly is hip hop? Hip hop is a complex culture, deeply rooted in the Black and Puerto Rican communities of New York City. However, a contemporary analysis of hip hop reveals the expansion of the music and culture beyond the Black and Puerto Rican communities of New York City. In such places as Tokyo, Japan, and Berlin, Germany, hip hop has taken on a new generation of fans and followers globally.

Most "hip hop heads" would locate hip hop into four essential elements: rapping or MCing; DJing; creating graffiti art; and break dancing. Through these four elements of hip hop, a culture has developed that is firmly entrenched into American and world culture.

The challenge of defining hip hop is similar to defining the meaning of life . . . it depends on who you are and where you are situated. In other words, the music of hip hop is much more political in France and in Palestine than what mainstream media plays on the radio in the United States. Nonetheless, hip hop can be best described as an expressive art form that embraces music, dancing, and artistic beauty through the collaborative efforts of MCs, DJs, graffiti artists, and break-dancers.

With roots in communities that have been historically oppressed, a definition of hip hop must include its foundation. More succinctly, hip hop, with all four elements centering the culture, the grounding of hip hop, from a historical perspective, is at its foundation a critique of issues of racism and classism. Rising up out of the pains and struggles of Blacks and Puerto Ricans in New York City, an integral part of the definition of hip hop is its original efforts to explore issues of racism, classism, and poverty.

Influence of Hip Hop and African American Boys

Hip Hop and Social Activism

In response to the 2007 *Jena 6* legal battle in Louisiana, hip hop artists were able to mobilize young people, especially African American boys, to lead marches and protests. These protests including those held on college campuses and universities were lead by Mos Def, Talib Kweli, and Dead Prez. While calls from veteran civil rights leaders like Al Sharpton and Jesse Jackson might have yielded a much broader cross section of the African American community, the connection of African American males to hip hop artist is unmatched. Most importantly, African American males were involved and intimately connected in an outcry against injustice and a contemporary civil rights struggle in the twenty-first century.

In 2003–2004, Kanye West led a national voter's rights campaign targeted at young minorities. In his campaign, *Vote of Die,* he challenged African American males to vote during the presidential election and thereafter to eliminate voter apathy among young African Americans. In order for African American males to vote, he maintained that they needed to be knowledgeable about the candidates and the issues most severely confronting African American people as a whole. As a result, many young African Americans voted during the national election; overall voter turnout among young inner city voters increased nationally.

Hip Hop and Entrepreneurship

Many of today's leading hip hop artists transcend negatively biased media stereotypes and perceptions of hip hop and its artists. The following points illustrating the evolution of hip hop, the leading hip hop artists, and the positive impact of hip hop on African American boys must be understood in order to appreciate hip hop:

1. Hip hop currently dominates the musical sales charts.
2. Hip hop is mainstream music for young people, which makes it cross-cultural.
3. Hip hop has a major influence on global economy via magazine sales, concert sales, musical sales, film and television, fashion, branding, and community service (social causes).

For African American boys and other minority boys who understand the three above points, hip hop translates into increased economic opportunities in ways to make money in the hip hop industry besides rapping. Although many of today's leading hip hop artists began as rappers, their trailblazing efforts on the rap circuit allowed them to transform into entertainment moguls and icons. More important, these entertainers no longer just work for record companies; now they own companies. They have given way to a new phenomenon of Entertainment-Chief Executive Officers, E-CEOs (pronounced EE-chose), hip hop artists owning multimillion dollar entertainment empires.

Some analysts believe that this idea is nothing more than a mere replication of the rock music genre of the 1960s and 1970s, an era that identified leading rock artists as rock stars. Unfortunately, many of the rock stars from the 1960s and 1970s were unable to transfer their celebrity status from being employed by the record label to being owners of the record company. E-CEOs have been able to launch brand extensions, to create subsidiary companies, to launch even larger parent companies, and to generate non-musical products that exceed music sales. Economists and business analysts refer to these types of e-CEOs as *serial entrepreneurs*. Serial entrepreneurs constantly create new businesses and enterprises for the most part, one after another. They routinely use their influences, professional networks, creative instincts, and keen business acumen to go beyond the most recent successful venture. If a venture fails to work, serial entrepreneurs move on to the next enterprise quickly; they neither personalize nor become paralyzed by the lack of a new venture's success.

Hip hop's most celebrated E-CEOs and serial entrepreneurs include Andre Young, Shawn Carter, Sean Combs, and the godfather of hip hop, Russell Simmons. Here is an abbreviated overview of some of their accomplishments:

In the late 1970s, what began as an attempt to vocalize and visualize dissatisfaction, experiences of alienation, social isolation and separation, unemployment, police harassment and brutality, and environmental and economic disenfranchisement in the streets of New York, hip hop became a mainstream genre' of music in the twenty-first century. Hip hop created social scenes and musical fan fare from the east coast to the west coast and every major urban city in between. Originally, viewed as a largely youth culture, hip hop has enlarged within a global market to include stakeholders from various age groups.

Those urban youngsters once regarded as merely break dancers, pop lockers, graffiti artists, gangsta' rappers, and overall menaces have now become social activists and people of positive influence who able to harness and motivate African American and other minority boys to engage in conflicts of social justice and civil rights. Hip hop artists have also been able to use their influence to eradicate voter apathy among inner city African American males.

Finally, many leading hip hop artists have morphed into E-CEOs and serial entrepreneurs. Some ownership among hip hop artists include: record labels, production companies, marketing firms, restaurants, sports teams, clothing lines, jewelry lines, magazines, and television programs. African American males and other minorities influenced by the hip hop culture will continue to be positively impacted as hip hop culture and hip hop artists continue to evolve.

Hip Hop Artists

Hip Hop Artist	Endeavors & Accomplishments
Andre Young (Dr. Dre)	• Late 1970s, introduced to Hip Hop as a dancer and DJ in group World Class Wrecking Crew. • Mid 1980s, collaborated with Easy-E forming the rap group N.W.A.; their first album sold over three million copies. • 1998, Dr. Dre was the first rap artist to host a television video show, *Yo! MTV Raps*. *Yo! MTV Raps* was the first hip hop television show broadcast on the MTV network. • 1992, Dr. Dre launched a solo album *The Chronic* on Death Row Records. • *The Chronic* remained a top-ten album for eight consecutive months, selling over 4 million copies (Light, Death Row Record, 1999). • Dr. Dre launched several mega hip hop artists as an executive producer: Snoop Dogg, Eminem, and 50 Cent.
Shawn Carter (Jay Z)	• Former Kentucky Fried Chicken cashier. • Partnered with Damon Dash and formed Roc-A-Fella Entertainment Empire. • Debut album *Resonable Doubt* went gold in the 1990s and platinum in the early 2000s. • 1998, Jay-Z's album *Hard Knock Life* peaked at number one on the Billboard Top 200 and won a Grammy Award for best Rap Album (Billboard, 2007). • By 1999, Roc-A-Fella earned more than $50 million. • Early 2000, launched Rocawear clothing line, which currently reports yearly earnings of over $700 million (Rocawear, 2007). • In 2001, Jay-Z was the first nonathlete to have a signature line of sneakers through Reebok. His shoe became the fastest selling shoe in Reebok history (Bhatnagar, 2004). • Joint venture between Roc-A-Fella and Def Jam (Russell Simmons) yielded 10 platinum albums. • In 2004, Jay-Z became president of and CEO of Def Jam Entertainment company. • In 2004–2005, Jay-Z bought a stake in New Jersey Nets professional basketball team.
Sean Combs (Puff Daddy / P-Diddy / Diddy)	• Began career as a dancer and extra in music videos. • In late 1980s interned for Andre Harrell of Uptown Records (Guy, Jodeci, Mary J. Blige). • 1994, CEO of Bad Boy Records and Entertainment. • First major negotiating record deal was with Clive Davis for over $15 million. • Puffy earns over $150,000 per track; if Puffy produces 12 tracks on an album, he earns $1.8 million for producing alone. • Puffy's production clients include: Mary J. Blige, Boyz II Men, Mariah Carey, Faith Evans, Jay-Z, MC Lyte, Notorious BIG, Usher, and many others. • Owner and proprietor of two restaurants, Justin's. • Owner of Blue Fame marketing company. • In 2002, P-Diddy was listed as #12 on Forbes America's Richest People under 40. • In 2004, Inc. Magazine estimated Bad Boys to be worth over $300 million, with Combs' personal wealth exceeding that worth (Lee & Turner, 2004). • In 2004, Sean John clothing line (Puffy's clothing line) had wholesale revenues exceeding $225 million. • Writer and Executive Producer of MTV's *Making the Band*.

Further Reading

Bhatnagar, Parija. Jordan, 50 Cent & Jay-Z: A Funky Fit? Cnn.com business Web site. Retrieved October 24, 2008 from http://money.cnn.com/2004/02/06/news/companies/retro_shoes/index.htm.

Billboard. Artist Biography: Jay-Z. Billboard.com Web site. Retrieved October 24, 2008 from http://www.billboard.com/bbcom/bio/index.jsp?pid=167256&aid=321824.

Lee, Elyssa and Turner, Rob. Top 10 Celebrity Entrepreneurs. Inc. Magazine Web site. Retrieved October 25, 2008 from http://www.inc.com/magazine/20041201/celebrity-combs.html.

Light, Alan. (Ed.). *The Vibe History of Hip Hop*. New York: Three Rivers Press, 1999.

Rocawear. About us. Rocawear Web site. Retrieved October 29, 2008 from http://www.rocawear.com/shop/aboutus.php.

Jumanne Sledge and Robert Simmons

Asian Boys and the Model Minority Label

He is the mythical Asian boy with a calculator in hand, whizzing through math calculations ahead of his classmates. He is the awkward Asian kid who can't seem to ever catch the ball but can do calculus in his sleep. He is the polite boy the teachers love to teach but the students never seem to embrace him as one of the cool kids. Eventually he grows up to study engineering or to be a doctor or to work at a bank. He would never walk in a political protest, he would never pick up a paint brush, he would never question his heterosexuality, and he generally would never make waves of any kind in the classroom or society at large when he grows up to be an Asian man. He is a model minority. Model minority boys are stereotypically characterized by qualities such as being intellectually gifted in maths and sciences, physically inept, lacking in social skills, quiet, passive, submissive, obsessively diligent, emotionally unavailable, and in popular culture terms, geeky or nerdy.

The images of the model minority Asian boy are not so hard to imagine because they have been engrained in our cultural consciousness through Asian characters in film, television, and print that embody and perpetuate this concept. The lead characters in the movie *Harold and Kumar Go To White Castle* are examples of a Korean American and an Indian American male character that are frustrated with the assumptions and expectations that society puts on them because of the model minority stereotype. The stereotype is not limited to boys in any way and affects female Asians as well; however I will focus on how the stereotype influences Asian boys in particular.

The archetype of the Asian model minority is a racial stereotype where all Asians are predisposed to academic and economic success because of their cultural values. It is implicitly assumed in the model minority myth that Asians are a homogenous cultural entity and that therefore they share a singular, or at least similar culture, that is Japanese Americans are assumed to share the same cultural values as Korean Americans, Filipino Canadians, or Samoan Americans to give an example of how far-reaching the umbrella term of Asian is. Although it originates with reference to Japanese and Chinese immigrants in the United States, it now has a broader cultural reference to Asians, South Asians, and Pacific Islanders at large.

Birth of a Stereotype

The idea that Asian immigrants were wired to succeed in the United States started to garner attention in the 1960s and grew in popularity in the coming decades with more and more media stories about the success of Asian immigrants. A *New York Times Magazine* article by William Peterson titled "Success Story: Japanese American Style" in January 1966 foreshadowed the use of the term model minority to capture the perceived innate ability of Asian American immigrants to succeed economically and academically. Similar articles followed such as "Success Story: Outwhiting the Whites" in *Newsweek* June 21 1971 and "Asian Americans: Model Minority" again in *Newsweek* on December 6, 1982. These articles were often published alongside pictures of young Chinese or Japanese students at an Ivy League university.

The model component of model minority stems from the fact that young Asian immigrants were held up as an example to other minority communities—namely African American and Latino American populations—as an immigrant American success story. The term implies that since Asian Americans enjoy academic and economic success/achievements/advancements, they are properly assimilated and can possess a degree of white Americanness. The message to African American and Latino American populations was clear: if they can do it, why can't you? The idea was that these Chinese and Japanese immigrant families were able to succeed without help in the form of government financial assistance or worker placement programs. Holding up these young Asians in the media as examples of how to properly assimilate was a way of America saying to itself at the time that the problems of immigration were not problems of America, but problems of the immigrants—problems that were proven to be fixable if the immigrants had the right tools such as these spotlighted Asians.

What these articles were contributing to was the racializing of success. Academic and educational success became outcomes solely associated with whiteness. Indeed the work ethic that the media praised Japanese and Chinese immigrants for was strangely similar to the Protestant work ethic. In this way although on the surface it may have seemed that the American media was recognizing the worth of other cultures' values, these articles really were only praising how much they thought these Asian students were like white Americans. Also, since whiteness was tied to success, then minorities who achieved this success somehow lost a degree of their minority status and became white.

Another less addressed effect of the model minority media explosion was that Asians as an immigrant group became a homogenous identity. The media press covered Japanese and Chinese youth but the jump from Chinese or Japanese to Asians in general was quickly made and rarely questioned. The reality is that the term Asian is a terrifyingly huge umbrella term. To say that there are many Chinese students in graduate programs and therefore Asians are doing well in higher education would not explain the low enrollment rates of Hmong Americans from Cambodia and Laos. Southeast Asians and Pacific Islanders face a unique battle when slapped with the stereotype of the model minority because it allows the public to ignore their continued struggles in the classrooms, on the streets, and in the workforce, simply because they are seen as Asian and therefore immune to these problems.

Sounds Like a Compliment to Me

We are used to stereotypes being negative attributions such as girls can't play sports. The model minority stereotype is a positive stereotype; that is instead of assuming Asian boys cannot do something, it starts with the assumption that they can do something. At first glance it does not seem problematic that a teacher would walk into a classroom and assume all the Asian kids were smart. A natural predisposition to academic and intellectual work is seen as a positive characteristic. Consequently the model minority occasionally goes unquestioned as a stereotype since it praises the character of Asian boys. Yet when we look deeper into the effects of this stereotype on boys we see that there is another side of the story to consider.

The problem with stereotypes is that they confine how an individual defines oneself and how society perceives that individual. Stereotypes limit. Young Asian boys are bombarded with the pressures of being a model minority from both the media and a society which has come to believe that the model minority stereotype is true and holds true for all Asian boys. It is enormous pressure for a young boy to have their identity dictated to them before they even have a chance to figure things out for themselves. Asian boys see themselves through this lens of a model minority and the consequences of that are endless: they could shy away from physical activities because they think that is not what they should be good at, they could place unrealistic academic pressure on themselves, or they could even base their subject choices and later on career choices on what they perceive is an appropriate career for an Asian male. As well, educators might not be aware of how their acceptance of the model minority myth influences their interactions with students. Teachers may also put unreasonable expectations on their Asian students in subject areas such as math or science and push them harder; conversely they may put little or no expectations on the same students in areas such as literature, art, or physical education and be satisfied with mediocre achievements.

As much as stereotypes limit they also mask and hide. As a result of the model minority perception in education many of the needs of immigrant populations such as the Hmong and Pacific Islanders such as Samoan Americans are going unnoticed or are overshadowed by the perceived success of their other Asian peers. Model minorities are supposed to be fully functional students without need for academic, emotional, or mental support from educators. Unfortunately, many young Asians are slipping through this large model minority crack because we have come to believe this stereotype as true, unquestionable, and universal. Asian North Americans ourselves have also grown up with this stereotype embedded in how we construct what makes a good Asian. When we stop questioning stereotypes we begin to turn away from problems and consequently from the Asian youth who are dealing with the pressures of the model minority.

The One-Dimensional Boy

Thinking that all Asians are inherently smart is not a compliment. It takes away from the achievements that many Asian immigrants and their children and grandchildren have accomplished in North America by writing it off to some sort of racial gene encoded for success. It does not allow young Asian boys the room to breathe, to grow, to make mistakes, and to simply make choices. The words model minority do not only imply that Asian boys are smart, they also implicitly assume that Asian boys are lacking in creativity, independent thought, athletic ability, and social ease. The term and its constant depiction in the media has one-dimensionalized the Asian boy who eventually becomes a one-dimensional Asian man if we choose to accept this stereotype as truth instead of as fiction.

Further Reading

Chin, Andrew. A Brief History of the Model Minority Stereotype [Online March 2008]. Model Minority: A Guide to Asian American Empowerment Web site <http://www.modelminority.com/article72.html >.

Lee, Robert G. *Orientals: Asian Americans in Popular Culture.* Philadelphia: Temple University Press, 1999.

Media Action Network for Asian Americans. Restrictive Portrayals in the Media of Asian Americans and How to Balance Them [Online March 2008]. Media Action for Network for Asian Americans Web site <http://www.manaa.org/articles/stereoBust_p.htm>.

Woo, Terry. *Banana Boys.* Toronto: Riverbank Press, 2000.

Wu, Frank. *Yellow.* Cambridge: Perseus Publishing, 2003.

Eloise Tan

Asian Males and Racism

The angry Asian male is an emerging concept. Asian males who are conscious that they have experienced racism and stereotyping self-identify as angry Asian males. These dynamics especially affect dating and relationships, partly due to the objectification of Asian women (also termed Asian fetish or yellow fever) through the perpetuation of Asian women stereotypes in the media.

Web sites and blogs, such as www.angryasianman.com and www.bitterasianmen.com, have emerged over the past decade. These Web sites reveal the effects of racism on Asian men. The creators of these Web sites, angry Asian males themselves, discuss how racism has impacted not only their personal lives, but how it has affected society. By expressing their thoughts and feelings about this topic, they are able to communicate to readers specific examples of racism in the media. They also give readers the opportunity to learn more about socially conscious works that expose racism in society.

The Model Minority Myth

Asian stereotypes often refer to the disaggregated Asian group, a large group that includes East Asians, South Asians, Southeast Asians, and Pacific Islanders. East Asians are those who are Chinese, Japanese, Korean, Mongolian, and Taiwanese. South Asia refers to the region south of the Himalayan Mountains. South Asians includes people from Bangladesh, India, Pakistan, and Sri Lanka. Southeast Asia refers to the region south of China, east of India, and north of Australia. Southeast Asians include Laos, Cambodia, and Vietnam. Pacific Islanders are natives of islands such as Guam, Polynesia, Micronesia, and Melanesia. The model minority myth is used to describe how one ethnic minority has been able to overcome obstacles in education and income to succeed. Asian Americans are considered model minorities when looking at academic and socioeconomic achievement. The myth of the model minority is often used in juxtaposition with other ethnic minority groups and subsequently, causes tensions among these groups. The myth often does not take into consideration Asian American subgroups that do not demonstrate academic and socioeconomic success. Asian Americans are not a monolithic group and some people feel that better categories should be created to better describe the subgroups and also to provide better support services for those Asian American subgroups that need assistance.

Asian Americans are overrepresented in higher education enrolment. This means that there is a greater percentage of Asians pursuing a college degree than the percentage of Asian Americans in the population. Asian Americans also have higher educational attainment rates than the national average. Asian Americans tend to be more highly educated than other ethnic groups, including whites. However, there is much diversity within the Asian American category that the U.S. Census Bureau uses to collect its data. For example, East Asians and South Asians tend to have higher educational enrolment and attainment rates than Southeast Asians and Pacific Islanders. Southeast Asians and Pacific Islanders are underrepresented in higher education and have lower educational attainment rates than the national average. Southeast Asian and Pacific Islander educational statistics more closely resemble those of African Americans and Latinos than they resemble their East Asian and South Asian counterparts.

Because the numbers for Asian Americans are aggregated, the needs of Southeast Asians and Pacific Islanders are not recognized. Southeast Asians and Pacific Islanders are not given special assistance or academic support that would help them compete with their more successful counterparts. The model minority myth is a divisive expression that creates tension within the Asian American population and between Asian Americans and other ethnic groups.

The U.S. Census Bureau also collects data for Asian American household income. The statistics show that Asian American households are making close to what white households are making. However, these numbers may be deceiving as Asian Americans tend to have larger household sizes. This means that more members of Asian families are working and making less money than White households. Asian Americans are also concentrated in urban areas where the cost of living is high and therefore, their incomes may reflect this differential.

Some Asian Americans are aware of the discrepancies in the statistics that support the model minority notion. These individuals are angry that Asian Americans are ignored in the public discourse. They feel that more research should be conducted to disaggregate Asian American data, so that educators and policymakers can get a better sense of how best to serve Asian Americans' needs. Some Asian Americans are unaware that the model minority myth is divisive. They may be accepting and proud of the concept. It would take them some time to encounter the negative effects of the myth, which will cause them to begin questioning race relations in American society.

Perpetual Foreigner

Asians have had a long history in the United States. They first immigrated to America as indentured servants in the 1700s. The Filipinos settled in Louisiana and worked as sailors. The Chinese and Indians worked on the plantations. In the 1800s, the Chinese also settled in the New Frontier. They worked on the goldmines, railroads, and farms.

Despite the contributions that these settlers made, there was much anti-Asian sentiment in the United States, with the settlement of any Asians known as the Yellow Peril. Whites felt that Asians threatened the wage earning abilities of whites as well as their standard of living. In 1870, the government excluded Asians from the amendment of the Nationality Act of 1790. The 1870 amendment allowed people of African descent to be naturalized citizens. The Chinese Exclusion Act of 1882 was passed to prohibit Asians from immigrating to the United States and made it illegal for American-born Asians to become American citizens. While the name of this Act referred to the Chinese in its title, the act limited all Asian immigration. Subsequent laws added to the limitations of freedom for Asian Americans. For example, the Scott Act of 1888 prohibited Chinese laborers who left the country to come back to the United States. The Geary Act was passed in 1892, which required that all Chinese laborers be registered into a catalog. Those who did not register within a year would be deported. The Immigration Act of 1924, also known as the Johnson-Reed Act, excluded Asians from immigrating to the United States though it allowed two percent of the number of people from each ethnic group in the country at the time of the 1890 census. In 1942, Executive Order 9066 was passed to place Japanese in internment camps during World War II. Over 100,000 Japanese were forced to leave their lives and move into these camps, so that they were not seen as a threat to the country. The United States fought the Axis powers in World War II, which included Japan, Germany, and Italy. Neither the Germans nor the Italians living in the United States were forced to move into internment camps.

Centuries have passed since the first wave of Asians immigrated to the United States, but the notion that they are not Americans still exists. Phrases, such as "go back to your country," "you speak English very well," and "what country are you from?" are used in everyday conversations and also are a constant reminder to Asians that they are unwelcome in their own country.

Asian Males in the Popular Media

As stated in the previous section, the Chinese Exclusion Act made it illegal for Asian immigrants to enter the country. The first wave of Asian immigration consisted mostly of men. Because these men were not allowed to sponsor their wives and families to the United States, they were forced to live in an almost all bachelor society. Whites were threatened by this predominantly male society, and they were afraid that Asian men would take their white women as wives. Asian males began to be portrayed in newspapers as sly, evil, hypersexual, and effeminate. Along with these characteristics, Asian villains were portrayed in media as kung fu masters and gangsters. Examples of evil kung fu masters are David Lo Pan from *Big Trouble in Little China,* Wah Sing Ku from *Lethal Weapon 4,* and the Axe Gang in *Kung Fu Hustle.* Asian Gangsters can be viewed on episodes of *Law & Order SVU, the Corruptor,* countless Jet Li movies including *Romeo Must Die,* and all three of the *Rush Hour* movies.

Perhaps the most well-known depiction of the evil Asian male is Dr. Fu Manchu. Fu Manchu is a fictional character created in the early 1900s. He is a cunning criminal that plots the murders of many and uses unusual weapons to annihilate his enemies. He is portrayed as a skinny, Asian man with small eyes, a long, thin moustache that draped below his chin, and long fingernails. Dr. Fu Manchu was so popular that he appeared in almost all forms of media for almost a century.

Sometimes Asian men are portrayed as heroes, but they often never have romantic scenes with their female leads, especially those from other races. Take for instance, Chow Yun-Fat and Mira Sorvino's characters in *The Replacement Killers.* Their characters were not linked romantically and they did not share an on-screen kiss. The same holds true for Jet Li and Aaliyah's characters in *Romeo Must Die.* At the end of the film, the couple hugs and they go on their separate ways. In season one of *Heroes,* Hiro Nakamura goes back to the past and develops a romantic relationship with Charlie Andrews, but they do not show the characters kissing on screen.

Along the same lines of never getting the girls, Asian men are also depicted as passive, sexless, and nerdy individuals. On *Law & Order SVU,* Dr. George Huang is a supporting character who is analytical. The show does not delve into his personal life, though it does with the rest of the characters. B. D. Wong has also publically stated that he has never shared an on-screen kiss with anyone in all of his years of acting. *Details* magazine in April 2004 published a picture of an Asian male who looked similar to John Cho's character in *Harold and Kumar.* The picture had arrows pointing to items of the man's clothing with patronizing comments. The caption for the picture was "Gay or Asian?" This was a racist illustration by *Details* magazine that played on stereotypes for both gay and Asian men as emasculated and passive. In *Harold & Kumar Go to White Castle,* Harold Lee is the epitome of the intelligent nerdy character who will not defy others. He fantasizes about approaching his neighbor in the elevator, but he does not follow through with it until the end. Harold turns into an angry Asian male. He is fed up with others for taking advantage of him and that is when he starts lashing out.

There is a lack of Asian male representation and a shortage of roles for them in the media. There are very few Asian males in leading roles on film or recurring roles in television. In film, Jet Li, Jackie Chan, and Chow Yun-Fat are known for their martial arts skills. In television, B. D. Wong and Daniel Dae Kim are known for being nerdy and aggressive, respectively. Asian males are presented in the media in dichotomous roles. They are rendered as evil and nice, hypersexual and sexless, or aggressive and passive. They are kung fu masters, gangsters, and nerds. Some of these elements are combined, but there are not many roles for them that defy the stereotypes.

Some Asian males are upset that they are not represented in the media; there are few Asian male faces on television and movies. When other ethnic groups have diversity in the characters that are depicted, Asians are forced into inflexible stereotypes. Asian characters in movies and television are not the best role models for younger Asians to follow. The way Asian males are depicted in the media presents a narrow and racist view of Asian men.

Just as in how heterosexual media has represented Asian women, gay media has objectified Asian males. Asian males are portrayed as exotic, submissive, and sexual servants. Gay Asian men in pornography are always depicted in the role of the bottom. They are placed in these roles to satisfy and serve the white men. They only exist to pleasure others while the white men are the audience and subjects of the works. This is an example of how the Asian fetish has extended to gay relationships, where white men are interested in dating Asian men. They see Asian men as desirable, obedient lovers. Many Asian men are offended that their media representations do not reflect the diversity of their roles in relationships.

The Future

The angry Asian male is a concept that some Asian males are familiar with while others are unaware of. Levels of awareness vary depending on how much they are exposed to the racism and stereotypes in society that are often perpetuated in the popular media. Some Asian Americans question why after centuries of building the United States and supporting the country economically, they are still regarded as foreigners.

Angry Asian males are an emergent group that are developing momentum as they speak out against the ways in which society has branded them. They are creating Web sites that educate audiences, many of whom are young males, about how racism has impacted how Asians are viewed. The Web sites provide their authors with a therapeutic way of relaying their anger and a means to connect them with a support network. These Web sites are also public forums where they can freely discuss the issues that the media have chosen to ignore.

Further Reading

Bitter Asian Men. Bitter Asian Men Blog [Online March 14, 2008]. Bitter Asian Men Web site <http://www.bitterasianmen.com>.

Chong, Kevin. All the Rage: Tracking the Trend of Angry Asian Men [Online March 14, 2008]. Canadian Broadcasting Corporation Arts Web site <http://www.cbc.ca/arts/media/angryasianmen.html>.

ModelMinority.com. Model Minority: A Guide to Asian American Empowerment [Online March 14, 2008]. ModelMinority.com Web site <http://modelminority.com>.

Yang, Jeff. ASIAN POP: Angry Asian Men [Online March 14, 2008]. San Francisco Chronicle Web site <http://www.sfgate.com/cgi-bin/article.cgi?f=/g/a/2007/05/08/apop.DTL.

Yu, Phil. Angry Asian Man Blog [Online March 14, 2008]. Angry Asian Man Web site <http://www.angryasianman.com/angry.html>.

Kimberly A. Truong

Boys' Day in Japan (*Tango no Sekku*)

Not many countries celebrate specific days that celebrate boys and girls. However, in Japan, Boys' Day, known as *Tango no Sekku*, is a Japanese tradition and national holiday (there is also a Girls' Day). On May 5 of every year, the Japanese celebrate the wellness and happiness of boys. In particular, it is a very special event for those boys celebrating their first Boys' Day. One's first Boys' Day is usually celebrated with extended family members. It becomes a large family event to celebrate the family's happiness of having a boy in their family. The significance of this holiday reflects Japan's male-dominated society where boys are more valued than girls.

Many Japanese traditions are based on symbolism. On Boys' Day, families with boys display traditional male dolls, Japanese-style helmets, or carp-shaped flags as part of the celebration. The dolls (known as *Kintaro*, a character from Japanese folktale) symbolize strength and sturdiness, the helmets (known as *Kabuto*) symbolize talismans to protect the boys from evil and misfortunes, and carp-shaped flags (known as *Koinobori*) symbolize hopeful future prospects. Boys also take baths in bathwater with iris petals and stems (as iris is a symbolic flower for Boys' Day) to cleanse their bodies and maintain their health. In addition, rice dumplings wrapped in bamboo leaves (known as *Chimaki*) and rice cakes wrapped in oak leaves (known as *Kashiwamochi*) are the special foods of the day. Japanese Boys' Day is also celebrated in many Japanese homes around the world.

The custom of *Tango no Sekku* originated in China and was first adopted by Japan's warrior class society in the feudal era. Prior to adopting the tradition, Japan already celebrated a custom of exorcism before the May rice planting season began. This existing Japanese custom and the Chinese custom combined to become *Tango no Sekku*. The event, however, was initially observed in a much different way. Women were made superior to men on that day; for example, women bathed before men and the men prepared meals for the women.

Around the *Edo* era, however, *Tango no Sekku* began to be recognized as Boys' Day. In *Edo* era, Shogun Ieyasu Tokugawa established May 5th as an important day, and celebrated the day by hanging a special flag or coat of arms, especially when a boy was born in his family. As this tradition was eventually adopted by general society, May 5th became Boys' Day. During this era, the symbolic display of items, such as the helmets, dolls, and flags, became associated with Boys' Day.

The word *Tango* originally means the fifth of each month, but does not specify the fifth month of the year. However, since the word *go* means five in Japanese, the holiday became the fifth of May. Iris (*Shobu*) became a symbolic flower for Boys' Day because of its seasonality and the belief that it could exorcise impurity and evil. In addition, the word *Shobu* (phonetically the same word, but a different Japanese spelling) means martial spirits, which corresponds with the idea of boys being strong and successful. Since the iris leaves are sword-shaped, the flowers also reflect the *samurai* culture in Japan.

Although Girls' Day is celebrated on March 3rd, it is not a nationally recognized holiday. Even today, the traditional societal ideology of highly valuing the male gender over the female continues in Japan. However, at the same time, Boys' Day is gradually becoming known as Children's Day (*Kodomo no Hi*) in Japan. Thus, the distinction between Boys' Day and Girls' Day is becoming both less noticeable and less controversial.

In today's Japanese society, Boys' Day is becoming less significant, formal, and traditional. This may be attributed to changes in family dynamics, such as the increase in single parenthood and the geographic distance between members of extended families. In addition, many Japanese have adopted a more modern living style and no longer value the idea of following old traditions and customs.

Further Reading

Ishii, Minako. *Girls' Day/Boys' Day*. Honolulu, HI: Bess Press, 2007.
Sosnoski, Daniel. *Introduction to Japanese Culture*. Boston: Tuttle Publishing, 1996.

Tomoya Tsutsumi

Ethnic Identities

As society becomes more ethnically diverse due to immigration and social changes, the issue of identity formation becomes more complex. In adolescence, both boys and girls confront the issue of finding or forming an identity. During this time, members of ethnic minorities may identify more closely with their ethnic group, rather than with their national citizenship. Since physical appearance is often our most identifiable feature, gender and ethnicity greatly affect one's identity formation. Many adolescents gather with students who possess a similar gender and/or ethnic background, which can establish a feeling of belonging and comfort, and enhance their identity formation as individuals and also as groups.

Ethnic identity is the part of a person's identity that reflects the racial, religious, or cultural group to which he or she belongs. Different societal values, meanings, and expectations (which may be referenced as stereotypes) are attached to each ethnic background. Through media and other social communication and interaction processes, people tend to attach both positive and negative connotations and societal values, meanings, and expectations to each ethnic group, which may not always reflect truth or fact. Such societal values, meanings, and expectations do not look at an individual's uniqueness, but rather at socially constructed group characteristics, labels, and identifications as a whole.

Some of the connotations and societal values, meanings, and expectations are unique to boys, but not applicable to girls, and vice versa. Black males, for instance, reflect different values, meanings, and expectations than Hispanic males or Asian males or even Black girls (e.g., hip hop culture is greatly associated with Black males; Asian males are believed to excel at math and science as compared to other ethnicities).

Just as the values, meanings, and expectations attached to different ethnicities greatly affect one's identity formations through social interactions between those of different ethnic backgrounds, there are analogous differences between boys (male) and girls (female) that can come from certain expectations of and assumptions about gender roles in society. One such assumption is that boys tend to be stronger and have more control of their physical space. Another assumption is that boys are the more active and assertive sex. As with ethnicity, gender roles are also constantly reinforced through social interaction, communication processes, and the media.

Identity formation is not solely an individual process, but rather is relational in nature. Societal values, meanings, and expectations can play an influential and crucial role in one's identity formation. Therefore, it is not simply a journey of finding one's identity, but also finding meaning and connection between one's self and society through interactions with the external environment. More specifically, people develop their identity by comparing and differentiating themselves from others to know where they belong and who they are. Ethnic identity can be formed through this similar process as well. Since peer cultures are a crucial part of adolescents' lives, they greatly influence the process of identity formation.

As set forth above, ethnic cultures and gender cultures are not only biological, but also have socially constructed meanings, values, and expectations attached to them. Thus, it is not a simple matter of whether you are male or female, or Black or Hispanic. Rather, it is a more complex and dynamic matter which should be understood as a social process. Moreover, over time, ethnic cultural characteristics and gender characteristics have intertwined together to create new schemas, which may not be simply characterized by looking at either ethnic or gender characteristics. These new schemas can also greatly influence identity formation.

Some boys resist, reject, or disassociate themselves from their own ethnic culture, gender role, or even the new schemas mentioned above because some of the societal values, meanings, and expectations do not match or fit with their own. This experience can be a struggle for them, and many boys may feel isolated, lost, and misunderstood by others. Since identity formation is relational and comparative, these boys may find it difficult to find their own place if they do not identify with one group or another (such groups can be ethnic groups, gender groups, or new schemas that are created by a combination of both groups).

Further Reading

Connolly, Paul. *Racism, Gender Identities and Young Children: Social Relations in a Multi-Ethnic, Inner-City Primary School.* London, UK: Routledge, 1998.

O'Donnell, Mike, and Sue Sharpe. *Uncertain Masculinities: Youth, Ethnicity and Class in Contemporary Britain.* London, UK: Routledge, 2000.

Stecopoulos, Harry. *Race and the Subject of Masculinities.* Durham, NC: Duke University Press, 1997.

Tomoya Tsutsumi

Immigration

The New Kid on the Block

There are approximately 3.1 million foreign-born children living in the United States (Kidscount.org, no date). This means that about 1.5 million immigrant boys are facing lives as new Americans and must learn to adapt to this culture. According to the estimates of the child welfare organization Kidscount.org, 2.2 million immigrant children had difficulty speaking English. The U.S. Census estimates that immigrant children are more likely to live below the poverty line than American-born children. (The poverty line is the official government marker of being poor; children who live below it face deep economic struggles that impact their emotional and physical well-being). Some boys migrate to the United States alone, knowing nobody. According to Refugees.org, over 7,000 unaccompanied immigrant children arrive in the United States each year.

Immigrant boys come for a variety of reasons. Many are sent to the United States because their families know that their homeland is not safe, particularly for a boy, as their home country is experiencing political violence or poverty. The oldest boy is often the child who is sent to the U.S. He leaves his homeland thinking of himself as the one family member who (with youth and maleness on his side) is most likely to be able to make use of opportunity in a new land.

He may also be, as the boy, the child who would be the first to be endangered by events in his country. Other boys are sent by their families to work in the United States to send money home. All too often boys are sent to the U.S. with the hope that they will have a better chance at life than the one possible for the families and communities they leave behind. They carry the hope and pride of their families with them. Many of these immigrant boys come from communities where they have little exposure to what America is really like. Taking their first plane ride ever, they arrive excited, hopeful, and nervous (especially when they don't speak English) and have almost no idea of what to expect.

Coming to America: Hollywood versus Reality

A boy who finds out that he is moving to the United States has to try to find out what lies in store for him. This often means asking anyone who has been to the United States to tell him what life is like there. In many of the communities where hardship (the violence of war, and/or other internal political struggles, or the danger of life threatening poverty) forces a boy to leave his homeland, there are few adults to ask who have been to the U.S. It can be difficult for a boy to get a real understanding of what to expect when he arrives in the U.S. Therefore, boys often use television for information. However, in many countries television and electricity are not available in most homes. TV shows that portray American life might not be easy to access in a language that the boy speaks. In addition, life in the U.S. on television can be very different from reality.

It takes a lot of adjustment to get used to living in the United States for an immigrant boy. Young boys can find being away from familiar surroundings and people very frightening. Boys who are of middle school age or older have expectations about their new lives that may not match reality; they may carry the optimistic idea that living in the U.S. is how it is portrayed on television as a land where everyone lives happily without struggle. Unfortunately, life in the United States does not look like how it is portrayed or seen on TV. Life in the United States is bewildering for the immigrant boy who arrives there, sometimes without a command of the languages spoken, and with his expectations shaped by golden images broadcasted by the media.

The buildings in the United States shown in the movies and on TV are tall, expensive, and spacious and where the streets are clean. In reality (unless the immigrant boy is exceptionally lucky), the buildings he will live in and see are not tall and expensive and the streets he will walk down are not clean and may not be safe (especially in poor urban neighborhoods). The food that an immigrant boy expects to eat in the United States from watching TV is good nutritious food; however, the food that he will eat is often cheap and strange to his taste. The style of clothing that a foreign-born boy thinks of as nice is usually not the style of clothing that an American boy sees as nice. Boys who don't grow up in the U.S. expect boys to wear shoes, not sneakers, and ironed trousers, instead of baggy pants. They may not know how to layer for the cold or what footwear to own. They have to learn how to dress for their new life. The picture of America that a foreign boy sometimes sees shows the United States as a country in which people are polite and there is no homelessness or discrimination. The U.S. census shows that immigrants are more likely to live in poverty than American-born children are, the immigrant boy may not have "a life of plenty." The United States that immigrant boys arrive to does not match the rosy picture of coming to "the land of opportunity, peace, and wealth." The reality is that the U.S. is often not an easy country to live in or to understand. It is complex; it can be hard on a new child. It is a country that has poverty, and also has opportunities and hardships. Immigrant boys have to learn to adjust their behaviors and expectations as they learn to live in the United States.

School Daze

Both the actual school and the ways that boys think about school are different in the United States than from other countries. In many countries, school is a luxury not a necessity. Worldwide, millions of families have to pay to send children to school; often only the boys or the oldest boys can go to school because it is too expensive for the family to be able to educate all the children. The boys are seen as the ones who should be educated. Children often have to work to help their families financially, so they may not have the opportunity to go to school. If these boys do not take school seriously, they risk being beaten by the adults who have made sacrifices to send them. For many immigrant boys, their home communities may have many people who did not go to school at all. For these reasons, immigrant boys often see schooling as more important than their American peers. But the transition to a new country, a new culture, and a new school is rarely easy. Often as a defense, immigrant boys are quiet and try to be invisible in their new schools.

American schools can often be better funded than schools from many immigrant boys' home countries. Schools may have proper lighting, reasonably decent toilets, school-provided lunches for students who need them, and seats for all students. An immigrant boy from a poor country may be surprised by the average American school. They will have to adjust to the way in which teachers and students interact in a classroom. American students are often informal with their teachers. Often, students in North American public schools do not wear uniforms. Adolescent American boys often view schooling as their right. Consequently, they may skip school or not study. Boys from other countries become quickly aware of American boys' different attitudes and behaviors in school. These new experiences, along with new materials and subjects, perhaps learning English for the first time, make the experience hard for immigrant boys. They may be unable to know exactly what to do and how to behave in order to succeed in school.

Muted Boys

Over a million immigrant boys in the United States have difficulty speaking English. The difficulties these boys face are often hidden, as they are unable to communicate (although they may speak more than one language that is not spoken in the United States). The struggles of adapting to a new culture are increased when a boy is silenced by language differences. Simple things such as getting from place to place, getting food, and not getting into fights when they are laughed at can become a problem when a boy does not understand what is being said and cannot speak a language that is understood. It is not unusual for a new immigrant boy to hide in the house because he does not know how to get around the neighborhood or how to use the transportation system. There is a fear of getting lost and not being able to ask for directions. Boys who do not speak the main languages in the U.S. cannot buy anything without great difficulty. They may stay hungry when they are not familiar with the food they see offered and do not know how to ask for it; when the currency is unfamiliar they also may not know how to pay and to be sure that their change is correct, or even able to speak out if it is not.

Immigrant boys who do not speak the language used in schools may have trouble adapting. They may be able to find a teacher who speaks their language but they cannot transition in the school community with ease. Other students in schools tend to ask new boys questions that they may not be able to understand or answer. Immigrant boys who speak and understand some English can find that they are viewed as representatives of their country. If their peers know little about that country, they may voice attitudes and ideas about the immigrant boy's homeland that he finds disrespectful. It is easy in these situations for him to feel insecure, humiliated, or angry. The boy who once knew everyone and was popular in school when removed from his native land can become the boy who does not speak and/or the boy who gets into fights. However, immigrant boys often seek the people and help that they need; they find that there are adults and peers who will assist them and they learn to eventually change their position, moving away from being muted boys.

Making Home

As an immigrant boy acculturates (becomes a part of the new culture), he may get used to living without his family, although retaining the desire to be reunited with them. Keeping in touch with home is often impossible as many rural areas around the world are without paved streets and house numbers, many families do not have phones that work consistently or computers, and often people cannot read. If the boy is from a rural part of the world, he may only be able to stay in touch with his family when he dreams of the places and people that once were home. Few places on the planet possess the abundance of objects to buy that America does, and an immigrant boy may never forget how shocking it was to first visit a supermarket and find dozens of variations of breakfast cereal (he may wonder why we need so many). If the boys have come to America at an age where they can still remember their homeland, they also possess a keen worldliness (sophistication about the world) as they have the perspective of more than one culture. They are aware of the ways that people can see and do things differently. Their perspective can help us all understand the contradictions between the images and reality of boyhood in the United States.

Further Reading

Children in Immigrant Families. Kidscount Data Center [Online February 2008]. Annie E. Casey Foundation Center Web site <http://www.kidscount.org/datacenter/>.

Nugent, Christopher. Protecting Unaccompanied and Immigrant Children [Online February 2008]. American Bar Association, Human Rights Magazine Web site <http://www.abanet.org/irr/hr/winter05/immigrant.html>.

The U.S. Committee for Refugees and Immigrants [Online January 2008]. USCRI Web site <http://www.refugees.org>.

Aboubacar Sylla and Carolyne Ali Khan

Latino Boys

In recent years, Latino/Hispanic boys have garnered considerable attention because of their vulnerability in terms of health, education attainment, and economic potential. Hispanic boys certainly have pressing issues central to their lives that stem from and contribute to some of the hardships that Hispanics (as a whole) experience through their subsistence in the United States.

While many use the terms Latino and Hispanic interchangeably to identify this subculture of boys, and some prefer one usage to the other, there is a difference in their meanings. The term *Latino*, which is condensed from *Latinoamericano,* represents boys whose origin is from Latin American countries, such as boys whose ancestry is rooted in Mexico, El Salvador, and Nicaragua. The term *Hispanic*, however, encompasses such boys worldwide who have the Spanish language in common. Boys from Spain, the Philippines, Chile, and so forth are considered Hispanic because they speak Spanish.

Federal data indicate that Hispanic/Latino boys are from the fastest growing group in the United States and are the largest minority. In fact, for the first time in our nation's history two Hispanic/Latino surnames—Garcia and Rodriguez—made the top 10 surnames in the 2000 Census. The Hispanic/Latino population size in 2006 was nearly 44.3 million, which was about 15 percent of the nation's population. It is projected that in 2050, approximately one-quarter of all Americans (102.6 million) will be Hispanic. Hispanic/Latino boys are concentrated in five states: California, Texas, Florida, New York, and Illinois.

There are more Hispanic/Latino males than there are Hispanic/Latina females (107 for every 100, respectively), which is a stark contrast to the general population (97 males for every 100 females). Two factors account for the Hispanic/Latino population increase: immigration from Latin American countries and relatively high fertility rates. About 11 million unauthorized persons have migrated to the United States seeking better opportunities (Pew Hispanic Center, 2006). Though migrants may find more improved lifestyles than their country of origin, they are likely to experience a host of problems associated with earning poor wages as an undocumented worker paving the way for a hard life for their family and children.

Even though most Hispanic/Latino boys today—about 64 percent—have Mexican (Chicano) roots, they are a heterogeneous group with distinct subcultures (U.S. Census Bureau, 2006). Several key factors account for their diversity, including: (a) the cultural heritage from their national origin (i.e., there are unique cultural celebrations and foods among the diverse origins); (b) the generational status (i.e., each generation removed from the direct immigration is more acculturated to the American lifestyle—a fourth generation Hispanic/Latino boy is far more likely to be Americanized than a boy who immigrated with his parents); (c) race (e.g., some Hispanic/Latino boys have African ancestry, and others have mixed heritage—known as Mestizo—combined from the natives and Europeans); (d) socioeconomic status in the United States and in their native country (i.e., an Hispanic/Latino boy may be treated differently and have varied experiences if his parents were well educated in their homeland and are wealthy than an Hispanic/Latino boy whose parents immigrated illegally and are poor); and (e) their legal status (i.e., undocumented families tend to experience burdens that include the fear of being deported).

Despite this diversity, Hispanic/Latino boys share some commonality. In general, Hispanic/Latino children live in poverty. In fact, the number of Hispanic/Latino poor children increased by about 500,000 between 2000 and 2006 (Children's Defense Fund, 2007). Recent census data indicate that about one out of three Hispanic/Latino children are poor. The statistics are discouraging for Hispanic/Latino children under the age of three as 67 percent live in households whose family income is 200 percent below the federal threshold for poverty. Living in poverty creates hardships that have lasting effects. For instance, a lack of health insurance is often associated with inconsistent or meager employment, which means that uninsured children are less likely to get medical and dental attention when they need it (so they are more likely to miss school for longer periods of time when they become ill) and are likely deprived of eyeglasses, braces, or preventative medicine because these can be costly. As expected, Hispanic/Latino children tend to lack health coverage. 2006 Federal data found that nearly 40 percent of all uninsured children in the nation are Hispanic/Latino. Early data indicated that of the uninsured children who were considered in poor or fair health, 68 percent were Hispanic/Latino, compared to 19 percent African American and 12 percent of their white peers.

About 45 percent of Hispanic/Latino students attend schools that are located in high poverty areas, which are often poorly financed, serve a large concentration of low-income students, are commonly segregated, and staff teachers who are marginally qualified to teach (Association of the Federation of Teachers, 2004). Additionally, in many low-income Hispanic/Latino communities there are no or few preschool programs available. It should be of no surprise that Hispanic/Latino children have the lowest rate of participation in preschool programs. Less than 12 percent attend formal preschool programs (National Council of La Raza, 2007). Hispanic/Latino children are even underserved by Head Start programs, which are federally designed to help needy youngsters develop school readiness skills. According to the National Council of La Raza, Hispanic/Latino families underutilize early childhood programs because there are too few of them available in their community, they may not be affordable, and they may not have bilingual and bicultural staff. As a result, Hispanic/Latino working families must rely on themselves or relatives for day care, but this puts Hispanic/Latino children at a disadvantage because quality early childhood programs prepare children with the skills to succeed in school. After-school programs are also scarce in Hispanic/Latino communities. About one in five Hispanic/Latino children care for themselves after school, and they (like their African American peers) spend more time unsupervised than any other children. With a meager income parents are less likely to purchase resources such as computers, Internet service, and other academic tools, which could enhance their children's school achievement. Studies have found that Hispanic/Latino children tend to have a significant less number of children's books in their homes than their white counterparts and are less likely to be read to than their white counterparts.

Being poor, having parents with low levels of education, not having adequate pre-primary preparation, and being an English language learner are general disadvantages that hit the academic achievement of Hispanic/Latino children hard. In fact, since the 1970s the educational outcomes for Hispanics/Latinos have not improved significantly as they (as a group) still maintain relatively low levels of academic achievement. The good news is that the achievement gap between Hispanic/Latino youth and their peers has decreased, but there still remains at least a 20-point gap in reading and math (Association of the Federation of Teachers, 2004). As examples, in 2005 Hispanic/Latino fourth graders lagged behind their white counterparts by 26 percentage points in reading, and Hispanic/Latino eighth graders lagged behind their white peers by 25 percentage points in math (National Center for Education Statistics, 2007). Moreover, one out of three Hispanic/Latino students performs below grade level, and by the time that many Hispanic/Latino youth are 17 years old, their math and reading skills are at about the same level as a 13-year-old white peer.

This gap has a direct effect on Hispanics/Latinos completing their schooling. While census data over the last 30 years show that the Hispanic/Latino graduation rate has increased dramatically, Hispanics/Latinos still have the highest high school dropout rate (28%) in the nation. This causes a number of egregious setbacks. As a high school dropout, a Hispanic/Latino boy is more likely to be unemployed, earns less than his peers who graduated, uses welfare social services, and is more likely to be incarcerated. (Research suggests that Hispanic boys born in 2001 have one in six chances of going to jail sometime in their lives) (Children's Defense Fund, 2007). These setbacks limit Hispanics/Latinos, especially boys, from attending college and earning a degree. Accordingly, the education attainment of Hispanic/Latino men from 1960 to 2005 is the lowest compared to men of other races (U.S. Census Bureau, 2007). Despite these figures, Hispanics/Latinos tend to have positive views about their schooling and education institutions, and desire the pursuit of higher education.

Indeed, Hispanic/Latino boys are a vulnerable population faced with many challenges. They need the urgent advocacy and support of political, business, community, and educational leaders if we expect their trajectory to be a hopeful one.

Further Reading

Association of the Federation of Teachers. *Closing the Achievement Gap: Focus on Latino Students.* Retrieved January 10, 2008, from http://www.aft.org/pubs-reports/downloads/teachers/PolBrief17.pdf.

Children's Defense Fund. *America's Cradle to Prison Pipeline*. Washington, DC: Children's Defense Fund, 2007.

Espinoza-Herold, Mariella. *Issues in Latino Education: Race, School Culture, and the Politics of Academic Success*. New York: Allyn & Bacon, 2002.

Garcia, Eugene. *Hispanic Education in the United States*. Lanham, MD: Rowman & Littlefield, 2001.

National Center for Education Statistics. *The Condition of Education 2007*. Washington, DC: U.S. Department of Education, 2007.

National Council of La Raza. *Buenos Principios: Latino Children in the Earliest Years of Life*. Washington, DC: Author, 2007.

Pew Hispanic Center. April 2006. *Estimates of the Unauthorized Migrant Population for States Based on the March 2005 CPS*. Retrieved January 10, 2008, from http://pewhispanic.org/files/factsheets/17.pdf.

Reyes, Pedro, Schribner, Jay, and Scribner, Alicia. *Lessons from High Performing Hispanic Schools: Creating Learning Communities*. New York: Teachers' College Press, 1999.

U.S. Census Bureau. *Facts for Features: Hispanic Heritage Month Sept. 15—Oct. 15, 2006*. Retrieved January 8, 2007, from http://www.census.gov/Press-Release/www/releases/archives/fact_for_features_special_edition.

U.S. Census Bureau. *The 2007 Statistical Abstract: The National Data Book*. Retrieved January 10, 2008, from http://www.census.gov/compendia/statab/education/.

David Campos

Latino Stereotypes

Media and general portrayals of Latino males in U.S. society have ranged from total disregard and absence to stereotypical depictions. The Center for Media and Public Affairs has shown that Latinos have only constituted 2 percent of the representation in media for the past 30 years. There has been less representation of Latino males especially with regard to prime time television shows. With the notable exception of Jorge Ramos, working with Spanish speaking station *Univision,* Latino news anchors are largely absent.

When Latinos are represented in U.S. society at large, it is usually in stereotypical portrayals that tend to be negative. Common terms referring to Latino males include *Latin lover, macho men, lazy drunks, gang banger,* or *drug lords.* Sexually, Latino males are perceived as exotic, erotic, hypersexual beings. From the *macho* perspective, Latino males are depicted as violent, abusive, drunk, and hypermasculine. From the intellectual perspective, Latino males are depicted as slow and deficient, but good at manual labor.

A quick perusal of *YouTube* will garner examples of clothed and unclothed examples of the *sexy hunk syndrome.*

Latino male masculinity is usually viewed in essentialized ways, meaning that it becomes a common expectation by people who are not from the Latino culture that all Latino males are supposed to be and act according to the stereotypical expectations. Antonio Banderas, Jimmy Smits, and others are usually used as examples that relay these stereotypical messages. Socioeconomic class expectations are also essentialized about Latina/os with either wealthy or poor exaggerations, that often become expectations, as depicted in a now-cancelled television drama titled "Cane." Similar to African American males, Latinos in sports are seen as being good at either soccer or baseball.

Newspaper accounts contribute to the narrow depictions of Latino men. Newspaper stories miss the complexities and subtleties of the daily-lived reality of Latino men and their families and children. The danger over these portrayals is that the population at large will believe the myths and misrepresentations that continue to add to the existing misunderstandings about Latinos and Latinas at large. These types of media portrayals often lead to negative misinformation that can be ultimately used against the entire Latina/o community. For example, CNN's news anchor Lou Dobbs consistently demonizes immigrants on a nightly basis as if it were a sports event.

Latinos and the Media Project (LaMP) housed at the University of Texas–San Marcos has compiled a data set with annotations of 263 items with negative depictions of Latina/os. The executive summary notes include:

- There are marked similarities between the concerns raised by critical observers in the 1970s and those discussed two decades later. Only a slight improvement in the portrayals of Latinos in the news is reported in the literature.
- Problem areas remain; among them the lack of attention received from the general market (mainstream) media, the oversimplified coverage using well-known stereotypes, and the tendency to portray Latinos in situations of crime and violence.
- The irresponsible and insignificant increase in the number of Latinos hired by news media organizations, not even enough to keep pace with the overall growth in newsroom personnel is part of this problem.
- Other worrisome trends in employment matters pertain to the continued lack of diverse voices in the newsroom and in U.S. society in general and the even greater absence of minorities in management positions.
- One area of positive change is the exponential growth in the attention given to this topic, especially in professional magazines, newspapers, and in academia.

In a study conducted by Urrieta, twenty-four informants reported that in their experience social studies courses in K–12 schooling often overlooked the presence of people of color in the curriculum, focusing exclusively on white versions of U.S. society, and used white models (whitestream) of education. The study found that Mexicanos/Chicanos in particular were: (1) invisible in the curriculum, (2) uncritically portrayed by educators, or (3) portrayed in negative or hostile ways, especially Mexican men, due to the U.S.–Mexico War.

Some of the participants in this study reported being influenced by the whitestream social studies curriculum and pedagogy in negative ways. This included not knowing that Mexicanos/Chicanos contributed to U.S. society in significant ways, Mexicanos/Chicanos were capable of attaining higher education, and by internalizing negative feelings about their personal selves, their culture (especially the Spanish language), and ideals of beauty.

The study concludes that these are the effects of a white supremacist society that are manifested in a whitestream system of education that systematically limits the educational aspirations of people of color by dehumanizing and demonizing, in this case, Mexican people and Mexican men in particular.

This is a quote from one of the participants:

> The El Paso experience, when I used to live in El Paso, Texas, that's really where I guess I have the most vivid memories of that [negative portrayals of Mexican men]. Porque (because) you know ahí en (there in) Texas you know está cabrón (it's hard) and shit. Fuckin' . . . the history that they teach you man, it's fucked up you know. It's the whole Texas pantheon of heroes, Moses Austin, Davey Crocket. . . . The kind of shit you go through every year. So, every time you see or talk about Mexicans or anything like that it would be like bad dudes you know? (Pedro)

Pedro explicitly mentions how the social studies (history) curriculum in Texas through heroification glorifies in a colonialist/nationalist way a set of white men as heroes (Loewen, 1995), subsequently reifying the stigma that Mexicans were/are *bad dudes* through negative curricular portrayals.

Media and general portrayals of Latino adolescent males influence not only how males are perceived but also tear away at the very spirit of young males. Parents raising young Latino males often find that their sons face many complexities in school, the community, and with their peers. When parents think about their sons, they know that they are not exotic beings; they are not thugs; they are not deficient. On the contrary, many Latino parents know that their sons are hard working with deep empathy for others.

There is also concern for young children in the Latino culture as well. Who represents the youngest generation? How will the complexity of the images they see impact their lives? How can we ensure that they will be treated with equity by the society at large? How can families and schools ensure that Latino and Latina children experience social justice in our lifetimes?

Further Reading

Loewen, James. *Lies My Teacher Told Me: Everything Your American History Textbook Got Wrong.* New York: Touchstone, 1995.

Rodriguez, Clara. *Latin Looks: Latino Images in the Media.* Oxford: Westview Press, 1997.

Urrieta, Luis, Jr. "Dis-connections in American Citizenship and the Post/Neo-colonial: People of Mexican Descent and Whitestream Pedagogy and Curriculum." *Theory and Research in Social Education,* 2004; 32(4): 433–458.

http://db.latinosandmedia.org/bibliography/.

http://www.cmpa.com/index.html.

http://www.youtube.com/results?search_query=latino+males&search_type=.

Lourdes Diaz Soto and Luis Urrieta, Jr.

Middle Eastern Boys

Middle Eastern boys in the United States, Canada, Australia, New Zealand, and Europe have become increasingly known for a media-driven image that either omits or depicts them as the caricatured *Other* in popular culture. Middle Eastern boys actually come from a diverse geographical, religious, worldview, ethnic, linguistic, and cultural background. Some of the countries that have been typically associated with the Middle East have been (and continue to be), for instance, Egypt, Iraq, Lebanon, Israel, Turkey, occupied Palestine, and modern-day Iran. In the recent *War on Terror,* countries such as Afghanistan and Pakistan have been commonly referred to as the Middle East, as well, by political powers and the media. Therefore, a Middle Eastern boy may have his geographical roots from Asia, Africa, or (even in the case of Turkey) Europe and may associate himself ethnically, for example, as Turk, Armenian, Kurd, Jewish, Persian, and/or Arab. Mother tongue languages that may be spoken by a Middle Eastern boy could be Arabic, Hebrew, Farsi (modern Iranian Persian), and/or Turkish. Among the many religions and worldviews, a Middle Eastern boy may be Muslim, Christian, Jewish, Baha'i, Zoroastrian, humanist, or atheist. Given the diversity of all of these factors, Middle Eastern boys can be culturally dissimilar and, in some areas, similar.

Because of the large areas of the world that encompass the Middle East, and the broad and changing definition of who belongs in it, demographics need to be carried out through specifics, such as the population of Yemen, as opposed to a whole. Tracking trends of Middle East immigration to such places as Canada and the United States also needs to be addressed in particulars, such as the percentage of people living in the United States who claim their heritage as Iranian. Despite considerable immigration of Peoples of the Middle East to North America and Europe that include long established communities (e.g., the Arab-American Community of Dearborn, Michigan), the overwhelming perception that Middle Eastern boys must confront is one of an outsider, foreigner, or Other.

In relation to the Middle Eastern boy experience, the Other refers to a group of people who have been put in a comparative or opposite position to a dominant group; meaning the dominant group develops a sense of who they are by agreeing upon what differentiates them from another, whether the differences are real or imagined, and imposes their perceptions of and on the Other. Sources of substantial power and influence, such as schools and the media, have shaped the representation of the Middle East and therefore the Middle Eastern boy as a monolithic or stereotyped, predominantly casting or defining them in the role as a generic *Arab,* militant, violent, and nonrational Muslim extremist. Despite the diversity of Middle Eastern boys, they must negotiate with a powerful image of self that is overwhelmingly and uniformly negative and has increased since the attacks of 9/11. The post-9/11 atmosphere has allowed an increase in the demonization of Peoples of the Middle East, with examples of influential U.S. public figures, such as Fox television's Bill O'Reilly and televangelist Pat Robertson (*The 700 Club)* speaking negatively about the generic *Muslim,* with little to no effect on their reputations or careers. Dehumanization of Middle Eastern people can also be observed by the news media's omission of or reluctance to report in any real and humane detail on the massive amounts of deaths of Middle Eastern people through the ongoing War on

Terror. In media sources that are associated with childhood (e.g., television, film, or comic books), Middle Eastern males are typically depicted as villains and Middle Eastern boys are usually nonexistent or (at best) peripheral props. In 2005, The Canadian Islamic Congress published a report summarizing the harmful media portrayal of Muslims in 2003 and used the term *image distortion disorder* to explain how the media has created a destructive sense of self among Peoples of the Middle East, but particularly Middle Eastern Muslim youth.

Schools in the United States, Canada, and Europe are also locations where the character of the Middle East, and by extension the Middle Eastern boy, is also maligned as curriculum either portrays them as inadequate, problematic, or does not refer to them at all. When addressed, common themes in curriculum and teachers' attitudes involve a view on the Middle East that teaches either an *us* as compared to *them* message or (in some cases) a sympathetic one that promotes the idea of helping or rescuing a group of people in need. Just as typical in schools is the absence of any curriculum that represents the Middle East, leaving the impression that it has not contributed to humanity, knowledge, or culture in any meaningful and positive way.

Understanding that the events of 9/11 have certainly intensified the negative portrayal and teaching of the Middle East, this has been a problem for the Middle Eastern boy that has existed for quite some time (e.g., consider the Crusades). The combination of non-formal and formal miseducation about the Middle East has resulted in increased risk of physical danger, mental anguish, and reduced opportunity for the Middle Eastern boy.

Further Reading

Children of Heaven, A film by: Majid Majidi, Miramax Films, 1999.

Kincheloe, Joe L. and Steinberg, Shirley R. (Eds.). *The Miseducation of the West: The Hidden Curriculum of Western-Muslim Relations.* New York: Greenwood Press, 2004.

Reel Bad Arabs; How Hollywood Vilifies a People, A film by Sut Jhally, Media Education Foundation, 2007.

Said, Edward W. *Covering Islam: How the Media and the Experts Determine How We See the Rest of the World.* Pantheon Books: New York, 1981.

Stonebanks, Christopher D. "Spartan Superhunks and Persian Monsters; Responding to Truth and Identity as Determined by Hollywood." *Studies in Symbolic Interaction*, 2008; 31.

Christopher Darius Stonebanks

Redneck Boys

Currently, young males, regardless of their place of birth, who are born into what are considered by some as lower or middle-class families and who live in rural areas often call themselves *rednecks;* or the term is used by others to describe them, sometimes in a derogatory manner. The term originates from the fact that people who made their living outside, especially the farmer and the farmer's family, were often exposed to the harsh rays of the southern sun. Sunscreen did not exist and often people, especially the males, would have a sunburned neck. Females usually wore bonnets or hats that shielded their necks, but the necks of the males were often exposed. Other parts of the body such as the arms and legs were usually covered by pants and shirts, so the neck and face of men and boys would often be starkly reddish in color. Because, in the U.S. South, those who labored in the fields were often poor measured against the wealth of the plantation or large farm owners and their families, they were considered to be of lower class and status by those who held power. Most of the small farmers and their children were not formally educated and were often considered ignorant and socially inferior, creating a further divide between the rich and the poor; thus, the term *redneck* began to be used by those with power as a way to describe a person, usually male, who was considered to be of lower class, uneducated, and unsophisticated in social and cultural graces. A redneck was not what one desired to be, though, as the culture of the South and other rural areas of the United States has evolved, many people, particularly males, have gladly claimed the term as a description of identity and a badge of pride.

In fact, some young males who are born into wealth claim the term. Redneck boys are associated with particular behavioral characteristics that are rooted in very traditional male gender roles and the old ways of the South. Namely, they are expected to lack formal education, enjoy the outdoors including hunting and fishing, have quick tempers, be aggressive and fearless fighters, dress in clothing appropriate to outdoor activities (jeans, boots, hats, etc.), and own vehicles that represent the farming heritage such as trucks, all terrain vehicles, tractors, and jeeps, with a gun-rack, complete with at least one gun, in the vehicle. Redneck boys are expected to exhibit all aspects of traditional masculinity, including fierce independence, strict heterosexuality, fearlessness in the face of danger, and suppressed emotions except for anger and rage. In relationships with females, redneck boys are expected to exhibit control and adhere to the idea that females are the property of the male—an ideology that may lead to domestic violence.

Redneck boys are often associated with racism, which is grounded in the traditional expectation that people only associate with others like them, a by-product of the strict divisions in race and class grounded in the historical culture of the agrarian South. Very often, redneck boys are expected to consume alcohol, in particular, low-cost beer, and there are fairly strict expectations regarding the consumption of food. A redneck boy would never consume food or a beverage that was associated with what some would define as more sophisticated cuisine or something associated with traditional femininity, such as a fruit-based cocktail or sophisticated cooking. Redneck boys often use tobacco products, such as snuff-like products or cigarettes. The use of illicit drugs, such as marijuana or cocaine, is not usually associated with being a redneck boy, though methamphetamine drug use is now popular in rural (and urban) areas, especially among lower-income people. In terms of work, a redneck boy is expected to engage in some form of labor, such as masonry, carpentry, factory work, or agriculture. Office work or jobs traditionally associated with females or with formal education are not acceptable. Despite very close relationships between and among friends, physical contact with other males is limited to fighting, contact in sports, or a slap on the back when something has been accomplished. Redneck boys avoid long involved conversations and stick to what some would consider simple phrases and expressions. Above all, redneck boys should never appear vulnerable in the face of danger or in response to a tragic life event. Strength, in a traditional masculine sense, is the foundation of being a modern-day redneck boy. In many cases, the strict rules of redneck boy culture create stress and anxiety for young men who are expected to adhere to this code of conduct, particularly when they find that it does not match with how they want to live their lives.

The origin of the word has its roots in the era before industrialization completely changed the way people lived, particularly in the rural southern United States. Before the age of factories and mass production of material goods, the United States was mainly an agrarian society. Money was made chiefly by growing crops of all sorts and selling them locally and internationally. In the southern United States, lumber, rice, and (a bit later) cotton became major export crops and material wealth became associated with the cultivation of thousands of acres of agricultural goods. As this way of life developed in the South, only a few people reached a point of great wealth. Most people were barely able to grow all that they needed to survive and life was centered on working the land and planning for times when the yield from the crops was limited. One of the first priorities of life at this time was to plant a garden and to raise livestock so that the family could eat. Once this was accomplished, the main task was to cultivate whatever crops would be sold for profit.

Many people grew relatively small fields of indigo (a plant used to make a blue dye), cotton, and tobacco. The owners of the plantations oversaw the development of large fields of such crops, sometimes having thousands of acres. The labor of slaves, most being of African decent, was essential in fueling the mass production of exportable products, and the great wealth of the plantation owners was the result of one of the most inhumane practices humans have ever known—owning and exploiting other people for the sake of increasing material wealth. While plantation owners often had hundreds of slaves to labor in the fields, most people did not have enough money to own slaves and they depended on family members to do the work. The social division that was created by the coexistence of enslaved people, the small farmer who was usually not wealthy and the owners of large farms and plantations who had great material wealth would create a great divide among people in the United States that still exists today as racism and classism.

Further Reading

Billings, Dwight B., Gurney Norman, and Katherine Ledford (Eds.). *Confronting Appalachian Stereotypes: Back Talk from an American Region.* Lexington, KY: The University Press of Kentucky, 1999.

Roebuck, Julian, and Mark Hickson III. *The Southern Redneck: A Phenomenological Class Study*. New York: Praeger, 1982.

Jay Poole

Rural Boys

The United States is a continuously growing, and changing country very different today from her agricultural roots. The Industrial Revolution that occurred in America during the 1800s caused a major shift in how goods were produced as well as where people lived. This time period saw Americans move from farms to cities. Although advances in machinery assisted with farming techniques, the population increase in urban centers changed America forever. Farming communities are still important in the functioning of America. Boys who grow up on the farm make up an integral part of our society and have unique experiences that make them special.

The U.S. government defines rural as areas with less than 2, 500 residents. In 2000, according to the U.S. Department of Agriculture, approximately 21 percent of Americans lived in sparsely-populated areas such as these. Although farms usually come to mind when talking about rural communities, ranches, mill, and mining towns fall into this category as well. Within rural areas, there are typically two primary groups: those who participate in agricultural production and those who provide services for the producers, such as school teachers, doctors, and lawyers. Farm boys have a deep understanding of the typical characteristics and people that make up a rural community.

Education

Some generalizations can be made about students living in rural areas and their involvement in school. However, as with all generalizations, it is important to realize that every student is unique and there are always exceptional individuals and circumstances. One generalization, for example, is that rural children largely excel in school in the areas of grades, standardized testing, and earning degrees. There is not much difference between rural and urban students regarding their secondary and college education, although there are likely some differences in the subject matter they choose to study. During their college career, for example, boys from a rural background may be more likely to study areas that assist with their role in the family business, such as forestry, horticulture, or animal sciences. Studies indicate that rural students are just as likely to graduate high school and obtain an undergraduate education as urban kids. In general, however, rural students are less likely than their urban counterparts to pursue a postgraduate degree, such as a PhD or an MD. This difference is most likely due to differences in life plans involving such things as future place of residence and desired occupation.

For example, not surprisingly, rural kids, especially boys, typically have strong ties to their community and family. A close-knit atmosphere where population is small and people depend on one another for goods and services is conducive to an intimate environment and an attachment to home. This close attachment to local people and places sometimes means that rural students are less likely to move great distances for schooling. When it is considered that there are limited options for graduate programs providing the postgraduate work and accreditation necessary for a medical or law degree, for example, this difference in likelihood to pursue a postgraduate degree is easily understood.

Technological advances, however, are reshaping the way in which America's students are able to learn. The traditional classroom does not necessarily have to be a physical space anymore. The Internet provides opportunities for distance learning and enables students to obtain an education from theoretically anywhere in the world. High-speed Internet access, however, is still not available in many rural areas, thus limiting the informational and educational opportunities for many citizens. This digital divide is shrinking though as advances in technology quicken and widespread demand for Internet access continues to rise.

Schools not only provide educational opportunities, but also offer avenues for participating in extracurricular activities. Organizations that cater to and focus on local interests, such as 4-H Clubs and Future Farmers of America, are popular activities. In addition, sports and athletics are very popular in rural community schools and provide opportunities for physical fitness, camaraderie, and healthy competition for rural boys and girls alike. The community often revolves around school activities, such as sports teams, especially football, basketball, and baseball, so there is a strong support system present. Communities provide helpful, necessary support for school programs, especially athletic activities. Supporting a successful school system can be expensive, however, and limited tax dollars must be spread out to meet various community needs. Therefore, communities offer the most support for those programs and organizations seen as coinciding with local values and interests.

Economic Challenges

Rural communities experience many economic challenges that urban populations do not share, even during hard times for urban areas. Although most rural communities can be divided into two groups—agricultural producers and those who supply services to the producers—the economic health of the entire population ultimately depends on the community's ability to produce goods. Factors such as the weather, pests, soil composition, availability of migrant workers, and machinery are just some of the important components in achieving economic prosperity. As globalization increases and competition becomes fiercer, some small farmers have suffered economically. Reports indicate that familial income for these small farmers has been declining in recent years. Additionally, rural communities offer fewer, less diverse employment opportunities than urban centers. They may also be centered around a few small businesses or factories, and if they have trouble, the area does, too. As a result, rural communities usually have relatively higher unemployment percentages than cities do.

In general, rural kids seem to be less materialistic than urban kids. Unfortunately for rural communities, however, children living in rural areas are more likely to live in poverty than urban children. It has been shown, however, that stable families can help curb poverty. Rural families are typically more stable and have lower divorce rates than urban families. This close family connection serves to keep poverty rates lower than they would be otherwise. For those rural kids that do live in poverty, however, the circumstances are dire. Rural children in poverty are more adversely affected than their urban counterparts. Although a specific, detailed examination of this disparity is beyond the scope of this entry, one possible reason is that most social services provided by both the government and private organizations are based out of urban centers. Cities typically house the bulk of resources and political power. Additionally, rural communities are usually spread out over large distances, which can make assisting poverty-stricken children more difficult. Researchers have also found that minorities living in rural areas are disproportionately impoverished, a situation that deserves further attention.

Community Life

Rural children grow up in communities that are oftentimes spread out over large geographical distances. In addition, rural boys carry great responsibility within the family and assist with many chores necessary to keep the household and family business running. Some researchers view the limited social interaction that can arise out of distance between friends and their extensive responsibilities as deficits in rural kids' development. However, rural children seem as happy and well-adjusted as their urban peers. In fact, rural kids are generally more accepting of their peers within the community. A strong sense of community identity, however, can create seemingly unfriendly or hostile conditions for an outsider.

It is important to recognize that farming is a way of life in rural communities, not just a way to make a living. In the smaller, rural communities, people's social, professional, and personal lives overlap. Kids often go to school and church with the same people and see other community members in multiple roles throughout their lives. Life in rural communities often centers on church and school functions, which provide gathering places and social events for residents. Rural communities are largely cohesive, stable entities that cooperate to provide and care for its members. Limited access to medical care, for example, can be an issue for rural citizens battling serious illnesses such as cancer. In such cases, it is not unusual for people in the community to come together to help their fellow member get the care he or she needs by providing transportation, babysitting services, or even financial support.

Family Life

As might be expected, rural children often grow up in a cohesive family unit with extended family often living nearby. The vast majority, around 80 percent, of rural marriages are still intact, contributing to a stable, strong family unit (Larson and Dearmont, 2002). A rural boy will likely grow up listening to stories told by his grandfather, who lives down the road, and might be kept after school in his younger years by his grandmother or an aunt. The extended family is often involved in child care duties of its younger members and works to pass along and develop community, religious, and family values as well. These values often include such aspirations as self-reliance, loyalty, hard work, and honesty. Religion and faith are also important attributes in rural family life. In keeping with the notion of a strong family unit, similar to a team, rural boys are protective of family information and seek to guard the unit from outsiders. A strong desire to keep assets and land in the family is passed down from generation to generation.

In general, rural boys have positive feelings toward their family members and exhibit a strong sense of attachment to the family unit. Their heavy involvement in familial duties and decisions, as compared to urban boys, likely contributes to this. Rural children have greater levels of responsibility and often enjoy much input in family decision making. Parents set high expectations for their children at a young age to fulfill and succeed in their role within the family. Generally, rural children benefit from the clear, set purpose in life that often accompanies growing up in a rural community. Their ability to accomplish their duties competently and the fact that they hold an instrumental role in the family are factors that contribute to resilience among rural children, which is often not found in such great degrees with urban children.

Changes and Challenges

Although rural children often benefit from scholastic success, stable family influences, and strong community support, there are some challenges affecting America's rural residents. It has been shown through research that rural children can be more fearful than urban youth. Although we can only speculate as to why this might be, some possible explanations include things such as heavy parental protection and limited exposure to realistic, potentially fearful situations. In short, rural youth might be more sheltered than urban youth and thus might not be able to confront and subsequently dismiss many frightening situations. For example, violent crime in rural communities is generally not as prevalent as it is in urban centers. If rural children only have *Law & Order* to base urban reality on, they might be fearful of entering large cities because rapes, murders, and kidnappings would seem to be much more common than they are in actuality.

Additionally, rural boys are more likely than urban boys to use illegal drugs, abuse alcohol, and smoke cigarettes, or use chewing tobacco. Such risky behaviors can result in serious health and crime problems for rural communities and families. Moreover, a population shift among rural youth may be happening with substantial differences expected between the sexes. Research shows that 50 percent of rural boys have said they would prefer to live in an urban area as opposed to the rural community they grew up in (Kuvlesky and Pelham, 1970). When rural girls were asked the same question, 66 percent said they would prefer to live in an urban area. If these kids follow through with their statements, not only will rural communities experience drastic population changes, but families, peer groups, and companionship options will be affected as well. This population shift would have consequences for economic factors as well. Lastly, the previously mentioned digital divide is still an obstacle for many rural communities' ability to receive information and thus limits opportunities. High-speed Internet access is a necessity for rural communities to benefit from the type of information and educational opportunities available to other Americans.

Further Reading

Conger, Rand & Glen Elder, Jr. *Families in Troubled Times: Adapting to Change in Rural America.* New York: Aldine de Gruyter, 1994.

Cromartie, John. Measuring Rurality: What is Rural? [Online March 2009]. United States Department of Agriculture Economic Research Service. http://www.ers.usda.gov/Briefing/Rurality/WhatIsRural/.

Elder, Glen, Jr., & Rand Conger. *Children of the Land: Adversity and Success in Rural America.* Chicago: University of Chicago Press, 2000.

Gibbs, Robert M., Paul L. Swaim, & Ruy Teixeira (Eds.). *Rural Education and Training in the New Economy: The Myth of Rural Skills Gap.* Ames, IA: Iowa State University Press, 1998.

Kuvlesky, William P., & John T. Pelham. Place of Residence Projections of Rural Youth: A Racial Comparison. *Social Science Quarterly,* June, 1970.

Larson, Nancy C., & Melissa Dearmont. Strengths of Farming Communities in Fostering Resilience in Children. *Child Welfare,* September/October, 2002.

Carly T. McKenzie

South Asian Boys

South Asian masculinity in North America is not monolithic. In North America, the term South Asian has come to signify the sociocultural practices of the diverse groups of people who have immigrated to the continent from a specific global geographic location. Although geographically most commonly associated with the country India, the term South Asian also incorporates people from surrounding countries such as Afghanistan, Pakistan, Bangladesh, Nepal, Bhutan, and Sri Lanka. Men who come from this geographic location speak different languages, have different religious backgrounds, and have diverse sociocultural practices. These men come from Muslim, Sikh, Tamil, Hindu, Buddhist, and Christian backgrounds to name a few. An estimated 1.5 billion people live in this region currently, 1.3 million people identified themselves as South Asian in Canada's 2006 census, and there are approximately 2.7 million South Asians living in the United States.

Despite the diversity within South Asian male culture, these men are usually represented in popular culture and media as model minorities or societal malcontents. It is within these extreme poles that South Asian masculinity seems to be essentialized, or given a certain common standard of categorization, in North America. Popular culture, media, and educational texts help cement these extremes as the only possibilities of what South Asian boys can aspire to be. South Asian boys in North America deal with the dichotomy between traditional cultural beliefs and the norms of dominant culture.

Issues around interracial dating, maintaining first languages, and keeping with religious customs of parents are some of the concerns facing South Asian boys. Participating in school-based activities around themes such as Christmas or Valentine's Day could be culturally difficult for some South Asian youth who do not celebrate the intent of these days. Playing on school sports teams at times poses difficulties because traditional attire such as turbans might be hard to manage. As evidenced by mainstream education in North America, it is clear that there is little in the way of curriculum offered in regard to various South Asian cultures and practices. Being left out of curriculum and being only partially identified through stereotypes may have a negative impact on South Asian boys.

South Asian boys have concerns about racism in society. Often they are scapegoated for loss of jobs in North America due to outsourcing. Other issues which may insight discriminatory attitudes from non-South Asians may be issues around the smell of certain foods and spices used in cooking, the wearing of culture-specific clothing, and religious practices such as praying five times, even in public. It is difficult for some South Asian boys to maintain cultural practices in a social context which may not welcome difference. Some of these issues manifest as a result of being in a culture whose media and educational texts speak very little to issues of concern to South Asian boys.

South Asian boys are often grouped into one category. Many youth complain about being lumped together by dominant culture into one group, instead of being acknowledged for diversity. When portraying this group of men as the same, it has the effect of making issues relevant to a specific South Asian group invisible. South Asian boys have complained that the general public has not been educated on differences between such diverse groups as Hindus, Sikhs, and Muslims. Teachers, cultural workers, politicians, media, and educational texts are considered possible starting points in educating society about the rich diversity within South Asian cultures. The lack of knowing the difference between groups comprising the category of South Asian males can have severe consequences. In Arizona a Sikh man, Balbir Singh Sodhi, was murdered after the 9/11 attacks in the United States because he had brown skin, wore a turban, and was mistaken for a follower of Islam.

There seems to be a Muslim/non-Muslim divide in perception of South Asian males in North American culture due to global events. Post 9/11 North American institutions have increasingly portrayed adolescent boys from Muslim cultures as dangerous potential terrorists who eventually will seek to undermine western values of democracy, liberty, and equality. Although most commonly associated with Arab countries, the Muslim population in South Asia is very large and falls under the general negative stereotype.

Often South Asian boys are portrayed as coming from cultures where male dominant behavior is encouraged, violence is a part of life, and females are mistreated. This poses a problem for many South Asian boys who may be labelled at an early age as violent misogynists, or men who have a hatred for women.

Media in Canada have often shown stories of young South Asian men engaged in various abuses toward women, such has gender-motivated beatings and even murder. North American culture is also saturated with images of brown skinned young men, turbans, beards, and religious extremism on television news programs. Images with captions such as Sikh militants, Muslim fanatics, and Tamil extremists are often used for preserving political agendas which seek to finance global efforts in punishing potential threats to North American society. Images of dangerous South Asian men have also appeared in television shows such as *Lost*, *24*, and *Generation Kill*. In Canada, particularly British Columbia, South Asian males have been linked to gangs, drug trafficking, and organized crime. News media outlets such as *The Vancouver Sun* and Channel M have assigned reporters to specifically cover South Asian boys and illegal activity.

Conversely, in North America where assimilating attitudes toward immigrant groups are often prevalent, non-Muslim South Asian males are sometimes viewed as a model minority. This label denotes their ability to assimilate into the dominant culture and gain prominence in middle- and upper-middle-class fields which are considered important by those in power. This label encourages South Asian males to achieve in fields of study such as medicine, accounting, engineering, computer science, and business. Pop culture reinforces these occupations for South Asian males. Television programs such as *ER*, *House*, and *Hopkins* (a television documentary filmed at Johns Hopkins University Hospital) have featured South Asian characters as doctors, and movies such as *The Life Aquatic with Steve Zissou* and *Superman Returns* show South Asians as technical engineers. The negative effect of this perception is the limiting of public attitudes of what South Asian males can accomplish and aspire to. Any South Asian male who does not follow a prescribed formula of what he should do may be considered uneducated, deviant, or simply not trying hard enough.

According to census data, South Asian men are among the most highly educated group in North America and their businesses and firms generate tremendous revenue. Their labor continues to be an asset in economies associated with farming, lumber, and railways. A criticism of some North American immigration policies toward South Asian men is that rules allow for prosperous, educated immigrants from South Asia to enter, and do not look favorably toward working-class men from this region. This has the effect of taking some of the most creative and astute young minds from South Asia and putting them to work for North American firms.

Despite achieving academic success and making headway monetarily in North America, popular films and television often portray South Asian males as comical small business owners, such as the characters Apu Nahasapeemapetilon from *The Simpsons* and Babu Bhatt from *Seinfeld*, or taxicab drivers. South Asian characters are often cast in subservient roles to white superiors, such as the character Punjab from the movie *Annie*. The comic relief offered by the finger wagging, eyes popping open, sharp tongued South Asian male, such as the character Mooj from the *40-Year-Old Virgin*, and the complete stoner character of Kumar from the *Harold and Kumar* franchise, seem to be a contrast to the reality of most of these men.

Mysticism and spirituality are also associated with South Asian men. Popular films such as *A Passage to India, The Guru,* and *Holy Smoke* show Indian males as overtly spiritual sages. The explosion of Bikram Yoga, the popularity of authors such as Deepak Chopra, and the increasing interest in Buddhist meditation in North America are examples where South Asian males are cast in positions of spiritual leadership. A criticism of western incorporation of South Asian spiritual practices is that it inevitably leads to turning spirituality into a material good for sale to the masses for profit, which is not the original intent of such a lifestyle. Movies such as *Indiana Jones and the Temple of Doom* go one step further and depict Indian spirituality as exploitive in nature and having a brainwashing effect.

South Asian boys have a very unique stereotype in North American society. On the one hand they are considered a model minority and on the other hand are considered a group that does not fit in with the societal norms. They are portrayed as deviant and are also viewed as aspiring university degree holders who will enhance fields of medicine, engineering, computer science, and politics. Prominent South Asian public figures such as former premier of British Columbia, Ujjal Dosanjh, and the current Attorney General of BC, Wally Uppal, also show how South Asian boys raised in North America have impacted politics. Governor Bobby Jindal of Louisiana is currently the highest elected South Asian politician in the history of the United States, and was considered a vice-presidential candidate for John McCain in the 2008 presidential election. South Asian boys raised in North America such as actors Waris Ahluwalia, Kal Penn, and Academy Award nominated director M. Night Shyamalan have achieved significant fame as well. All of these examples add to the dichotomy that represents South Asian boys in North America.

Further Reading

Aalgaard, Wendy. *East Indians in America.* Minneapolis, MN: Lerner Publications, 2005.

Böck, Monika, & Aparna Rao (Eds.). *Culture, Creation, and Procreation: Concepts of Kinship in South Asian Practice.* Oxford, UK: Berghahn Books, 2001.

Ghuman, Paul Avtar Singh. *Coping with Two Cultures: British Asian and Indo-Canadian Adolescents.* Bristol, UK: Multilingual Matters, 1993.

Maira, Sunaina. *Desis in the House: Indian American Youth Culture in New York City.* Philadelphia, PA: Temple University Press, 2002.

Prashad, Vijay. *The Karma of Brown Folk.* Minneapolis, MN: University of Minnesota Press, 2000.

Kal Heer

South Asian Boys: Desi Boys

Desi boys are as diverse as the concept of *Desi,* which is a slang term referring to South Asian immigrants and derives from the Sanskrit word meaning "from/of the country." The term is primarily used to refer to South Asians living in North America and the UK. The term was legitimized by first appearing as an adjective in 2003 and now appearing as a noun in the *Oxford Dictionary of English*. South Asians are people who are descendants from the countries of India, Pakistan, Bangladesh, and Sri Lanka. People from these countries also call themselves *East Indians* (as opposed to *West Indians* who are from islands in the Caribbean).

Second generation Desis are often called *ABCD*, meaning "American-Born Confused Desi." The term relates to the dual-identity cultural struggle many young second and third generation South Asians/East Indians face living between their traditional South Asian roots at home and the Western culture of North American society outside of their home. They derive from multiple lands, speak multiple languages, enjoy various foods and music, and have diversified stories to share. Their life experiences and consequently their *culture* depend largely on geography. Are they living in rural North America, or in major cosmopolitan centers like New York and Toronto? And even within these metropolitan centers, whether they reside in homogeneous suburbs densely populated with other South Asians (such as Surrey, British Columbia; Brampton, Ontario; or Queens, New York) or in heterogeneous communities where turf is shared with other immigrant populations or dominated by whites, the Desi experience is diverse.

Despite the diversity—whether rural or metro, Bengali or Punjabi, Muslim or Hindu—Desi Boys have all experienced growing up between two cultures. Those who have assimilated with their *western* peers are often labeled by others as an ABCD or as a *coconut* (brown on the outside, white on the inside). Others who have conformed to their parents' traditional ideals are often associated as being *FOB-ish* (Fresh Off the Boat—referring to those young Desis who are either new immigrants or typically have accents and enjoy their curry a little too much). This cultural confusion is exaggerated for third generation Desis who use Bollywood, India's entertainment industry, to associate with their South Asian identity, and find their native homelands more westernized than their parents want to believe.

Desi Boys who grew up in the 1980s and 1990s were all too familiar with the racist slurs of *Paki* (meaning from Pakistan, but usually a label for anyone who looks South Asian, whether actually from Pakistan or not) and coconut. It was these experiences that alienated Desi Boys (and girls) from their South Asian roots and consequently led to a South Asian revolution in the early 1990s. It was during this time that the Desi Boy persona really took root. The growing popularity of Apache Indian, a hip hop/bhangara artist from the UK, hailed solidarity and pride among young Desis, especially Desi Boys. DJing and club promoting became popular pastimes of these young men who immersed themselves in the "Desi DayJam Scene" in Toronto, Canada. DayJams were parties held at major night clubs in Toronto during the day, typically starting at 10 a.m. and going until the early afternoon (just in time for young Desis to get home as if they were at school all day). Call it rebellious or entrepreneurial, but thousands of young South Asians found ingenious ways to ditch school so that they could party to both the traditional bhangara tunes and mainstream rhythms of the 1990s. Schools in Toronto were often missing many of their students on those days.

Desi Boy culture from the 1990s gave way to a sense of belonging and pride among second and third generation Desis today. Apache Indians' success gave way for new artists such as Punjabi by Nature and today's Punjabi MC. In fact, now more than ever before, young South Asian boys are proud to announce their roots. Not only do we hear traditional bhangara beats remixed with mainstream hip hop and other forms of music, but the South Asian community has also been labeled as the *Model Minority* in the United States. This model minority is now the second wealthiest ethnic group living in the United States. Along with labels come a heighten awareness of the community and a genuine interest in all things Desi. Many Desi Boys have hopped on the entrepreneurial Desi train and have found ways to commercialize on Desi *coolness.* Desi Boys have changed the way other Desis dance, drink, and date. Log onto one of the many Desi chat rooms to find a mélange of Desi clothing lines (such as DesiWear, who's owner was once a Desi Boy enjoying Apache Indian tunes at sold-out DayJams in Toronto), bhangara remixes from popular artists such as Nelly Furtado working with popular artist Punjabi MC, and dating Web sites where the idea of an *arranged marriage* has been reinvented.

Initially, Desi Boys adhered to the common expectations of being studious, conscientious, and timid—future doctors or future engineers of immigrant parents. Desi Boys in the early 1990s rejected these ideals and reinvented themselves. Some even formed gangs such as the Punjabi Mafia who embraced a more aggressive *thug* life and refused to accept the racism they had subserviently endured in the past. Gautam Malkani's *Londonstani* describes Desi Boys gone *gangsta.* Today the solidarity among Desi Boys created among South Asians during the cultural revolution of the 1990s has led to a continued hype of Desi pride. Desi Boys at Penn State University have even chartered their own fraternity: Delta Sigma Iota. These boys even compete among the best in step dancing competitions, typically dominated by African American fraternity brothers. Desi Boy culture has become a fusion of South Asian and the mainstream and has even nudged its way into becoming *cool.* Bhangara, cricket, and even curry are part of the popular lexicon which gives way to a new generation of Desi Boy culture and pride.

Further Reading

American Desi, a film by Pitus Dinker Pandya, Blue Rock Entertainment, and American Desi Productions, 2001.

Lahiri, Jhumpa. *The Namesake.* New York: Houghton Mifflin Books, 2004

Maira, Sunaina. *Desis in the House: Indian American Youth Culture in New York City.* Philadelphia, PA: Temple University Press, 2002.

South Asian Student Alliance [January 2008]. <www.sasaweb.org>.

Ramona Parkash Arora

Urban Boys

In some urban settings, many boys find themselves growing fast and not cared for; rather, they find themselves being the caretakers of their families and of themselves. The responsibilities for these boys can be huge, and the odds against them can appear overwhelming, as poverty and violence often combine with the difficulties of being left alone. Boys who grow up in this situation are not alone for a short period; they are instead children who have been permanently forgotten and/or abandoned by the adults in their families. Boys in this situation struggle for emotional and physical health, as depression and other symptoms of living with stress make their days hard and their nights long.

This Ain't Disneyland

Boys who grow up without adult care may get involved with drugs, drug dealing, alcohol, gangs, and violence. They may suffer from the effects of stress. Instead of love, these boys experience neglect, and they try to find direction in the world without adult protection and guidance. The media and many adults do not look kindly on such boys. They are often blamed for their lives and the choices they make, as if they had chosen to *grow up hard*. But from these experiences, some boys grow strong; from the knowledge they gain on the streets, they develop a complex and deep understanding of right and wrong. Some boys who grow up without parental supervision and care, use their knowledge of a hard life to fight against unjust circumstances and they act as protectors and guardians for their grandparents and younger relatives. Understanding these boys is complicated as all boys are not the same. In addition, their lives do not follow the traditional *good-boy* versus *bad-boy* stories of the boys often in books, on TV, and in the movies. Boys who grow up urban and poor have to deal with complicated lives and adult concerns. They have to constantly remind themselves to "keep ya head up" because "this ain't Disneyland."

Knock Knock: Who's There?—Hard Knocks: Who's Not There?

Children have parents, unless they are orphans. It may be unusual for most people to think about children and not assume that there are parents who protect and care for them. But in the home of a poor urban boy, sometimes the question to ask is not "Who's there?" but rather "Who's not there?" Many children who grow up poor and in urban environments (or just poor) do not have a responsible parent living in the house with them. They may live with their mother (or less often their father), but that parent may not be able to fulfill that parental role. They may not be in the house to guide their children, they may not listen to their children, they may harm (verbally or physically abuse) them instead of protecting them, they may not even feed their children. Increasingly, poor boys are left to take care of themselves.

Parents

There are many reasons a poor urban parent might have a child and not take care of it; and this has a particular effect on boys. In some families, the parent or both parents are in trouble. Boys often see all of the male adults in their communities as in and out of jail. They see life as being involved with jails and courts as normal. If a boy does not have anyone to take care of him he can get involved in stealing (or other illegal activities) and he may find himself in jail at a young age. Other parents can't take care of their children because they may be ill, or work too much to be at home. Some parents are teenagers themselves and too young to be able to take care of a child, even though they want to (although many teenagers are great parents). Another difficulty that a boy may face is that he may have parents who are drug addicts or alcoholics and can't look after themselves, much less him. In this case, the parents just *party* all the time and get high, and consequently, they also set a bad example for their child who learns to do the same. In all of these cases, boys grow up in homes with no positive adult role models.

No Parents, but Family Instead

Some parents send their children to live with their grandparents so they can go back to living a childfree life. It can be very hard for a boy to only see his mother occasionally on visits, especially when she does not call to see how he is or remember his birthday. It is also hard for an elderly person to take care of a child; many older people have health issues and they need to be helped and cared for themselves. Often the grandparent works and has more then one child in the house; the older boy then becomes the caretaker in the family. In this case, a boy may have the job of being *the man in the house,* even though he might only be 15 years old. Boys who are neglected just grow up as best they can and fend for themselves. They make their own *family,* as *the streets* take care of helping them grow up more than their biological parents do. Young boys may stay out late and act like they think adults or older boys act. They learn how to *be grown* (men) from people they meet, and from the school of hard knocks.

Pressed

Boys who have to grow up without care are under huge amounts of stress. Some of this stress is about the physical world of things. They may find themselves hungry with no one cooking for them and nothing to eat in the house. They wear clothes that are too small or unclean because no one does their laundry. They worry about their family getting kicked out of the home because nobody can pay the rent. Often there is no hot water or heat. Frequently, a boy's health may be poor condition when needed medication or eyeglasses are not available. Similarly, they can face physical harm by a member of their household and the list goes on and on. Compared to the happy family we see on TV, boys who *grow up hood,* are often angry. The unfairness of these circumstances is not missed by these youth. They find it almost unbelievable that children are living such a difficult life in this land of plenty.

Stressed

In addition to physical concerns, emotional stress is also hard on boys. Boys are expected to be strong in our culture; this means that they often believe that they should be able to deal with (but stress over) violence. They worry about younger siblings getting in trouble with other kids or the law. They find themselves in situations that require that they *step up* as the older brother or cousin to protect a family member in danger of a fight. They have the stress of worrying about caring for other younger children in the home, to make sure everyone eats and stays out of trouble. They experience the stress of boredom, not having anywhere safe to go or anything positive to do. All of these worries can lead to a feeling of being weighted down—so depressed that it becomes hard to get out of bed. And on top of all this, they have the worry about being strong because "weak minds don't last long." We are all told that stress kills; they stress about being stressed. They stress about not going to school and worry about not being able to get out of the situation they are in—ever.

"They Say I Gotta Learn, but Nobody's Here to Teach Me"—Coolio

Boys who grow up in poor and urban neighborhoods often do not have someone to consistently tell them right from wrong; they have to figure out good and bad choices for themselves. Therefore, it is difficult to make good choices about life when you are a boy who does not see good choices in the world. Boys who have drug-addicted parents are often told that they are not worth anything. They try to find other ways to increase their self-esteem. If nobody cares about a boy's life, he may find it hard to care about someone else's. This cycle is dangerous. The urban streets are not safe for boys who are young and alone. They can easily get involved in gangs and gang violence. Many start using drugs and/or alcohol early. They smoke cigarettes when they are in elementary school, don't eat nutritious food, and do not get enough sleep. In this context, they may not go to school because they are tired or hungry, or simply do not have someone to make them get up in the morning to go to school. These young men find themselves at odds with adults who may be too loud late into the night, or with younger siblings whom they must care for. They may find while just walking home that they are around boys who have something to prove by hurting others. If no one cares about a boy's stresses, they just build up until the boy is ready to explode. If he does, he may harm himself or others. Adolescents are legally not adults, but for many boys, even preadolescents, it is no child's world.

Being a Man

Adultification means becoming like an adult when you are still a child. Boys who are adultified have many responsibilities. They have adult responsibilities and concerns while they are still young, with many people in the home depending on them. Along with the responsibilities already mentioned, they may be responsible for cleaning the house and the dishes, making sure that the bills are paid, translating for a grandparent, helping family members with legal paperwork, making sure their grandparents take their medication, watching the younger children, even bringing in money for the rent and food.

Outside of the home, the ability to be tough and violent or to have a lot of money (from dealing drugs or stealing) is one way that boys earn respect on the streets as men. Many boys never have had a chance to just be a kid.

Hope and Courage—Peace Out

Boys who have been through a lot learn a lot from their experiences. They have a wisdom that is beyond their years. During these experiences, they have had to be many different people and learned to change how they behave in their different roles on the streets, as caretakers, as students, as *the man of the house*. Some of these boys use what they have experienced to counsel younger boys. They know how difficult it can be to trust. They know how to be tough and they know how tough can be treacherous; they are aware of the many dangers that exist for young boys. These young men work to educate those who have not had their experiences. Boys who have been to jail often talk about reflecting on their lives during this time, about coming out determined to do the right thing and care about the people they love, and not "just be another statistic." Boys who grow up through hardship and have had to be adults at a young age are often emotionally and physically strong from their upbringing. Although they may regret a particular decision (who does not?), they do not regret what their lives have taught them. Entering manhood they have learned to "keep ya head up" even when the world is a hard place. These boys may be some of the strongest, most realistic, yet positive people that any city has.

Further Reading

Coolio. *Gangasta's Paradise,* on *Gangsta's Paradise* (CD), 1995.

Nikkah, John. *Our Boys Speak: Adolescent Boys Write about Their Inner Lives.* New York: St Martin's Griffin, 2000.

Christian Almonte and Carolyne Ali Khan

SECTION 3

Boys and Looks

Emo

Emo refers to a style of music that is directly associated with a visual style. Much like mods from the 1960s, an emo's clothing will reveal almost exactly the kind of music that he or she listens to. Emo boys in particular cross aspects of gender norms in their appearance, and, like mod rockers, they do embody an interesting assemblage of stereotypically masculine-rocker and feminine mod (1960s) or new-wave (1980s) styles. The emo boy can usually be recognized by his look. He has shaggy, generally darker hair, often dyed jet black or sable brown, with heavy bangs, and wears a fitted T-shirt, sweater or vest, blazer or hoody, often a white cloth belt, and super-skinny jeans. He frequently sports eyeliner, termed *guyliner,* especially at night, as he wears wrist accessories like bangles, bandanas, and/or wrist bands. The emo boy might wear a neck bandana, a back pocket bandana, a series of pins which reveal his favorite bands and/or images, and he wears canvas shoes such as Chuck Taylors or Vans. As well, he is frequently adorned in star, lightning bolt, or skull patterns. He can sometimes be androgynous, as the cliché of the emo boy is, but often beneath his tailored clothing can be a lithe body, and he is frequently just as masculine or boyish as he seems androgynous. In short, the emo boy blurs gender boundaries, much like his mod and new-wave predecessors.

Emo makes direct historical reference to a genre of punk(ish) music that split from typical political punk of the late 1970s and early 1980s, releasing what has been deemed an emotional punk genre, from which the term emo has been coined. Accordingly, early forms of emo subculture were not always from the upper middle classes. Emo boys once frequented thrift shops to acquire and redesign clothing that would produce their desired effect, although presently emo is adapted by rebellious youth, regardless of class background. Emo, within the confines of this entry, falls into two larger categories. The first, beginning in the mid-1980s in Washington, D.C., existed until the latter 1990s. This kind of emo boy was often a more stylized version of his punk contemporary and had no sexuality prejudice associated with him. The second category, moving past the influence from bands such as *The Rites of Spring* to *My*

Chemical Romance and the onslaught of emo bands that began releasing their music in the late 1990s and the earlier years of the new millennium, became associated with the aforementioned gender-bending and androgyny. A strong example of a present emo band with a higher level of success is *Fall Out Boy*.

Within a very contemporary understanding, emo boy and gay boy have become synonymous, and thus emo and homosexuality have become intertwined. Nonetheless, there remain plenty of young men within emo subculture who are emo boys and straight. Emo and queer are not meant to be tantamount, even though contemporary youth do interchange these terms, but emo boys do, regardless of their desires, cross, bend, and mesh gender norms and create an outlet or option for boys who identify with punk, alternative, or edgy-independent rock music. Furthermore, emo boys have also become associated with sadness, melancholy, and even suicide. The possible reason for this could be the prejudice linked to being visually different or gay in high school. This would make sense to both the anger and the emotion found in emo music, and therefore the music would not only link the emo boy to his favorite bands but also to a mood or temperament that reveals how he feels about his place in the world. While the emo boy will respond to confining images of masculinity or heterosexuality, he is not necessarily liberated from this parallel. Hence, the emo boy's musical tastes and his look reveal how he feels and the frustrations he might embody.

Further Reading

Greenwald, Andy. *Nothing Feels Good: Punk Rock, Teenagers, and Emo.* New York: St. Martin's Griffin, 2003.

House of Emo, <http://www.houseofemo.com/display/ShowJournal?moduleId=243819&currentPcur=2>.

Photo Bucket, "Emo Boys Kissing," <http://s4.photobucket.com/albums/y118/EmoBoysKissing/?start=all>.

Simon, Leslie, and Trevor Kelley. *Everybody Hurts: An Essential Guide to Emo Culture.* Toronto, CAN: Harper Collins Canada, 2007.

Straight-Edge Fag, "What Is Emo?," <http://www.faqs.org/faqs/cultures/straight-edge-faq/section-21.html>.

Brian M. Peters

Goth

They always tend to wear black clothes and seem to be in a dismal mood. This could be a common description for people considered to be *goths*. Goth culture or the dark scene opens a great variety of possibilities for self-expression and identification. In the 1980s goth split up from the punk scene and the development of its own subculture started. The term *goth* was first established in the United Kingdom for this subculture. Today the gothic scene has become international but great inputs still come from the United Kingdom, Germany, and North America. The scene offers many possibilities for goth boys to transcend gender expectations.

During the 1990s the dark society grew and goth music became a fusion of gothic rock, dark wave, synthpop, electronic body music (EBM), industrial, medieval music, and neo- or dark folk music. Popular international bands were, and still are Siouxsie and the Banshees, Sisters of Mercy, Depeche Mode, The Cure and VNV Nation. Generally goths meet each other in special clubs, at home, or organized events in *mystical* places. The biggest events are the "Wave-Gotik-Treffen" in Leipzig, "The Whitby Gothic Weekend" in the United Kingdom, and the "Chamber's Dark Art and Music Festival" in the United States. As the names imply, these events are meetings to watch favorite bands as well as to share and buy gothic art, furniture, and, of course, fashion.

In addition to the different types of music available, the various styles of fashion can also be separated. It is possible to name six main styles: the wave style, the 1980s style, the medieval or romantic style, the common style, the gothic-punk style and the fetish style. The wave style and the 1980s style consist of wide clothes, spiky shoes, and wild hair. Males often wear the so-called *Mohawk* haircut. The wave style integrates a military look, and the 1980s style incorporates capes and a lot of chains. The medieval or romantic style consists of a fashion reminiscent of days gone by, such as Victorian and Edwardian modes of dress. The common style indicates people who just wear black clothes, such as leatherwear. Leather is also part of the gothic-punk style and the fetish style. Gothic punks wear boots, leather jackets, and frazzled clothes. The fetish style also incorporates black, latex, and leather and veers toward the erotic. Within all styles goths tend to apply a contrasting approach to makeup, such as white powder for the face, black eyeliner, dark lipstick, and/or dark nail polish. Piercings and tattoos are also wide spread among the subculture. It should also be noted, though, that there are numerous styles differing from country to country, and almost from individual to individual.

What could be classed as unique and particularly individual for goth men? For men, it is possible to mix feminine and masculine looks and create a personal style, for example, wearing skirts, boots, and makeup, as well as having long hair. Furthermore, the scene offers the possibility of showing emotion, which is not generally seen as being a part of a strong masculine stereotype. Suffering and sadness as emotions go along with a reflection on personal problems, life, sin, and mortality. In modern societies, these topics are often looked upon as taboo. Displaying oneself as the *walking death* could be interpreted as a provocation or schism.

Being a goth can also be enjoyable, taking pleasure in the music, the clothes, and one's own particular status in the world. Besides fashion and music, there are a lot of other pastimes within the scene. Goths spend their leisure time with several activities, for one example, reading. Favorites range from classical literature such as Oscar Wilde, Edgar Allen Poe, or Bram Stoker's *Dracula* to modern fiction or fantasy literature such as J.R.R. Tolkien's *The Lord of the Rings* or Anne Rice's *Interview with the Vampire* and others in that series. Goths are very creative, and not only in the arrangement of their own individual style. Nearly all Goth magazines contain extra sections where poems, artwork and pictures can be published. Computer games and live-action role-playing are common activities, too.

In contrast to other subcultures, goths do not want to change society as a political movement. In most cases, goths are seen as apolitical. Another important attribute is nonviolence. Sometimes journalists connect the goth scene with violent behavior. The school shootings of Columbine and Dawson are an example of such false connections. Later investigation showed that the perpetrators were not serious goths.

Beyond that, there is also a darker side to the dark scene suggesting hints of Satanism and racism. Symbols as aspects of simple yet somewhat sinister decoration can be misinterpreted. Religious and mythical animals are favorite symbols, such as Celtic crosses, ankhs, Wiccan pentacles, dragons, bats, skulls, and many more. Wearing such symbols does not have to extend to a deeper meaning or significance, even though some symbols do have ancient religious origins, and some carry more the burden of an additional secondary provocative connotation; for example, the inverted cross, which could indicate Satanism as well as being an early Celtic symbol, or Thor's hammer, which could be interpreted as a relatively modern symbol for racism, as well as having a completely different meaning in mythology. Although such minorities might call themselves goths, there is no real connection to the common gothic subculture.

The mood and aesthetics of the *dark side* of life have overwhelming importance for those involved in the gothic subculture. Also typical for goths is their fascination of and attraction to ancient times, as well as the world of fantasy and darkness. This documents a reflection of one's own personal life, containing both the good and the bad sides of goth culture: its history, practices, stereotypes, religious connection, and other aspects.

Further Reading

Kidzworld, Get the Goods on Goth style [Online April 2008]. http://www.kidzworld.com/article/4095-get-the-goods-on-goth-style.

Morrison, Richard. Whitby Gothic Weekend Is a Lesson in British Tolerance. http://entertainment.timesonline.co.uk/tol/arts_and_entertainment/whats_on/article3797569.ece.

Porter Smith, Alicia. A Study of Gothic Subculture: An Inside Look for Outsiders [Online April 2008]. http://www.gothicsubculture.com/.

Sina-Mareen Koehler

Grunge

The fashion of the 1990s witnessed an entry to the scene that brought to the foreground a "wear what you will" attitude, but one that was best characterized by plaid, jeans, Doc Martens shoes, and high top running shoes. It was a fashion of comfort and regional specificity with a nod to the climate and a "who cares" response to a slowing economy of the time. Though anti-establishment, the look of grunge was quickly marketed to the Generation X crowd. But rather than be the antiestablishment, anti-fashion it was intended to be, grunge eventually went mainstream from the inexpensive, thrift store clothing of plaid hoodies, plaid shirts, and striped leggings to a more upscale appearance on the shelves of such stores as American Eagle. *Grungies*, as they became best known in the fashion world, had crossed from the music arena to find themselves tailored and tucked in the fashion industry.

Prompted by the band Nirvana and influenced by Kurt Cobain from the Seattle music scene, the trend of layering clothes in a haphazard manner was born as a response to the establishment. The music, like the fashion, was dishevelled and distorted by perceptions. The lyrics reflect distrust and disdain for all that was powerful. The layering of mismatched plaids and stripes, and stone-washed blue jeans, not to mention the standard clunky Doc Martens or high tops, spoke loudly in a rebellious, "who cares" attitude determined to reject all that was fashion. The eighties had passed and so had the tolerance for elitism and power dressing. Grunge took the scene with the most notable lead band being Nirvana, followed by others including Pearl Jam and Alice in Chains, whose lyrics were smattered with the angst and despair prompted by a spiraling economy.

If the colors of grunge reflected anything it might be a tone despair taken from a color palette that was unremarkable, neither shocking nor muted, with its attention to plaids, stripes, and a range of colors from dark green to maroon, to indigo and dark colors that variously combined for a heavier, more resistant, strong force. For all intents and purposes, grunge was a unisex fashion, though there were hints of differences where, for example, girls already had the straight, long, hair, which went with the grunge style; boys were not so quick to adopt this coiffure fashion.

Though grunge held on and was catapulted by the music industry through to 1994, there was a noticeable slippage of its couture grip in fashion by the time of the mid-1990s. The hippie-driven fashions of the grunge era complimented one another, but gradually grunge was replaced by Polo shirts and an obvious absence of plaid in the industry. Punctuated by the death of Kurt Cobain in April of 1994, grunge slowly faded from the music and fashion industry.

Further Reading

La Ferla, Ruth. Smells like grunge again [Online August 2008]. *The New York Times* Web site <http://www.thefashionspot.com/forums/f49/smells-like-grunge -again-967.html>.

The 1990s in fashion [Online August 2008]. All Experts Encyclopedia <http://en .allexperts.com/e/0/1990s_in_fashion.htm>.

Tredre, Roger. Money can't buy you grunge [Online August 2008]. *British Studies* Web site <http://elt.britcoun.org.pl/elt/y_grunge.htm>.

Michael Kehler

Jeans

If there is an anchor in fashion that continues to hold on, and on, and on, and literally hold on, whether they be on your hips, or low-risers, the baggy, the tight-fitting, or the boot cut, jeans remain a dominant fixture for most boys and men. Once called *dungarees,* worn initially by sailors and later by workers in the United States, jeans have since crossed fashion boundaries to be coupled with dress shoes and a sport jacket, flip flops and a T-shirt, or sneakers and a polo shirt. As jean fashion transgressed boundaries it also shifted in degrees of acceptability. The initial notion of jeans as representative of rebellion and disdain for conformity was reflected in shops and theatres that refused entry to people in jeans. That too has passed as jeans and the donning of them is widely accepted and indeed more symbolic with associations to celebrities in both the fashion and music world. After being introduced in various shades and hues from black to blue, sand-blasted, faded, and acid wash, from distressed to utility style, and pressed to ripped, jeans have been formed and transformed over decades as one sure and safe item all men and boys will have worn at some time. In fact, jeans are reportedly the most popular pant of choice among the average male with some sources noting the average American owns seven pairs of jeans.

The appeal of jeans to boys and men in particular is not easily answered. Akin to traditional qualities of masculinity often ascribed to boys, jeans are tough, durable, resistant, and come with a long history as de rigueur for *cool poses.* Think James Dean or Marlon Brando and you get an early rebellious and rugged landscape of cool poses for men in jeans. The new millennium has witnessed the jeans tighter and leaner with a return to the rock 'n' roll style of the seventies and eighties. Some boys and men want the hug and snug fit that captures at least one aspect of masculinity up front. There has been a shift over the decades as styles have emphasized and de-emphasized the physical body. For men and boys, jeans have gone from stove-pipe styles, to baggy, loose, and relaxed fits, to recent versions of a low-rise jeans popular with boys 14 to 23 years of age who invariably put jeans as the fashion framing on masculinity. In short, the masculine physique has been both tightly and loosely captured in passing fashions on the jeanscape. More recently skinny jeans for men and boys are taking hold and designers are responding with leaders in the field including Rogan, and slowly following the trend is Diesel and G-Star. With the standard brands of Levis, Lee, and GWG dominating the jean scene for decades, designers are also securing a high-end niche market including Calvin Klein, Rogan, and a host of others. Jeans are not only for boys but they are for appearing in fashion for older men as well. The versatility and flexibility of jeans across fashion streams, social classes, and ages is perhaps what makes jeans most enduring and notable. Jeans are for men and boys and reflect the toughness stereotypically valued in the world of tough, working men sailors and laborers; but as the history of the industry has evolved, it is evident that jeans are more than the mere bolt of cotton it once was and are now an emblem of fashion, class, and agelessness among men and women.

Further Reading

Creativity, Style & Comfort: Denim Remains a Worldwide Volume Driver [Online August 2008]. Cotton Incorporated <http://www.cottoninc.com/LifeStyleMonitor/Denim-Issue-Lifestyle-Monitor-2007/?Pg=3>.

The Denim Blog. See <http://www.denimblogs.com/>.

Lehman, Peter. *Masculinity, Bodies, Movies, Culture.* New York: Routledge, 2001.

Michael Kehler

Preppy

Clothes are an important way in which boys express their identities. Style of dress has the ability to link boys with particular social groups—generally, conformists or nonconformists. Their apparel is a reflection of who they are or who they desire to be. Boys can be accepted or rejected by their peers based on their appearance and material possessions—from what they wear, to how they style their hair, to what type of cell phone they have. The clothes boys choose to wear also make an impression on those around them. For example, the 1960s were a time when many youths chose to wear beads, sandals, flowers, and fringed leather in resistance to middle-class normalities. In this way, they were recognizable among each other, and society at large, as sharing similar values. Historically, since about the 1970s, youth have even been categorized according to dress as jocks, punks/punk rockers, nerds, or preppies. The latter, *preppies*, present a clean-cut, upper-class image and tend to hold a higher status among peers than lesser dressed boys due to their perceived fashion sense and wealth.

Preppy, or preppie, boy fashion derives its style from the uniforms of preparatory school students in the New England area of the United States. The fashion itself is an expression of social conformity. Though distinctly American, the style mirrors that of London teenagers and collegians in the 1950s and 1960s. Made popular in the 1950s, the preppy style of clothing includes such garments as the Polo shirt, button-down shirts, khaki shorts, and seersucker pants. The preppy look also popularized the act of layering clothes. Boys sporting the style may wear an outfit including one or more cotton shirts, a tie, a crew- or v-neck sweater, and a blazer or coat with a scarf.

Ralph Lauren, a fashion designer and icon worldwide, is often credited with making the *preppy* boy style of fashion common in the United States beginning in the 1980s. He is probably best known by his Polo fashion label, which includes clothing, accessories, and fragrances. Other brands designed by Ralph Lauren include Ralph Lauren, Polo Jeans Co., Polo Sport, Ralph Lauren Sport, Ralph, Lauren, Polo Golf, RLX, Double RL, and Chaps. Born Ralph Lifshitz in New York on October 14, 1939, Lauren was the fourth child of Russian immigrants Frank and Frieda Lifshitz. As a child, he was the typical American boy, enjoying stickball games in the park and idolizing baseball great Mickey Mantle and actors such as Cary Grant. What set Lauren apart was the importance of image—flawless movie star hair and making a masterpiece of the clothes he had to create the perfect look.

Growing up in New York, Lauren was exposed to the best in films and fashion. One of his early jobs as a waiter and a camp counselor in the Catskills also allowed him a look into the lives of the upper middle class. It was during this time that Lauren developed an appreciation for the character and appearance of the upper echelon of society. The confidence he found at the camp had a major impact on his life, even prompting him to write "millionaire" as his future profession under his high school yearbook photo.

In 1967, Lauren finally got his own clothing line as a division of the company Beau Brummell. He decided to name his line Polo because of its international appeal and touch of elegance. Initially, Lauren had to create the line entirely by himself, from purchasing and designing to selling and shipping.

Lauren's eye for fashion and powerful influence on the industry is illustrated in the changing of the nation's clothing choice in the late 1970s and the 1980s from *hippie* fashion to more straight-laced and crisp fashions often referred to as the *preppy* style. The popularity of this new preppy style faded in the 1960s and 1970s era of hippiedom, but re-emerged in the 1980s. The 1980s became the platform for this classic look that has again resurfaced emphatically in the beginning of the twenty-first century.

Preppy attire is associated not only with higher income, but also with a sense of better education and increased confidence. Those wearing preppy boy attire are usually well groomed with manicured nails and shaved faces and very social, similar to the description one may have given Lauren during his teenage years. They also have the reputation of being descendants of wealthy families and partakers of the lifestyle that goes along with that. Thus, the clothes associated with the preppy style are designed to reflect the lifestyle of more affluent Americans. In that respect, you will notice that many of the clothing items are associated with the pastimes of the elite in society—polo, golf, sailing, and tennis. The fashions are also offered in an array of classic colors as well as increased use of pastel colors. In fact, an early ad for Lauren's Polo T-shirts boasted that they were offered in 24 colors. These colors ranged from the all-American red and blue to the bright (and often male-shunned) colors of pink and lime green. Today, these colors continue to abound and are supplemented with plaid and flowered styles atypical of traditional male clothing.

The fame of the preppy style prompted authors to write books, such as *The Official Preppy Handbook* and *A Privileged Life: Celebrating WASP Style,* which provide information on the clothing, social, and eating patterns of preppy elites. Today the style still persists, but is often broken down into subcategories of preppy attire such as hip hop preppy. Boys now create variations on the trend by mixing patterns (plaid, seersucker, paisley, etc.) and styles (preppy with non-preppy clothing). No matter how diverse the preppy look seems to be in the twenty-first century, the look is still a classic one traced back to designers such as Ralph Lauren and Paul Stuart, and stores such as Brooks Brothers, J. Crew, and Lacoste. Preppy fashion is sometimes associated with such brands as Abercrombie & Fitch and Aéropostale, though these brands would not fit in with the traditional notion of preppy clothing.

Lauren's Polo label reigns as one of the largest fashion brands in the United States with over 35 boutiques nationwide. The Polo clothing line for boys ranges in price from $30 for the classic mesh polo to over $100 for specialty clothing. What is priceless about Polo is the impact it has had on boys' clothing, prompting a more classic look for American children. Lauren is also a part of the fashion generation that aided in the widespread introduction and acceptance of fashion advertising for everyone from boys to men.

Further Reading

Gross, Michael. *Genuine Authentic: The Real Life of Ralph Lauren.* New York: Harper Collins, 2003.

Lurie, Alison. The Language of Clothes. New York: Henry Holt, 2000.

McDowell, Colin. *Ralph Lauren: The Man, the Vision, the Style.* New York: Rizzoli International Publications, 2003.

Mia Long

Pretty Boys

Combining the Korean words for flower (*Kkot*) and handsome guy (*Mi-nam*), the newly popular Korean term *Kkot-mi-nam* reflects the current fascination with pretty boys in Korea. Traditionally considered a girl-specific area of concern, boys are now actively participating in beauty talk in a world where digital cameras, cell phones, and Internet culture place the emphasis on people's appearances. Boys carefully follow up-to-date fashion, hair, and face or body types, and then try to embody those ideal standards by going to beauty salons and fashion stores, and even undergoing plastic surgery.

This aspect of teen culture can be witnessed with the *Mom-zzang* (best body) and *Err-zzang* (best face) contests that occur among Korean teens on the Internet. *Err-zzang* and *Mom-zzang* are cultural phenomena reflecting teenage boys' and girls' idolization of external beauty. Once teens upload the best pictures of themselves on the Internet, they engage in self-promotion so that other teens will favorably judge and vote on their posted pictures. These teen *Zzangs* become very popular, and actually there are some examples of teen *Zzangs* who have gone on to careers in TV and movies based on other teens' support.

Today's Korean boys in both North America and Korea have started to blur the boundaries of girlhood and boyhood by revealing their inner desire to look *prettier*. Their desired wistful appearance is hard to generalize, but mostly the boys strive to achieve a smaller contour of their face, silkier whiter skin, bigger eyes, long eyelashes, a higher nose, and a moderately skinny body. This change of boys' attitudes toward appearance reflects a transition in the masculine ideal: previously, boys tried to look tough, but now the emphasis is on appearing cute, pretty, and younger-looking.

The mass media is reinforcing this fascination with *Err-zzang* and *Mom-zzang,* particularly among boys. In 2006, a Korean singer, *Rain* (known as *Bi* in Korea), was featured in *Time* in the "Time 100: The People Who Shape Our World." His impact on Korean boys has been significant: portrayed by the media as a *Kkot-mi-nam* and a good role model, teen boys now seem to be enthusiastically taking care of their appearance to look like *Rain*.

Similarly, in 2009, *Boys over Flowers* (*Kkot-bo-da-Nam-ja*) first aired on Korean television. The TV drama is based on a Japanese anime, *Hana Yori Dango,* which had been successful in other Asian media markets such as Japan and Taiwan. The four main male characters are called *F4 (Flower 4)* and are depicted as *Kkot-mi-nams* from extremely wealthy socioeconomic backgrounds.

Why is socioeconomic background relevant? Regardless of the specific TV drama, becoming pretty is not attainable without consuming accepted beauty products and services. In order to look attractive, teen boys do up their hair, wear male-appropriate makeup, go shopping for clothes and accessories, and sometimes decide to change their appearance with the help of plastic surgery. By earning money from part-time jobs or asking parents for money, many teen boys go to plastic surgeons and say, "I want a face like *F4.*" However, plastic surgery done at an early age sometimes has to be redone because bones and flesh are still growing. It is easy to become addicted to plastic surgery, because when one part of the face or body is changed, it can lead to an imbalance of the whole, which makes further surgeries necessary. And what will happen when the *Kkot-mi-nam* trend changes, as all trends do? Teens would require even more plastic surgery to keep up.

There are both positive and negative arguments about the *Kkot-mi-nam* phenomenon. Some say that Internet *Zzang* culture is meaningful because it is a youth-generated culture and is mostly free from the influence of adults or private entertainment companies. In addition, it is inspiring to see that there has been a change in gender roles for boys. Teen participation on the Internet is conceptually influenced by media culture where they consume time, money, and conformed culture. The media depicts *Kkot-mi-nams* as a conformed culture in contemporary society, and teen boys are more and more wannabe-*Kkot-mi-nams.*

Further Reading

Johnson, Jason. "Boys over Flowers: The Movie." *First,* September 2008.
Walsh, Bryan. "Rain." *Time,* April 2006.

Myunghee Kim

Shaving

From a full beard to goatees, to tufts of facial hair, the meanings of facial hair on a boy or man reflect messages about masculinity. Historically beards and facial hair have been deeply associated with religiosity and the presence of facial hair connected to the image of God. Other versions and images of masculinity can be traced in history to figures of Anglo-Saxons and notions of toughness while conversely men who shaved were linked to accusations of effeminacy. These earlier associations between shaving and facial hair have given way to more recent times in which the shaved face has been seen as a public display and prevalent cultural sign or signifier of masculinities. Sculpting of facial hair requires attention and intention from boys and men who are purposefully engaging with the face as an indication of masculinity. Not too dissimilar to earlier historical links between the shaved face and effeminacy, the physical development and growth of facial hair and shaving are synonymous with signs of puberty and virility, which for many boys are rites of passage into manhood. The image of boys watching dads shaving in the mirror and pretending to do as they do vanish when young boys see the first growth of *peach fuzz*. Jokes about the cat licking the milk off a boy's face are quickly replaced when a young boy speaks of the *five o'clock shadow*. In North American culture, shaving represents a level of manliness akin to a public billboard suggesting that "I am man enough to shave" and moreover "don't need the milk moustache of my youth."

Recent shifts within the media have seen the rise of the male body in advertising and the public gaze toward male bodies as desirable and enviable not only by women but also by other men. The marketization and commercialization of male bodies as representational tools of masculinities clad in various product lines from shaving creams to body washes to makeup has grown significantly. Though still associated with being a particular kind of man, the recent onslaught of beauty products is striking and shaving creams and shaving tools are no stranger to the fashion industry. There is a shift in how and why the shaved face and the practice of shaving is interpreted and commodified in the public domain, but the signification and the level of understandings about masculinity and shaving remain ripe with interpretation. As history and cultural meanings dictate, if one is a man he has the ability to shave, but the practice of shaving is deeply rooted in the politics of such practices. The goatee, for example, is not the strict and exclusive domain of gay men, but rather an alternatively expressive canvas upon which some men make public statements. Resistance and managing of the shaving and how one shaves, in addition to where one shaves, are open to an ongoing interpretation as well as politicization of the male body. Facial hair is symbolic but its symbolism has emphasized a patriarchy and issues of control and masculine identities routinely connected to how one cares for and maintains the public face that is masculine and the ongoing struggle for meanings of masculinity captured in the aesthetics of the masculine face.

Further Reading

Gill, Rosalind. "Rethinking Masculinity: Men and Their Bodies" [Online, August 2008], http://fathom.lse.ac.uk/Seminars/21701720/21701720_session2.html.
Middleton, Jacob, "Bearded Patriarchs." *History Today,* February 2006.
Pinfold, Michael, "'I'm sick of shaving every morning': or, "The cultural implications of 'male' facial presentation" [Online, August 2008], http://www.mundanebehavior.org/issues/v1n1/pinfold.htm.

Michael Kehler

Skaters

Skateboarding and skater culture evolved within the United States beginning in the late 1950s and represents an exemplary example of boy culture as a predominantly post–World War II Western phenomenon because it is thoroughly steeped in the rugged individualism and hypermasculinity of settler-state societies of European extraction. Skateboarding, in its current manifestations, did not just appear out of nowhere, but has a rich and complicated history—a history of which too few of today's participants are aware (Malott, 2003).

A common observation is that the simple act of having *fun* is inherently human, transcending age, ethnicity, gender, national origin, and so on, and is at the heart of skateboarding culture. Because the act of having fun is essentially human, people have been seeking new and freer ways to fulfill that need since the beginning of humanity. Skateboarding has been characterized as a source of fun; not just fun for the sake of fun, but fun against the boredom and oppressiveness of mainstream structure and rules represented in its institutionalized sports, schooling, and economy. Skating is particularly apt for the creation of subversive fun because "skaters create their own fun on the periphery of the mass culture" (Weyland, 2002, 187).

Underscoring the original and ongoing appeal of skateboarding, Weyland (2002) argues that from the beginning the resistance-oriented fun inherent within skating lay in "the thrill and potential for danger" (28) it embodies, which dominant society has consistently attempted to control through such acts as constructing *safe*, regulated parks, and rendering *natural* skating terrain (e.g., drainage ditches and handrails) unskatable and illegal.

However, skateboarding, as many people know, originated from southern California's surfing community. Indigenous to Hawaii's native population, surfing before colonial rule was an activity reserved for the nobility. Brought to southern California by U.S. troops, surfing (as with its Hawaiian predecessors) was reserved for the wealthy. With the introduction of foam and fiberglass construction and the subsequent decrease in the price of surfboards, surfing became a viable activity for California's working class.

Skateboarding was invented as a way to practice one's surfing skills on land when the waves were too small to ride. During the 1970s skateboarding was a mainstream activity of the dominant society. As the value-generating potential of skateboarding as part of the socially engineered consumer culture of capitalism began to wane it was left to the die-hards who continued to ride regardless if anyone was paying attention or not. By the 1980s, however, skating was fundamentally transformed with its marriage to punk rock. Underscoring skaters attraction to punk rock, and its faster, more aggressive counterpart, hard core, Weyland (2002) explains that "the sound of the music wasn't the only attraction of hardcore; it was just as much about the attitude, the anti-everything lyrics, the disgust with society's hypocrisy, the thrashing and energy and dancing and slamming that skaters (even if they weren't that into the music) could relate to" (186).

As a result, throughout the 1980s, skateboarding unified with punk rock, spawning a generation of skate punks at the forefront of youth rebellion (along with rap music) with transformative potential (Malott and Peña, 2004). It was the underground network of skaters combined with the political analysis and commentary of punk rock that made the skate punk movement so volatile. Situating skate punk in the sociopolitical context of the 1980s, which was marked by Reagan's trickle-down economics that resulted in higher levels of unemployment and poverty (especially among people of color), the threat of nuclear war, and a popular culture that failed to capture the minds of many a disgruntled youth, Weyland (2002) nostalgically argues that "punk rock was actually a movement of substance and importance, not the watered-down artistically bankrupt genre that it is today. It was new and scary and against everything establishment" (153).

This fiercely independent sense of resistance translated, very centrally, into style and dress. That is, the emerging skate punk uniform was intended to be the anti-uniform for its drive was informed by the desire to offend and break from dominant society's perceived sense of aesthetics and taste. First and foremost, the lyrics of punk music, which had already proven their offensiveness to the sensibilities of the white, middle-class mainstream, were copied directly onto clothing and the skin by individual skate punks themselves, oftentimes from head-to-toe, literally. Because early punk rock skateboarding first blossomed in southern California in neighborhoods with an abundance of recession-induced empty swimming pools that happened to be located in the heart of Los Angeles' working-class Chicano/Mexican American communities, the fashion associated with the genre clearly found inspiration from the Vato culture of Chicanismo. For example: the white T-shirts; the flannel shirts with only the top button connected; the trucker baseball cap with the partially upturned bill; the pressed Dickies cut off right below the knee; the flat deck shoes (i.e., Vans); the white tube socks with stripes pulled up just below the knee; and the black sunglasses known as *locs* were all adopted from Chicano skateboarders and popularized by the skater-led skateboarding industry. Other non-skateboarding marketers saw an opportunity for profiteering and contributed to these tendencies. Even the style of writing was copied from what we might name *street gang Cholo art*, most widely known through the style of the Venice Beach-based 1980s punk rock band The Suicidal Tendencies and their EP, Possessed to Skate. Skateboarding's sense of being *counter to* or *resistant toward* white mainstream society found a blueprint and leaders, such as 1980s pro skater Christian Hosi and many other less well-known skateboarding Vatos, within Brown counter-culture.

These *clean* and very militant elements from Chicanismo were combined and blended with punk rock messages—for example, *everything society stands for is wrong so lets destroy it by destroying ourselves as punk rock cultural suicide bombers*—and the punk rock look of the Sex Pistols and the Ramones. From them, skate punks drew on different aspects. For example, the Sex Pistols embodied the chains, spikes, and black leather taken from England's underground fetish culture. The attitude can be described as a snarling bravado coupled with a complete open sexuality and public performance promiscuity. This shameless raunch and complete disregard and rejection of puritanical conceptions of sexuality was a bold statement that found profound transgressiveness and meaning in sex-shop symbolism, including tight leather and a wide array of bondage equipment crowned with tall colorful spiked hairdos such as the Native American-inspired Mohawk. The Ramones' punk rock message was also *anti*, but their image was that of the New York City bad boy, working class, street gang of European descent. Their look included black leather motorcycle jackets and blue jeans with long, shaggy hair.

Today this skate punk look and resistant attitude is commonly identified as *old school*. Those who sport this style tend to be those who came of age during the mid-to-late 1970s and the 1980s. That is, most old school skate punks who sport the style originally and not as a throw back purchased as a commodity at major shopping centers average in age between 35 and 45 (Malott, 2003). These individuals can be identified by their old school Vans, wide boards, big wheels, Dog Pile shorts, oversized knee pads, and skate punk sound tracks, including the U.S. Bombs and The Faction. New school skateboarding style, on the other hand, is typically identified as taking inspiration primarily from Hip Hop culture—both music and dress. Whereas old school skateboarders specialize in *big vert*, that is, large half pipe ramps and bowls that stand as much as 12 to 14 feet tall, new school skateboarders are primarily street skaters and therefore excel at handrail riding and flat-ground tricks. New school skateboarding fashion consists of oversized, baggy pants and shirts and large shoes with lots of padding and cushion, unlike old school Vans which are sleek and minimal. New school skateboards, which are arguably part of the fashion, are substantially shorter and narrower, as much as three inches, than old school boards. The new wheel sizes are also much smaller. The graphics on many new school boards have clearly been influenced by urban graffiti art associated with Black counterculture. It is argued that this new school style has been depossessed of its transgressive aspects and is therefore the result of cooptation and marketization rendering it safe within mainstream conventions.

Further Reading

Malott, Curry. The Revolutionary Potential of Sk8punk Countercultural Forma-tions in an Era of Global Capitalist Exploitation and Cooptation: A Call to Action. *Taboo: The Journal of Culture and Education* 7, no. 2 (2003): 95–102.

Malott, Curry, and Milagros Peña. *Punk Rockers' Revolution: A Pedagogy of Race, Class and Gender.* New York: Peter Lang, 2004.

Weyland, Jocko. *The Answer Is Never: A Skateboarder's History of the World.* New York: Grove Press, 2002.

Curry Stephenson Malott

Sneakers

Thirty years ago, sneakers were reserved for PE class. Style was not the trade-mark of a running shoe because there was a fairly limited selection of brands and designs that really were considered gender neutral. The sneaker was not seen as a fashion statement or a symbol of cultural materialism but a piece of functional apparel worn just for sporting activities. Ironically, wearing "run-ning shoes" as everyday footwear for fun and style has been making a peren-nial *comeback* since the plain, white sneaker originally made its way out of the gym to the schoolyard. The running shoe has evolved beyond its original use as athletic footwear to a form of cultural and symbolic capital with implica-tions for identity and the performance of gender.

The aerobics exercise boom of the 1980s saw the dawn of *work-out chic* com-plete with legwarmers, lycra leggings, headbands, over the shoulder sweat-shirts, and high-top, white Reeboks. The fashion was popularized in the disco-hangover flicks *Flashdance*, starring Jennifer Beals, and *Staying Alive*, John Travolta's miserable sequal to *Saturday Night Fever*. And to a certain extent, the work-out gear made you look like you were going to or coming from a gym and running shoes naturally began spilling out into the streets. In the 1990s sneakers went *haute couture* along with the infamous designer track suit and leisure footwear that made their debut as the Eurotrash equivalent of the good old, American sweatshirt thanks to Fila, Sergio Tachini, Kappa, and Umbro. Now one sees everything from high heeled Converse and plaid, slip-on booties to canvas loafers and patent leather, wing tip high-tops that have redefined running shoe style. The consumer craze for cool kicks—whether *old school, high tech,* or *totally phat*—has become big business, and sneaker manufacturers have carved out a healthy niche in the popular footwear fashion scene outside of PE class. The quest for *the perfect shoe* drives a billion dollar industry with plenty of famous faces and bodies taking part in the cutthroat competition to satisfy the tastes of urban male youth and to keep them coming back for more *kicks.*

The sneaker wars have taken quite a few fashion victims and hostages. There is tremendous competition for manufacturers to put a recognizable face or name together with a new shoe to get it noticed by adolescent male consumers. The vulcanized rubber three—Nike, Adidas, and Reebok—have a stable of celebrities guaranteed to bring a running shoe addict to their knees. The drawing power of a star helps focus attention and create desire for a product. Run-DMC unintentionally started the trend of celebrity running shoe marketing with their song "My Adidas," a rapper ode to their favorite kicks. Before hip hop became the dominant purveyor of youth culture and fashion, it was a street genre that big business was either unaware of or unwilling to endorse because of its rogue image. When Adidas execs saw thousands of fans waving their unlaced shoes up in the air at a Run-DMC show in 1986, a lightbulb went off. The band was offered a lucrative sponsorship deal in the neighborhood of $1.5 million to promote their hip look and a mock gangsta pose generated for city style and urban consciousness. With the rapid rise of the fashion oriented *street sneaker,* there has been a change in sport footwear marketing strategies. Recently, rappers and actors have been credited with helping to raise the retail fortunes of everything from soda to shoes. The bigger the star, the more exclusive the deal. Reebok signed 50 Cent to a lucrative contract for a G-Unit shoe named after the gangsta-style rapper. Jay-Z's Carter sneaker was reportedly one of the quickest selling lines in the company's history, marking one of the first times that a shoe by a nonathlete has flown out of stores so quickly. Reebok launched a global campaign based around the slogan "I am what I am" with the likes of Allen Iverson, Yao Ming, Lucy Liu, and Andy Roddick added to its celebrity spokesperson roster along with mainstays Jay-Z and 50 Cent. The rappers by themselves brought in over $100 million dollars in sneaker revenue. Reebok is not the only running shoe manufacturer hopping on the celebrity endorsement bandwagon. Linkin Park, Halle Berry, Robert Downey Jr., and Matt Dillon have been photographed in Skechers. Pro-Keds has Damon Dash and Grandmaster Flash.

The power of rappers and actors to hawk sneaker style and the quest to find "I have cooler than you footwear" cannot be questioned. Yet it is a sports superstar who truly created a must-have athletic shoe for older boys and teenagers. In 2005, the Air Jordan XX—the granddaddy of all celebrity shoes—sold record numbers in three days after its debut at the NBA All-Star Game; not a big surprise. Thanks to meticulous brand management and careful product reinvention, these basketball shoes have been flying off the shelves for more than 20 years. Today the popularity of Air Jordans is still based on the appeal of the name behind the product and the legacy of the celebrity. Basketball star Michael Jordan is a legend. He is also a role model and a marketing product as well as a cultural icon. Many would argue that Michael Jordan helped build the "House of Nike." The marketing format for the Air Jordan shoe has been unique and basic at the same time. It focused on the charismatic star's overpowering, almost superhuman, athleticism. The "jumping man" silhouette—a likeness of the high-flying Jordan (His Airness) going to the hoop that is emblazoned on the sneakers—is as famous a logo as the Nike swoosh. Even now, when the highlight reels are gone and the star has kept a surprisingly low profile, the shoes remain. Michael Jordan has been called the greatest basketball player of all time. Was it the shoes? Not very likely. But Air Jordans certainly toppled the cult-like status that Converse enjoyed among urban youth with its high-cut, canvas Chuck Taylor All Stars. Part of the Air Jordans appeal came from the hype of commercials directed by Hollywood filmmaker Spike Lee, which used the tag line "It's gotta be the shoes!" Advertisements would show Michael Jordan defying the laws of gravity and soaring over opponents on the basketball court. The footage was simply astounding. No one since Julius Erving (Dr. J.) could execute a backboard-rocking monster jam on a 15-foot leap from the foul line. By the end of the Nike commercials, it was hard for viewers not to believe that if they were wearing Air Jordans, they too could fly like Mike—or, at least, wish they could. The first Air Jordans shoes initially sold as *must-have* basketball sneakers. The marketing worked perfectly. Rumor has it that Jordan himself was paying $5,000 a game to wear the new patent leather shoes because the shoe was not licensed for wear in the NBA because of the league's licensing agreements. The exposure was well worth it. Soon after, every self-respecting male—school kid, college freshman, and over-the-hill, weekend roundball warrior—was wearing Air Jordans in the self-deluding hope of *sky-walking* to the rim like Mike.

The shoes gradually made their way into casual urban fashion and moved from the court to the sidewalk. Thanks to media saturation because of rap videos and the return of leisure hip, the Jordan brand has become a cultural phenomena associating sportswear with athletic prowess and social success. But because of mass consumption, in 1997 it became a spin-off division of the Nike business model grossing roughly $500 million dollars in sales (Andrews, 2001). Air Jordans became sought-after fashion accessories. Young people have been buying the sneakers for their material value as a social marker of success and a healthy dose of street cred as a trademark of urban style. Air

Jordans are still among the most popular lines of shoes in the world. There are many styles and specializations available that will take care of locomotion needs from walking and jogging to cross-training and loafing. The shoes have evolved from strictly sports specific models to become leisure wear and are even collected as historical memorabilia.

The Air Jordans have been a huge moneymaker for Nike since their inception. The first line of the sneaker was priced at $65. Since then, Air Jordans have been priced as high as $500, or higher for limited edition models. Although not available in snakeskin or allegator, you can find oxblood red trainer high-tops with *Swiss cheese* perforated leather. Or a pair of classic-styled Air Safaris done up with a blend of khaki brown suede and red cloth uppers that can be worn for all occasions. The 20th edition Air Jordans designed by Tinker Hatfield cost $165. That seems cheap in comparison to a pair of $800 Swarovski crystal-studded Adidas shell tops that don't have the MJ mystique. Or the laser-etched strap adorned with a tattoo of game highlights commemorating an all-star career. Are sneakers overpriced? Many believe so, but for most boys Air Jordans are styling, so being fashionable demands a sacrifice, especially if everyone has them or wants them because of the star quality they radiate simply by putting them on your feet.

The consumer is the focus of over 3,000 advertising messages a day (Resnick and Stern, 1977). Approximately 15 percent of those are celebrity endorsements (LaFerber, 1999). It would make sense then that stars act as commercial vehicles to market taste and huck fashion to the masses of adoring fans with varying amounts of disposable income. It is as if the aura of celebrity pervades the clothes that are being advertised and magically transfers its qualities, good or bad, from the person to the thing being sold, then on to the consumer.

Further Reading

Andrews, David L. (Ed.). *Michael Jordan Inc.: Corporate Sport, Media Culture, and the Late Modern America*. New York: SUNY Press, 2001.

Breward, Christopher. Fashioning Masculinity: Men's Footwear and Modernity. In Shari Benstock and Suzanne Ferriss (Eds.), *Foot on Shoes*. New Brunswick, NJ: Rutgers University Press, 2001, pp.116–134.

Cheskin, Melvyn P. *The Complete Handbook of Athletic Footwear*. New York: Fairchild, 1987.

Girotti, Eugenia. *Footwear*. San Francisco: Chronicle Books, 1997.

LaFeber, Walter. *Michael Jordan and the New Global Capitalism*. New York: W. W. Norton & Company, 1999.

Resnick, Alan, and Bruce L. Stern. An Analysis of Information Content in Television Advertising. *The Journal of Marketing* 41, 1 (Jan 1977): 50–53.

Vanderbilt, Tom. *The Sneaker Book*. New York: New York Press, 1998.

Walker, Samuel Americus. *Sneakers*. New York: Workingman Publishing, 1978.

Wolkomir, Richard. The Race to Make a "Perfect" Shoe Starts in the Laboratory. *Smithsonian*, September 1989.

Peter Pericles Trifonas

PART II

Bodies, Minds, and Power

SECTION 4

Boys and the Physical

Health

ADHD

Attention Deficit Hyperactivity Disorder (ADHD) is a condition that causes an individual to have difficulty paying attention, controlling impulses, and controlling his or her body. There is a concern that boys are being diagnosed with ADHD when their behaviors are actually the result of other issues such as learning disabilities, depression, or a stressful home life.

Symptoms of ADHD include hyperactivity or the inability to sit still, difficulty controlling impulses, and increased difficulty paying attention. There are three main types of ADHD. Someone with the hyperactive-impulsive type of ADHD will have challenges controlling impulses but will be able to focus and pay attention. Someone with the predominantly inattentive type of ADHD has a difficult time focusing but does not have problems controlling impulses. Someone with the combined type of ADHD will have challenges focusing and controlling impulses.

Deciding whether someone has ADHD is a complicated process. There are no hard scientific tests that can diagnose ADHD. If a child is suspected of having ADHD, the family and teachers are interviewed and a qualified specialist, such as a psychologist or psychiatrist, assesses the child's behaviors and decides whether those behaviors are a result of ADHD. Some experts feel that the current methods of identifying ADHD are inadequate because they are not based on hard scientific tests. Boys with ADHD are more likely than girls to exhibit behaviors such as the inability to sit still in school, getting easily frustrated over tasks, and talking out of turn. Usually, boys are referred for ADHD evaluations between the ages of five and seven and as a result many boys with ADHD spend the majority of their educational experiences aware that they have ADHD. Because boys with ADHD have behaviors that are often disruptive in a classroom setting, they may feel as though their behavior is being focused on more and that they are being targeted by their teachers. This can lead to boys with ADHD having lower self-esteem and feeling self-conscious about their behaviors. Also, boys whose ADHD leads them to have physically unsafe and impulsive behaviors are more prone to depression than their peers who do not have those behaviors.

The effects of ADHD continue into adolescence, making the already difficult teenage years more challenging for boys with ADHD. They may have increased difficulty withstanding peer pressure and handling the demanding academic workload in high school and college. They may also feel alienated from their peers who do not have those same difficulties. As a result, many boys with ADHD begin to exhibit more signs of depression during their teenage years. Also, boys whose ADHD causes them to have impulsive behaviors often have a more difficult time controlling their impulsivity during adolescence when hormones and social factors make impulse-control even more challenging.

Medication is commonly used to treat ADHD. Stimulants, which work to increase alertness and awareness by affecting the nervous system, are considered to be the most effective drugs for treating ADHD. There are many types of stimulants marketed to those with ADHD. Research studies have not provided conclusive information about the long-term effects of the medication. As a result, there has been increased interest in alternative treatments for ADHD that focus on creating structure and schedules to help those with ADHD stay focused. None of these methods can cure ADHD but many experts recommend combining prescription medications with structure, such as schedules, and physical activities to help those with ADHD stay focused and feel in control.

ADHD affects all areas of boys' lives, especially because the behaviors that boys with ADHD exhibit are often more noticeable than the behaviors that girls with ADHD show. Boys may feel that they are falling behind in school, doing more work to keep up with their peers, and that their teachers and parents are harder on them. These factors can lead to depression, anxiety, and low self-esteem, which can manifest as frustration and aggression. When boys exhibit these frustrations, it can be easy to view them as symptoms of ADHD instead of as a reaction to an understandable frustration. Fifty years ago, boys' difficulties in focusing on school work, disruptive behaviors, and impulsivity may have been considered normal boy behavior. Now, those behaviors are often viewed as symptoms of an underlying disorder such as ADHD. This shift in how educational experts and schools view these behaviors affects the way boys are educated. They may be put on special education plans or behavior plans and they may be put in special classes designed to accommodate their needs. These things may cause boys to feel self-conscious about themselves and their behaviors, which can lead them to question whether their feelings and impulses are normal or if they are symptoms of a condition such as ADHD. Although the social shift toward being more aware of ADHD has helped many people cope with the disorder, that same awareness has also affected the way society thinks about and responds to boys' behaviors.

Further Reading

Attention Deficit Hyperactivity Disorder [Online April 2008]. National Institute of Mental Health <http://www.nimh.nih.gov/health/publications/adhd/complete-publication.shtml>.

Sax, Leonard. *Boys Adrift: The Five Factors Driving the Growing Epidemic of Unmotivated Boys and Underachieving Young Men.* New York: Basic Books, 2007.

Silver, Larry. Why Boys with ADHD Need Their Dads [Online April 2008]. *ADDitude Magazine* Online <http://www.additudemag.com/adhd/article/707.html>.

Meghan Guidry

Asperger's Syndrome

Asperger's syndrome (AS) is one of the pervasive developmental disorders (PDD), also known as autism spectrum disorders (ASD), which are characterized by difficulties in areas of social interaction and communication and restricted areas of interest. Individuals with AS have average or more typically above average IQs with higher verbal scores than performance and processing scores. Most have gathered particularly detailed information about their focused interests (e.g., trains, hurricanes, numbers, natural disasters) but have difficulty grasping more abstract thinking and concepts. The diagnosis of AS is usually made by a psychiatrist, a neurologist, a developmental pediatrician, or a neuropsychologist who is familiar with the diagnostic characteristics. There appear to be increasing numbers of individuals, both children and adults, but particularly boys, who are identified with AS and with autism each year.

Asperger's syndrome is the professional term used to describe individuals who have some of the defined behaviors and/or characteristics that make them appear socially odd and different. They are more often young boys than girls who "just don't get it" socially and don't fit in; but they can be extremely intelligent in special areas of their own interest. They are often the youth who never fit in the school environment and often seem out of it, and in their own world. They don't seem to care about the way they dress and sometimes may ignore their personal hygiene.

In elementary school children may think some of the things that students with AS say or responses that they make are weird and funny because Asperger's students are quite literal. As they continue through middle school and high school and into college many of these students become more and more withdrawn and wrapped up in their own world of thoughts. They frequently become depressed and unhappy because they really do not understand how and why they are different, cause problems, or do not fit in. They become frustrated, especially when taunted by others and can react with sudden outbursts of anger and acting out. They interpret things that are said and written by the basic, literal meanings of the words, not understanding any implications for subtle additional meanings or uses. They miss the hidden meanings of many words their peers will use in everyday casual small talk or slang. They also seem to miss the social actions or reactions of their peers, those things that most people never really have to talk about and just understand or learn through mistakes. For students with Asperger's syndrome, these cues for better social living are sometimes called "the hidden curriculum," because their rules are neither obvious nor taught, and the AS students just don't get it. That is why they are the perfect set up for inappropriate jokes, such as being told to share an off-color joke with a teacher. Wanting to fit in and to be part of the group, they follow the suggestion and may end up being punished for something they did not realize was out of place because of a lack of social judgment. They can be taught some of the hidden curriculum, but will always have to work at keeping up with the social changes as they become adolescents and then young adults who are beginning to socialize and date.

Their learning style is frequently referred to as literal or concrete. They interpret things that are said and written by the basic meanings of the words. They miss the hidden meanings of many words, the implications, innuendos, and themes. When they are studying or learning new material they have difficulties understanding the concepts that are abstract or that we envision internally. Yet they may be very capable of doing intricate math or science problems rapidly and without being able to explain step by step how they got the correct answer.

Seeing details as separate entities is another struggle for boys with AS. They will focus on one part of a larger project, an assignment, or even a picture or activity and not see the whole picture. Tests have shown that those with AS typically follow the movement of things, even down to others' mouths moving when they talk. So when they go to the movies or simply watch TV they will miss all the things that may be happening around the people talking—the expressions given through their eyes or movement. Most people express themselves and communicate with others using more nonverbal signs than the actual words themselves. More than half of a communication message is sent out by the way people stand, gesture, move, turn their heads, or look (e.g., eye-contact and expressions) at others. Another third of communication comes from the tone and changes in the volume and quality of the voice. That leaves less than 10 percent of a message to be communicated by the actual words. And words are used in many different ways, as there are times when we don't mean exactly what we say or we don't say exactly what we mean. Individuals with AS do not see the nonverbal communications, nor do they appreciate the differences in the tone of voice; they just don't get it. The end result is that children with AS are trying to understand and navigate through the social world using less than 10 percent (the words) of the communication process.

What Helps Children with Asperger's Syndrome?

There are many things that professionals and researchers are learning that begin to help individuals with AS. Efforts are being made to recognize these people with AS when they are still very young, even babies or toddlers so that there can be early interventions to help them learn to socialize appropriately and introduce an understanding of what the larger world can be. Professionals who have studied Asperger's syndrome know those early interventions can make a big difference in how these students progress in school. They also know the importance of having peers understand that this a neurobiological disorder and the challenges the students present can be helped by guidance from others, especially their classmates. When those things are put in place, and students, teachers, and families work together to help, everyone can begin to appreciate the good qualities and even extraordinary capabilities these students may have. They can be great science lab partners or members of debate teams. They can actually be very funny when they are comfortable and share some of their unintended humorous problems with words that they create with their literal use of language.

Many students will receive different types of therapy to address their areas of weakness. They can work with occupational therapists and physical therapists to improve their movements and coordination and handwriting. They can participate in social skills groups to introduce the more appropriate social skills for interactions. They may also work with speech and language therapists and psychotherapists who specialize their work around individuals with AS needs. A cognitive behavior approach where individuals are taught actual skills and techniques for improvement and then receive positive behavioral re-enforcements seems to be the most effective way to help. It can also help develop organizational and time management skills that are crucial to their success.

History

Asperger's syndrome was first identified in 1944 by Hans von Asperger, a physician in Vienna, who wrote about a group of boys he worked with who did not understand nonverbal communication skills; they appeared to lack empathy for others and also had an odd gait and clumsy movements. About the same time in the United States, Dr. Leo Kanner was documenting similar patients he had with more severe characteristics and limitations that he termed *autism.*

In the 1980s Dr. Lorna Wing discovered Dr. Asperger's writing while researching a group of boys in England who had similar symptoms to Asperger's patients. Dr. Uta Firth translated Dr. Asperger's writings into English, and more people started to become familiar with this syndrome. Dr. Christopher Gillberg in Sweden, Dr. Tony Attwood from Australia, and Dr. Digby Tantam from the United States were among early writers from other countries to identify more patients and detail their findings with an expanding variety of characteristics.

It was not until 1994 that Asperger's syndrome was recognized in the *Diagnostic and Statistical Manual of Mental Disorders (DSM-IV)* and the *International Statistical Classification of Diseases and Related Health Problems (ICD-10).* The two professional manuals differ in their diagnostic criteria, which highlights and contributes to the ongoing confusion of the AS diagnosis. Some of the confusion may be attributable to the fact that more than 50 years of formative research has been with individuals with autism, while detailed research with AS has been limited to more recent years. As a result, professionals continue to question and debate whether there are distinct (diagnostic) differences between AS and high-functioning autism (HFA). Thus, the present *DSM-IV-R* (APA, 2004) criteria should continue to be considered a work in progress, while more formative data is gathered and universal standards for characteristics are accepted and used with consistency.

Diagnosis

A variety of different scales and measures are being used in the diagnosis of ASD and AS. Many are more dependent upon qualitative interpretations of diagnostic criteria and do not differentiate between ASD, PDD, and AS. The characteristics that are most commonly used in the diagnosis of AS include (1) an impairment in the use of multiple nonverbal behaviors (e.g., eye contact, facial expressions, body postures and gestures regulating social interactions); (2) restricted repetitive and stereotyped patterns of behavior, interests, and activities, including routines or rituals, repetitive motor movements (e.g., finger or hand flapping or twisting movements); (3) no clinically significant delay in speech development; and (4) no significant delays in cognitive development or self-help skills.

Other disorders that occur with AS include obsessive compulsive disorder for approximately 25 percent of those with AS, with the other 75 percent having an attention deficit disorder profile. Although many of the social interaction issues may diminish with age, a coincidental increase of clinical depression is reported to be as high as in adolescents and adults.

During the 1990s other syndromes that shared some of the fundamental similarities with AS began to appear in the professional literature that have added further confusion to differentiation and accurate diagnosis. These have included semantic-pragmatic disorder, right-hemisphere learning disability, nonverbal learning disability, and schizoid disorder.

Prevalance

The past decade has revealed alarming increases in the number of individuals with both autism spectrum disorders (ASDs) and Asperger's syndrome. The question of whether there are actually increasing numbers and why is being discussed and intensely investigated today. Some researchers feel there are more individuals identified because more doctors are aware of AS and thus more correctly diagnose individuals who might formally have been labeled with other disorders—e.g., mental retardation—or completely overlooked. Others are concerned there are environmental factors(s) effecting fetal or physical development, resulting in autism and AS. Childhood vaccinations, pollution, and viruses are among the possible causes being considered. Still others attribute the increase to a combination of factors: better identification, genetics, and possible physical and/or environmental components. Research continues to explore all these possibilities and search for more.

The Centers for Disease Control, in 2004, sited the incidence of AS to be roughly 1 in every 300 children, a remarkable increase from the 1996 report of 1 in 1,500 children. More recent sources give numbers that range from 1 in 350 to 1 in 150 and the possible incidence of AS actually outnumbering all ASDs combined. Likewise, the ratio of boys to girls varies. Presently there are more boys reported, with a ratio of 4 boys to 1 girl, but some question whether girls may present differently from the original boy-based criteria. Girls with AS may appear quiet, shy, withdrawn, and less disruptive and physically assertive. Researchers find girls to be more observant of social interactions, which they interweave into compulsive fictional reading and fantasy escapes.

Characteristics

Social Functioning

Individuals with AS struggle to understand simple daily social interactions and reciprocal social interchanges. They are socially awkward and clumsy, and are usually at least two to three years behind in social awareness and skill development. They do not learn intuitively from their peers or from their mistakes. They may do reasonably well in one-to-one exchanges with an adult, an occasional peer, or older child, but they find classrooms or small groups of peers very challenging to navigate. They will use repeatedly inappropriate attempts to make a friend and at the same time will often fail to respond to or try to dominate overtures from others. It can be difficult for them to distinguish between accidental or deliberate physical contact from a peer(s), and they can over-react with disruptive, even aggressive, confrontations. Their repeated and inappropriate acting out along with the unsuccessful attempts at socializing lead to ostracism, isolation, sadness, loneliness, and ultimately withdrawal and depression.

Social skills groups where small groups of students are taught the step by step intricacies of social interactions, rehearsal of skills, and role play have been reported by researchers to be effective. However, parents and school officials and outside activity leaders report general levels of carryover of these skills to be less successful, even lacking.

The Internet has offered individuals with AS a new venue to establish friendships in an environment where they are not as stressed with too much sensory input or where they have to struggle with face-to-face social signals. It is also an environment that allows them time to process what they are reading or writing and the possibilities of supportive interchanges with others who may be contending with similar issues.

Theory of Mind

There are many theories geared to understand these social deficits. The theory of mind is one of the most frequently referenced theories, which is characterized by an inability to recognize the individual perspective and thinking of another person; children and adults with AS or ASD simply assume that everyone else has the same perspectives and, therefore, the same thoughts as they do. This results in them appearing to be very egocentric with a very literal interpretation of the world and using very concrete intellectual reasoning of emotions. They can be rude and abruptly honest in their comments, with a general lack of self-consciousness or introspective thought of the impact of their behavior on others.

Language

Parents frequently report a delay in the onset of speech that will typically start rather abruptly around the second year with the use of two or more words and the onset of speech can quickly become normal or even accelerated in their language. Children with AS are frequently described as pedantic or referred to as "little professor" because of their formal, stilted, one-sided style of speaking with superficially precocious expressions. Looking more closely at their conversations, one notices that they are frequently tangential or off topic with their comments and use repetitive patterns of speech and idiosyncratic words.

Until recently, testing materials had not been sensitive to intricacies of the child with AS speech and language understanding and use. It is also recognized that there is dramatic contrast between performance in the quiet, guided setting where tests are conducted and the daily environment of the classroom or playground where multiple sensory stimuli and complex demands of language use prevail. All assessments for children with possible AS should include observation and evaluation of the student in his typical settings.

The literal interpretation of life experiences includes the understanding of language. Their comments are usually direct, honest, with a lack of social sensitivity that easily offends others. Figures of speech, the double meanings and innuendoes, or the peer use of certain words make the interpretation of spoken and written language a serious challenge. In addition, they do not recognize the speaker's shift in tone, inflection, emphasis, or volume, thereby missing many of the subtleties used throughout daily interchanges.

Cognitive Abilities

Students with AS have distinctive learning styles: they pay excessive attention to the details but struggle to grasp the whole picture or the overall concept. They are strong rote learners, especially with structured and factual information. They usually do well in the areas of learned facts, that is, math, science, and history. Often they are quick in providing answers to difficult problems, but struggle with simple explanation of the step-by-step solution. Organization abilities with both physical materials and internal categorizing can be extremely compromised, which impacts cognitive processing and academic learning and simply getting things started or handed in. The need for perfection and the inability to cope with making mistakes can be an obstacle to moving ahead. Because they typically do not learn from their mistakes and will repeatedly use incorrect and unsuccessful strategies, this easily leads to frustration and anger and acting out. Likewise, the introduction of new learning material, new topics, and new approaches (called "novel learning") add to their challenges—with change and the need to be able to intellectually process and integrate new information into their rigid internal structures for learning and coping.

Sensory Sensitivity

Work with individuals with AS has increased awareness of the complexity of sensory issues for this population. Young children with AS can be hyper-vigilant to sounds, lights, smells, touch, clothing, tactile experiences, and taste and texture of foods. As they grow with continued exposure to these sensory inputs, they often appear to adapt and be less disturbed or upset by them. However, at times of stress, tension, or insecurity, the hypersensitivity can abruptly reappear. Sudden, unexpected, high-pitched and continual sounds, and complex or multiple sounds contribute to sensory overload, even for older children and adults with AS. Accommodations that reduce the intensity of these stressors (i.e., wearing sunglasses in bright settings, including classrooms or dentist offices, or sponge earplugs in noisy settings) help individuals to begin to cope.

Movement

New studies continue to look at the physical development of individuals on the autism spectrum, including AS. Occasional involuntary and poorly planned movements along with an uneven or unsteady gait makes these chil-dren and youth, even adults, appear awkward and clumsy. Likewise, weak neuromuscular development of the spine and upper extremities has been found to be a common developmental deficit. This makes it difficult to sit on the floor without support, throw balls, play many sports, and run. It also con-tributes to poor handwriting—large, poorly formed letters and spacing.

Treatment

At the present there is no specific treatment for AS, and interventions to address the most pronounced symptoms and adaptations to independent liv-ing and daily living skills are available.

Further Reading

Robinson, John Elder. *Look Me in the Eye: My Life with Asperger's*. New York: Crown Publishers, 2007.

Santomauro, Josie, and Damian Santomauro. *Asperger Download: A Guide to Help Teenage Males with Asperger Syndrome Trouble-Shoot Life's Challenges*. Shawnee, KS: Autism Asperger Publishing Company, 2007.

Jeanne Angus

Boys' Health

Although most people may believe that boys and men are healthier, stronger, and less likely to get injured than girls, this is not the case. Males die an aver-age of six years earlier than females, experience more injuries and illness, and commonly engage in behaviors that threaten their health (Courtenay, 2003; Gibson and Denner, 2000). From an early age, boys learn that certain practices or behaviors are more highly valued than others. Being tough, aggressive, competitive, and avoiding all things viewed as girly or feminine are ways that boys learn to demonstrate their masculinity. Not asking for help, hiding pain and emotions, and continuing to play sports while injured are also ways in which boys may prove their manliness. Unfortunately, all of these behaviors can have a negative impact on the health of boys and men.

Young males are less likely than young females to take care of themselves. Boys engage in fewer behaviors that can prevent injuries or illness than do their female counterparts. For example, boys are less likely to wear sunscreen, seatbelts, or to drive safely, and are more likely to smoke, drink, and eat unhealthy diets. Because boys and men experience poorer health than girls and women, there is a need to explore the many ways in which boys' masculine beliefs and behaviors can influence their health. By doing this, boys may become better able to lead healthy lives.

Recently, *men's health* has become focused on the interrelationship between masculinity, men's health, and their health care practices. In particular, the ideal or hegemonic version of masculinity, which is associated with traits such as aggression, physical and emotional strength, and competitiveness, is one that men and boys attempt to measure up to through practices that prove they are *real men*. Boys and men are well aware of the penalties of not measuring up to the ideal or hegemonic standard of masculinity. Given the association of illness with weakness and vulnerability, boys' and men's perception and experience of illness and lack of health care seeking can be understood as their avoidance of anything feminine or demasculinizing. In this way, hegemonic masculinity itself is a health risk for men.

Measuring Up and Taking Risks

For boys and men, physical risk is often naturalized, promoted, and celebrated. As a result, research indicates that boys are twice as likely to visit emergency rooms for injury/poisoning, and are three times more likely to die from accidental injury, including car accidents, than girls or women. Examples of measuring up through risk-taking behaviors include:

1. Reckless Driving

Boys are less likely to wear seatbelts in a motor vehicle or wear a helmet when riding a bicycle. Injuries as a result of skateboarding are also common. Boys have significantly higher rates of motor vehicle and bicycle fatalities and injuries. Statistics indicate that motor vehicle collisions are the number one cause of death for young men (Ramage-Morin, 2005).

2. Sexual Risk Taking

The rates of sexually transmitted infections in Canada have risen substantially over the past decade. Nearly two-thirds of all new HIV infections are found among men, with half of these infections occurring among men who have sex with men (Boulos et al., 2006; Centers for Disease Control and Prevention, 2007).

Research indicates that twice as many men engage in high-risk sexual activities than women, that men are more likely to have more sexual partners, to have sex while under the influence of alcohol or illicit drugs, and to be non-monogamous during adulthood (Courtenay, 1999). Men have also been found to not use condoms consistently, and some men report not using them at all. In fact, a health report published by Statistics Canada in 1998 indicated that 29 percent of men between the ages of 15–19 and 44 percent of those between the ages of 20–24 reported not using condoms. Consequently, boys' and men's high-risk sexual practices have been identified as being largely responsible for the continued spread of sexually transmitted infections.

3. Substance Use and Abuse

On average, 20 percent of Canadian boys report heavy drinking (five or more drinks consumed on one occasion). However, it is apparent that geographic location influences alcohol consumption among young men: 13 percent of boys in major metropolitan regions report heavy drinking compared to boys in some rural regions reporting up to 30 percent (Mitura and Bollman, 2004).

4. Mental and Emotional Health

Suicide is the second leading cause of death for young men between the ages of 15–25, and is only narrowly surpassed by motor vehicle collisions (Discussion Paper for the Development of a Suicide Prevention Strategy for the Winnipeg Health Region, 2003). Although rates of depression and attempts at suicide are much higher among girls and women, boys and men are four times more likely to successfully commit suicide and employ violent methods to do so. Hanging, firearms, and poisoning are the top three methods of suicide among young men. Boys' and men's greater likelihood of dying as a result of suicide is particularly evident among young people in Canada, as four out of every five suicides are committed by men.

Men report lower rates of depression; however, this may not indicate better mental health among men, as many researchers suggest that depression is greatly under-diagnosed and under-reported among men. Researchers have found that men are far less likely to seek help for mental health problems, especially depression. Research indicates that boys are happier than girls, and have better self-esteem, confidence, and decision-making ability. Boys also claim to feel less depressed and less lonely than girls. However, boys and men who experience depression often do not ask for help because of the association of depression with unmasculine qualities such as weakness, helplessness, and a lack of emotional control.

5. Sports and Health

In Canada, boys and men are much more active in sports compared to girls and women (39% vs. 23.4%) with the gender gap being most evident during the teenage years between 15 and 18 (80% boys vs. 55% girls) (Sport Canada,

2000). An important consideration in relation to boy's health is that high-risk and physical contact sports are dominated by boys and men. This results in school age boys having significantly higher rates of injury and more severe injuries.

6. Seeking Help

Several researchers have reported that boys and men seek health care services far less frequently and are less interested in being informed about their health than are girls and women. When boys and men fail to access health care or acknowledge their health care needs, they are able to demonstrate the characteristics of physical strength and invulnerability associated with hegemonic masculinity. In this way, boys and men reinforce strongly held cultural notions about what it is to be a man—that is, stronger, less vulnerable, and better able to handle problems than girls and women. This has important implications for the health of men and boys.

Some researchers argue that men's reluctance to seek help may be directly related to the way that men are socialized. Boys and men are taught to be strong, independent, and to conceal their vulnerabilities, all of which may present substantial barriers to seeking help. In addition, men are socialized to believe that revealing emotional or physical distress is indicative of weakness and that enduring physical pain demonstrates toughness; it is also viewed as an inherent part of being a man. Simply put, men are taught to *take it like a man*.

Boys' and men's practices of avoiding preventative care, paying less attention to health information, delaying treatment, and not following physician recommendations can all be understood as practices that affirm an ideal or hegemonic masculinity.

The greatest factor that determines individual health is behavior. This statement is particularly significant for young men, given that masculinity shapes perceptions of health and illness and their subsequent health care practices. Hegemonic masculinity and traditional beliefs about manhood are the strongest predictors of individual risk behavior over time for men.

The World Health Organization (2002) acknowledged the need to pay greater attention to the shorter life expectancy of men. A lack of understanding of the role of masculinity in shaping boys' and men's expectations, behaviors, and health was identified as a primary causative factor for the health disparity between men and women. There are also health disparities among boys and men that remain largely invisible and unexplored.

Further Reading

Boulos, D., Yan, P., Schanzer, D., Remis, R., & Archibald, C. Estimates of HIV prevalence and incidence in Canada, 2005. *CCDR, 32*(15). <http://www.phac-aspc.gc.ca/publicat/ccdr-rmtc/06vol32/dr3215a-eng.php.>

Centers for Disease Control and Prevention. *HIV/AIDS Surveillance Report, 2007.* Vol. 19. Atlanta: U.S. Department of Health and Human Services, Centers for Disease Control and Prevention, 2009. <http://www.cdc.gov/hiv/topics/surveillance/resources/reports/.>

The Disaster Center. Deaths and death rates for the 10 leading causes of death for people 15–24 years all causes: United States, preliminary 1996. <http://www.disastercenter.com/cdc/111riskd.html.>

Discussion Paper for the Development of a Suicide Prevention Strategy for the Winnipeg Health Region. (2003, November). <http://myuminfo.umanitoba.ca/Documents/2069/Discussion%20Paper%20for%20the%20Development%20of%20a%20Suicide%20Prevention%20Strategy.pdf.>

Courtenay, W. (2003). Key determinants of the health and the well-being of men and boys. *International Journal of Men's Health, 2*(1), 1–30.

Courtenay, W. (1999). College men's health: An overview and a call to action. <http://www.menweb.org/courtney.htm.>

Gibson, M., & Denner, B. (2000). *Men's health report 2000. The MAN model. Pathways to men's health.* Daylesford, Victoria, Australia: Centre for Advancement of Men's Health.

Men's mental health: A silent crisis [Online June 2004]. *Medical News Today* Web site <http://www.medicalnewstoday.com/articles/9475.php>.

Mitura, V., & Bollman, R. (2004). Health status and behaviours of Canada's youth: A rural-urban comparison. *Rural and Small Town Canada Analysis Bulletin, 5*(3). <http://dsp-psd.communication.gc.ca/Collection/Statcan/21-006-X/21-006-XIE2003003.pdf.>

Ramage-Morin, P. (2008). Motor vehicle accident deaths, 1979–2004. *Health Reports 19*(3), 1–7. <http://www.statcan.gc.ca/pub/82-003-x/2008003/article/10648-eng.pdf.>

Sport Canada. (2000). *Sport participation in Canada—1998 report.* Ottawa: Minister of Public Works and Government Services Canada.

World Health Organization. A literature review on the health and development of adolescent boys. What about the boys? [Online 2002]. World Health Organization Web site <http://www.who.int/child_adolescent_health/documents/fch_cah_00_7/en/>.

Blye Frank, Joan Evans, and Derek Leduc

Circumcision

Male circumcision is the removal of the foreskin of the penis, which is the region that covers the glans. The surgery is widely practiced in the United States and, to a lesser extent, other English-speaking countries such as Canada and Australia. All male and female children are born with foreskins. For the male child, the foreskin adheres to the glans, or head, of the penis. For females, it is the fleshy area that covers and surrounds the clitoral nerve endings and forms part of the clitoris. The male foreskin is attached to the head of the penis and, if it is not removed, can be retracted from the head of the penis when a boy is roughly around three years of age. The penile foreskin of Jewish or Muslim boys is often removed in infancy in keeping with religious tenets. Circumcision for religious reasons is both a Jewish and Muslim religious rite, most recognized as being associated with Jewish spirituality in the United States. For Jews, this religious custom refers to the Old Testament of the Bible, which constructs circumcision of the penis as representative of a sacrificial circumcision of the heart. Socially, this practice served to separate Jews from gentiles, or non-Jews.

Medical Notions

Disjointed from any direct religious connection, the foreskin of U.S. infants is often removed within hours or days of their birth due to the idea that there is a relationship between circumcision and potential medical benefits. In the United States in the late 1800s, circumcision gained popularity among non-Jews for nonritual reasons. Early arguments for circumcision were ludicrous by modern standards. For example, male masturbation was believed to cause a host of ills, including blindness, hernia, gout, and insanity. The medical community posited that the removal of the male foreskin would prevent masturbation, which in turn would eliminate the numerous pathologies that masturbation was alleged to cause. Additionally, the association of masturbation with spiritual or moral impurity helped to cement the views of both the lay public and health care practitioners that masturbation was a male adolescent behavior that needed to be eliminated.

Over time, the masturbation link between foreskin and sickness became blurry, and the foreskin itself was soon constructed as a direct cause of various pathologies and implicated as engendering a general lack of penile cleanliness. The sheer number and variation of illnesses and otherwise disturbances that circumcision was thought to cure or prevent are worth noting. This list includes but is not limited to phimosis, gangrene, tuberculosis, hip-joint disease, hernia, gout, nervousness, impotence, convulsions, and epilepsy.

Nearly all late-1800s arguments that were mobilized in favor of male circumcision have since been retired in favor of new medical theories, not the least of which being the current argument that removal of the foreskin may lower HIV/AIDS transmission from heterosexual intercourse and other STDs. Additionally, a decrease in the already low (0.001) frequency of urinary tract infections in the first year of life is given as a reason to circumcise, despite the incidence being almost as high in circumcised males (0.01), and most significantly the highest in female infant, for whom there is no surgical recommendation. Despite specific and continuing medical justifications for the practice, it remains officially, medically contra-indicated since 1971. In other words, although it is a widely performed elective surgery, it is officially regarded by all major medical associations as not medically necessary. Rates of circumcision hit a peak in the 1970s and 1980s, having hit close to 90 percent. In the 1990s, the rates started to fall and are currently, on average, at roughly 60 percent (Denniston, 2002). Possibly contributing to declining circumcision rates are counterclaims to the benefits of the procedure.

Those who argue against the medical efficacy of the procedure include a variety of individuals. Scholars, activists, medical personnel, and lay people have started to doubt the necessity, utility, and even legality of male circumcision in the United States. Detractors of circumcision argue that circumcision is medically unnecessary, harmful, and physicians who perform them outside of medical necessity are violating their Hippocratic Oath to do no harm to patients.

Those who protest the procedure argue that the foreskin is a healthy and natural part of the penis with several known functions. They note that in the diaper period, far from being infectious and dirty, the penile foreskin actually protects the head and opening of the penis from urine and feces. Additionally, the foreskin, far from being the useless extra flesh that proponents of circumcision argue it is, has several sexual functions that it serves. They posit that the foreskin is wrought with sexual nerve endings and acts as a dam during intercourse; this makes intercourse more physically pleasurable for men and less chafing for both partners. Also, it serves as a protective sleeve for a penile head that is only meant to be exposed when erect—instead of also being exposed when flaccid, like a circumcised penis. Without the protective sleeve of the foreskin and the additional lubrication, coverage, and blood flow that it enables, the head of the penis becomes keratinized, calloused, experiences decreased blood flow, and, ultimately, loses much of its sexual sensitivity. Lastly, they argue that circumcision can be dangerous, as one or two babies die or lose their penises per year from circumcision-related infections or surgical errors.

Arguments used against circumcision are not only medical, but legal and ethical as well. Those against circumcision note that, although U.S. female minors are now protected from medically unnecessary genital surgeries, males are not. They state this to be a violation of the Equal Protection Clause in the 14th Amendment, and as a violation, male circumcision is technically illegal. Ethically, critics argue a right to what they call *bodily integrity,* which champions the rights of infants and children to intact and unmutilated bodies, despite the potential wishes of parents, physicians, or religious leaders.

Despite the fact that the politics of circumcision have become increasingly contested, many medical doctors and lay people continue to advocate for the procedure and assert that evidence suggests that said benefits outweigh the alleged risks and dangers. Others in the medical and lay community remain ambivalent, arguing that whether or not to circumcise is and should remain a social, religious, or cultural choice left to families to make. For the families who choose to circumcise in absence of a personal investment in medical argu ments, what factors go into their choices to circumcise their male infants?

Social and Cultural Notions

Bodies and Masculinity

Notions of masculinity, as well as those of femininity, are understood largely in terms of bodies. There is a widespread media emphasis on attractive bodies, and the impact of these narrow beauty standards on girls has been well documented. Girls who are slender with large breasts, a small waist, and big hips are identified as attractive and socially desirable. Girls who have larger body sizes are represented as unattractive and unhealthy. Boys are also constrained by cultural constructions regarding what makes a male body attractive. These body image standards, in part, determine who gets to be identified as a masculine, socially desirable male. Male bodies that are deemed culturally and socially desirable are expected to exemplify certain physical traits, which include being tall and muscular, and having a certain penile length and girth. It is considered socially and sexually unattractive to be short, overweight, bald, or to have a small penis.

The penis, as the male organ, holds special symbolism in terms of its relationship to masculinity. Men who do not meet the minimum requirements regarding penile acceptability often command societal ridicule and are the butt of many jokes and humiliating media representations. As a result, masculine identity is heavily wrapped up in penile size and shape, erectile functioning, and sexual performance.

Circumcision and Masculinity

As all aspects of the penis are symbolically representative of masculinity and manhood, whether or not the penis is circumcised has also found itself serving as a subject of debate in both public and family spaces and mainstream culture. For example, in absence of any investment in medical arguments that support circumcision, fathers often report a desire that their son's penis look like their own, and cite this as a primary motivator in choosing to circumcise their sons. This is a social choice rather than a medical or religious one, and it supports the idea that the penis can be used to symbolize an intergenerational continuity of cultural representations of masculine bodies.

Not being circumcised can cause anxiety and preoccupation regarding how one's status measures up to the status of other boys—for example, the proverbial "boy in the locker room" preoccupation: that a boy does not want to be the only boy in the locker room who is uncircumcised for fear of isolation and derision from peers. Although few, if any, boys actually experience being teased for looking upon another boy's exposed penis, the scenario holds its own threat to the maintenance of masculinity and heterosexual identity; the dialogue itself reflects a broader cultural preoccupation both with the uncircumcised penis and its relationship to both masculinity and conformity and deviance.

Deviant Bodies

For certain bodies to be culturally condoned as appropriate, desirable, and attractive, there need to be contrary categories to compare them against. In other words, we cannot know what is advantageous and sought after without knowing what is unsatisfactory and stigmatized. Old, overweight, misshapen, heavily scarred, mutilated, or disabled bodies are identified as deviant bodies, or bodies that do not confirm to conventional societal notions of acceptability.

Bodily atrocities can be seen as outside of an individual's control, in which case she or he may be viewed with compassion or sympathy, as in the case of an amputee or one with a horribly burned or disfigured face. In other cases, the bodily deviance can be enmeshed with ideas of character weaknesses. For example, overweight people may be seen as deserving to be overweight because they are over-indulgent with food and lazy. Because self-restraint and physical movement through exercise are valued as positive in American culture, to be identified as not possessing of those traits is stigmatizing. In other words, you may be doubly stigmatized. In either case, having a deviant body impacts the way the deviant interacts with others, and the way those others interact with her or him.

Deviant Penises

Over the last 10 years, circumcision rates have dropped from an all time high of almost 90 percent to approximately 60 percent nationwide (Denniston, 2006). In light of these new and more balanced national averages, one might argue that one or the other would not be designated a deviant penile form. After all, both circumcised and uncircumcised males make up the U.S. population in a near 50/50 split. However, even though rates are down to about 60 percent nationwide, circumcision rates are both very high and very low depending on the region in question. For example, rates remain at around 80 percent in the Midwest, while they are at slightly above 30 percent in the far western states (Circumcision Information Research Page, 2008). Depending on the area of the country, an expectation toward circumcision may dominate attitudes and expectations.

This can still be readily identified through language, stereotypes, and mythologies still associated with the uncircumcised penis. For example, foreskin is still widely held in certain circles to be implicated in the harboring of bacteria and seen as generally less hygienic. This can easily be transferred to the characterization of a boy or man more generally as dirty or less able to keep himself clean as a result of his deviant genital anatomy. As cultural or medical circumcision is largely a U.S. practice, men from Europe, Asia, and Latin America have low circumcision rates by comparison. Therefore being uncircumcised can also serve to reinforce the practice as a marker of ethnic or national deviance. A foreign identity—coupled with ideas that the circumcised penis is the cleaner, safer, healthier, and more hygienic choice—could designate foreign boys and their respective cultures as primitive, barbaric, or backward. Additionally, jokes geared toward the uncircumcised penis—that is, calling the foreskin an elephant trunk—with no comparable disparaging language ever applied to the circumcised penis points to the idea that an uncircumcised penis is still a deviant genital form. This, in absence of compelling medical evidence to circumcise, helps explain continuing high rates of the surgical procedure.

That being said, in regions of the country where circumcision has fallen out of favor, a circumcised boy may find himself questioning his circumcised state in relation to his largely uncircumcised peer networks. In essence, a deviant labeling process has nothing to do with whether or not a man is or isn't circumcised, but rather, how he is defined, and subsequently, defines himself, in relation to a larger group. Either a circumcised or uncircumcised boy may be labeled genitally deviant depending on the context, time, and place in which he finds himself.

Further Reading

Circumcision Information and Resource Pages [Online March 2008]. <www.cirp.org>.

Denniston, George. *Doctors Re-Examine Circumcision.* Seattle, WA: Third Millennium Publishing Co., 2006.

Goldman, Ronald. *Circumcision—The Hidden Trauma.* Boston, MA: Vanguard Publications, 1997.

Goffman, Irving. *Stigma.* New York: Touchstone Books, 1986.
National Organization of Circumcision Information Resource Centers [Online March 2008]. <www.nocirc.org>.

Melissa F. Lavin

Drinking

Use and abuse of alcohol continues to be a problem affecting American youth. However, boys are particularly vulnerable to alcohol abuse. When considering drinking over an entire year, there is little difference between boys and girls. However, boys are more likely to drink on a monthly basis. Boys are also more likely to binge drink, which means to consume more than five drinks in one sitting. Beer remains a particularly more popular beverage for males than for females.

Problems that typically arise from drinking are more prevalent among boys than girls. Boys report higher incidents of drunken driving, car accidents, fighting, and difficulties at home or school. Studies of children from the time they are 14 or 15 until they are adults show that boys are more likely than girls to become drinkers, full-blown alcoholics, and have problems with alcohol-induced aggression. The same study also showed boys had more drinking problems after graduation than girls.

In 1984, the U.S. Congress passed the National Minimum Drinking Age Act, which requires states to adopt laws prohibiting the sale or the possession of alcohol by anyone under the age of 21. States that do not comply risk losing federal money. However, despite laws restricting the sale of alcohol to minors, alcohol still finds its way into their hands. According to the University of Michigan's 2007 Monitoring the Future survey, 44 percent of high school seniors, 33 percent of high school sophomores, and 16 percent of eighth graders had an alcoholic drink in the 30 days prior to the survey.

As two-thirds of adults in the United States drink alcohol, most boys will grow up watching their parents drinking at home or at social functions (Newburger, 1999). Moreover, fathers with substance abuse problems, including alcohol, are more likely to have children with similar problems. In similar fashion to their parents, teenagers will also partake in alcohol at their own social functions, often as a way to fit in and ease transition into high school. Alcohol is a common factor among many high school cliques. Often children will experiment with alcohol before moving on to harder substances.

The reasons why people drink range from using alcohol as an aid in socialization, to using it as a stress reliever, to using it to obtain the euphoria and freedom from inhibitions that comes from intoxication. The last motive is a particularly powerful one for boys. First, a lack of inhibition can lead boys to pick fights or act out aggressively and use their intoxication as an excuse. Second, a lack of inhibition can lead boys to find the nerve to approach an object of their affection or even to sexually assault someone. Again, intoxication makes for a handy excuse or rationalization.

Family and friends may not be the first introduction children have to alcohol. American children have been inundated with alcohol advertisements from a young age. Alcohol advertising may be responsible for 10 to 30 percent of the children who drink (Strasburger, 2001). Many of these advertisements are directly targeted at young males. They use male-centric devices, such as sports, attractive female models, or a combination of the two to hawk their wares. More than two alcohol advertisements appear during a sports program per hour compared to one in four hours of primetime TV. And the crown jewel of sports advertising is the Super Bowl, which is laden with beer advertisements directed at the predominantly male audience.

Further Reading

Johnston, Lloyd D., Patrick M. O'Malley, Johnston G. Bachman, and J. E. Schulenberg. Overall, Illicit Drug Use by American Teens Continues Gradual Decline in 2007 [Online March 2008]. University of Michigan's Monitoring the Future Web site <www.monitoringthefuture.org>.

Newburger, Eli H. *The Men They Will Become.* Cambridge, MA: Da Capo Press, 2000.

Strasburger, Victor C. "Children, Adolescents, Drugs, and the Media." In Dorothy G. Singer and Jerome L. Singer, eds. *Handbook of Children and the Media.* Thousand Oaks, CA: Sage Publications Inc., 2001, pp. 415–46.

Robert Andrew Dunn

Sexual Awakening

Boyhood sexuality is perhaps the least understood aspect of boys' experience. It includes considerations of anatomy (physical make-up) as well as gender (the social meaning the body has been given). The standard accepted view is that his genetic sexual difference from girls becomes apparent to a boy at around four to six years of age and that identification with an older male (usually the father) serves as the psychological mechanism leading to his self-recognition as a boy/male. This early version of a gendered self is revisited in adolescence after the growth spurt and puberty when one's overall identity as a man is finalized. As in most cultures, the sexual element of identity is primary in the Western world and is usually assessed in terms of the boy's fantasies and sexual interactions with females (usually age mates). Sexual attraction to one or the other sexes is apparent to the boy at about age 10, which coincides with adrenarche (the period of development that comes right before puberty, which causes, among other things, pubic hair growth and changes in the chemistry of sweat). This attraction occurs several years before the boy can fully participate in sexual intercourse or other forms of sexual behavior leading to orgasm and ejaculation.

Since Freud, it has been assumed that there is infantile or childish sexuality, which is different from adult sexuality and is part of every boy's life from the early years of life on. Psychological experiences of infantile sexuality are associated with other body functions and activities (eating, eliminating) and distinguished from adult genital sexual behavior. These sexualized functions are associated with ideas and fantasies about the bodies of other males and females. Infant (and prenatal) boys regularly experience erections, in response to a full bladder or bowel, general excitement, physical stimulation by caretakers who clean the boy's body, and while dreaming. By the early childhood years, most boys have learned to stimulate themselves and experience a form of heightened arousal leading to orgasmic feelings (without ejaculation). This also regularly occurs while playing. For example, the simple event of bouncing on someone's knee or the regular rhythm of rocking back and forth on a swing may stimulate such feelings. Although Freud thought these feelings were pregenital (infantile sexual), it is more likely that boys first associate feelings of genital pleasure with episodes of play. Only much later do sexual ideas enter the picture.

At adolescence, sexuality takes on a serious tone. Semenarche (first ejaculation) is always a profound experience for a boy and is the equivalent of menarche in girls. Because it occurs privately, however, and is usually not discussed until much later after the event (compared to a girl's first menstrual period, which is nearly always discussed with an adult almost immediately), semenarche does not have the significance of being a defining moment in the boy's life. The fantasy that accompanies the first ejaculation and the setting in which it occurs will have lasting significance for a boy, who usually continues to bring the fantasy to mind while masturbating. Boys who do not masturbate are unusual and the absence of this behavior may be a sign of emotional and expressive inhibition.

Genital feelings and sexuality are closely related to gender, which is a complex combination of factors, including genetics, the influence of hormones on the growing brain, assigned sex at birth, attitudes and expectations of parents about expectable boyish behavior, and broader social expectations about masculine behavior that the boy is expected to display. A boy's sexual orientation is a combination of preference for the male or female body, his sexuality, and his gender. Much has been written about sexual orientation and the possible influence of traumatic experiences on its formation and the determination of his gender identity. None of the research is conclusive and all of it refers exclusively to Western attitudes.

It is clear that no single experience is determinative of either a boy's gender or sexual orientation. What determines whether an experience engaged in actively or passively (usually with elements of both) is registered as pleasurable or harmful (or a mixture of both and reacted to with ambivalence) varies from boy to boy and situation to situation. It is easy for a boy to misinterpret a sexual advance for aggression. Punishments may also be confused with the sexual advances of an older child or adult. The incest barrier usually excludes parents from these scenarios, although some boys may experience ordinary caretaking procedures as sexually stimulating, and lively play as aggression. A mother's affectionate feelings toward her son are decisive for his ability to feel lovable. A father's feeling of engrossment toward his son is essential for the initial process of identification (mentioned above) to proceed, but just as important are a boy's first self-initiated loving feelings toward his father, which likely serve as a template for the affectionate aspect of all of the boy's later relations with friends and sexual partners of either sex. Boys require the loving attention of a mothering figure during the first years of life and the opportunity for affectionate interactions with a father figure in early and middle childhood. But evidently during later childhood and adolescence, they also gain a great deal from homosocial relations with other boys and older males such as coaches and teachers. In highly gender dimorphic cultures such as ours, these experiences are essential for a feeling of belonging to one of the genders. Feeling psychologically as though he is a girl or female (gender dysphoria) is not well understood. In the West at this time, however, the feeling allows a boy fewer options than it does girls. Childhood play and adolescent exuberance provide many opportunities for close physical contact with other boys. Some of the "real boys" experiences may be perceived as sexual, but for the most part they are experienced as playful. A boy's gender and sexual orientation remain malleable through the late teens and early twenties as meaningful rites of passage are missing in boys' lives.

Further Reading

Brongersma, Edward. *Loving Boys* (2 vols.). Elmhurst: Global Academic, 1990. Originally published in 1986.

Maccoby, Eleanor. *The Two Sexes. Growing up Apart, Coming Together.* Cambridge, MA: Harvard University Press, 1999.

Pollack, William. *Real Boys. Rescuing Our Boys from the Myths of Boyhood.* New York: Henry Holt, 1999. Originally published in 1998.

Miles Groth

Sexual Development in Culture

The sexual life of boys has often been and continues to be an important problem for American parents and teachers. American boys' sexual escapades and experiments have been historically informed by Puritan, "muscular Christian," psychoanalytic, "social hygienic," pediatric, feminist, and men's studies perspectives, among others. Accordingly, what should be considered "healthy," "normal," "necessary," or "proper" sexual behavior, experience, or attitude is a much debated, and ultimately irresolvable, question. What has remained pretty much constant over the centuries is that boys' and male sexualities have always been thought of as indicative of, and of outstanding importance to, their masculinity. This importance, however, has received much criticism over the past decades.

What is to be considered worthy of attention regarding boyhood sexuality has shifted considerably over centuries. In the Southern world of plantations, problems such as youths experimenting with animals and female slaves occupied parents' minds. Later on, masturbation, venereal (sexually transmitted) disease, and liberties with prostitutes were major concerns for urban area families. In the twentieth century, issues such as homosexuality, metropolitan teenage hustling, use of pornography, sexual abuse, and harassment became major issues. Currently the range of *new media* (Internet, cell or mobile phones, Web cams) invite parental and legal scrutiny with regard to "exposure" to pornography, "grooming" of minors, and graphically explicit computer games.

Twentieth century theories and psychological concerns about sexual development have had a largely Germanic, particularly psychoanalytic, heritage. Stanley Hall, a key figure in the late nineteenth and early twentieth century child study movement, had introduced America to the psychoanalytic theories of Sigmund Freud about psychosexual stages, theories that centralized the Oedipus complex in boys. It focused mainly on infant male affection and ambivalent attitudes toward parents, their management, and the boy's ultimate resolutions. The years up to puberty would be "latent," or void of overt interest in matters of intimacy and reproduction.

Puberty would present a second dangerous trajectory toward normal, "healthy" heterosexuality. The overall effects of this male-, family-, and biology-focused theorizing have been mixed. Much of the original Freudian ideas are no more widely endorsed; for instance, the notion of a dormant stage before puberty has been refuted time and again. However, it can be argued that thinking about boyhood sexuality is still very much focused on psychology, the family, and the biological effects of puberty on the brain. Psychoanalysts also had much to say about the normality of masturbation, or at least genital play, and generally found it indicative of disturbance only if it persisted into adulthood. However, as in Europe, even into the 1950s, masturbation was commonly viewed as depleting a boy's vigor as well as his juices, leading parents to warn their children about blindness and hairy palms, if not threatening to "cut it off." Even a late 1960s study showed that particularly lower-class parents told young boys that their sexual part would "drop off," or smacked them if they caught the children in the act.

Another pervasive concern dealt with the question of whether same-sex sexual experiences were normative and expected in the adolescent years, or whether they were "ominous" for later gay identity. A chapter in the influential 1948 Kinsey report on *Sexual Behavior in the Human Male* stirred some specific commotion here, as it suggested that homosexual experiences (among other nonheterosexual experiences) were very common among young boys; it also suggested that "one in ten" males could be called homosexual. Arguably these debates, centering around the question of whether early same-sex experiences necessarily lead to enduring same-sex preference, continue today in the lay imagination, though it is now generally argued by sexologists that such experiences don't have significant consequences. The early twentieth century notion of an *adolescent homosexual phase*, however, was, in the 1970s, largely abandoned for psychological models of "normal adolescent homosexual development." Such models have been mirrored by models of "heterosexual development." Regardless of these models, the notion of *being gay* remains a serious concern for most Western boys from grade 4 onward, be it in the form of jokes, slander, or genuine anxieties about masculinity. In one 2001 British study, 377 fourteen- and fifteen-year-olds listed the pejoratives they heard at school and identified the ones they considered most taboo. As some of the most vitriolic items reported, homophobic (antigay) pejoratives accounted for 10 percent of the 6,000 items generated.

In the second half of the twentieth century a broader range of concerns took center stage, including the effects of absence of fathers as role models on sexual identity; the clinical and social significance of "sissiness"; the prevention and punishment of sexual harassment of girls; the long-term effects of circumcision on sexual satisfaction; boys' conduct at dating; and boy-sensitive issues in cases of child sexual abuse. Enduringly popular research topics include boys' sources of sex education (mostly peers and media), the age of first sexual intercourse, attitudes to condom use, and (after President Clinton) "what counts as sexual behavior" among boys. Topics that have received little attention in comparison to girls are attitudes to male virginity, to pubertal changes including the capacity to ejaculate, and to teenage fatherhood. For instance, only heterosexual intercourse is considered worthy of the terms *sexual initiation* and *losing one's virginity*. Consequently it is known as the last of four bases in popular analogy to baseball. But, of course, there is much sexual behavior going on among boys before this event.

No singular American pattern of "sexual development" can be discerned, however. Clearly the experience of growing up sexually has been markedly different in North America, depending on where a boy grows up, whether in a lower socioeconomic neighborhood, or an upper-class suburb, or among Americans, or in Hawai'i. African American and Latino boys' sex practices and attitudes have traditionally differed from white middle-class experiences. Furthermore, differences *among* ethnic minorities may often be larger than *between* ethnic minorities. These seeming ethnic differences have a lot to do with housing, access to formal sex education, and access to domestic channels of less formal information.

Still a number of issues have distinctly American aspects. Media-hyped scandals may display "American" cultural values regarding the nexus of sexuality, masculinity, and youth: antigay policies of the Boy Scouts of America, boys' sporadic liaisons with female school teachers, a wave of pedophilia incidents in the Catholic church throughout America, and so on. Some of these issues can be studied in the context of conservative and Christian opinion on the one hand, and on the other as related to a myriad of aligned political stakes. The attention to the role of the father in boys' psychosexual development may be understood as arising from father's rights issues raised by the 1980s and 1990s American men's studies movement. Circumcision has been widespread as a routine neonatal procedure in America, resulting in an enduring clash between the medical community and the anti-circ (anti-circumcision) movement that hosts conferences, rallies, anti-circ days, and numerous Web sites. Child sexual abuse is at times regarded as a feminist theme arising first and most pervasively in the 1970s United States, but only sporadically has it been considered as inviting specific attention to boys. Most of the politics around sexual abuse deals with boys in terms of "children" even if they are well into their teenage years, and while a range of aspects of dealing with sexual experience are clearly different for boys and girls. For boys, experiences may present problems of labeling their experience (as abuse or as sexual initiation), problems of identity (gay or straight or both or not yet any of these), and problems of making sense of the relations between important—though abstract—cultural notions (sexuality, masculinity, intimacy).

These and other issues trickle down profusely into the popular culture. Film has become one of the most important media, reflecting and influencing cultural opinion and imagination. Many American movies deal with boys' "coming of age" (a phrase often used to imply sexual maturation) from *The Blue Lagoon* (1980) and the *American Pie* trilogy (1999–2003), to lesser known movies with same-sex (*Wild Tigers I Have Known*, 2006) and cross-generational (*L.I.E.*, 2001; *Mysterious Skin*, 2004; *The Heart is Deceitful Above All Things*, 2004) themes, to more symbolically complex dramas about male development (*Burning Secret*, 1988; *Blue Velvet*, 1986). Controversial films by Larry Clark such as *Kids* (1995) and *Ken Park* (2002) have been widely considered to be among the most daring and extreme representations of American boys' sex lives. Other films such as *Boys Don't Cry* (1999) illuminate the problems of transsexual growing up.

Further Reading

Dennis, Jeffrey. *We Boys Together: Teenagers in Love before Girl-Craziness.* Nashville: Vanderbilt University Press, 2007.

Janssen, Diederik. Main Index: Atlas (Volume 1) [Online January 2008]. Growing Up Sexually: A World Atlas <http://www2.rz.hu-berlin.de/sexology/GESUND/ARCHIV/GUS/GUS_MAIN_INDEX.HTM>.

Pomeroy, Warren. *Boys and Sex Revised, 3rd Edition.* New York: Delacorte Press, 1991.

Renold, Emma. *Girls, Boys, and Junior Sexualities: Exploring Children's Gender and Sexual Relations in the Primary School.* London; New York: RoutledgeFalmer, 2005.

Diederik F. Janssen

Tourette Syndrome

Most people know about people with Tourette syndrome from movies or TV shows that depict people shouting out obscenities at inappropriate times or twitching their bodies in strange ways. Unfortunately, this kind of joking representation does not explain what Tourette syndrome is or what can and should be done when someone has it. People typically find out they have Tourette when they are young, usually before they turn 18, and statistics indicate that males are three to four times more likely to have Tourette than females.

Gilles de la Tourette first identified the disorder in the 1800s and it was named after him. Tourette syndrome is a neurological disorder characterized by motor tics, or involuntary body movements, of the face, arms, legs, or trunk. There are also vocal tics such as grunts, throat clearing, whistling, shouting, and snorting that most often happen alongside motor tics. Symptoms vary from person to person and range from mild to severe. Tics can be simple (one or a few tics) or complex (a lot of tics happening simultaneously). Tics often come in clusters. For example, a person could snort, twitch his/her arm, and hop in place—all at the same time or one right after another. Tics are like sneezes; people can feel them coming but they cannot prevent them.

There are no scientific tests to diagnose Tourette, but doctors look for tics that occur for a long period of time, typically a year, and that they happen every day, usually several times a day. Most often it starts with a simple tic, such as an eye twitch or the involuntary urge to touch something. Symptoms change in location and type and wax and wane (they come and go) in frequency, intensity, complexity, and severity. People with Tourette often also have ADHD (attention deficit hyperactivity disorder) and/or OCD (obsessive compulsive disorder). Obsessions and compulsions (persistent thoughts or urges to jump or touch something) feel like tics and are also involuntary—people can't stop them even if they want to, no matter where they are. Because it's a neurological disorder, there is usually a family history of Tourette, ADHD, or OCD. Males are three to four times more likely to have Tourette than females.

Sometimes, but not always, people with Tourette also have learning disabilities. Tourette has nothing to do with intelligence or ability. There is no reason why a person with Tourette cannot be successful at whatever she or he wants to do. The main problem is other people who do not know about Tourette and do not understand what's going on. Sometimes people laugh, tease, or stare when they see or hear someone's tic. This sort of treatment can be embarrassing and lead to depression and low self-esteem.

School can be particularly difficult for people with Tourette. Rules about sitting still, listening for long periods, focusing on one task at a time, and not talking are virtually impossible to follow. People with Tourette can sometimes suppress tics for certain periods of time, but they must be given time later to express the urge. However, because tics are involuntary, boys with Tourette are often in trouble at school or in other public settings. Punishments, such as suspensions or time-outs, don't work and are an inappropriate response to tics and compulsions. Excessive attempts at control can lead to a buildup of anxiety that results in an explosive tantrum or other release. These episodes produce stress, and stress of all kinds significantly increases tics. Either the child's parent or the child himself or herself has to be proactive in teaching school personnel and peers about Tourette so these kinds of reactions can be stopped.

Further Reading

Dornbush, Marilyn, and Pruitt, Sheryl. *Teaching the Tiger.* Duarte, CA: Hope Press, 1995.
Haerle, Tracy. *Children with Tourette Syndrome: A Parent's Guide.* Rockville, MD: Woodbine House, 1992.
Handler, Lowell. *Twitch and Shout.* New York: Penguin, 1998.
Tourette Syndrome Association [Online July 2008]. <http://www.tsa-usa.org/>.

Joanne Larson

Sports

Baseball

Perhaps the ultimate North American dream can be traced back to imagining a career in baseball, playing in the Major Leagues. Unlike other sports, there is something about baseball, which engages boys from every social class. A relatively inexpensive sport to play, boys have been playing different forms of baseball for almost two centuries.

It is difficult to pinpoint exactly when the sport of baseball originated. Early paintings record people hitting a ball-type of shape with long sticks. However, modern baseball was first played in 1838 in Ontario, Canada. This is ironic, in light of the notion that baseball has been called *the* American sport. In fact, popular sayings often include using baseball as the American simile: "it's as American as baseball," and naming it the *national pastime.* The history of urban sports in North America includes stickball, which, as it sounds, is a game where children use any type of stick and a round object to replicate a ball. Stickball is often associated with young people who don't have access to team sports or equipment; it can even be played with rolled newspaper and crumpled paper.

In the 1860s, baseball became so popular that semi-professional teams began playing it—this included men who kept their "day jobs," but also played baseball. Professional baseball began in 1869 with the Cincinnati Red Stockings as the first team. For over a century, North American baseball has been associated with boys and men, large stadiums, summer, peanuts, and singing "Take Me Out to the Ballgame" in the seventh inning stretch. Baseball is considered a male sport. Females may excel at softball, but baseball is primarily male. Early baseball was segregated, and professional baseball had two leagues: Major League Baseball (white) and the Negro League (Black). Baseball was slowly integrated when Jackie Robinson was drafted to play for the Brooklyn Dodgers; unfortunately, it has taken many decades for all races of men to become somewhat equitable. Famous early white baseball players include Babe Ruth, Shoeless Joe Jackson, Honus Wagner, Ty Cobb, and Cy Young. Great African American players were Cool Papa Bell, Satchel Page (who later played in the Major Leagues), Josh Gibson, and Dick Lundy. The history of baseball has always been shadowed by the difficulties that Black players encountered when playing. After integration of the leagues, Black men, and then Latino men began to populate the Major Leagues, and now many ethnic groups are included in American Major League Baseball.

After a series of incarnations, professional baseball has evolved into two major leagues: the American League and the National League. Although the majority of baseball teams are in the United States, the Toronto Blue Jays are a part of the American League and won the World Series in 1992; they became the only team outside of the United States to play in and win the World Series. Famous modern baseball players include Jackie Robinson, Mickey Mantle, Ted Williams, Yogi Berra, Joe DiMaggio, Willie Mays, Henry (Hank) Aaron, Jim Palmer, Sandy Koufax, Whitey Ford, Don Drysdale, Al Kaline, Roger Marris, Roberto Clemente, Johnny Bench, Joe Morgan, Dennis Eckersly, Ozzie Smith, Don Mattingly, Barry Bonds, Mark McGuire, Mike Schmidt, Pedro Martinez, and Sammy Sosa. Baseball is unique in that professional managers (like coaches) are also public figures and idols: John McGraw, Connie Mack, Casey Stengel, Earl Weaver, Sparky Anderson, Tommy Lasorda, Joe Torre, Tony La Russa, and Bobby Cox. Even though there are many amazing baseball teams, many argue that the New York Yankees are the ultimate American baseball team. In fact, in the 1950s, a musical film, *Damn Yankees*, dealt with an aging baseball player who sold his soul to the devil to play in the World Series. The title of the film shows the anger that non-Yankee fans continually felt through the many New York championships of the 1950s and early 1960s. A novel published in the 1950s, *The Year the Yankees Lost the Pennant*, was a "fantasy" about the Yankees *not* winning the championship in a particular season.

Many little boys are raised with dreams of becoming baseball players. Organized teams are created for boys as young as three with tee ball; when they attend school, they join the midget leagues, and then Little League. Some boys continue playing baseball through high school and on to college; however, professional baseball is definitely *the* spectator sport within North America (unlike football, which is the leading NCAA sport). The notion of baseball is, in itself, somewhat romantic compared to other sports. It is not particularly dirty, not a contact sport, and is not timed. A nine-inning game can be as short as two hours, and as long as almost six hours. Baseball culminates every fall with the World Series, where the two leading teams (one from each league) play the best out of seven games in alternating stadiums. Although the World Series and Major Leagues are still in North America, baseball has become a global sport, and teams in Japan, Korea, China, The Dominican Republic, Mexico, and scores of other countries are exceedingly professional and engaging. Baseball became an Olympic sport in 1992. However, as global as baseball has become, the prediction is that it will always be *the* American sport.

Further Reading

Aaron, Hank. *I Had a Hammer.* New York: Harper Perennial, 2007.

Editors of Sports Illustrated. *Sports Illustrated: The Baseball Book.* USA: Sports Illustrated, 2004.

Kahn, Roger. *The Boys of Summer.* New York: Harper Perennial Modern Classics, 2006.

Shirley R. Steinberg

Basketball

Three, two, one . . . the shot is up, "swish," and the crowd goes wild. This is one of the most common boyhood play scenarios; it easily rivals the superhero, cowboy, and rock star fantasies that eternally show up in boyhood play. In the parks, gyms, and driveways, the "wanna-be" superstars of the hard court emulate the heroics of their favorite basketball players. You have to wonder, what encourages a three-and-a-half-foot tall boy to repeatedly attempt to hurl a seven pound ball ten feet into the air in order to make a single basket. It is a marvel to observe but even more engaging when you think about what is happening in the mind and emotions of the youngster. Consider the subject who is a third of the height of the goal, throwing an object that is a sixth of his weight into the air. As if that wasn't enough to think about, consider him attempting to throw this object into and through a ring only slightly larger than the object itself. Witness the subject's successive failure as the task unfolds. Often times the ball never makes it to the rim, much less into and through it, but he continues to count and heave. In that moment where all the necessary actions are in unison, something truly special happens. The boy who has been thinking of himself as Kobe Bryant, LeBron James, Steve Nash, Tony Parker, Kevin Garnett, or Allen Iverson is now the star, taking center stage, jumping up and down, and accepting the adoration of his imaginary arena-filled crowd of onlookers. The euphoria is short lived as in less than five minutes he is back in front of the goal toiling again in blissful athletic optimism.

History of Basketball

Most boys today, the future "kings of the court" are more familiar with the contributions of "Doc" Rivers and Dr. J than with Dr. James Naismith, founder of the game. As time changes all things, it has also changed basketball, from the layup, jump shot, and pass-oriented game to its gravity-defying dunks, long-range three-point shots, and its off-the-dribble lobs. Basketball only became popularly recognized after Naismith invented it in 1891 as a physical fitness requirement in the sound mind and body based curriculum of Springfield, Massachusetts's Young Men's Christian Association (YMCA) International Training School. However, it is worth noting that there are ancient cultural games, such as Tlatchtli and Ulama, played by the Aztecs, Olmecs, Mayans, and other cultures, that bear a striking similarity to the modern game of basketball. Dr. Naismith developed the game of basketball to fulfill academic requirements rather than cultural needs. Boys participating in the YMCA were often labeled the Young Muscular Christians because of their rigorous physical preparation.

Over the last 100 years the game has followed the spirit of the original, but the players have brought a heightened level of physical demands and an unimaginable level of creativity in defense, dribbling, and scoring. Comparisons of greatness between players from the past and the present day are flourishing in the global game.

Arguments can be heard from the press box to the barbershop about who is the greatest of all time, while some of the "experts" fuel the statistical comparisons between players that seek to preserve the mystique and nostalgia of the game. The boys that sit on the sidelines of all the courts, from the backyard to the college bench, hoping to get their shot realize that someone has to forge new paths and perform the unimaginable, so why not them?

The Mystique of the Game

This romanticized "daring to dream" notion can be found in most any sport around the world, but basketball surpasses them all because it reinforces the idea that an individual needs to do his or her part and prepare for interactions with the group. At its core, basketball is an individual game, like golf, where you compete against yourself to score a goal. It is also a team-based game dependant on strategy and defense. Many other sports, such as football, base-ball, tennis, golf, and soccer, have also had a special place in the minds and hearts of boys. Football and baseball have taken their turns at being the most historic sport of all boyhood fascination. But basketball brings a new level of experimentation and creativity that has dominated against the growth of other major sports. The little league parks used to be filled every year with boys planning to emulate their professional heroes by running faster and hit-ting harder than any other boy on the planet. As the leaves changed color and the weather became harsh, boys raring to go would suit up in their football gear to "clean the clocks" of their best friends, then grab a soda and walk home together with helmets in hand, all the while planning to come back the next day and do it all over again. This ritual would continue well into winter. But with the budding of spring a transformation takes place in these young gladiators. They drop the helmet and pick up their gloves. They seem to instinctively know it is time for baseball practice. This cycle continues today but with fewer boys suiting up from year to year. The dwindling numbers may be recognizable in the Major League slogans for each game. Football takes a sacrificial attitude to the game by saying that it is all "for the love of the game." The long-lived baseball institution expresses its attitude and expectations with two statements: "catch the Fever" and "what a game. . . ." Basketball makes its league aspirations less epic with a more personal slogan: "I Love This Game."

We are certainly in a new era; today's game is unquestionably basketball. There is no change from season to season. The young athlete plays year round because the game is both an outdoor and indoor sport. The remarkable thing about basketball is that every level and every region is filled with legends that are recognized and celebrated for their on-court accomplishments. Football, baseball, and basketball have had movies and video games made celebrating their amateur ranks, yet basketball has become a rung in the ladder of pop cul-ture. Every top basketball player has a nickname, worn as a badge, and earned on the court. Young boys are quicker to recognize the players' nicknames before the players' real names. In the ranks of playground legends, names such as Earl "The Goat" Manigault, Richard "Pee Wee" Kirkland, and Rafer "Skip to My Lou" Alston are a part of the common boyhood basketball vocab-ulary. When a shot is being made by a future basketball great, he may call out "Pee Wee" as if he was summoning the super natural powers of a legend to guide the ball through the hoop. The boys that grow up shooting and calling out the names of the greats are also the innovators for the future of the beloved game.

Unlike other sports, the major game changes rise up from the amateur ranks. The boys from the playground become the men of the boardrooms. They still carry the dreams of hitting that last-second shot or dunking in the open court after a breakaway steal. As adults they live out these fantasies in the local YMCA or gym. The largest change to the game not fostered by the National Basketball Association (NBA) is the creation of streetball. The grow-ing subculture of streetball has intertwined itself with other innovations of boyhood such as hiphop, sneaker culture, sports apparel, and many other forms of youth entertainment. In recent years streetball, basketball's sister game, where the rules are loosely interpreted and the one-on-one creativity of the players is celebrated during team games, has grown among boys all over the world. Because streetball is the popularizing of playground-style basketball, some streetball legends include the old-school players of the 1960s and 1970s, but a new business-minded crop of amateur players have helped create an industry out of this playground-style game. Some recognizable names from the "mixtape" (current) generation of streetballers are Philip "Hot Sauce" Champion, Waliyy "Main Event" Dixon, and Grayson "The Professor" Boucher. The streetball enterprise has fueled the imaginations of boys that see the players' star quality, style of the apparel, and the respect of knowing "who's got game."

Becoming Professional

The road to the NBA is a narrow one. Many young boys carry their hardwood dreams well into their manhood. There is a group of players that hone their game on playgrounds and high schools in hopes that a college scout will give them that shot to play for their favorite university team. Eager freshmen recruited to play college ball are ushered into new academic settings and end up playing a game that hardly resembles the one they loved in high school. They soon realize that other players surrounding them are as good as they are or better. This is a maturing moment for many young players, where they step their game up and learn how to play as a squad. It is rare for a single college player to have all the necessary talent and tools to carry a university team to the prized NCAA championship. The focus is now off the individual performance and refocused on skills that help him make his teammates better. This lesson is difficult to learn and takes many youngsters years to exhibit.

Coaches become teachers and players become students, and the lessons are intended to win games and also to build character. Although this setting has its structure and is focused much less on the abilities of any single player, a select few shine and earn that coveted nickname symbolizing his exceptional skill for the game. Some easily recognized players that moved through the college ranks to have successful pro careers where Wilt "The Stilt" Chamberlain, "Pistol" Pete Maravic, Earvin "Magic" Johnson, Jr., and the amazing Michael "MJ" Jordan.

As an example, Michael Jordan is argued in barbershops to be the world's greatest pro basketball player of all times. He is the measuring stick by which pro players such as Dwayne "D-WADE" Wade, Lebron "King" James, and Kobe "The Black Momba" Bryant are judged. But even "MJ" played in an orchestrated team system lead by Dean Smith, one of college basketball's greatest coaches. It has been noted in many interviews that Michael was a special college player, but no one knew how special until his championship runs at the professional level with the Chicago Bulls. As young boys learn these stories, they very quickly see the passion, maturity, and discipline necessary to be successful on and off the court at any level.

Cultural Issues

In identifying some pivotal figures in basketball, it is also essential to discuss political and societal issues associated with them. The game was a racially segregated sport in its early years when white males dominated the popular organized teams. Basketball remained segregated from 1891 until 1950 when the Boston Celtics drafted the first African American player, Charles "Chuck" Cooper. Cooper, Nat Clifton (of the New York Knicks, and the first African American player to sign a contract with an NBA team), and Earl Lloyd (of the Washington Capitols, and the first African American player to play in a game) initiated the integration of professional basketball leagues such as the National Basketball League (NBL) and the National Basketball Association (NBA). Lloyd's controversial debut was followed a day later by Cooper's and Clifton's four days later. Their greatness was not in their game performances on those nights; rather they exhibited greatness through their endurance of racial slurs and death threats, even as they continued to show up and compete, as well as through their endurance of the fans' nightly questioning of their right to be there.

As an example of the game's accelerated change, merely 20 years later, an NBA team drafted the first international players. The Atlanta Hawks chose Mexico's Manuel Raga and Italy's Dino Meneghin in the 1970 Draft. The league would still have to wait to feel the impact of such players on the game as the Hawks could not afford to buy the players out of their overseas contracts. Eight years later, Mychal George Thompson of Nassau, Bahamas, was selected the number 1 pick in the NBA Draft. Although the Thompson draft would not be representative of the varied international recruitment into the NBA (much of his high school and college basketball was played in Florida and Minnesota), he does reflect the NBA's goal to find the best players in the world. In the 2007 NBA playoffs, there were 60 international players representing 26 countries and territories on 15 of the best-record teams. Some of the international players such as Steve Nash, league MVP for two consecutive years, have demonstrated individual talents that have placed them at the top of the game.

There is another level where the names of Bill Russell, "Pistol" Pete Maravich, Wilt Chamberlain, Jerry West, Larry Bird, Magic Johnson, Michael Jordan, and many others of similar accomplishment are reserved for boys dreaming of NBA stardom and barbershop bragging rights. This is the land of superstars where talent is replaced by the individual's absolute will and his resistance to losing. Basketball's elites survived the early years where the much revered baseball was only second to religion. Basketball greats somehow continued to shine through the political and social controversies during the 1960s and into the early 1980s when everyone thought basketball was limping along wounded and fated for death. The tickets weren't selling and the seats were empty, but the game kept progressing, albeit slowly, and great basketball continued. The kings of the hardwood court experienced a fan-based rebirth in the late 1980s. The basketball trinity was about to descend upon us. Magic Johnson's LA Lakers were about to turn the tide on Larry Bird's Boston Celtics, amplifying the game to the stature of legend. The Lakers went on to win the playoffs twice during the eighties. The last component needed to ensure the successful growth of basketball was the entrance of the noted basketball wonder, Michael Jordan, into the NBA. The Jordan era brought new fans to games and new marketing opportunities to players. Nike had its finger on the pulse of the game. They realized that the fan loyalty was with the players, not with the team itself. This new pulse was loud enough for the manufacturing, marketing, and ad agencies to wake up and take notice.

Basketball Gear for Boys

Popular culture could not get enough of basketball. Boys went to school in NBA official team jerseys and their hero's sneakers. Team logos were on the shirts, jackets, caps, and shoes of fans and those with an eye for fashion. The sneaker companies made sure any player that had a fan following in the NBA had a shoe to sell to those fans. When there is a mixture of this type of commercial energy, a strong product, and a public with expendable cash, a dark side to the story seems to surface. The demand for "gear" grew with the game and soon American culture was faced with boys violently attacking each other to steal a pair of $60–$200 sneakers sponsored by NBA players. Converse, Nike, and Fila lead the way in the "shoe war," while Adidas, Reebok, and Etonics were all trying to pair a shoe with an NBA giant. Parents were looking for someone to blame. High schools were running scared, with the administrators placing students in uniforms in order to decrease waves of youth violence in the name of style. The greatest form of social recovery didn't come from the parents, politicians, or teachers. It came from a few NBA players, who, in protest against the violence and high prices placed on the merchandising, made deals with manufacturing companies to produce price-conscious gear for kids to wear. It took some time for the public to settle down from the frenzy and fashion and get back to focusing on the game.

The Present and Future

By 2000, the league had a mass of new talent along with loads of game excitement and drama. The three-point shot had been in place for about five years and the NBA, never known for its defense, actually had lock-down defensive specialists that changed the game by blocking shots, stealing the ball, and hitting the glass to rack up rebounds. Offense will always fill the seats of the arena but defense wins playoff titles. As such, teams were being built on this concept. Jordan's Chicago Bulls were the ideal model for offense and defense in balance. Michael Jordan, Scottie Pippen, and a cast of support players handled the offense but they shared the court with a player not known for his offense but his defense, Dennis Rodman. His job night in and night out was to go out and prevent the other team from scoring, get every loose ball, and grab any rebound that bounced off the rim. It is not that this was the first time a team had this dynamic; however, it was the first time for fans to create celebrities out of the team's specialists and role players. Charles Barkley said it best, "Everybody in the NBA has talent." So there must be something else that separates the great from the talented.

The NBA playoffs are the stage for much of the players' heroics. Fans follow their teams and support regional or traditional favorites. Their faithfulness is called into question when they are cheering the last-second pass and shot from any of the true superstars of the game. At that point it just boils down to an appreciation of talent, skill, and desire. Just as boys did in the 1940s, when baseball was truly the nation's game, the dreams of a few lucky people to play a game that they loved became the dreams of millions of boys all over the world. They mimic how players wear their socks and headbands, how they set their feet at the free throw line, all the way down to an individual player's game face. The game is now bigger than the court. It is easy to understand the players denial of this pressure when they say, "Hey man, I'm just a basketball player." They realize the responsibility that the game's increased role and context demands and the impact this has on their lives. Still, when they lace up and step on to the court it's still "3, 2, 1 . . . perfection." With every blink of the clock there are boys in parallel spaces going through the motions of their favorite players. Their dreams unrealistically seem within arms reach as they witness the influx of younger players drafted into the NBA. So they keep trying to beat the odds of making the shot and making it big.

Further Reading

ABAlive.com [Online]. <www.abalive.com/>.

Batchelor, R. (2005). *Basketball in America: From the Playgrounds to Jordan's Game and Beyond.* New York: Routledge.

Lane, J. (2007). *Under the Boards: The Cultural Revolution in Basketball.* Lincoln, NE: Bison Books.

Moran, J. (1991). *Nothing But Net!: An Essay on the Culture of Pickup Basketball.* San Antonio, TX: Full Court Press.

NBA History [Online]. <http://www.nba.com/history>.

Streetball.com [Online]. <http://www.streetball.com/>.

Roymieco A. Carter

Bodybuilding

Though bodybuilding is both a lifestyle and sport, boys often first look to it for answers to self-esteem and body image issues. In part these perceived shortcomings are manufactured by American society and a supplement and magazine industry that center around bodybuilding and fitness and seek to define what is sexually desirable. We live in a country where boys are told winning isn't everything (with the usually unspoken but implied corollary that it is the only thing) but a "bigger is better" mentality—from larger cars and paychecks to fuller muscles—suffuses the land and boys' impressionable psyches.

It is important to understand the differences between bodybuilding as a healthy lifestyle of clean eating and exercise centered on weight training—what is sometimes referred to as physical culture—versus competitive bodybuilding, a sport where genetically gifted athletes transform their bodies into cartoonish dimensions through hardcore training, nutrition, and drug use. The competitive physique of the bodybuilder has evolved from late nineteenth-century circus side-show attraction as exemplified by Prussian strongman Eugen Sandow to today's 260-plus pound of shredded physiques (eight-time Olympia champion Ronnie Coleman was documented as weighing 296 pounds onstage at the 2005 contest). Arnold Schwarzenegger single-handedly popularized the bodybuilder look by piggybacking his acting career off the muscles he amassed as seven-time Mr. Olympia (weighing 230 pounds) in such films as *Conan the Barbarian* and *Commando,* ushering into the 1980s the era of big-muscled action movie stars. It is ironic that today's Olympia winner takes home a Sandow trophy in a sport where a Sandow or even Schwarzenegger-like physique no longer stands a chance of success.

There are a lot of misconceptions that bring boys to bodybuilding. Though big muscles may intimidate some opponents, they do *not* make you a better fighter. Nor do they necessarily slow you down as in the stereotypical muscle-bound weight lifter caricature, except in extreme cases such as off-season bodybuilders who carry around 300-plus pounds of water retention and bloat. Nor is the hardcore bodybuilder-type physique one most women find desirable, though magazines routinely feature enormous bodybuilders with fitness models on their covers. Though everyone has six-pack abdominals, these can only be seen when body fat levels are low enough to render those muscles visible, a product more of dieting and individual body fat levels and composition than of any weight training regimen.

Steroids and other sports drugs alone will not impart massive muscles, though the gargantuan inflated look of today's professional muscle builders is not possible without them. The advertisements in magazines and online usually couple a bodybuilder with a supplement that had little, if anything, to do with the bodybuilder's muscular development. All this aside, weight training along with a sensible diet and supplements is an excellent regimen and will impart to its practitioner a better quality of life as well as help with other sports. Through a consistent weight training program and bodybuilding lifestyle, most boys find they are able to double or triple their strength within two to three years of picking up a weight and add anywhere from 10 to 20 pounds of muscle naturally.

The supplement and magazine industry, while preying upon people's self-esteem, hold out the false promise that weight training will impart a Herculean build. Nothing could be further from the truth. Genetics play the most important role in bodybuilding. Genetic potential sets the limits of how much one will respond to everything from training to dieting to supplementation, including drug use. Everyone who trains with weights stands to benefit and will see improvements, but not everyone who trains will hit a baseball as far as Barry Bonds, run as quickly as Ben Johnson, or have the muscles of Mr. Olympia Jay Cutler. That said, one's genetic potential is not obvious until one starts following the bodybuilding lifestyle.

Whether bodybuilding depends more on drug use than other sports is debatable. What is not questionable is that bodybuilders are *perceived* to be drug dependent, a view that has long stigmatized the sport. Where doctors in the field of hormone replacement therapy routinely prescribe 200 mg weekly doses of testosterone to men over 30 with diminished testosterone levels, it is not uncommon for bodybuilders to inject 2–5,000 mgs of testosterone per week, stacked with various other drugs that work synergistically (together) with it, including growth hormone and insulin (which has become quite popular among athletes in the past decade due to its highly anabolic or muscle-building effects). In the United States of America, steroids, including testosterone, are labeled class III drugs. Their possession and sale without prescription are punishable by fine and/or imprisonment. They also carry possible short- and long-term risks to one's health. Despite this, it is estimated that 3–6 percent of American high school students use or have used steroids without a doctor's prescription (Manning, 2002).

Advertisements for Charles Atlas' *Dynamic Tension* program in the 1940s comic books promised boys a body that would scare off sand-kicking bullies and win them the attention and affection of girls. Today's supplement industry promises them much the same with a glossier veneer of science. With the success of violent action movies starring Arnold Schwarzenegger, Sylvester Stallone, and Jean-Claude Van Damme, big muscles became cool. Being built came to be synonymous with manliness and virility, with the ability to take care of oneself in all walks of life, from fighting to the ladies. And indeed, individuals with higher levels of testosterone coursing through their systems—either naturally or exogenously (supplemental) supplied—report greater levels of well-being and confidence. Muscular, defined physiques sported by celebrities such as rappers soon caught boys' eyes and helped spread the message that such a look is desirable.

There are three main components to the bodybuilding lifestyle. Weight training is essential to bodybuilding but there are differing ideas on what constitutes an effective routine. Some practitioners advocate a greater number of sets and repetitions (high volume), whereas others favor a high-intensity routine of heavier weights, lower reps, and fewer sets. In the last 15 years, the importance of not overtraining has led to the adoption of routines that see each body part trained once a week or once every 10 days, whereas in Schwarzenegger's heyday, bodybuilders would lift weights five to seven days a week, sometimes twice per day.

Diet, in the sense of proper nutrition and not as a corrective, is now recognized as perhaps the most important aspect of the bodybuilding lifestyle. Competitive bodybuilders routinely eat six to eight small meals. These meals are centered around protein, the building block of muscles, in the form of lean chicken, fish, beef, or supplemental shakes. Most experts argue that for each pound of bodyweight, one should take in anywhere from one and a half to two grams of protein per day. Along with diet, cardiovascular exercise is recognized as necessary for shedding excess body fat and bringing out the detail in one's muscles. In addition to proper eating, recuperation in the form of adequate sleep is a necessity for the bodybuilder, as muscles grow during one's sleep.

Though bodybuilding can help a boy feel better about himself and result in discernable muscle mass and strength gains, an underlying sense of inadequacy that often drives many youngsters to the weights in the first place is not dispelled by pumping iron. More studies are detailing body dysmorphic disorder in males, from teens to professional bodybuilders, who feel they are not big enough or muscular enough. The supplement and magazine industries do not help this situation by offering up as exemplars of masculinity drug-addled models with enormous physiques. One certainty is that bodybuilding will not make one rich. Whereas the median National Football League player salary in 2007 was $770,000, the first place prize at the 2007 Mr. Olympia was $155,000 (*USA Today,* 2008). Professional bodybuilders are not unionized and their professional organization, the International Federation of Bodybuilders, does not offer them health insurance or a retirement plan.

Further Reading

Llewellyn, William. *Anabolics 2007: Anabolic Steroids Reference Manual.* USA: Body of Science, 2007.

Manning, Anita. Teenagers' Steroid Use "At an All Time High." *USA Today.* Accessed July 23, 2008, from http://www.usatoday.com/sports/bbw/2002-07-11/special-steroids2.htm.

Muscular Development Magazine [Online June, 2008]. <http://www.muscular development.com/>.

Paris, Bob. *Gorilla Suit: My Adventures in Bodybuilding.* New York: St. Martin's Griffin, 1998.

Schwarzenegger, Arnold, and Bob Dobbins. *The New Encyclopedia of Modern Bodybuilding.* New York: Simon & Schuster, 1999.

USA Today. Pro Football Salaries Database. Accessed July 23, 2008, from http://content.usatoday.com/sports/football/nfl/salaries/default.aspx.

Zinkin, Harold, and Bonnie Hearn. *Remembering Muscle Beach: Where Hard Bodies Began, Photographs and Memories.* Santa Monica, CA: Angel City Press, 1999.

Tony Monchinski

Boys' Behavior and Body Image

Because so much focus of concern is on girls and their body images, we often forget how these images influence boys. Boys have always been encouraged and influenced to achieve some sort of masculine physique. In a phenomenon called reverse anorexia boys as young as 10 years old are now turning to steroids to enhance their bodies and obtain the same physique that they see in the media. Along with this hypermasculine body image boys are also discouraged to express emotions or show any kind of personality traits that can be construed as emotionally weak or not man enough. Boys are told not to cry or show too much emotion and to *man up* when things become tough or difficult. In many ways, kindness in boys is equated with weakness, and boys are not to be weak. Although girls are allowed and encouraged to show emotion, boys must to be emotionally strong and stoic or suffer ridicule and be considered fragile. Today a lot of emphasis in society is placed on a girl's body image and how this body image is heavily influenced by the media and peers. We constantly hear about body image disorders that girls experience, such as anorexia and bulimia, but little is discussed about boys, their body images, and how they perceive themselves and each other. Children today are inundated with images on how they should look. Corporations have unfettered access to the airwaves and bombard children with physical images that are unrealistic and unattainable. Through television shows, movies, and images on the Internet and in magazines, both boys and girls are fed a steady diet of body images that become hypersexualized and can be devastating to self-esteem, self-image, and self-worth.

Throughout media, boys are fed a steady diet of hypermasculinity and emotional toughness. Boys watch movies and play video games that encourage violence and value strength, while traits such as compassion and empathy are scorned. Boys' idols are to be war heroes or adult males that can exhibit physical strength and stoic emotions, with anger being the only acceptable emotion allowed to show through the emotionless exterior. Media critic and theorist Douglas Kellner calls this male caricature in the media the Rambo effect, referencing the Rambo character portrayed by Sylvester Stallone and Rambo style movies that were so prevalent in the 1980s. These movies profiled men that were hypermasculine, larger-than-life individuals with gleaming muscles and stoic personalities. They were portrayed to be the ideal man. These men were practically indestructible and they could face down huge armies and defeat them single-handedly with little or no physical injuries.

These were the movies that many grew up with in the 1980s: *Rambo*, *Commando*, and *Top Gun*. These movies became propaganda for the military, because boys would see these movies and want to emulate these characters. Patriotism was standard in these movies, and the media encouraged the boys that consumed these images to become like these men, or at least as close to them as they could get, which meant becoming soldiers. The image of a masculine boy implied a slim, strong physique, tall height, full head of hair, bravery, recklessness, and strength. Boys in essence were being groomed for military service. But this did not just start in the 1980s with the advent of *Rambo*. This militaristic image of masculinity has been around for years and has been and continues to be used by governments and the media as a way to encourage boys to join the military. Long before *Rambo* and *Commando* influenced teenagers in the 1980s, there were mythic war heroes, such as those portrayed by John Wayne, who tapped into boys' desire for adventure. Now with the proliferation of technology and media outlets, there are a fleet of hyper masculine heroes to influence boys to become toy soldiers, from movies, to television, to video games.

But we cannot completely lay the blame of overt masculinity and stoic reserve at the altar of the media and government. The psychological community has had an influence on what would be considered the proper behavioral patterns for boys and which body image they should adopt. *The Diagnostic and Statistical Manual of Mental Disorders* (currently in its technically revised fourth edition: *DSM-IV-TR*) has long held sway over professions that deal with the mental and psychological well-being of children. Professionals from medical doctors (mainly psychiatrists) to school counselors and social workers are well-versed in the *DSM*. They have had training in this text in relation to their respective educational programs. Most of these mental health and educational professionals must demonstrate proficiency in the *DSM* and mental health issues of children to qualify for state licensure required for employment. The *DSM* is a text that is used to diagnose individuals with mental disorders that may require some form of psychological intervention such as counseling or medication. As text that has been around since the 1950s, the *DSM* is released by the American Psychiatric Association (APA) and is written and compiled by highly qualified professionals in the mental health field (psychiatrists, psychologists, psychotherapists, social workers).

Gender identity disorder (GID) is a mental disorder in the *DSM* that boys may be diagnosed with if they do not engage in stereotypical gender-assigned behaviors of masculinity. The *DSM* has a detailed explanation of GID that equates boys that do not engage in traditionally assigned gender roles with behaviors of girls. The *DSM* is actually very specific in detailing some behaviors that are considered to be abnormal and should raise concern if a parent or professional sees a boy exhibit these behaviors. Boys can be diagnosed with GID if they exhibit the following:

A strong attraction for the stereotypical games and pastimes of girls. They particularly enjoy playing house, drawing pictures of beautiful girls and princesses, and watching television or videos of their favorite female characters. Stereotypical female-type dolls, such as Barbie, are often their favorite toys, and girls are their preferred playmates . . . They avoid rough-and-tumble play and competitive sports and have little interest in cars and trucks and other nonaggressive but stereotypical boys' toys.

This overt image of masculinity affects boys in a negative way, including a disconnection from their own emotions, a lack of empathy, and less regard for others and their feelings, not to mention the potential use of steroids in adolescent males. Of course, the place for this hypermasculine idea and behavior, as presented by the media, is also found in stereotypes that include sports, ultimate sports, and the military. Boy soldiers are training as toy soldiers to become real soldiers. These characteristics that boys are expected to adopt not only influence how boys view themselves, but it also affects how they view girls and how they treat them. To be the stoic Rambo or G.I. Joe, willing to die for a cause, one has to suspend the notion of love. Not only are the traits and characteristics presented by the *DSM* and the media the only ones that boys must adopt, interest in girls is the only acceptable expression of love. But as love is a girl's trait, boys are expected, then, to express something more like lust. Stoicism is very important in the shaping of a boy soldier, because then he does not really question how he is to look or act. He also does not question orders that will be eventually given to him in a military setting. Girls are viewed less as beings with feelings and senses and more as just physical objects, which in turn influences how girls perceive themselves. Athletes, like soldiers, are expected to be stoic, devoid of emotion and "softness," and controlled in their manner, diet, and relationships. Indeed, many athletes are instructed to not see or touch their romantic partners before a big game. There is an expectation of deprivation, and that a real man can "do without" the softer side of life.

Whereas boys are to be hypermasculine, girls are to be hypersexual. Not to be left out, girls are also profiled in the *DSM* with possible GID, and these are girls that do not engage in stereotypical girl behaviors and act more masculine than they should. For every characteristic listed for boys in the *DSM*, there is a counterpart for girls. This in turn means that girls demand that any boy they are interested in adhere to a hypermasculine ideal if they are to garner the interest of that girl. The girl in turn will attempt her best to adopt the physical characteristics that any boy soldier would want her to have, just as long as he does not show too much emotional interest. The media and psychological community work together to create a vicious cycle where boys attempt to adopt unattainable physical characteristics. Likewise, boys expect girls to adopt unattainable physical characteristics and vice versa.

Taking into consideration the development of male body image is an important factor in the health and development of children. We have to do more than just focus on how the media and society place demands on girls and their self-image; we must also look at how the media and society place demands on boys' body image and on how they appropriately share their feelings and emotions. To do this we will need to take a strong, critical look at not only the media and their presentation of adolescent body images, but also at institutions and individuals that are there to provide emotional and physical support for children, such as schools and mental health professionals. Children should be provided a supportive community where they are able to develop and grow and establish normal and obtainable images of themselves and others.

Further Reading

Campbell, Joseph. *The Hero with a Thousand Faces.* Princeton, NJ: Princeton University Press, 1949.

Diagnostic Statistical Manual for Mental Disorders, Fourth Edition, Technical Revision. Washington, DC: American Psychiatric Association, 2000.

Egan, Timothy. "Body-Conscious Boys Adopt Athletes' Taste for Steroids." *The New York Times.* November 22, 2002.

Kellner, Douglas. *Media Culture: Cultural Studies, Identity and Politics between the Modern and the Postmodern.* New York: Routledge, 1995.

Daniel Rhodes

Dance

The 2000 film *Billy Elliott* (later a Broadway musical) brought to mainstream audiences worldwide the vision of an 11-year-old boy who rejects his family's traditions and his town's expectations by choosing to go to ballet class instead of boxing lessons. With the guidance of an understanding ballet mistress, a large amount of skill, and a strong awareness of the joy and excitement that dance offers him, Billy goes on to win his family's approval, a scholarship to the Royal Ballet School, and the principal role in a successful all-male version of *Swan Lake.* Although its ending shows a celebration of this particular boy who dances, much of the film depicts Billy's struggle to gain acceptance as a dancer and to pursue dance as a worthwhile activity for boys.

For much of the past century, classical or art dance has carried the label of being an activity reserved for girls, and many boys who dance have lived experiences similar to those of the fictional Billy: when they have chosen to pursue dance, they have discovered the pains of not being accepted by their peers or adults. The history of ballet suggests, however, that this perception of dance as not worthy of boys is a relatively recent phenomenon. At its beginnings in Renaissance Italy and its subsequent development in the French courts, not only were boys selected as star pupils for eventual high-paying roles, but they were also encouraged by their families to study dance in order to gain prestige and favor. France's Louis XIV danced ballet during much of his long reign as monarch, and in 1653, at the age of 15, he performed the signal role of the sun god Apollo in the *Ballet de la Nuit* ("Ballet of the Night"), thus solidifying for his courtiers his image as the Sun King. Boys throughout Europe learned dance as a skill, alongside reading, writing, and fencing, all of which would make of them more honorable and honored men. Historians have proposed that it may have been in the nineteenth century, as women were placed onto the pedestals of the newly developed pointe shoes, that art dance began to be perceived as an activity worthy only for females. Leaping onto the stages of Paris in 1909 as principal dancer with Serge de Diaghilev's Ballets Russes, having already danced leading roles in St. Petersburg's Mariinsky Theater as a teenager, the strikingly talented, strong, and muscular Vaslav Nijinsky showed the world again that boys who dance could make significant contributions to the art.

Billy Elliott reminds us that this reclaiming of the stage as a respected space for boys and men is not yet fully complete, and the more general acceptance of the moves of the b-boys in school playgrounds and on screen may stand in sharp contrast to some of the struggles lived by the art dancer. Certain contemporary boy cultures reach out to embrace the art dance, however. Boys-only classes have sprung up across North America, for example, created by ballet companies in an express effort to show that boys who dance may have unique contributions more appropriately developed alongside those of other boys. A movement toward reappraisal of the physical skills developed in dance has led schools and professional enterprises to send athletic teams to ballet class; it is becoming increasingly common to see high school football players doing deep *pliés* as a way to forestall injury and to develop agility. Online communities, through Facebook, MySpace, or other social networking systems, have offered significant camaraderie for those boys in towns or cities where other boy dancers might not exist. Furthermore, the conscious reappropriation of stereotypes, as in the t-shirt slogan, "Hey Sissy Boy, Real Athletes Dance," may well undermine conventional ideas and point to the notion that some boys who dance, such as Louis XIV and Nijinsky before them, have learned to celebrate their difference, their skill, and their strength.

Further Reading

Au, Susan. *Ballet and Modern Dance.* New York: Thames & Hudson, 1988.

Billy Elliott, DVD. Directed by Stephen Daltry. Screenplay by Lee Hall. London: Universal Studios, 2000.

Burt, Ramsay. *The Male Dancer.* New York: Routledge, 1995.

Gruska, Denise. *The Only Boy in Ballet Class.* Layton, UT: Gibbs Smith, 2007.

Charles R. Batson

Extreme Sports

The term *extreme sports* came to prominence in the mid-1990s to refer to a unique collection of physical activities performed mainly by youthful male participants that involved taking risks, seeking thrills, pushing personal limits, breaking rules, and having fun as part of the sports experience. Sports as different as skateboarding, snowboarding, sky surfing, bungee jumping, street luge, wakeboarding, BASE jumping, Eco-challenge, mountain biking, and BMX and Moto-cross dirt jumping have been labeled as *extreme* sports. Participants in these activities consciously defined themselves and their sporting cultures as different from more traditional, mainstream American team sports such as baseball, basketball, or football. Extreme sports often appeal to athletes because they allow participants greater control over their sporting experience, as extreme sports usually lack coaches and formal team structures. While many sporting activities that have come to be understood as "extreme sports" have been around for decades, prior to the 1990s, there was little, if any, shared community between participants in these activities. But with Entertainment and Sports Programming Network's (ESPN) creation of *The Extreme Games* in 1995, extreme sports became commercialized and institutionalized, resulting in a number of new formal and informal associations between many of these sports.

Birth of Extreme Sports

The birth of extreme sports is due to a number of social conditions. First, extreme sports are a product of the contemporary emphasis on youth, leisure, and lifestyle that originated in the post–World War II era of American prosperity. As more and more middle-class Americans enjoyed a relatively prosperous life with new opportunities for leisure, more individuals created new sport forms in which to express and challenge themselves as individuals. Seeking to escape the hierarchies and individual constraints offered in traditional team sports, alternative sport participants created a host of informal activities that emphasized participant freedom, cooperation among group members, risk taking, individual progress, and seeking thrills and excitement.

Extreme sports are also a product of the expansion of cable television—specifically of ESPN's efforts to expand its programming through the launching of ESPN2. ESPN2 was originally created to be a younger, hipper version of ESPN. To promote their new fledgling channel, the network created *The Extreme Games,* an Olympics-like competition featuring sports such as skateboarding, sky surfing, street luge, bungee jumping, and BMX bike riding, among others.

Third, the birth of extreme sports was influenced by the cultural interest in Generation X during the mid-1990s. Generation X, popularized by American media and marketers of the time, referred to Americans born between the years of 1961–1981. Generation Xers were imagined as youth interested more in leisure than career-oriented work and who appeared to be seeking different and alternative lifestyles than their parents. As extreme sports were imagined at this time as sports enjoyed by a younger generation of boys who preferred expressing their own individuality through sport, playing without adult authority figures, and rebelling against social norms, extreme sports became regarded as the sports of this new generation. The idea of generational differences was particularly championed by marketers at the time who were interested in tapping into an increasingly lucrative young male market. The rapid emergence of extreme sports during the 1990s was partially the product of corporate and media elites seeking to develop programming that would reach the highly coveted 12–34-year-old male demographic, which marketers estimated as possessing $700 billion in spending power. During the 1990s, extreme sports and the "extreme" ethos were used to sell a wide range of products from soft drinks to snacks to automobiles to tennis rackets to clothing.

Finally, the extreme sports phenomenon is a product of the United States' new awareness of, and interest in, cultural diversity during the 1990s. This new awareness of racial representation and opportunity in American culture and society led many to ask critical questions about how people of color (including whites) were represented in the media, as well as who had access to high-status positions in American society (i.e., government, law, medicine, etc.) following the civil rights movement. American professional sports were hardly immune from this critical analysis. Sport sociologists have noted that extreme sports, which are performed by and largely represented in the American media through stories and images of young white boys and men, emerged on the American national sporting scene at a time when public concerns arose about the numeric and on-field dominance of Black athletes in the traditional American team sports. The rapid rise of extreme sports during the 1990s is interpreted as part of a cultural struggle over which American male professional athletes would become the sporting idols, influencing the dreams and aspirations of the next generation of American boys—an increasingly Black and brown set of men playing traditional American sports such as basketball and football, or a set of white boys and young men participating in these new extreme sports. At the same time, other scholars point out that as extreme sports and their participants were imagined as rebellious, strange, nonconventional, and, in a nutshell, "different," these young white boys and men came to symbolize a different sort of white male who embraced cultural difference. Thus, extreme sports are implicated in the United States' contemporary struggle over the extent to which we have made meaningful progress on racial matters in and beyond sports in the post–civil rights era.

A Decade of Extreme Sports

Most would mark the origin of extreme sports with ESPN's creation of *The Extreme Games*. The brainchild of ESPN director of programming, Ron Semiao, executive director, Jack Weinert, and general manager, Chris Stiepock, *The Extreme Games* were first held in Newport, Rhode Island, in the summer of 1995. Close to 200,000 spectators attended the first event. The following year, ESPN decided to change the name of the event to *The X Games* because of the over-exposure of the term extreme. In 1997, ESPN took another step in following the sporting model of the modern Olympic Games by adding the *Winter X Games* to its summer version. This first *Winter X Games* was held at Snow Summit Mountain Resort in California. As of 2008, not only does ESPN still annually hold the summer and winter installments of the *X Games*, but it also holds *X Games* internationally as well, signaling the fact that the *X Games* are now a global brand.

In 1999, NBC sought to capitalize on the popularity of extreme sports by creating its own extreme sports competition called *The Gravity Games* (with summer and winter versions) to rival the popularity of the *X Games*. Extreme sports programming became a staple of afternoon programming for ESPN and Fox Sports networks in the late 1990s. Further evidence of the popularity of extreme sports and their integration into the sporting mainstream is the International Olympics Committee decision to add snowboarding as a medal competition in the 1998 Winter Olympics held in Nagano, Japan.

In 2008, images of extreme sports and extreme athletes became ubiquitous throughout American media culture. Films such as *Dogtown and Z Boys, Lords of Dogtown, First Descent, XXX,* and *Blue Crush* feature extreme sports such as skateboarding, snowboarding, sky surfing, and surfing. Extreme sport participants such as skateboarder, Tony Hawk, skateboarder and snowboarder, Shaun White, and big-wave surfer, Laird Hamilton, are as well known to young boys as traditional team sport athletes such as football player, Peyton Manning, or basketball player, LeBron James. Today, the best athletes in marquee extreme sports such as skateboarding, snowboarding, surfing, and BMX bike riding and Moto-Cross become wealthy through earnings from prize money and endorsement deals.

Seeking to profit from the lucrative market of home-made skateboarding and BMX videos made independently by young male skaters and riders in their local communities, Music Television (MTV) has from the late 1990s to the present offered a number of programs featuring young white males, programs in which participating in extreme sports such as skateboarding are a central part of the show. This trend began with the pain-inducing, masochistic pranks performed on one another by the cast of *Jackass* and skateboarder, Bam Margera's spin-off show, *Viva La Bam*. More recently, less edgy shows such as *Rob &*

Big and *Life of Ryan* feature the lives of professional skateboarders, Rob Dyrdek and Ryan Sheckler, respectively. MTV has also become the place where some of the icons of extreme sports athletes such as youthful male skateboarders, Tony Hawk and Bob Burnquist, as well as BMX riders, Mat Hoffman and Dave Mirra, are regularly featured on their popular show, *MTV Cribs,* which showcases the prosperous lifestyles of young actors, musicians, and athletes.

When skateboarding, snowboarding, in-line skating, and BMX riding first hit the scene in the mid-1990s, participants in these activities debated the virtues and pitfalls of having their sports co-opted and taken over by media conglomerates such as ESPN/ABC/Disney and other corporate/commercial interests. Although a few participants sought to maintain the outsider and subcultural status of these activities, many of the best performers could not refuse the big money being offered to them to participate in competitions such as the *X Games* or to endorse various products. Today, American media and corporate interests have thoroughly invaded and reconstituted extreme sports. It is impossible not to consider extreme sports as part of the mainstream of a modern global sporting culture. Indeed, extreme sports are now a global phenomenon and boys across many Westernized countries such as Brazil, Japan, South Africa, New Zealand, and Norway now participate in extreme sports.

Further Reading

Greenfeld, Karl. "Life on the Edge." *Time,* December 6, 1999.

Howe, Susanna. *(Sick): A Cultural History of Snowboarding.* New York: St. Martin's Griffin, 1998.

Koerner, Brendan. "Extreeeme." *US News & World Report,* June 30, 1997.

Price, S. L. "Whatever Happened to the White Athlete?" *Sports Illustrated,* December 8, 1997.

Rinehart, Robert. *Players All: Performances in Contemporary Sport.* Bloomington and Indianapolis, IN: Indiana University Press, 1998.

Rinehart, Robert, and Synthia Sydnor, eds. *To the Extreme: Alternative Sports, Inside and Out.* Albany, NY: State University of New York Press, 2003.

Weyland, Jocko. *The Answer Is Never: A Skateboarder's History of the World.* New York: Grove Press, 2002.

Wheaton, Belinda, ed. *Understanding Lifestyle Sports: Consumption, Identity, and Difference.* Oxfordshire, Great Britain: Routledge, 2004.

Kyle Kusz

Football

Jim Brown, Joe Namath, Red Grange, George Gipp, Johnny Unitas, Walter Peyton, Gale Sayers, Dan Marino, John Elway, Joe Montana, Jerry Rice, Tom Brady, Terry Bradshaw, Franco Harris, Roger Staubach, Emmett Smith, Barry Sanders, Brett Favre, and Peyton Manning are names that immediately conjure images of males covered in padding, helmets, going into huddles. Internationally, several sports are referred to as "football"; however, this entry discusses North American football, specifically American football. The term is also used to describe what non–North Americans call soccer and rugby. Canadian and Australian football is related to American football but retain particular definitions and rules.

Anthropological research reveals that there were games in China that resemble current football. As early as 500 BC, Cuju, the earliest known form of football, was developed in China, where players kicked a ball over a goal; the game spread to other Asian nations, and different adaptations of the sport took hold. Along with ancient Rome and Greece, aboriginal peoples also played variations of this game in their societies. The games universally contained some sort of ball that was manipulated by a team in order to score a goal.

It is traditionally acknowledged that William Heffelfinger from Pennsylvania organized the first football games in 1892. The American Professional Football Association played its first game in Ohio in 1922. The National Football League (NFL) was created, and it continues to this day.

The biggest differences between American and Canadian football are in the size of the field and in the number of downs played. American football fields are 100 yards in length, and at the end of each rectangular field there is a goal. Yard lines are drawn, usually by chalk, every five yards down the field (origin of the word gridiron). The goalposts are usually made of steel, and vary in size, depending on the division of football (high school, college, or NFL). Each football team has 11 players on the field at once, but the bench may contain up to 35 additional players. Football is played in four quarters, with a halftime break after the second quarter. Many times, the halftime show or activities become as important as the game in college or professional football.

Non-Professional Football

Although some Canadian universities have football teams, when one refers to college football, the words are clearly associated with four-year American university football. Within the NCAA (National Collegiate Athletic Association), divisions are created, reflecting the skill level of each team. The NCAA organizes all sports teams in higher education into conferences (groupings of teams in geographic areas or skill levels), and they control rulings, championships, media, and recruitment and retention rules. The NCAA has conferences in basically five different categories: Division I, Division II, Division III, Division I-A Football Bowls, and Affiliate Member Organizations. College teams play within their own conferences during the fall season, and winners from those conferences play in bowl games that begin in mid-December and end the first week of January. Bowl games are held in the southern part of the United States, as the winter in the North is too harsh. The most well-known bowl games are "The Rose Bowl," "The Orange Bowl," "The Fiesta Bowl," and "The Cotton Bowl." Since 1998, the larger bowl games rotate the national NCAA championship game.

College football players are usually recruited by the schools based on the players' high school performance. Most American high schools highlight football as their key sport—whereas Canadian schools often do not have a school football team. Young American males begin playing football in boys' organizations and during elementary school. Pop Warner Football is an organized nonprofit group created to promote football for boys. Established in 1929, the Pop Warner (named after Coach Pop Warner) has assisted many young men in football careers.

Professional Football

During the NCAA season, professional football recruiters travel to find the best draft choices for the spring football draft. Professional teams are given draw positions to select their choice players. The lower-ranking teams draft their choices first, in an attempt to keep the NFL competitive. Not all college players end up in the NFL, and unfortunately, many are injured during their careers and do not last. A myth of riches surrounds football players, and many assume that all professional players are rich. Actually, although playing in the NFL does pay a good salary, it is only the stars who make millions. If one is injured in play, and is not a star, that player can be looking at a very difficult change of career.

In 1960, the American Football League (AFL) was formed to be a competitive league to the NFL. During the 1960s, many memorable games, coaches, and players came from both leagues. However, in 1969, the AFL folded back into the NFL. In 1967, the AFL and the NFL played the first Super Bowl, and this continued until 1970 when the Super Bowl became the NFL championship game. The Super Bowl is the quintessential championship game and Super Bowl Sunday, now played in late January or early February, is a North American phenomenon. Not only football fans, but also families and friends gather in the day-long ritual of not only watching football, but also the premiere of unique television advertising and multi-million dollar halftime shows.

Popular culture has used football battles in many films and TV programs, and one can easily see cheerleaders, large stadiums, overhead lights, and loudspeakers as they watch films such as *The Longest Yard, Any Given Sunday, Brian's Song, Jerry Maguire, Knute Rockne: All American, Everybody's All-American, North Dallas Forty, Remember the Titans, Rudy, Varsity Blues,* and *We Are Marshall.* In fact, football films are usually a guaranteed Hollywood success and draw audiences of all ages and interest levels.

It would be difficult to not name football as the all-American sport, from little toddlers kicking a ball around the backyard, to joining Pop Warner, to watching Friday night high school football games and the late-winter Super Bowl. Both men and women love football, but as far as school football, NCAA, or NFL is concerned, football is a male performance sport, most probably due to the need for bulk, size, and physical power in the game.

Further Reading

The American Football Coaches Association. *The Football Coaching Bible.* Champaign, IL: Human Kinetics, 2002.

Fleder, Rob, ed. *Sports Illustrated: The Football Book. Sports Illustrated,* 2005.

Fundamentals of Youth Football: Basic Skills and Practice Drills, DVD. Directed by Bill Richardson, www.sportsvideo.com, 2004.

Shirley R. Steinberg

Hockey

Just as baseball is considered to be the American national pastime, Canadians hold hockey up as "their" game (even though officially, lacrosse is the Canadian national sport). Hockey is a team sport that is fast-paced, physically rough (often to the point of violence), and requires tremendous strength; as such, it embodies traditional Western notions of masculinity.

The National Hockey League (NHL), which is the professional hockey league in North America, started in 1917. This league began with five Canadian teams: the Montreal Canadiens, the Ottawa Senators, the Toronto Arenas, the Montreal Wanderers, and the Quebec Bulldogs. However, by 1942, some of these Canadian teams folded while new American teams were created. The six franchises of 1942, which are now known as "The Original Six," still exist today: the Boston Bruins, the Chicago Blackhawks, the Detroit Red Wings, the Montreal Canadiens, the New York Rangers, and the Toronto Maple Leafs. The NHL is comprised only of male players (Manon Rhéaume, a female goalie, played in preseason games with the Tampa Bay Lightening in 1992 and 1993).

The sport's primarily male fan base has always been fiercely loyal, which was partly due to the unfair labor standards in the National Hockey League in the 1940s: the owners of The Original Six teams worked together to ensure that the players were not paid very much money, so it was quite rare for players to be offered higher wages to play for another team. As such, players were rarely traded and they often played for one team for their entire career. This means that fans strongly identified with *their* team's players: for example, Montreal fans worshipped Maurice "The Rocket" Richard, Jean Beliveau, Elmer Lach, and Toe Blake, while Chicago fans looked up to Bobby Hull, Stan Mikita, and Bill Mosienko. As the labor standards changed and ensured much higher wages and more mobility for the players, most players came to be traded several times throughout their careers. These days, fans root for their favorite team (whether it is their hometown team or not), and there is somewhat less intense hometown hero worship among hockey fans than in the earlier years of the NHL (although notable players, such as Wayne Gretzky, Mario Lemieux, and Martin Brodeur, have garnered huge fan bases both in their teams' cities and in other cities as well).

Unlike Canadian hockey fans, Americans took longer to adapt to the sport and create its fan base. Still today baseball, football, and basketball are the true "American" sports. Recent success with American NHL teams has stirred up interest and inspired many young boys to join amateur and local hockey teams. And since 1993 American NHL teams have taken the Stanley Cup home every year: New York, New Jersey, Detroit, Colorado, Tampa Bay, Carolina, and Anaheim. These championships have exposed hockey to young people and allowed the NHL to market the sport to this generation of young American boys. It is common to see the NHL sponsoring local hockey tournaments and promoting amateur hockey in hopes of keeping and fostering a larger fan base. The fresh young talents of Pittsburgh Penguins' Sidney Crosby and Washington Capitals' Alexander Ovechkin have created a great following and their contribution to amateur hockey encourages young boys to continue playing. Both players are actively involved with local hockey organization to keep boys off the streets and playing sports. For example, Sidney Crosby is actively involved with Tim Hortons Timbits Minor Sports Program,

> Tim Hortons currently sponsors over 200,000 children who play on hockey, soccer, lacrosse, t-ball, baseball and ringette teams across Canada and in the United States. Each sponsored team is supplied with Timbits Minor Sports jerseys or T-shirts. Timbits hockey teams are often given the opportunity to play on-ice scrimmages during intermissions at Junior, American Hockey League (AHL) and National Hockey League (NHL) games. Timbits players are also given the opportunity to play in their own "Timbits Jamboree," a fun-filled Tim Hortons sponsored event where everyone receives a prize, food and beverages. (Tim Horton's Web site, 2009)

It is these initiatives that create a buzz and keep young boys investing time and energy in a sport they love. It is also important to mention that just like every other sort of fan base, there are many young boys who do not actually participate in hockey but are interested in following and cheering for a team. It gives them a sense of belonging to a team—the fan base—and many of these fans are the ones who produce and generate fan videos online, create fan-based groups in social networking sites, and so on.

Even in the early days of the sport, when it was still largely the domain of an elite class, hockey was heavily influenced by a traditional British public-school sensibility (Gruneau and Whitson, 1993). Unlike basketball or soccer, it is a sport that has always required a lot of specialized equipment, which has historically meant that at a professional level, it has been a game for boys from the upper and middle class. Roy McGregor (1986), a writer who has written several books about hockey, puts it this way: "The family of modern hockey too often means two parents, two cars, money for registration, money for equipment, money for ice time, tournaments, jackets, parties, and snack bars" (22). It is not a sport that is necessarily accessible to all boys, so many make do with what is available to them: some play street hockey with a tennis ball, hockey sticks, and an improvised goal rather than joining a local organized hockey team. Others will play pick-up games at their local outdoor rink during the winter. And interestingly, there are several stories of hockey-playing boys from the working class who eventually made it big: In the 1930s, a boy from Owen's Sound, Ontario, strapped Eaton's Department Store catalogues to his shins as goalie pads, because he couldn't afford to buy pads. That boy was Harry Lumley, who went on to play as a goalie in four of The Original Six teams. Another boy from Truso, Ontario, often slept in his hockey uniform (except for his helmet), woke up before dawn, and snuck into his local broken-down arena to practice his technique before going to school. That boy was Guy Lafleur, who is one of the most dynamic players the NHL has ever known (Turowetz and Goyens, 1986).

Further Reading

MacGregor, Roy. *The Home Team: Fathers, Sons, and Hockey.* New York: Viking Press, 1986.

Turowetz, Allan, and Goyens, Chris. *Lions in Winter.* Hoboken, NJ: Wiley, 1986.
Whitson, David, and Gruneau, Richard. *Hockey Night in Canada: Sports, Identities, and Cultural Politics.* Aurora, ON: Garamond Press, 1993.

Giuliana Cucinelli

Martial Arts

Many North American boys participate in traditional martial arts classes primarily as a hobby or sport. As in football or hockey, practitioners train in groups, and often focus on learning specific self-defense techniques through mental and physical conditioning. Such training can help build self-confidence, socialization skills, self-discipline, and positively impact physical and mental health. Some examples of traditional martial arts include karate, tae kwon do, wushu, and aikido.

As a practical means of self-defense, many martial arts focus primarily on realistic strategies and skills to avoid physical confrontation or escape physical harm. Boys can benefit from training in such martial arts to the extent that they learn to recognize risky situations and prevent physical violence, while at the same time retaining the ability to defend themselves. For younger boys these martial arts typically focus on personal safety skills, anti-bullying, self-esteem building, and fun social activities. For older boys most martial arts begin to focus more on physical conditioning, training in specific techniques, and discipline. As a result the same martial art can be learned and taught in a number of different ways, depending on the age and specific needs of the students. For example, sparring exercises between training partners is reserved for older boys in certain martial arts, while in others it is adapted and changed to suit younger students. Many martial arts are adapted to a wide variety of situations including those not based on formal classes or training.

In popular media, martial arts are portrayed as entertainment rather than a sport that is taught for practical application. Martial arts movies make up an entire film genre; film stars including Bruce Lee, Chuck Norris, Steven Seagal, Sylvester Stallone, and many others have considerable impact on boys' fascination with specific martial arts. For example, Lee is known in North America for popularizing various forms of kung fu including a hybrid form of martial arts that he founded called *jeet kune do.* More recent cable television and Internet based multimedia broadcasting combative martial arts competitions has popularized mixed martial arts (MMA), which consists of a blend of several styles of martial arts and is often seen in televised contests. Commercial competitions such as the Ultimate Fighting Championship, Pride, Elite Xtreme Combat, International Fight League, and many other similar organized contests maintain a considerable following of mostly young male viewers. Surrounding such competitions are public concerns over the extremity of violence, the safety of the competitors, and the effect of fighting contests on young viewers. Although publicized martial arts competitions are nothing new, these modern MMA competitions appear to challenge the conventions of many traditional martial arts. Kickboxing, wrestling, grappling, and other competition-oriented styles of martial arts can be combined, resulting in a more flexible system of rules and acceptable techniques. And although MMA and other hybrid martial arts styles can lead to innovation in the technical aspects of organized competition, refining styles in this way increases the risk of losing important noncompetitive aspects of traditional martial arts.

The historical, cultural, and spiritual connections held within many traditional martial arts offer more than technical lessons in self-defense. The origins of individual styles of martial arts are often particular to one region, town, family, or historical period. As a result, some martial arts retain unique words, concepts, and customs specific to their historical context; this places emphasis on cultural traditions, values, and beliefs over training and preparation for competition. Some examples of this include practicing meditation, spiritual contemplation, philosophical inquiry, and physical artistic expression. Such features are present in a variety of forms across many martial arts and especially characteristic of styles such as tai chi chuan, iaido, and capoeira.

Further Reading

Anglo, Sydney. *The Martial Arts of Renaissance Europe*. New Haven, CT: Yale University Press, 2000.

Green, Thomas A., and Svinth, Joseph R., eds. *Martial Arts in the Modern World*. Westport, CT: Praeger, 2003.

Lowry, Dave. *In the Dojo: The Rituals and Etiquette of the Japanese Martial Arts*. Boston, MA: Weatherhill, 2006.

Rosenbaum, Michael. *The Fighting Arts: Their Evolution from Secret Societies to Modern Times*. Boston, MA: YMAA Publication Center, 2002.

V. W. Goebel

Parkour

Parkour (PK) is a physical form of movement, which can also be regarded as an "art of displacement." Obstacles are overcome as one tries to follow a straight line from a starting point to a goal. Buildings, walls, or other obstacles are overcome as surely and effectively as possible by running, climbing, and jumping.

Parkour was founded by David Belle and his friends, Sébastien Foucan and the actor Hubert Koundé. The latter created the name from a form of military training called *parcours du combatant* that is used to practice escaping from opponents over various terrain. The participants are known as *traceur* (female: *traceuse*), which translated from the French means "they who leave a track," or "they that smooth the way." Suitable training areas for parkour are marked with spots.

Parkour was developed from a modification of *methode naturelle,* which David Belle learned from his father. Developed by Georges Hérbert around the beginning of the twentieth century, this artistic form of movement is supposed to unite athletic abilities with personal characteristics such as helpfulness, and subsequently train the body and spirit together along such lines. Natural obstacles should be overcome during movement in harmony with nature and the environment. At the end of the 1980s, David Belle transferred such techniques to the suburb of Lises, Paris, where he lived.

The philosophy of parkour is to regard objects in public areas as obstacles that one can overcome. Thus the public area in its rigid and often commercialized function is reinterpreted, occupied, and recovered in a different manner. It is important for the traceur to respectfully manage the urban or natural environment and their fellow man, on whose understanding they are dependent upon in the long run. The basic idea of parkour is to recognize and overcome the limits set by the human body and the environment. No aids may be used and the obstacles may not be changed or altered. It is also important not to push toward risk-taking, but to remain within the context of one's own mental and physical capabilities.

Degrees of difficulty are only slowly increased through long training, which is advantageous for avoiding injury or causing undue risks. Due to the high level and years of training necessary, parkour cannot be regarded as a trend sport, or as a sport in the actual sense of the word, as competition is not involved. Efficiency, or the aim to surpass an obstacle with as little effort as possible, is closer to the actual credo of parkour. All movements should be implemented as flexibly and as dynamically as possible. Superfluous moves, such as salti, turns, and so forth, are considered a waste of bodily resources and are thereby declined.

It is only in a variation called *freerunning* created by one of the joint founders of parkour, Sébastien Foucan, that such supplementary acrobatic and/or aesthetic elements play a larger role. In this variation, rather than being looked upon more as an art of displacement, the beauty of movement, along with elements of dance and other spectacular moves are more effectively characterized. Parkour is represented internationally by the Parkour Worldwide Association (PAWA), which functions as a union of like-minded practitioners and fans alike.

Parkour and other related arts have become well known through the media and marketing of films, music videos, and video games. In 2001, the feature film *Yamakasi—The Samurai of the Modern Age* and in 2004, *District 13*, in which David Belle participated, are good examples. Likewise film scenes including parkour such as *Live Free or Die Hard* with Cyril Raffaelli, a friend of David Belles, or the James Bond film *Casino Royale* (2006) with Sébastien Foucan have further established its familiarity.

There are also various other examples such as the music videos Jump and Hang Up by Madonna. In the world of video games, parkour elements are widely represented, beginning with Prince of Persia right up to Spider Man, Tomb Raider, or Free Running, which is based primarily on the movement art form of the same name.

Further Reading

American Parkour [Online]. <http://www.americanparkour.com>.
Parkour North America [Online]. <http://parkournorthamerica.com>.
Pourkourpedia [Online]. <http://www.parkourpedia.com>.
Wilkinson, Alec. "No Obstacles. Navigating the World by Leaps and Bounds." *The New Yorker*, April 16, 2007 [Online April 2008]. <http://www.newyorker.com/reporting/2007/04/16/070416fa_fact_wilkinson?currentPage=all>.

Maren Zschach

Skateboarding

Skateboarding is a popular American extreme sport that has become an important element of youth culture, particularly boy culture. More than just a hobby or activity, skateboarding has become an important lifestyle choice for countless young men, particularly white teenage boys. Throughout its history, there has been a tension between the image of skateboarding as a legitimate sport and its image as an underground movement, a tension that has become more intense as skateboarding has become more commercial.

The roots of skateboarding can be traced to the early decades of the 1900s, when teenagers created milk crate scooters out of wood and steel roller skate wheels. The first commercially produced skateboard was the Roller Derby Skateboard in 1959. Although skateboarding became popular throughout the United States, early skateboarding was closely linked to surfing, and California quickly became the epicenter for skateboarding activity. Larry Stevenson, publisher of *Surf Guide*, produced the first professional skateboards with pressed wood and clay wheels in 1963 through his company, Makaha. Stevenson also formed a skate team and sponsored the first skateboard competition in Hermosa, California, in 1963. Early skateboarding style, called "freestyle," was very different than skateboarding today, and resembled ballet or ice skating using a skateboard. Notable skateboarders from the era include Danny Berer, Woody Woodward, and Torger Johnson. In spite of its early popularity, interest in skateboarding had faded by the mid-1960s due in large part to inferior technology and growing safety concerns.

In 1972, Frank Nasworthy invented urethane skateboard wheels and began producing them through a California company called Cadillac Wheels. Unlike clay or steel, urethane wheels were more stable and soft, and offered more grip. Better boards sparked a whole new interest in the sport, which evolved throughout the 1970s into the skateboarding we know today. The famed Zephyr Skateboarding team was formed in 1975, and included Tony Alva, Jay Adams, Stacy Peralta, and Peggy Oki. The Zephyr (or Z-Boy) style of skateboarding was more like surfing than the freestyle skating of the day, and their low and smooth style became the basis for modern skateboarding. Peralta depicts the experiences of the Zephyr team and the growth of 1970s skateboarding in his 2001 documentary *Dogtown and Z-Boys*. The Zephyr team was notable for skating in empty swimming pools, the basis for vertical or *vert* skating. In 1978, the skater Alan Gelfan (nicknamed "Ollie") revolutionized the sport by inventing the ollie, a maneuver that forms the basis for almost all street-skating tricks. All the advances in technology and techniques led to a growing interest in skateboarding as an exhibition sport. Several skateboarders including Tony Alva, Russ Howell, and Ty Page began to claim sponsorships and endorsements. During the 1970s, skateboarding began to emerge as both a real, legitimate sport as well as an underground, rebellious movement, a far cry from being just the popular American hobby it had been in the 1960s.

In the 1980s, skateboarding solidified its reputation as an urban, alternative youth culture. Despite the fact that skate parks had existed for several years, skateboarders became known for practicing illegally in public spaces, as well as abandoned buildings and parking lots. Skating became associated with punk music, even inspiring a subgenre of skate-punk (also called thrash or skate-core) that included notable bands such as the Descendents, Agent Orange, Bad Religion, and Suicidal Tendencies. Two magazines devoted to skateboarding began publishing: *Thrasher* magazine in 1981 and *Transworld Skateboarding* in 1983. *Thrasher* was started by Fausto Vitello, owner of the Independent Truck Company, and promoted the underground culture of skateboarding with a "skate and destroy" mantra. Larry Balma founded *Transworld Skateboarding* as a direct response to the anti-establishment attitude of *Thrasher,* and geared the magazine toward positively promoting the sport. Skateboard videos also became popular in the 1980s. Stacey Peralta formed the Bones Brigade Team in 1984 and produced several videos featuring skaters such as Tony Hawk, Steve Caballero, and Rodney Mullen. The vast majority of skateboarders were young men, and skateboarding culture reinforced the accepted notion that skateboarding was almost strictly a boy's world. Girls did participate in the sport, and were periodically featured in magazines or videos, but when skating superstars began to emerge, they were almost inevitably male. Skateboarding offered young men the opportunity to participate in a sport with a "hard core" attitude, but many also regarded the sport and its culture as a way to express themselves. Many skaters also discovered an entrepreneurial opportunity in skateboarding, and many young men started their own skateboard and merchandising companies. During this time, street skating became immensely popular, overshadowing vert skating.

Skateboarding took a more prominent position in popular culture starting in the mid-1980s, expanding well beyond its booming population of skaters. Skateboard fashion, including baggy jeans, oversized shirts, and graffiti-style logos, became more popular. The Beastie Boys, skate-punk hip hop artists, released *Licensed to Ill* in 1986. Films about skateboarding were released, including *Thrashin'* in 1986 and *Gleaming the Cube* in 1989. In 1987, the animated series about skateboarding and pizza-eating *Teenage Mutant Teenage Turtles* began appearing on television to skyrocketing popularity. Bart Simpson, perhaps the most notorious pop culture skateboarder of all time, debuted as part of the *The Simpsons* in 1989. In 1991, director Spike Jonze, who had done photography for *Transworld,* teamed up with editors from several small skateboard and BMX magazines to launch a magazine called *Dirt,* a spin-off of *Sassy* magazine that was targeted to skateboarding teen boys. *Dirt* never caught on in popularity, and Jonze moved on to producing skate videos and co-founding Girl Skateboards.

Even as it maintained its bad boy reputation, skateboarding became even more popular and commercially successful as the teen market increased throughout the 1990s. In 1995, ESPN debuted the *Extreme Games* (renamed the *X Games* in 1996), legitimizing skateboarding as a sport while also maintaining its rebellious, counterculture status. Both street skating and vert skating were featured in the games, and vert skating regained popularity as a result. The *X Games* also ushered in a new era of extreme commercialization, as major sponsors such as Taco Bell and Mountain Dew began to represent their products as essential markers of youth subculture. Since the late 1990s, skateboarding has become even more mainstream, and although it still retains its edgy reputation, the appearance of skateboard shops in shopping malls, skate parks in suburbs, and children's skateboards in department stores are signs that the sport has become an accepted and more conventional part of teen culture. In 2001, Stacy Peralta produced the popular skateboard documentary *Dogtown and Z-Boys*, which won the Audience and Directing Awards for Documentary at the Sundance Film Festival as well as the Best Documentary Award at the Independent Spirit Awards. Peralta later adapted his documentary into a screenplay for the film *Lords of Dogtown* in 2005.

There are many famous professional skateboarders, including Rodney Mullen, Bob Burnquist, Bucky Lasek, Andy MacDonald, Shaun White, Mike McGill, Andrew Reynold, Chad Muska, and Elissa Steamer. The most well-known skateboarder is Tony Hawk, who capitalized on his highly influential vert skating career by becoming a successful entrepreneur and role model. Hawk is widely regarded as the most influential vert skater; he invented a number of famous tricks in addition to being the first skater in recorded history to land a 900 at the 1999 *X Games*. Hawk successfully bridged the mainstream and counterculture elements of skateboarding to gain mass appeal. He is the owner of Birdhouse Skateboards; a film and production company called 900 Films; and Hawk clothing lines. His action sports tour, Tony Hawk's Boom Boom Huck Jam, regularly tours the United States. Hawk also worked with Activision to produce the wildly popular Tony Hawk's Pro Skater line of video games.

Further Reading

Brooke, Michael. *The Concrete Wave: The History of Skateboarding*. Los Angeles: Warwick Publishing, 1999.

Davis, James. *Skateboarding Is Not a Crime: 50 Years of Street Culture*. Buffalo: Firefly Books, 1999.

Rhinehart, Robert, and Synthia Sydnor. *To the Extreme: Alternative Sports, Inside and Out*. New York: State University of New York Press, 2003.

Tammy Oler

Soccer

Soccer, or football as it is known outside of North America, is a beautiful game, an international passion, a sport at once tactical, tough, and elegant. Boasting the highest youth participation levels of all team sports in North America, it ranks far behind (American) football, baseball, basketball, and hockey as a fan sport. It does, however, have a strong and passionate fan base in North America's varied immigrant communities. This becomes particularly evident during major international tournaments such as the World Cup and the European Cup, and to a lesser extent during the African Cup, the Asian Cup, and the Copa de las Americas.

Why soccer is popular among boys, or how it becomes a passion for many, is not a question that is easy to answer. (Soccer has a strong following among girls and women, but that is outside the parameters of this discussion.) To a great extent it is a family and community tradition, handed down from generation to generation; a cultural practice for some members of the many diasporic communities in North America; and an idiosyncratic love or passion for some families.

Soccer is a game played by two teams of eleven players. It is a game that relies on teamwork, on letting the ball do the work. It is also a game of direct one-on-one encounters where individual skill and flair can make the difference. Ball control, dribbling, passing, and shooting are kinetic skills. These skills are body knowledge that can be improved through verbal instruction, and can only be perfected through practice.

For soccer players, the love of the game is born through this kinetic engagement. Of course, each of the team sports played by boys in North America breeds tactile, kinetic, and emotional attachments. Although kicking a ball around differs from tossing the pigskin, shooting some hoops, batting a few fly balls, or shooting some pucks on net, it also shares elements with these other sports.

The soccer ball that is juggled (keep ups) or flicked over the head from behind (over the rainbow) is as much directed by the heart as the head. The curving, arcing shot on goal is a physical strike, but it is also a caress. Many coaches of juvenile players ask them to carry the ball around with them for a week, to walk it at their feet, and to sleep with it in their bed. One can only know the attachment to the game by living it.

For soccer fans, various elements come into play. The sport is tactical like chess. It is a thinking person's game. It is also a game of elegant movement, a dance of sorts, but one that combines the violence of collision with the grace of the deke (a technique or a move intended to deceive the opponent into moving out of position or to maneuver around an opponent). It is the game of the efficient movement, of short, sharp passes that "let the ball do the work" and of the impossible—balls that curve and dip in mid air and body dekes that let a player slip past another.

The professional soccer player is a star, an idol for many. The two individuals named Players of the 20th Century by FIFA, the world governing body of soccer, were Pele and Diego Maradona. These players were dramatists of the game, inventors of moves that had not been seen before, and leaders who took their respective national sides, Brazil and Argentina, respectively, to World Cup glory. Pele had a big impact on the internationalization of the game, but, in terms of breaking racial barriers, Pele's impact on soccer was not like Jackie Robinson's impact on baseball. Contemporary African-born soccer players are to some extent still trying to break the racial barriers. And contemporary players such as Ronaldinho are less Black than Brazilian, a slippery race-neutral zone perhaps pioneered by Pele.

Two contemporary players, Wayne Rooney and Christiano Ronaldo, both members of the world famous club team Manchester United at the time of this writing, embody two classic visions of the soccer player. Stocky and brutish, a bull dog with a snarl, Rooney's raging temper and punishing style make him the target of opponents looking to gain an advantage. Rooney is a ruthlessly effective striker who will take the ball to the net when given the opportunity. His teammate, Ronaldo, is silky smooth, a svelte and good-looking player who can dribble through a crowd, find the open man to pass to, or shoot on net himself. Christiano Ronaldo has it all—bearing, balance, skill, and imagination—and at the time of this writing, is considered the best soccer player in the world.

Further Reading

Hornby, Nick. *Fever Pitch.* New York: Riverhead Books, 1998.
Lanfanchi, Pierre, Christiane Eisenberg, Tony Mason, and Alfred Wahl. *100 Years of Football: The FIFA Centennial Book.* London: Weidenfeld & Nicolson, 2004.

Michael Hoechsmann

Sports and Masculinity

Through sports, boys learn a particular form of masculinity that is rooted in strength, courage, determination, and discipline. Furthermore, through participating in violent sports, boys are socialized to accept violence as a normal part of their masculine development. As such, violence and aggression can become ingrained into the identity of some boys as a means of achieving social prestige or status. This particular form of violent masculinity that is developed within the context of sports can be termed *sporting masculinity*.

The ideals of sporting masculinity can emerge in a number of ways. These include, although are certainly not limited to, overbearing fathers, disciplinary coaching styles, narratives of heroism, the promotion of violence, the social prestige of sports stardom, and strictly male interactions. Each of these aspects contributes, in greater or lesser degree, to the development of sporting masculinity for boys.

The overbearing father, or mother, within the world of sport, is one who endlessly pushes the child to excel. They attend every game, critique their child's play, and heckle the referees, coaches, and other fans. Their concern is not for their child, but for their child's success in sport. Examples of the overbearing father could include, for example, the hockey dad who gets into a physical altercation with the referee after the game because of a call involving his son, or the football dad who screams at his son to hit the opposing players harder. The child of the overbearing father is abused psychologically, emotionally, and/or physically, with the end of sporting success in mind.

Much like the overbearing father, the disciplinary coach pushes his or her players with reckless abandon to achieve team success in a given sport. They treat winning as the objective of sport, rather than having fun, meeting friends, and learning to live a healthy lifestyle. Examples of the disciplinary coach could include the coach who forces his football players to run five miles in excessive heat without letting them drink any water, or the volleyball coach who has his or her players spike balls at another player on the team who has missed a serve. Those children who play for disciplinary coaches rarely have fun, but they learn to win at whatever cost.

Young players come to accept the physical, psychological, and emotional abuse that is prevalent in many sporting contexts because of the social grandeur that is created through narratives of sporting heroism. Stories are often relayed to young athletes about the basketball player who tore several ligaments in his ankle but still returned to play in the final quarter of the game, heroically leading his team to victory; or about a hockey player who stopped the potential game-tying goal by diving in front of the net and taking the puck in his abdomen. Stories of such heroism, whether authentic or not, make all of the pains of rigorous sports worthwhile to some young athletes.

Tied to this notion of heroism in sport is the idea that the young athlete becomes a violent warrior of sorts. In some competitive sports such as football, rugby, lacrosse, and hockey, violence is not only an accepted part of the game but it is also often promoted. Young athletes are often taught to hit opposing players in ways that will temporary immobilize them or take them out; young athletes can also have parents and fans yelling at them to hit the opposing players harder. Harming other players through violence becomes a normal aspect of the sport.

The heroic warrior in sports is often given enormous social status or prestige. The high school basketball player who hits the game winning shot is often featured on the front page of the local community newspaper, while the professional hockey player who scores 50 goals in a season is rewarded with a multi-million dollar performance bonus. Athletes are given a measure of celebrity in North American culture. As such, the pains they endure in practice, the violence they commit on the field, and the many limits they push to achieve success—all these actions become accepted, and often promoted, by the larger society.

The sporting contexts of many young male athletes is often dominated by the presence of other males who have either played sports for much of their lives or are currently playing sports. Male sports is often a social institution that restricts the involvement of women. After the age of 10, it is rare to see both female and male hockey players sharing the same ice, and it would be even more of a unique occurrence to see a woman coaching a high school football team. In these contexts, young men interact primarily with other men and have less involvement with women.

These factors, among others, lead to the formation and perpetuation of sporting masculinity. Some boys in sporting contexts come to accept the physical, psychological, and emotional abuse from their fathers and coaches, believing that that is all part of winning and becoming a great athlete. They come to learn, adopt, and later perpetuate a masculine sporting identity where winning and personal excellence are the only things that matter. This identity is learned not only on the field or in the locker room, but in the car ride home from games, in school, in the media, and in the larger community.

Adopting a masculine sporting identity can have negative consequences on the players involved, as well as to others. Sports, when taken to these extremes, is often unhealthy for the players because they are forced to push their bodies to harmful limits by playing injured or injecting themselves with dangerous performance-enhancing substances. Furthermore, they are asked to go out and deliberately harm the players on opposing teams.

Such behaviors are then often exhibited off the field as well. Women, like their opponents, can become mere objects to male athletes. The power hierarchies of the sports world place women at the bottom, which may lead some male athletes to treat them as lesser beings through physical and sexual abuse. Furthermore, many athletes come to abuse one another physically, sexually, and emotionally in a number of ways—for example, through acts of hazing or initiation rituals.

Further Reading

Fine, Gary. *With the Boys: Little League Baseball and Preadolescent Culture.* Chicago: University of Chicago Press, 1987.

Messner, Michael. *Power at Play: Sports and the Problem of Masculinity.* Boston: Beacon Press, 1992.

Sabo, Donald, and Ross Runfola, eds. *Jock: Sports and Male Identity.* Englewood Cliffs, NJ: Prentice-Hall, 1980.

Curtis Fogel

Surfing

The beach is deserted. The sand is damp and the ocean is churning angrily after a storm. A figure appears in the distance, walking feverishly and scanning the length of the beach. The person comes to a stop and abandons shoes and a shirt in a heap, pulls on a wetsuit, and heads straight for the water, surfboard in tow. No one is on the beach to watch the surfer, there are no contests or prizes or big corporate sponsors to impress. The figure is riding wave after wave, carving up and down the wall of water, driven to surf by his or her awe of nature and the sense of self-respect found while surfing. Surfing, in this form, is pure enjoyment.

He'e nalu is the Hawaiian word for the act of wave riding, or surfing. The first half of the word depicts the transition from solid to liquid, and the second half represents the surging of the wave. Surfing originated as a recreational sport, a way of celebrating nature and its supreme beauty. As early as 1000 AD, surfing became an integral aspect of Hawaiian culture. Surfing and board making were treated as religious rituals. The ritual of board making dictated that surfboards be made from the wood of three types of trees: the wili wili, the ula, and the koa. The ocean was thought of as a god and the act of surfing was considered to be the point at which man joined nature, man succumbing to nature's power and learning how to harness and use this power for recreation. Utilizing nature's power and adapting to the constant change of the ocean's topography were seen as the beauty of surfing and the source of the exhilaration that surfing provoked.

History has multiple accounts of foreigners coming to different lands to "teach" the Christian faith to island locals, and Hawaii was no exception. In the early nineteenth century, Christian missionaries began appearing in Hawaii. They discouraged surfing because it was seen as a sinful distraction from Christianity. Surfing disappeared from the islands until the dawn of the twentieth century when the missionaries began to leave. Also, when interest in tourism increased, surfing increased again in the need to attract tourists to the islands. Tourists began to frequent the Hawaiian islands, and lifeguards were assigned to attend to them.

Duke Kahanamoku (1890–1968) was a beach lifeguard who often taught tourists how to surf. His infectious love of surfing brought the ancient respect for the sport to the U.S. mainland. Hawaii is often credited with surfing's origin because the Hawaiians introduced surfing to the rest of the United States. Surfers George Freeth and Duke Kahanamoku promoted surfing on the U.S. mainland, both having lived and surfed in Hawaii. Tourists from the mainland, inspired by the Hawaiian natives and their sport, brought surfing back to California where the sport exploded in popularity, but it wasn't long before surfing evolved and the ancient purpose of surfing began to disappear.

As expected, a new era of surfing emerged when the sport was brought to the mainland. The heavier wooden boards were no longer regarded with spiritual importance and were instead seen as a burden. The wooden boards were difficult to steer in the water and often weighed up to 150 pounds. After World War I, a man named Tom Blake invented the hollow board. Blake drilled hundreds of tiny holes into the redwood board to make it lighter. A thin layer of wood was placed over the board to cover the holes and then the board was shaped. This board was almost 50 pounds lighter in the water, making it easier to steer. With each new modification to the surfboard, surfing as a sport was modified as well.

Because surfboards continued to be made lighter, different tricks and surfing styles emerged, along with each new surfboard style. Surfboards changed dramatically after World War II and the discovery of new materials led Hobie Alter and Dale Velzy to make boards out of foam and fiberglass. This lighter material was easily accessible to the board makers and the boards could be made quickly, allowing the boards to be mass-produced at a cheaper rate. Although this type of surfboard became more accessible to the public, it affected the spiritual aspect of surfing.

The ancient Hawaiians surfed to feel a connection with the power of the ocean, to attempt to claim the title of the ultimate wave rider. The ultimate wave rider respected the ocean and learned to work with nature instead of against it. When surfing became part of pop culture, the ancient purpose of surfing changed. Surfers began to covet brand name surf clothing and used these brand names to identify themselves as surfers, as if simply surfing was not sufficient evidence.

Mass production of surfboards was the first step toward commercialization of surfing. The new fiberglass and foam surfboards were light in the water and easy to maneuver, and they immediately became popular among surfers. Jack

O'Neill, Alter, and Velzy all saw an opportunity to create these boards and sell them, and by 1956 they all had surf shops in California that sold these boards. With the success of the fiberglass board, companies began making products geared toward the need of the surfer. The wetsuit, a suit made of foam neoprene to keep the body warm in cold waters, was marketed to the average surfer by the Jack O'Neill company. Leashes or "kook cords" were also invented by O'Neill in 1971. The surfer strapped the leash or cord to his ankle and was thus attached the surfboard. Many expert surfers disapproved of the leash and felt that because surfers did not have to swim to shore to get their boards, surfing required less expertise and a lower level of fitness, and the use of the leash allowed too many beginners, or "kooks," out into the waters with the more experienced surfers.

With the introduction of new products, demands for these surfing-related items began to grow. Many people were drawn to these new products because they represented the surf lifestyle. When movies such as *Gidget* and *The Endless Summer* debuted, the surf lifestyle was represented by the image of the laid-back, attractive man, who nabbed all of the ladies and had the flashiest style in the water. The surfer was considered to be a hipster and was central to pop culture's image of cool in the 1950s, making it easy for companies to market products that would immediately induct nonsurfers into the cool crowd. Wearing surf clothing and owning surf gear was a way for some to feel a part of the surf culture, despite the lack of surf knowledge or ability. The surfing craze rode in to the tune of The Sufaris' "Wipeout," and didn't stop there.

Because the surfer identity became popular, the masses enabled surf companies to continue marketing surf products beyond the 1950s and 1960s. In 1970, Hurley began making shorts, called board shorts, specifically for surfing. Wetsuits and other beach gear began to sky rocket in sales and the demand for these items and for the beach lifestyle began to increase. Surfing not only was a sport during the 1960s and 1970s, it was also a marketed lifestyle. Companies jumped at the opportunity to market an entire lifestyle to young people and produced clothing, shoes, sunglasses, and anything else that was thought to represent the surfing culture. These companies sold a way of life as a fashion, and the sport became less about surfing for fun and for reveling in the beauty of nature and more about wearing the cool surf clothing and having a great surfboard, even if the owner had never set a foot into the ocean.

Evolving from a sacred Hawaiian ritual, surfing assumed a different role after it became central to pop culture. It seemed as though people surfed to win contests, to win fame, and to assume the lifestyle that every young person at the time dreamed of. Surf contests for professionals began after the International Professional Surfers (IPS) group began organizing global tours. The organization started out on a low budget, but soon expanded after contests became popular. Surfing contests further propelled the profits of the surfing industry, but these popular contests also blurred the ancient Hawaiian meaning of surfing: to achieve a *lokahi,* a harmonious unity, an exhilarating connection with nature. The surfers that saw past the commercialization of the surf culture and were acutely in tune with nature were called soul surfers. Today, despite being bombarded by endless billboard images and advertisements, labels and companies, and by promises of cool-crowd status, soul surfers still exist. These people surf for the same reason the ancient Hawaiians surfed: for the love of the sport, the surge of the wave, and the transition from solid to liquid.

Carving the face of one last wave before riding into shore, the surfer hops off the board into knee-deep water, scoops up the surfboard, and begins to trudge back to the place where the surfer had shed his clothing in a hurry to ride the early morning sets. The surfer gathers up the pile of clothing and shoves a pair of sandy feet back into the pair of well-worn shoes. A group of men steps onto the beach from the boardwalk and approaches the surfer, slapping the surfer's back and exclaiming, "That was awesome, bro; you really ripped out there." Turning around as she pulls her hair out from a tight bun, she thanks them. The men stand there with startled looks on their faces as the woman laughs, trotting up the boardwalk. She carries her surfboard and a sense of *lokahi* that a soul surfer finds after making the transition from solid to liquid.

Further Reading

Brisick, Jamie. *Have Board, Will Travel: The Definitive History of Surf, Skate, and Snow.* New York: HarperCollins Publishers Inc., 2004.

History of the Surfboard [Online July 2008]. The Club of the Waves Web site <http://www.clubofthewaves.com/culture_surfboard.php>.

Young, Nat. *The History of Surfing.* Palm Beach, NSW: Palm Beach Press, 1983.

Sadie Hewitt

Wrestling (Professional)

Many may question why anyone would want to watch professional wrestling in the first place, considering the fact that it is a choreographed spectacle. But its remarkable popularity worldwide as a form of entertainment is indisputable. Yet there are also those who dismiss professional wrestling as an event that exploits the strongest of human emotions—love and hatred—for profit, not for the edification of the spectator. It is easy to reject professional wrestling on aesthetic or moral grounds. Shapely females with ample lung capacity buttress their weighty cleavage with the tiniest of band aids while groping the slippery thighs of an equally stunning opponent for a firm hold during a corn oil match to the death. Long-haired bodybuilders in spandex tights strike menacing poses for the frenetic females (and males) in the audience as they recount with surgical precision the anatomical details of last night's slaughter of a fellow wrestler who was "taken apart, piece by piece." Tales of betrayal, adultery, greed, jealousy, and even theft abound. But what is it about professional wrestling that appeals to its main demographic, adolescent males?

There is more to professional wrestling than meets the eye. Understanding its appeal to adolescent males—their main market share demographic—is like trying to explain why one stops to look at an accident. Audiences thrive on spectacles. Spectacles that display the struggle between luck and destiny heighten reality and bear witness to the tragedy of an unknown other. So witnessing the aftermath of a traffic accident in order to unconsciously reaffirm a personal sense of safety and well-being is affirmed by the suffering of another. In professional wrestling, the sense of survival is conveyed through the spectacle that is admittedly fake. There is no point in watching a match with an obviously fixed outcome, other than to facilitate the release of anxiety through a scapegoat, the bad person who suffers for another's sins. Perhaps that is why the simulated violence of professional wrestling appeals to adolescent males, at a stage in their lives when finding a sense of identity becomes a key issue between, on the one side, good, and on the other, evil. The spectacle becomes a choreographed drama of characters who allow the spectator to watch and vicariously live out the outcome of particular actions and story lines that demarcate heroes and villains—like characters from stories one read in childhood and in popular cultural narratives such as comic books.

Professional wrestling is peculiarly interesting with respect to masculinity and male identity. The big sweaty men in tights are more than their muscle-bound, greased, and hairy selves. Notions of "what is good" and "what is bad" are symbolized through the dress, speech, and actions of characters who are combatants in the ring. For this reason, professional wrestling cannot be classified as a sport: that is, a true competition among equals. Like a play, professional wrestling is scripted. The outcome is determined in advance of actual matches. A sport's entertainment value derives from the fact that the contest is always up for grabs, the destiny of the players not known. Sports is drama. Anything can happen. Some would say that sports is "honest." But unlike professional wrestling, sports in general does not present a morality play. The concept of good against evil is not part of the strategic intentions of a soccer game.

Professional wrestling has to appeal to its audience and so presents the adolescent male spectator with images that are designed to affirm specific aspects of masculine identity. Professional wrestling is an artificial contest—not real life. The enjoyment of professional wrestling increases through witnessing the raw spectacle of life's great stories acted out in the ring as a play of moralities—not to mention the ethical decisions, free psychologists, pop philosophy, and generous smatterings of sexual counseling that make up the narrative thread of each and every match and entangle the stories of the wrestlers with our own lives. Wrestling consumes life. Nothing more, nothing less. The outcome of a match becomes secondary because the power of wrestling lies in the ability of the wrestlers to stage the event, the struggle, which is a real product of conflicts in human affairs outside the ring. Who wins does not really matter as much the release that the spectacle provides, which is why professional wrestling appeals to adolescent males who want to experience forms of a heightened masculinity and use them as vehicles for agency and self-actualization.

In the ring, the melodrama flourishes, with the wrestlers acting as performers, not simply athletes. The spectator is forced to take sides according to the moral codes and cultural values of a society. For example, "good" characters are referred to as "technically accomplished athletes." They are well-spoken defenders of dominant ideals like "the family," "the American way," "civil rights," "justice," and "democracy." Professional wrestling in the United States during the Second World War depicted clean-cut "good old boys" of unimpeachable character taking on monocled Nazi caricatures with bad German accents. The nationalistic spirit of the times made it possible to exploit the situation of real violence that was being experienced on the battlefield for the purpose of entertainment and patriotic moralizing. American wrestling heroes exacting symbolic revenge on the representative of an enemy nation was indeed a cathartic experience for a nation in turmoil. The good guy always won! Consequently, there was hope that evil would not triumph in the real world.

"Bad" characters use "dirty tricks" to subvert what the "good" characters stand for, in order to bring about a "New World Order"—which incidentally was also the name of a wrestling cohort of evildoers and misfits. This group of characters walk on the dark side of the fine edge between good and evil, and they usually have a fetishistic obsession attached to a prop (e.g., a shrunken head, a snake, a baseball bat, a branding iron, etc.). They talk with profanity, and make homophobic and misogynistic references—that is, if they speak at all. Sometimes menacing grimaces, guttural growls, the pumping of fists, and the gnashing of teeth are enough to make a point that professional wrestling is a man's world separating the good from the bad. These "less than savory" characters might include a satanic high priest, an ex–porn star, or even a raving lunatic who, having escaped from an unidentified asylum, wears a mask to conceal his identity. Whether it be raising the dead, seducing a wrestler's companion, or talking to a sock puppet, the wrestlers' actions are exaggerations of real life episodes intended to make visible the inner state of their troubled souls. Nothing is left to the imagination. We see and hear everything except the depth of the capacity for the evil that men do.

There is always a "good" character and a "bad" character. Morally upright male figures never fight each other. Never! One of them has to turn "bad" and betray the trust of the other. These explosive situations involve double-crosses, seducing a wrestler's mate, or just plain, old jealousy. Even though we know the world of wrestling is a stage-managed sport, its excessive scenes of human experience—its exhibitions of pain, suffering, betrayal, guilt, treachery, cruelty, desire, and elation—allow young men to identify with the main actors. Some of the wrestlers' symbolic names also facilitate stock responses, names such as "the Rock," "Stone Cold," "the Undertaker," "The Phenom," "Mankind," "The Patriot," "Sergeant Slaughter," "Kane" (the man whose face no one has ever seen!), and, of course, "Vader." The whole point is to recognize these men as humans who have raw emotions and experiences that audiences can relate to. The audience quickly has to take sides for the spectacle of wrestling to be effective. They are separated into communities of "the good" versus "the bad."

Wrestling exploits mythological archetypes when, for example, a darkly masked figure, a face of evil, squares off against a crowd favorite who displays and defends all that is good in a culture. A match feeds on the audience's sense of right and wrong. Even spectators are publicly judged—praised or mocked—according to their display of sympathies and choices about what it is to be a man fighting another man for his principles. Any rejection or show of support reveals a response that is morally categorized as "good" or "bad." The saleable commodities that accompany the marketing of professional wrestling—T-shirts, belts, flags, hats, pins, pens, belt buckles, stickers, water bottles, coffee mugs, bikinis, etc.—brand the sport and sell its ideas and values for public consumption.

Professional wrestling allows the audience to gloss over the unsavory elements of violence and verbal abuse that is enacted in every match by forcing the audience to think about the moral and ethical values of it. The reward of finding the goodness of truth in such an unlikely place would redeem the spectators from the sense of guilt they feel watching the spectacle of professional wrestling. Masculinity is made so clear in the ring that any child can understand the meaning behind the symbolism. We all know that "good guys don't wear black." And never will!

Further Reading

Ball, Michael R. *Professional Wrestling as Ritual Drama in American Popular Culture.* Lewiston, NY: Mellen, Edwin, 1990.

Dell, Chad Edward. "'Lookit that Hunk of Man!': Subversive Pleasures, Female Fandom, and Professional Wrestling." In *Theorizing Fandom: Fans, Subculture and Identity.* Edited by Cheryl Harris and Alison Alexander. Cresskill, NJ: Hampton Press, 87–108, 1998.

Elliot, Keith, and Elliot Greenberg. *The History of Pro Wrestling: From Carnivals to Cable TV.* Minneapolis: Lerner Publishing Group, 2001.

Peter Pericles Trifonas

SECTION 5

Boys in Mind, Boys in Relationships

Boy Talk

Boys have ways of talking that are specific to them—called *genderlects* (Blair, 2000)—and different from how girls talk. Boy talk shares all of the features of spoken English such as grammar and vocabulary generally, but it has its own unique features in terms of the social uses of language. This talk is representative of the boys' gender, of what it means to be a boy, and, at the same time, this talk also contributes to the construction and maintenance of the gendered identity of being a boy.

Boy talk (Blair, 2000) includes both the topics (what they talk about) and the tools of talk (the way they talk). The topics of conversation among boys differ, of course, by age, but there are some constant elements. Topics such as games, sports, gadgets, or vehicles, which could range from bicycles to cars, appear to have remained quite consistent over the years.

Boy talk has its own set of social rules—rules for what, when, and how boys talk; when it is right to talk or not talk; what silence is; and who gets the floor to speak. In this way, boy talk is used to establish and maintain relations among members of a group and between groups. These power differentials can often be seen in classrooms. For example, in one eighth-grade classroom that I observed, it became evident early in the school year that the gendered dynamics of talk were established clearly: those who spoke first and the loudest, interrupted the most, made side comments to classmates, or mocked previous ideas were most often boys. This public talk to establish status was a tool that the boys had learned; they used it, and it worked to maintain their dominance in the classroom talk.

Boy talk also includes numerous homophobic references, and calling someone gay or a fag was one of the worst insults. The idea that able-bodied, white, heterosexual men are "real guys" and that that's "normal" was perpetuated. There was little room for any other interpretation of ways to be a boy, and name calling worked as a reminder. Maybe the issue was more about a tough-guy image for boys, given that there aren't many alternative images for boys in society today to emulate. The image of a quiet, gentle, caring, and smart boy just doesn't get the same ratings. What images are portrayed in the media—in news, sports, or entertainment?

Boy talk also erodes the classroom cohesion, silences the voices of many of the girls, and disrupts the comfort of the quieter and more effeminate boys. Talk remains a very important component of classroom participation, and if this access to talk is closed for some, there can be a number of ramifications for the ways in which youth develop literacy and demonstrate their learning.

This is not to say that boys intend their talk to be intimidating or take up a lot of space. For the most part, they are not conscious of the role that their talk plays. All children learn talk, and they acquire different forms of it from their interactions with adults and other youth. Boys and girls each take on the talk patterns that they see among the gendered group with whom they identify, so boys who aspire to be like the men in their lives subtly and slowly take on the talk patterns and styles of men as they are growing up Boy talk in itself is not necessarily a dangerous entity, but when it impacts the talk of girls and the less powerful and vocal boys, it can be dangerous. It reinforces the notions of a macho masculinity as the norm to the exclusion of other ways of being.

Further Reading

Blair, Heather. 2000. Genderlects: Girl Talk in a Middle Years Language Arts Classroom. *Language Arts,* 77(2): 315–23.

Heather Blair

Brothers

Biologically, brothers are male siblings; boys who share the same parents. Brothers can also be half-brothers—which means they share one parent—or step-brothers, which means they are brothers because a parent of one of the boys married a parent of the other boy. Children who are brothers may live in the same house, may live apart, or may live in the same house some of the time. The relationships of brothers are complicated and unique, and can't be summarized or characterized easily; however, there are certain experiences and emotions that are typical of the connections between brothers. The term *brother* goes far beyond the biology of being male siblings, and represents a complex variety of situations and relationships.

He's Like a Brother to Me

Brother is a word that is used to represent boys who are siblings, but it can also mean much more than a biological or a family relationship. Brother is used to represent boys and men that have a connection or a close bond of some sort. "My brother" is an expression that many boys and young men use to refer to their close friend, and it is commonly used to mean friends that have special attachments. Brother is used in the expression "brother from another mother," which refers to a close friend, often a friend that has been known for most of one's life.

The members of a fraternity also call each other brothers. A fraternity is a social organization, usually at a college, into which a person has to be initiated and accepted. When you are a member of a fraternity, you are a "fraternity brother" to all other members of that fraternity, and this connection may last long after graduation from college.

A brother can also be a member of a church. Many religious groups call all male members of their community brothers. For example, Buddhists often call other Buddhists "brothers" and "sisters." Additionally, many Christian groups call the male members of the group "brethren," as they see each other as brothers in God. The Catholic religion uses the term brother not to refer to all members of the religion, but to represent a religious man who is not a priest.

"Brothers in arms" or "band of brothers" are expressions that represent people who are soldiers in the armed forces, usually soldiers who have fought in a battle, or who have fought together. Brothers in arms are considered to have a strong bond that comes from their shared experiences and dedication to the same purpose.

When people talk about the connection between nonrelated brothers, they refer to a brotherhood. This word is most often used to represent a religious brotherhood, a fraternity brotherhood, or a trade brotherhood, which usually implies members of a labor union. Basically, a brotherhood can mean a community of people that are connected by having something in common.

Brotherly love usually means getting along with people who are close to you and often different from you. The U.S. city of Philadelphia has as its motto "The City of Brotherly Love," thought to have originated with the founder of the city, William Penn, who hoped that all who lived there, regardless of their personal histories, could live in peace and harmony. These are just some of the common uses of brother to symbolize a bond between two or more boys or men. This word means more than a relationship that is determined by being a part of a biological family; it goes beyond genetics, and implies friendship and kinship.

"He Ain't Heavy. . . . He's My Brother"

"He ain't heavy, he's my brother" is an expression possibly originated by a magazine writer in 1924, which is now well-known and has been used over and over in pop culture, illustrated in movies, poems, and songs. It was popularized as the main refrain from a pop song in 1969 and performed and recorded by a variety of people and bands throughout the years. The expression implies that brothers will sacrifice and endure hardships for each other without much complaint. The expression is also part of the logo of an organization for homeless boys called Boys Town. In Omaha, Nebraska, the founding place of the Boys Town organization, a sculpture of one boy carrying another boy has the caption "he ain't heavy, he's my brother." The sculpture represents one model of brotherhood that romanticizes the relationship between boys who are brothers or who come to care for one another as brothers.

My Bro'

Brothers are people who usually have many shared experiences. Boys who are brothers have a wide variety of emotions that they feel about each other, and with each other. Some brothers get along really well, and some don't. Although all brothers' experiences are unique, there are certain characteristics that are consistent in many brothers' relationships. These features can be consistent and remain so even as the boys age. Some brothers' relationships may change and evolve over time, or they may stay exactly the same as they grow older.

A brother can be a source of companionship; he can be a person who is always by your side. Sometimes brothers feel like they always have someone to play with, someone to share time with, and someone to share interests with. Brothers who are close companions may enjoy playing games, or sports, or with toys together. They may create their own special types of games, and some boys grow up with their own private "language" that they have created. They may have secret clubs, and create secret messages. In these kinds of moments, brothers feel emotional security through having a buddy, a comrade, who is by their side. A brother can be someone to admire, someone to look up to. A brother can also be a confidante: someone to confide in, to tell fears to, to share secrets with, and to turn to for help with problems.

Sometimes brothers see each other as rivals, and may feel the need to compete. Competition can happen during sports or when the brothers try to get the attention of someone else, like a parent. Having a brother can feel like a healthy competition, in that the brothers use competition to push each other to focus. Competition can be positive, when it feels like it is something that motivates people to work harder at something. But competition can also feel bad and create a negative situation when brothers have to be rivals and fight about everything, especially if one feels that he is always being compared to someone and being criticized. When boys are growing up, it can be frustrating to feel that a brother is better at something, but it is part of life that we all have different things that we are good at, and sometimes brothers need to try to figure out what each brother's strength is.

Regardless of whether a brotherly relationship is mainly built on companionship, admiration, competitiveness, or rivalry, brothers may spend time having lots of laughs as well as lots of arguments and disagreements. The arena of brotherhood can be a space for lots of different relationships and emotions to develop and be explored.

A Brother's Roles

Some brothers feel that a brother is someone they can share their problems with and tell their secrets to. You can play with a brother, and know he is always by your side. A brother is someone you can annoy, and pester, and tease. A brother is a person who you may know well enough that you finish each other's sentences, or know what the other is going to say next. A brother is also someone you might talk down to, and not want to be with. A brother is a person you can look up to, and strive to be like. Sometimes being a brother can mean you get mixed up in a bit of all of this. And sometimes you want to be just like your brother, while other times you may not want to even be with him at all. Being a brother means being in a relationship that is unique, that will never be like a relationship with anyone else.

The New Brother

There are classic and perhaps nostalgic images of brothers in books and movies showing brothers as boys who cause mischief and are inseparable, an image that seems fairly time-honored, but it appears to be changing. The images of brothers portrayed in popular culture today are more antagonistic and often show brothers who are extreme rivals who try to interfere with each other's happiness. Where the images of brothers are heading is debatable, and only time will tell how culture moves to define what it means to be a brother.

Further Reading

History in Philadelphia [Online]. *Philadelphia and the Countryside* http://www
    .gophila.com/C/X/385_/Things_to_Do/211/History/209.html>.
Latest News [Online]. *Telegraph* <http://www.telegraph.co.uk/news/main
    .jhtml?xml=/news/2006/03/03/ntwin03.xml&sSheet=/news/2006/03/03/
    ixhome.html>.
Sudano, Glenn. Why a Laybrother? [Online]. <http://www.franciscanfriars.com/
    religious%20brothers/cfrreligousbrother/llaybro.htm>.

Christina Siry and Liam Siry

Depression

Depression is an illness. It can be defined as a lasting state of distress, which lasts over a period of two weeks or more. It is an illness that affects the whole individual—mentally, physically, and emotionally. Due to the broad range of symptoms that can occur, depression is often a confusing illness to diagnose. There are three categories of depression. In general, depression ranges from mild to moderate to severe. Mental health workers use rating scales that help them distinguish with some accuracy the different ranges. There is also a fourth category that applies mainly to adolescents (used here to indicate the age range from 12–20), comorbidity, meaning depression that occurs in combination with other disorders. These include drug use, anxiety disorder, conduct disorder, hyperactivity, or anorexia nervosa. Comparative data from Canada, the UK, and New Zealand indicate that major depression rates have been increasing. They also show that since 1945 the onset of depression has been occurring at an earlier age, especially among young men (born since the 1960s).

Depression in young people can be similar to adults in many ways. Depression has biological and social causes. Biologically, it results from chemical imbalances in the brain. There are numerous social causes, which will be outlined below. Some common mental symptoms are persistent sadness, lack of concentration, unfounded guilt, and pessimism. Common physical symptoms include insomnia or unexplainable and persistent fatigue; loss of appetite; weight loss; and reduced interest in sex. Although these symptoms are common for adults and adolescents, young people may *express* the symptoms of depression differently than adults. This can lead to depression in young people going unnoticed and undiagnosed. Adolescence is a particularly difficult time, with a number of added potential causes for depression. It is a time of transition between childhood and adulthood. It is a time of significant emotional and physical changes for young people. It is also a period where young people may struggle with their identity as they enter into adulthood. In addition, there are the new pressures of relationships and establishing sexual identity, as well as severe academic pressures as college or university enrollment approaches.

Adolescent males in particular face unique pressures in a world where changing gender opportunities have altered the dynamics of competition, as well as social norms. Today young women are more free to be many things (athletes, scientists, etc.), while boys are not sure about who or what they are supposed to be. They face unparalleled pressure from many directions. Expectations for male success are extremely high, though there is far less certainty about male success in the college race. Careers and life paths are not as obvious as they were for previous generations, resulting in heightened confusion and uncertainty for young men in this transitional phase. Adolescent males are also more likely to struggle with issues of sexuality and gender identity. An added risk for young men is their difficulty in comprehending and communicating their feelings, as well as their reluctance to seek help or treatment, as compared to females.

Although depression in young men has unique causes and is expressed differently than in young women, male and female depressions are not necessarily two different things. Currently there is no evidence for an altogether different kind of "male depression." However, there is evidence that certain symptoms of depression occur more frequently in males than in females. These include aggression, increased loss of control, greater risk-taking, irritability, and sudden anger. Before puberty, boys and girls are equally at risk for depressive disorders (Nolen-Hoeksema and Girgus, 1994). However, after age 14, girls are twice as likely as boys to have major depression. This is quickly changing though. For the first time in the United States, depression among adolescent males is almost as prevalent as among adolescent females. This is cause for alarm as young men are more likely to abuse drugs and alcohol as a way of coping with depression than young women. There is an increased risk of suicide for adolescents with depression, especially for boys. Research shows that although girls *attempt* suicide more than boys, boys *succeed* more often than girls. Thus the death rate from suicide is higher for boys than girls. This suggests that even though the incidence of depression among young men is less than among young women, young males are more likely to attempt to cope with depression in self-destructive and fatal ways. Suicide is the second highest cause of death among older teens in Canada and the third highest cause in the United States (Blum and Nelson-Mmari, 2004; Cutler, Glasser, and Norberg, 2001).

Because young men experience depression differently than others, they have unique treatment requirements. First, however, they have to overcome barriers to treatment that are unique to males. It is still largely culturally unacceptable for males to show emotions such as sadness and fear. This may account for why young men are less likely to see a doctor or pursue treatment than young women. Nonetheless treatments specifically more suited for boys are available. Pharmaceutically, young men are treated similarly to other groups, with antidepressant medication. Psychologically, on the other hand, boys have special needs. Cognitive behavioral therapy has been shown to help young men to alter negative thought patterns into positive ones, which can reduce the pressure men feel about their capabilities and thereby increase their confidence. In general, therapy can help adolescent males understand their feelings and makes them better able to handle their depression.

Further Reading

Blum, Robert W., and Kristin Nelson-Mmari. The Health of Young People in a Global Context. *Journal of Adolescent Health* 35 (2004): 402–418.

Cutler, David M., Edward L. Glaeser, and Karen Norberg. Explaining the Rise in Youth Suicide. *Harvard Institute of Economic Research* No. 1917 (March 2001): http://www.nber.org/papers/w7713.

Fact Sheet: Depression in Teens [Online]. Mental Health America Web site <http://www.mentalhealthamerica.net/go/information/get-info/depression/depression-in-teens>.

Men and Depression [Online]. National Institute of Mental Health Web site <http://www.nimh.nih.gov/health/publications/men-and-depression/complete-publication.shtml#pub8>.

Nolen-Hoeksema, Susan, and Joan S. Girgus The Emergence of Gender Differences in Depression during Adolescence. *Psychological Bulletin* 115, no. 3 (May 1994): 424–443.

Teenage Depression and Suicide [Online]. The Kelty Patrick Dennehy Foundation Web site <http://www.thekeltyfoundation.org/depression-facts .htm>.

Ghada Chehade

Empathy

Psychologists who work with boys argue that many boys do not develop their empathy sufficiently. Empathy can be defined as the capacity for identifying with the feelings of others or experiencing what the other feels. Kindlon and Thompson believe that boys lack an emotional education in their socialization to masculinity. Stephenson argues that boys need rituals of passage to learn about connectedness and the real meaning of manhood.

According to Kindlon and Thompson (2000), two destructive assumptions influence the way teachers and parents interact with boys, which ultimately contribute to boys' emotional difficulties. Boys are often viewed as either wild animals or entitled princes. Perceived as a wild animal, a boy appears to be out of control with no capacity for self-restraint. This view often elicits harsh punishments and strict measures of control from care-takers, which diminish a boy's self-esteem. When viewed as an entitled prince of future leadership, a boy is more easily excused for his bad behavior and the work involved in making amends. He is held to a lower standard of accountability and let off the hook more easily, and he does not learn the lessons of empathy. This view places boys at risk for becoming arrogant and insensitive. Adults who interact with boys unconsciously respond to their behavior according to these gender-related assumptions, either asking too much of boys through perfect behavior or not enough. Additional social and cultural expectations of masculinity reflected in popular culture affect boys, involving the idea that *real men* are strong, stoic, and self-reliant. Kindlon and Thompson (2000) call this the "culture of cruelty" that requires the suppression of feelings to achieve the impossible standard of manhood. Boys learn to obey the "code of silence" to keep their feelings hidden, so as not to appear feminine or be ridiculed, while also keeping silent when witnessing acts of cruelty done to others.

What is the cost to boys when their emotional life is suppressed in service to cultural ideals of manhood? What is the cost to society? It is well known that some boys have problems with alcohol, drugs, sexual aggression, anger management, violence, criminality, suicide attempts, and more. Boys need to have the experience of being empathized with, to be able to openly develop their capacity for empathy, and to be socially expected to act empathically. Cruelty needs to be openly addressed and the code of silence broken.

Stephenson (2006) believes that boy energy should be channeled into rituals. He argues that boys need boundaries and structure to test their strength and that they need to be initiated into manhood. In many non-Western cultures, boys are prepared for a life of hard work, danger, and difficult decisions. Around the age of 13, they go through an elaborate and rigorous initiation that often involves segregation from the community, a physical and psychological challenge, and an element of risk or danger. The elders, usually a group of initiated men, plan, organize, and supervise the ritual. After the initiation ceremony, boys return to the community as adult members. They are expected to behave in adult ways and are given new responsibilities. The initiation is meant to speed up the process of growing up. Stephenson argues that Western teenage boys indulge in self-destructive patterns because they feel like a useless class of society, and they have too few responsibilities. They are aimless, have little positive regard for adult life, and are angry at society. Their dangerous, thrill-seeking, antisocial activities are efforts to initiate themselves into manhood, which represents an archetypal need for belonging that is not being met. Boys feel empowered when they view their behavior from an archetypal perspective. This gives meaning to their internal drives and offers a positive view of masculinity.

Adolescent boys' developmental challenges include the following: the search for identity, individuation and leave-taking, dealing with paradox and abstraction, egocentrism, idealism, a sense of pride, puberty, sexuality, and seeking non-ordinary states of consciousness. Organized rituals of passage help address these needs in healthy and structured ways supported by family and community. Boys are not left alone with their issues and the elders guide the outcome.

Stephenson (2006) suggests that families, teachers, and therapists prepare an initiation ceremony for boys they live or work with, based on the "Hero's Journey." Its stages are the following: conventional slumber, the call to adventure (including crossing thresholds of difficulty), discipline and training, culmination of the quest (including crossing thresholds of difficulty on returning), and return and contribution. Initiations are meant to spark feelings of responsibility and commitment in boys, qualities that are so much a part of manhood and fatherhood. Boys are encouraged to dream bigger dreams, think bigger thoughts, and move beyond stereotypes into the world of emotional connectedness, community involvement, and spiritual development. Intellectual and empathic development is accelerated.

The function of the rite of passage is to provoke an ego death by challenging each boy with a test, evaluating his skill, making him face an ordeal to learn the courage of a man. Rituals are meant to push boys to their limits and out of their comfort zones so that a life-changing shift can occur. Wilderness settings are particularly appropriate for rites of passage that may include sweat lodges, rock climbing, river rafting, mask-making, artwork, and storytelling. Kindlon and Thompson (2000) and Stephenson (2006) strongly believe that boys want to feel like men and aspire to be responsible members of society. Their needs for emotional literacy and connectedness are strong.

Further Reading

Kindlon, Daniel, and Michael Thompson. *Raising Cain, Protecting the Emotional Life of Boys.* New York: Ballantine Books, 2000.

Stephenson, Bret. *From Boys to Men, Spiritual Rites of Passage in an Indulgent Age.* Rochester: Park Street Press, 2006.

Heather M. Veltman

Friendships

As toddlers, boys are usually unaware of gender. Their play and close friendships are formed primarily around shared interests: trucks for boys whose interest is in wheels, or playing house for boys who find interest in role-play in this context. Boys befriend those who share their interests, as opposed to those who are of a particular sex. Thus, cross-gender play is common when there are shared interests, and within-gender play takes place around the object of the play itself. Friendship forms from these common bonds.

In the United States in general both play and close friendships between boys and between boys and girls are often differently valued. Starting at preschool, boys may be encouraged to perform within-gender play, and to not actively engage in those activities associated with girls' interests. Thus friendship opportunities between boys and girls may be limited, and when they do occur, may be seen as a problem. A boy who develops interests associated with girls, such as dance, gymnastics, or even playing the violin, may be encouraged to associate with more traditional boy objects and activities. When young boys do form close friendships with girls as a result of common interests, the relationship will often be interpreted as a romantic one. In such instances the boy may be told by adults or older siblings that he has a "girlfriend" and be teased into confusion about the nature of the relationship.

Boys' Friendships at Different Ages and within Different Cultures

Like girls, boy's friendships take on differing expressions depending on age, family, culture, and peer groups. Toddlers and preschool boys will openly show affection for their closest male (or female) friend. Very young boys will hug, wrestle playfully, and share close physical space with another boy, such as riding together on a sled or sitting close together as they play. Young boys are likely to display their vulnerability, cry in response to being hurt, or openly express anger as well as affection to another boy. Close, tender friendships and a high level of physical and emotional closeness are often encouraged in very young boys. Yet this encouragement is in stark contrast to what is expected in their friendships with other boys, and with girls, as boys get older.

As boys develop, the emphasis in their friendship will tend to be less overtly intimate—particularly in public. This appears to be a result of cultural influences. Boys in cultures where public display of intimacy between males is permitted will display greater propensity to touch and also express affection for their male friends than boys living in societies such as the United States where such displays are generally discouraged. In some Middle Eastern, African, and European cultures, young men—and males of all ages—will publicly display physical closeness by, for example, holding hands in public, kissing on the cheek when greeting, or walking arm-in-arm. Boys raised in the United States in families who come from such cultures are more likely to practice these expressions within their close friendship groups. In cultures where close friendships between boys and girls are discouraged, boys will be less likely to engage with girls overall, and unlikely to share close physical or emotional interactions.

Boys, like all humans, will respond to the conditions of their social setting. A boy whose father is warmly physical and emotionally supportive will likely be similarly expressive toward his friends. It is the boy's early exposure to relationships, to norms, to expectations, and to opportunities that shape his life's friendship experience. In the United States, as in Europe and other countries experiencing a breakdown of the separation of the sexes, older boys are increasingly likely to have close female as well as male friends. Boys often report having an easier time talking to girls about their feelings and personal problems, fearing that their male friends will tease or not understand. Indeed, in part because boys do not often witness expressions of vulnerability or the need for emotional support among the male peers or older men in their lives, they come to feel awkward, embarrassed, or personally inadequate when they do experience such feelings. Girls, then, may be a safer source for support during such periods.

When a boy forms an emotionally close friendship with another boy, the private aspects of the relationship often take different form than the public display. In private boys will share details of their lives and be vulnerable in ways that cannot be expressed in public. In public, however, boys are likely to de-emphasize their physical and emotional closeness and place greater emphasis on activities, posturing, teasing, and kidding around, with less overt expression of sincere affection. Although boys tend to have a strong sense of loyalty in their friendships, overall, they are less likely to have as many same-sex friends as girls. Boys in their teenage years can find themselves without the vocabulary or awareness to express empathy to another male. However, expressions of love and affection may take the form of sharing an activity, sitting in silence, or joking in order to distract the boy who is struggling with his emotions.

From about middle school on, there is increased emphasis on boys to engage in competitive game playing and idea sharing—in sports, computer games, or adventure-play in the form of creating fantasy games or simulations. Depending on the boys, this can mean having a common interest in classical music, acting, other expressive arts, or in sports, cooking, mechanics, or the sciences. Such activities serve a developmental need in boys to negotiate life with increased independence and to experience different roles, identities, and ways of interaction with peers. Boys organize their relationships around these roles, identities, and interactions—tennis players or other athletes or the boys who become involved with service learning opportunities take on ways of being that help them experience relationships in varying contexts—with the focus on doing, producing, or contributing to an activity. These interactions build friendships along the way.

Teenage Friendships

In their teens, boys are influenced substantially by their male peers. As a result, and depending on the situation, they could advance their range of activities to accommodate peer expectations, but also limit them. Like girls, boys worry about rejection and are vulnerable to conforming and adapting to social pressures; boys will opt out of band or orchestra if such activities are not valued by other boys in their friendship group. Or boys will find their friendships among others in their preferred activity group—a sure way to get support for what the boy enjoys doing. It is not uncommon for boys who are not interested in traditional "masculine" activities to have more friends who are girls. Boys will find greater acceptance from them in pursuing their interests in areas such as the arts and humanities.

Boys who are able to have close friendships with girls throughout their developing years are likely to have greater respect for women overall and greater engagement in women's lives. Such boys are less likely to view girls and boys as "opposites," they will often appreciate ways in which the sexes are similar, and value what boys can learn from girls.

There are drawbacks when boys do not experience the type of friendships where there is safety for sharing emotions, being vulnerable, and experiencing trust. Males overall are at greater risk than females for feeling isolated from others, committing violence, of bullying and being victims of bullies, and not finishing high school or pursuing college education. Males are at greater risk of committing suicide. Males are also less likely to pursue counseling or seek other support for problems they are having. Close friendships can be a valuable training ground for building trust, and for receiving and expressing love, affection, and acceptance. They are qualities that occur naturally in most young children, and yet are not always encouraged, or held up as models, as boys grow up. If their close physical and emotional friendships with other boys and with girls are affirmed by male adults around them, adults who also embrace those value and act as role models, boys will find comfort in close friendships throughout their lives.

Further Reading

Canada, Geoffrey. *Reaching Up for Manhood: Transforming the Lives of Boys in America.* Boston, MA: Beacon Press, 1998.
Connell, Raewyn W. *The Men and the Boys.* Sydney: Allen & Unwin, 2000.
Kindlon, Dan, and Michael Thompson. *Raising Cain: Protecting the Emotional Life of Boys.* New York: Ballantine Books, 2000.

Robert Heasley

Gay Fathers

Boys raised by gay fathers are one of many groups of boys whose experiences typically receive little attention in the media, in parenting books, and in research. One of the reasons this occurs is that many people still assume that gay men can't or don't have children. Unfortunately, some people also believe that gay men shouldn't have children. Despite this, increasing numbers of gay men are starting families in the context of gay relationships, while others continue to parent once they leave a heterosexual relationship and "come out." As a result, more and more boys live with or are in some way parented by gay men.

Myths about Gay Fathers

Much of the research on gay fathers responds to four quite common myths about gay parents: (1) gay men are pedophiles; (2) gay men will raise children who are "confused" about their gender; (3) gay men don't have stable relationships; and (4) boys raised by gay men will grow up to be gay themselves. Myths such as these are dangerous as they stop us from actually understanding all the good things about gay fathers and the boys they raise. It is worthwhile looking at these myths a bit more closely and at the problems associated with them.

Myth 1

Unfortunately, this myth is associated with a whole range of negative assumptions about gay men. These include the assumption that being gay means being sinful, or unhealthy, or mentally ill, or generally deviant. In other words, when those who want to stigmatize gay men label gay fathers as pedophiles, they prevent us from better understanding what pedophilia actually is, and the many differing family forms where abuse occurs. As such, associating gay fathers with negative stereotypes is a red herring that distracts from an understanding of the abuse of boys in the broader community.

Myth 2

All children explore for themselves a range of identities and will eventually settle on the one that best works for them. Children are adaptive in the ways they learn about the world, and their skills in knowing what is best for them is underappreciated. It is only when society wants to prescribe one particular identity as being "the right" one for boys that it runs into trouble. Boys with parents of all sexualities and genders may at some stage experiment with their gender identity, and many of these identities will not necessarily conform to a particular gender stereotype. This is not the "fault" of their parents or of the children themselves. Rather, it is the child or young person actively making choices in his or her life.

Myth 3

Much like all families, the families that gay men create take many differing shapes. Some are formed by two men, while others are headed by a single gay father. Some gay fathers may choose not to be in a long-term relationship, but may have short-term relationships that fit in around their parenting, while others may have a number of "significant others" that support them as parents and as sexual beings. Whatever the family configuration gay fathers were raised in, it is nonetheless the case that most gay fathers, like most parents in general, will actively consider their children's needs, will ensure that their children understand where they fit in the context of the father's relationships, and will help them to understand the changes that their family experiences in regard to its composition. As research on parenting continues to demonstrate, it is process, not structure, that results in happy children. In other words, it is the care that parents give to children, not the relationship structure that they live in, that makes a difference.

Myth 4

In regard to the final myth, it is important to ask why anyone would be concerned if the son of a gay father grew up to be gay. Are people typically concerned when heterosexual parents raise heterosexual children? If we accept the points made in regard to the first and second myth, then the problems that are attributed to the fourth myth are irrelevant: if boys do grow up gay, it is not only acceptable for them to do so, but it in no way reflects deviancy or an illness on the part of either their parents or the boys themselves. If we accept all boys, regardless of their sexual identities, then this myth becomes redundant.

Research on Gay Fathers

Although much of the existing research on gay fathers takes as its starting place the above myths, and attempts to disprove them through scientific evidence, research nonetheless does tell us a lot about the positive and indeed beneficial aspects of having a gay father. For example, in regard to gay men who parent in the context of a gay relationship, research has shown that such couples undertake parenting in more equitable ways than do heterosexual couples. Research has also suggested that the considerable financial, legal, and emotional work required of many gay men to become parents often results in such men being more aware of their responsibilities as parents than hetero-sexual fathers, and as a result potentially displaying greater attention to meet-ing the needs of children.

Although the majority of research on gay men who parent has focused on men who parent post-heterosexual divorce, a growing body of research has focused on the experiences of men who become parents through fostering, adoption, surrogacy, and shared parenting arrangements with women. Gay men are also involved in some instances as known sperm donors to couples or single women and may often have some form of ongoing relationship with the children born of such arrangements. These many differing roles that gay men play in the lives of children have been shown to be beneficial not only for providing children with a broad range of experiences of parenting and inter-actions with adult males, but also serving to challenge the myths and stereo-types held within society more broadly about gay men who parent.

Research on Boys with Gay Fathers

Much of the research on children of gay fathers involves the sharing of stories or narratives about growing up in a gay-headed household. Such stories pri-marily focus on the experiences of adult men whose fathers came out as gay after separating from their mothers. As such, many of the stories focus on issues of loss and grief—of simultaneously working through issues of parental separation and coming to terms with the father's new sexual identity. Boys whose fathers come out during the boy's adolescence often report having to deal not only with their own feelings about their father's sexual identity, but also the prejudices held by society against gay men and their families.

Increasingly, as more gay men have children in the context of gay relation-ships, there has been a focus on other experiences of growing up with a gay father or gay fathers. Boys raised by gay parents may still be confronted by the societal prejudices held against their family, but these boys will most often do so in the context of a family unit that these boys consider the norm—although families may have changed over the years, children born into gay-headed families will understandably see the world as always having gay-headed fam-ilies. It should therefore not be surprising that some boys with gay fathers will not have had to deal with significant issues of loss or grief about their parent's sexual identity (though they may well have dealt with loss or grief over changes in family structure such as the break-down of a gay relationship). Boys raised in such families thus offer society unique perspectives for under-standing prejudice against gay men and their families: They remind us that such prejudice is only normal or justifiable to those who seek to perpetuate it. For every child, his or her own life will be the marker of what is normal, and for boys who live happily and healthily in gay-headed households, prejudice against gay men may reflect the norms of the society they live in, but does not reflect their own experience of living in a family unit.

Representations of Gay Fathers and Their Sons

One place to see examples of the prejudices held against gay fathers in society is in movies. Two examples of these are *Hollow Reed* and *The Next Best Thing*. Both of these movies feature gay men who are parents, and both movies show examples of gay men having to fight for their parental rights, and being discriminated against in the process.

Hollow Reed is the story of a gay man who, having once been heterosexually married with a child, is now living with his male partner, while his child is cared for by his ex-wife and her new male partner. The film primarily focuses on his desire to have his child live with him when he finds out that the child is being abused by his ex-wife's new partner. A court battle ensues, with many examples of discriminatory language being used against the gay father.

In *The Next Best Thing*, Madonna stars as a heterosexual woman alongside Rupert Everett who plays a gay man; they are two best friends who, following a drunken night of sex, find that one of them (Madonna) is pregnant. The two decide to live and raise the child together, but as the years go by, they find it difficult to live together as parents who are friends rather than lovers. Madonna eventually meets a heterosexual man and wishes to leave the state in order to move in with him and the child. When Rupert Everett's character contests this, it is revealed that he is in fact not the biological father, and a court battle ensues where the language of biology and rights plays a large part.

These two movies both provide a clear picture of how particular stereotypical understandings of gay men are perpetuated. In both movies the courtroom scenes feature the gay fathers taking the stand. In both movies the men are interrogated by the children's mother's lawyers about the fathers' sexual activities, the places they go to meet other men, the length and exclusivity of their relationships, and other such questions that are used to demonstrate that gay men should not be granted parental rights. In *The Next Best Thing,* Rupert Everett is asked whether he has "performed oral sex in front of his son." Although this may seem like an outrageous question to any parent, in the context of legal rights for gay parents, these sorts of questions are often the norm. This use of language that implies deviancy, promiscuity, and danger is used to depict gay fathers as inherently unable to care for their children.

Fathering and Raising Boys Books

Another place where negative images of both boys and their fathers are perpetuated is in books on fathering and raising boys. A recent review of these books suggests that none of the general books written on fathering include any mention of gay fathers or gay parent–headed households. Many of the books are explicit in their use of language that focuses on heterosexual fathers, such as choosing the term partner to refer to "wives, fiancées, or girlfriends," and constantly referring to the "mother of the child." Although these assumptions may hold true for many of the readers of fathering books, they actively exclude readers who identify as gay fathers. Importantly, however, there are a growing number of books being published on gay fathers. These books provide support for men seeking to start a family, and also for men dealing not only with coming out, but also with parenting after (typically heterosexual) divorce.

The same review also found that only a small selection of the books on raising boys included a chapter or section on gay boys, with all of the books using examples and images of heterosexual boys to describe the experiences of *all* boys. Many of the books used terms such as *sissy* and *wimp* to refer to boys who do not engage in behaviors that are thought to be appropriately masculine (such as fighting, climbing trees, and playing superheroes). The association of behaviors other than those deemed appropriate with derogatory terms such as *sissy* teaches parent-readers and boys themselves that men who do not embrace appropriate boy behaviors are deserving of discrimination.

In many of the books examined in the review, references to gay men or gay boys were often negative. Some of the books suggested that for a parent to find out that his or her child is gay is "like a death," while others suggested that giving birth to a child who is gay is similar to giving birth to a child with tumors and cataracts. As such, these books reinforce the idea that being gay is somehow negative, and in so doing they exclude gay men who read the books; these books also teach all parents that there is something not quite right about their gay sons (who may one day become gay fathers).

Understanding Gay Fathers and Their Sons

As this entry suggests, there are many differing ways to understand gay fathers and their role in raising children (and in particular boys). Some of these understandings are negative, and include a range of stereotypes about gay fathers. Other understandings, based on research findings, seek to challenge these stereotypes and explore the positive aspects of gay fathering. Some research has explored the ways in which prejudice against gay fathers is perpetuated, for example, in negative images in movies and in books on fathering and raising boys. All of these approaches provide different images of gay fathers, at the same time as many of them implicitly or explicitly provide images of what are deemed to be "normal parents"—heterosexual, married couples.

New avenues of research on gay fathers continue to be explored, with some of these being conducted by gay men themselves. These areas focus specifically on how gay men create families through fostering, adoption, and surrogacy; they focus as well on how a wide range of men negotiate identities as gay fathers, and what it means to be a gay father who experiences other forms of prejudice, because they do not identify as white, middle class, or able-bodied. These new avenues of research tend to be less focused on refuting stereotypes, and more on celebrating gay families and validating the benefits for boys growing up with gay fathers. These benefits include, for example, access to a wider range of gender and sexual role models upon which to navigate the boys' own identities; greater awareness of social injustices and often a commitment to challenging it; and greater knowledge of the diverse ways in which families are formed; and respect for this diversity.

Importantly, many gay fathers are no longer just ex-husbands, but are often now primary caregivers, sole fathers, fathers with multiple relationships, fathers living in varying forms of nuclear families, and, most important, fathers who are caring parents. Boys with gay fathers, like all boys, will live in a range of family forms, and will develop their own expectations of the world around them based on their experiences. Although some boys with gay fathers may see more instances of prejudice, their fathers and family could provide them with safe spaces from which to understand prejudice, but nonetheless recognize the validity and importance of their own family.

Further Reading

Children of Lesbians and Gays Everywhere [Online January 2008]. <http://www.colage.org/>.

Gottlieb, Andrew J. *Sons Talk About Their Gay Fathers.* New York: Haworth, 2003.

Mallon, Gerald P. *Gay Men Choosing Parenting.* New York: Columbia University Press, 2003.

Rainbow Families Council [Online January 2008]. <http://www.rainbowfamilies.org.au/>.

Riggs, Damien W. *Becoming Parent: Lesbians, Gay Men, and Family.* Teneriffe: Post Pressed, 2007.

Damien W. Riggs

Invisible Boys

Invisible boys are not seen or recognized by those around them. Boys become invisible when they hide from the world or are dismissed by it and seen as not counting in the way "real" boys do. By definition, invisible boys are not easy to find. If they choose to be invisible, then they know how to hide; if they are made invisible because they are ignored or victims of prejudice, then they live in a world that hides them from recognition.

Boys who *seek* invisibility often do so because they feel they don't fit in with all the other boys (who are seen) in the world. Society limits the way boys are supposed to behave if they want to be considered normal. This pushes boys to hide if they are "different."

Boys may become invisible because they do not want the world to notice that they are vulnerable, frightened, overwhelmed, worried, or depressed. (Depression is more than sadness; it is a medical illness that leaves a person feeling hopeless, helpless, and without energy.) Young and older boys can become depressed, and this can make them "disappear" from normal life activities. It can also place them at risk for suicide.

There are many things that a boy may feel are not emotionally safe for him to show to his community. As he tries to hide a *part* of his life, he may decide that his best option is to make *all* of himself invisible—especially in social situations where he is not comfortable, such as school, family gatherings, or community celebrations.

Invisible boys hide behind hats, or "hoodies," with hair covering their eyes; they hide within headphones that drown the world out and prevent interaction; they hide behind sleepiness and spaciness; they hide in bed, in corners, and at the back of the room. They hide in the shadows of parks, roofs, parking lots. They use their silence as camouflage, and hope not to be noticed.

The ranks of invisible boys include those who are shy; poor; a member of an ethnic, racial, or religious minority; BGTQ (bisexual, gay, transgender, or questioning/queer); disabled; hearing or vision impaired; disfigured; addicted; illiterate; physically abused; sexually abused; or neglected and uncared for at home. Boys may become invisible because they are thrown out of their homes, have run away, or are homeless. A boy who is invisible because of hardship feels that his world is not normal; this feeling then isolates him from others. He may not realize that the normal happy childhood is a myth for many boys.

Invisibility can be a dangerous place or a safe one. Some boys choose invisibility as a way to be strong and independent. They enjoy being left alone, often with books, music, or art. They may not agree with the behaviors and activities expected of boys. They refuse to participate in a world they do not agree with.

Invisible boys surround us, and when seen, they should be treated with sensitivity; their worlds may be fragile.

Further Reading

The National Center on Family Homelessness, Web site [Online February 2007]. <http://thunder1.cudenver.edu/cye/factsheets/outcasts.pdf>.

Teen Depression, Web site [Online February 2007]. <http://www.teendepression .org/>.

Carolyne Ali Khan

Psychology of Boyhood

After more than a century of observation by developmental psychologists, who mapped out stages of development for Western children in general and noted a number of gender differences in boys' behavior unique to the technologically developed Western world (for example, general activity level, play style, sexual activity after puberty), we still know very little about the experience of being a boy. Direct observation created a rather simplistic and crude model of typical boyhood deportment that was useful for grouping and classifying boys in school in an era of compulsory education. The developmental model produced expectations among parents who were influenced by widely known experts (for example, in the 1920s, the behaviorist John B. Watson and, beginning in the 1940s, the psychoanalyst Benjamin Spock). Parents were instructed about when to anticipate certain milestones in a son's overall functioning, but especially his cognitive and psychomotor skills. In describing the unique way in which boys negotiate what Freud called the Oedipus complex, psychoanalysts pointed to one way in which boys experience the world differently than girls. Given the earlier dominance of behaviorism, however, and the problem of nonrefutability of psychodynamic claims, we are left with a simplistic schematic account of boyhood psychological life, epitomized in the epigenetic psychosocial model of Erik Erikson, which at least takes into consideration cultural differences in raising children.

To remedy this, a phenomenological method has been introduced to elicit descriptions from boys of the meaning given to their experience. Qualitative studies based on this method promise the first authentic account of boyhood, but such an account is a long way off. Given such descriptions, most presuppositions we have made about Western boyhood will have to be abandoned.

Although there are undoubtedly some dispositional differences between boys and girls based on levels of prenatal circulating hormones and even small differences in brain structure affected by these during the growth of the fetal brain, these differences are most certainly subject to management by programs of socialization carried out by parents and other educators. In the case of girls, we have seen that revisions in socialization practices led, for example, to the elimination of the concept of the tomboy, which has been replaced by our recognition and acceptance that girls are by nature capable of holding traditionally masculine perspectives on objects and people, and therefore of engaging in traditionally boyish activities. Revisions of similar scope have not yet occurred in connection with our conception of boys, but cross-cultural studies have made it obvious that the absence during boyhood of signs of emerging traditional masculinity is as much a matter of what is expected of boys as of any inborn imperatives, so that changes in what we do not expect from boys will alter their experience and behavior.

We must study just how certain anatomical and physiological differences—for example, skeletomuscular bulk and the male body's higher center of gravity, his exposed genitalia—are experienced by boys and how they determine the way their bodies are in the world. This is work still to be done, as is study of the presumed differences in childhood play patterns among boys and their sexual behavior after puberty. Our assumptions will have to be tested in light of what boys tell us about their experience in these areas. In 1945, Jean Piaget first published findings about play based on his unique model for eliciting and making sense of children's thoughts about their games. Further study modeled on this method of gathering data that combines direct observation and interviewing techniques is needed to elicit boys' reports of their life experiences.

By comparison to what boys do, very little attention has been given to their emotional lives, especially as distinct from their sexuality. Recent widely disseminated popular treatments of the topic include works by Michael Gurian, and Daniel Kindlon and Michael Thompson, but these are, once again, based on a view from the outside, based on established behavioristic or psychodynamic models of development, and prescriptive. Close attention must be given to understanding how and why boys feel as they do, and only they can tell us this.

In short, a new psychology of boyhood must be developed without recourse to simplistic presuppositions—whether behavioral, psychodynamic, or biological—and reductionist *explanations* based on them. Instead we must attempt to *understand* how and what boys experience as they move, think, play, feel, and imagine. We must work our way into their unique spatial and temporal world and learn what it is like to become a boy. We will then be in a position to revise our socialization practices if we choose to do so.

Further Reading

Erikson, Erik. *The Life Cycle Completed.* New York: W.W. Norton, 1998. Originally published in 1982.

Gurian, Michael. *The Wonder of Boys.* Los Angeles: Tarcher, 2006. Originally published in 1996.

Kindlon, Don, and Michael Thompson. *Raising Cain: Protecting the Emotional Lives of Boys.* New York: Ballantine Books, 2000. Originally published in 1999.

Piaget, Jean. *Play, Dream and Imitation in Childhood.* New York: W.W. Norton, 1962. Originally published in French in 1945.

Spock, Benjamin. *Pocket Book of Baby and Child Care: An Authoritative, Illustrated, Common-Sense Guide for Parents on the Care of Children from Birth to Adolescence.* New York: Pocket Books, 1946.

Watson, John Broadus. *Psychological Care of Infant and Child.* New York: W.W. Norton, 1928.

Miles Groth

Relationships

Although more attention has since been given to boys' gender socialization and its impact, for instance, on boys' relationships, there has been a tendency to overlook and underestimate boys' relational capabilities, or what boys are capable of knowing and doing in relationships. When boys' relational capabilities are addressed, it is mainly in terms of their deficiency in comparison to girls. Consistent with cultural stereotypes, boys, and especially adolescent boys, are typically depicted as emotionally impaired and/or relationally incompetent. For example, the media often portray boys as being less attuned to emotions, including their own, and less responsive in relationships. Likewise, research studies indicate that older boys and adult men report having fewer close relationships and experiencing lower levels of intimacy within their relationships.

In attempts to explain boys' alleged shortcomings, the literature on boys has tended to emphasize either nature or nurture. On one hand, those focusing on nature suggest that boys' physiology, or biological make-up, causes them to be less able to recognize and express a full range of emotions and less interested in relationships. However, infant studies have shown that both boys and girls are born with a fundamental capacity and primary desire for close, mutual, responsive relationships. For instance, infants as young as three months old demonstrate the ability to detect, as evidenced by their emotional distress, interactive mismatches that occur when a caregiver's behaviors are inappropriate or inconsistent with the infant's expectations, as is common among depressed mothers. Thus, we know that boys are not inherently less capable of being emotionally attuned and relationally responsive.

On the other hand, those focusing on nurture suggest that boys' gender socialization toward norms of masculine behavior that emphasize physical toughness, emotional stoicism, and projected self-sufficiency leads boys to devalue and disconnect from their emotions and relationships. In societies and cultures where masculinity is defined in contrast to femininity, the development of a masculine identity rests in part on a boy's ability to distance and differentiate himself from all things feminine. For instance, there is the expectation that, in order to become men, boys must separate from their mothers and deny their own need for the kinds of nurturance and care that the mother-child relationship provides. In this sense, boys' development is associated with a move out of or away from relationships. However, boys' relationships with their mothers do not suddenly disintegrate, and there is evidence that boys continue to desire and seek closeness in their relationships, so we know that there is something more going on.

Although it is certainly useful to understand how biology and culture can influence boys' development, it is also important to consider boys' agency. As active participants in their learning and development, boys can mediate the effects of their biological predispositions (e.g., temperament) and cultural influences through the ways in which they make meaning of and respond to their experiences. For instance, individual boys demonstrate the capacity to resist as well as yield to cultural messages about masculinity and societal pressures to conform. Moreover, variations in boys' developmental contexts, including access to information and resources, can contribute to group and individual differences in how boys' intrinsic tendencies and socialized inclinations manifest.

Research that focuses on boys' agency to examine boys' experiences from boys' perspectives reveals that, contrary to cultural stereotypes, boys have certain relational capabilities that reflect the capacity and desire for relationships observed at infancy. For example, when given the language and permission to communicate their personal thoughts, feelings, and desires, boys as young as four years old can be articulate, in terms of naming clearly what they know about themselves and their relationships; direct, in terms of expressing their meanings and intentions in a forthright manner; authentic, in terms of representing themselves in ways that are true to their sense of self; and attentive, in terms of listening carefully and responding thoughtfully in their social interactions. Similarly, within relationships characterized by trust and acceptance, adolescent boys demonstrate the ability to be fully present and genuinely engaged in the sense that they are self-aware, sensitive to others, and keenly attuned to how their social and cultural contexts affect their interactions.

At the same time, boys are also reading, taking in, and responding to their culture, including constructions of masculinity that manifest in their everyday interactions with peers and adults. It is primarily through and within interpersonal relationships that masculine norms are introduced, incorporated, and perpetuated in ways that become personally meaningful and directly consequential to individual boys. Starting at early childhood (or earlier) and continuing through adolescence, boys learn through observation and experience what is considered appropriate and desirable behavior for boys. To the extent that boys are interested and invested in fitting in (e.g., being one of the boys) and be accepted (e.g., being with the boys), or just avoiding the negative consequences (e.g., ridicule, rejection) that can ensue when they deviate from the norm, boys begin to emphasize qualities that liken them to other boys (and downplay those that set them apart).

For boys, it is often the case that their peer group culture and broader social contexts are not conducive to developing and expressing their relational capabilities. For instance, adolescent boys typically describe their peer group culture as being competitive, antagonistic, and therefore unsafe for genuine self-expression. As a result, they learn to be guarded in their social interactions and selective about what they reveal about themselves and to whom. Likewise, because relationships are considered feminine, boys may come to regard their relational capabilities as a weakness or liability, learn to cover them up, and project instead an image of obliviousness and indifference (e.g., as evidenced by the frequent claim, "I don't care"), which simultaneously protects their vulnerability and affirms their masculinity.

Under circumstances where sharing genuine thoughts, feelings, and desires not only makes you vulnerable but where others are likely to take advantage of your vulnerability, a boy's decision to be strategic about how he expresses himself and engages in relationships could be considered socially adaptive. Nevertheless, there is a sense of loss as boys learn to introduce nuance into their behaviors and become savvy in their interactions in ways that make their relational capabilities more difficult to detect. Whereas boys are capable of being clear and upfront about their feelings, they become cleverly disguised and self-protectively hidden. Although boys demonstrate the capacity for thoughtful self-reflection and deep interpersonal understanding and express a desire to feel truly understood and valued for who they are, they begin to appear as though they are incapable of and/or uninterested in close relationships. In other words, as boys modify their behaviors and styles of relating to align with cultural assumptions and expectations regarding masculinity, they begin to look like stereotypical boys.

Importantly, boys do not appear to lose their relational capabilities as a result of their gender socialization; there is evidence that boys' relational capabilities persist beyond early childhood and through adolescence, at least. However, over time, the need to shield or withhold certain parts of themselves from their relationships can ultimately constrain their ability to realize, as well as their ability to express, a full range of thoughts, feelings, and desires, and hinder their ability to develop the types of close relationships that have been linked to psychological health.

As we understand that boys have relational capabilities that are not always apparent, it is crucial that we reconsider our assumptions about what boys are capable of knowing and doing in relationships, which starts with listening to boys in ways that allow us to hear and see them in a new way. Likewise, as we understand boys' relational capabilities to be an asset rather than a liability, it is necessary that we refocus our attention and redirect our energy toward bolstering this resource instead of trying to compensate for presumed deficiencies in our efforts to support boys' healthy development. It may be helpful to remember that in fostering boys' relational capabilities we are not asking them to be something they are not nor teaching them something new. Rather, the point is to help them to recognize, give value to, and draw upon sources of strength to which they already have access but that they may have, in learning to navigate the cultures of boyhood, forgotten were theirs.

Further Reading

Kimmel, Michael S. *The gendered society.* 3rd edition. New York: Oxford University Press, 2007.

Ryan, J. "Boys to men." *San Francisco Chronicle.* March 22, 1998.

Way, Niobe, and Judy Y. Chu. (Eds.). *Adolescent boys: Exploring diverse cultures of boyhood.* New York: New York University Press, 2004.

Judy Y. Chu

Social Homelessness

Although there are many large cultures defined by general descriptions (i.e., American culture, African culture, European culture), there are also subcultures that exist that further shape the traditions of families (i.e., Christian culture, hip hop culture, Southern culture). With each layer of culture, there are more and more traditions and expectations that shape the identities of boys. During the early years of development, boys are often unable to see the influences of their culture on their identity, therefore a part of their identity can easily feel prescribed.

Gender and sexuality are also significant parts of one's identity that are determined during this early stage of life. Although a significant number of children are either born male or female, approximately 1 percent of births are of intersexed babies (Fausto-Sterling, 2000). Although there has been much controversy about the issue of sexuality and the factors that influence sexuality, the American Psychological Association (APA) noted that an individual's sexual orientation is determined at an early age. During the early years of their lives, boys' families teach them important lessons—about their identities, and about how the families value them—that carry over into their adult lives.

As boys develop, there are many factors that contribute to their identity. With each new day, they are bombarded with new information that influence the people that they choose to be. Although they process the new information subconsciously, they are constantly pruning away the characteristics that do not align with the identity they choose to embrace. Their style of dress, their speech patterns, and their choices in music are three simple examples of how their surroundings influence the ways in which they live their lives. During the developmental years of adolescence, preteens and teenagers turn to many different places to find representations of the identities they wish to live out. Popular magazines, television, the Internet, and peers play significant roles for adolescent boys in defining the parts of their identity that they can control. With their peers, boys construct identities that seek to represent their understanding of normalcy.

Identity and Inferiority

The factors that influence an adolescent boy's identity fall into two categories: fixed and fluid. Fixed identities are those that are innate at birth or during the early years of childhood and that are interpreted as unchangeable (race, gender, sexuality). Fluid identities are those that are adopted by a person through life experiences and are interpreted as changeable (education, political affiliation, religion, style, class, speech patterns, sexuality). Sexuality is purposefully added to both lists. Some believe that sexual orientation is predetermined, while others believe that life experiences, culture, and environment are significant factors. The individual perception of identity determines whether it is fixed or fluid. For example, if a teenage boy believes that homosexuality is a choice, he will likely believe that his identity as gay is fluid. Each identity carries cultural capital that is shaped by the influences of the larger society. Cultural capital refers to the advantages, access, or privileges that lead to a higher status in society. In American society, white, male, heterosexual, Christian, educated, middle-class identities carry the most cultural capital. Because of the white, patriarchal (male-dominated) norms that govern our society, there is a greater amount of cultural capital assigned to identities that are more closely aligned to the dominant society. Boys have more cultural capital than girls because of gender; however, if there are two students that are both girls and one is a Christian and the other is Muslim, the Christian will have more cultural capital because her religion follows the dominant norms.

If identities that mirror dominant norms yield cultural capital and promote individuals up the hierarchy of society, then identities that do not represent a white, male, heterosexual, Christian, educated, middle-class demote individuals in society. This phenomenon furthers a sense of inferiority in adolescent boys that is internalized and reinforced by much of the popular culture they turn to in defining their fluid identity. Adolescent boys who feel inferior have accepted society's views on identity and use them as benchmarks for comparison. When comparing fluid identities (education, style, speech patterns), boys will often attempt to reshape their identity to match those of the wider society. This can lead to feelings of inauthenticity, which fail to end the perception of inferiority. For fixed identities, boys can easily feel trapped by their identity and take on a posture of self-loathing.

Types of Social Homelessness

Individuals' identities help them form connections with others with similar characteristics within society. Schools are microcosms of the larger society. Like adults, students have multiple identities that they claim for themselves and use to create social categories in schools. The categories used as identifiers are not based on individual identifiers; rather students recycle the social tropes that are given to them by their peers to identify themselves. Students understand the significance of the many identities that shape the ways in which they experience their world. In schools, gender, race, ethnicity, sexuality, class, religion, culture, age, ability level, political affiliation, and geographic location are just some of the social categories that blend together to define students. Students link with students who share similar identifiers.

As students align themselves based on common identities, they form social groups. The dynamics within social groups are unconsciously governed by the members of the group and influenced by the norms of the dominant culture. In addition to an adolescent boy's fixed identities, the social groups he claims add another layer to his fluid identities. Social identification leads to stereotypical perceptions of self and others. Couched in these perceptions are the notions of the in groups and the out groups. Because of the white, patriarchal norms that govern our society, there is a greater amount of cultural capital assigned to categories that are more closely aligned to dominant society. Dominant groups are more in than marginalized groups, which recreates in schools the stratification found in society. Aiming to be considered an in group, each group composes an unwritten set of rules or standards that are necessary for participation. In many cases, the rules are very simple, and are focused on the fluid identity of the group members. Some groups require an initiation from its members to gain entry or force its members to perform actions to remain in the group. Gangs often initiate members through acts of violence, and then require the members to continue acts of violence. In many cases, the fixed and fluid identities of individuals determine whether they will be considered as a gang member or not, despite the performance of the required initiation.

Although there is no way to include an exhaustive list of the informal social groups available for adolescent boys at schools, the following list includes those that have a direct connection to some of the aforementioned fixed and fluid identities: racial/ethnic affiliation (African Americans, Asians, Latinos, Indians, Native Americans, etc.); music choice (pop, punk rockers, emo, hip hop); style of clothes (preps, thugs, goth); education/academic ability (gifted and talented, special education, geeks, nerds, college prep (CP), advanced placement (AP), international baccalaureate (IB), dropout); religious affiliation (Christian, Jewish, Muslim, Buddhist, Hindu, Wiccan, Atheist); and sexual orientation (heterosexual, homosexual, bisexual, asexual, undetermined). Each of these groups has a set of rules, norms, or expectations that are often based on stereotypes. For example, entry into the African American social group may require an adolescent boy to be Black but may also have expectations that he listen to hip hop music and enjoy sports. Entry into the AP social group may require adolescent boys to achieve academically at a certain level but may also have expectations about race, class, and dress. The informal rules extend beyond the parameters that define the group.

Because there are multiple layers of identity, and because social identity is fluid, adolescent boys can simultaneously be a part of multiple social groups. They can also choose to move their affiliation to a different social group. Social homelessness is a term that is used to describe an individual that is not a part of any social group. The condition of social homelessness describes one who, upon first glance, should be wholly accepted in one or more social categories. However, the individual is unable to fully participate in the life of the social group because of competing identities. One example of social homelessness is found in the fictitious example below.

Case Study

Tyrek was excited about his first day at his new school, Cardinal High. Although moving meant he had to leave his friends and the high school he had attended for two and a half years, he was certain that he would make the 20-mile commute for regular visits. Tyrek was especially excited about competing against his former school in the Math Olympics, which was led by his long-time boyfriend, Dustin. As Tyrek entered his first period AP Calculus class, he could tell that the students were surprised. He was used to being stared at for being four inches taller than the majority of his classmates but he quickly realized that he was the only African American student in the class. In fact, besides the two Asian American students sitting in the back, he was the only student of color. After exchanging introductions and taking attendance, the teacher, Ms. Jensen, highlighted some of the announcements made by the principal on the loud speaker. She commented on how she was excited to begin practices with the Math Olympics team this Thursday. After an awkward pause, she said, "Don't forget basketball tryouts begin on Thursday right after school. Tyrek, I know you are new, so if you need someone to help you find the gym, I will be happy to get one of these lovely young ladies to help you! I can see the way they have been looking at you since you've walked in. They would also be great at tutoring you for this class."

In the scenario, Tyrek could have been a part of multiple social groups. Although the scenario only mentions three (African American, AP, and gay), Tyrek could have continued to uncover layers of his identity as he studied at Cardinal High. Although this scenario was only a snapshot of Tyrek's first moments at a new school, there is potential that Tyrek will experience or already has experienced social homelessness. The traditional view of homosexuality by the African American community has been negative. African American social groups often marginalize gays and lesbians. Advanced classes in high schools are overwhelmingly white, and African American males are underrepresented in AP classes. Although the acceptance of gay and lesbian adolescents in a school is heavily shaped by geographic location, gay culture (in mainstream society) is often typified by young, white males, leaving African American men unrepresented. Therefore, Tyrek's identities could cancel him out of full participation in any of the above social groups, leaving him socially homeless.

Although society values identities that follow white patriarchal norms, individuals should not be forced to prioritize their identities, whether they are fixed or fluid. An adolescent boy who is socially homeless must either ignore one or more of the layers of his identity or create a new home for himself that does not have the rigid rules based on societal stereotypes for entry.

Further Reading

Fausto-Sterling, Anne. *Sexing the Body: Gender Politics and the Construction of Sexuality*. New York: Basic Books, 2000.

Horne, Arthur M., and Mark S. Kiselica. *Handbook of Counseling Boys and Adolescent Males: A Practitioner's Guide*. Thousand Oaks, CA: Sage Publications, Inc., 1999.

Social Identity Theory [Online March 2008]. University of Twente Web site <http://www.tcw.utwente.nl/theorieenoverzicht/Theory%20clusters/Interpersonal%20Communication%20and%20Relations/Social_Identity_Theory.doc/>.

Rydell Harrison

Spaces

The role of space in boyhood studies has many facets. Psychologists have noted that boys use spaces such as playgrounds, classrooms, and hallways differently than girls. Boys are known to use more space, use open spaces more often, and may be granted more space by parents or teachers. Furthermore, sociologists suggest that space is used more often among boys than girls for the purpose of establishing, policing, and contesting of zones. This making of competitive space is to some extent formalized through games and contests. Sports popular among American boys often entail ventures into enemy space, while "holding ground" against enemy incursions (football, baseball, basketball). Thus, spaces are often important elements (whether as territories, arenas, or stages) in the development of boys' sense of masculinity. Researchers have long observed this in primary schools, Little League, elite boarding schools, as well as in cultures around the world. For instance, North African boys are banned from the women's hammam (bath house) when they are said to develop "a man's stare" at about age four to eight. According to anthropologists, with this event, "a cosmic frontier splits the planet in two halves": male and female.

In contemporary America, matters of space seem less cosmic in proportion. Still, historians observe that books, card games, and videogames marketed to boys have long been situated in realms historically occupied mostly (or most visibly) by men: the frontiers of wilderness exploration (the Wild West), borders of expanding colonial empires, war fronts, crime scenes, and outer space. The traditional *boy book* genre has always been about "adventurous" space, exploration, and annexation. Around 1900 popular experts on boy life ("boyologists" as some called themselves) generally had much to say about appropriate spaces for boyhood activities and upbringing, especially the role of the home, "the street," the city, boarding schools, and the ranch. Today teachers still debate the appropriateness for boys of spaces such as cyberspace, co-ed schools, and summer camp. Also, temporary change of space (inner city boys to forests, for instance) has long been considered a necessary tactic in social reform projects directed toward boys.

Ideas about space offer diverse ways to interpret its relation to boyhood. Several schools of thought in American culture have at one time or another endorsed and centralized outdoor rural activities, be it in the form of scouting, summer camps, survival weekends, wilderness "initiation rites," or fishing trips. Rather than simply *beneficial,* spaces have also been theorized as essentially *entitled,* meaning that boys' development would be stunted if not allowed the spacious exuberance and rowdiness traditionally associated with normal boyhood. Some authorities on brain research say boys may learn better if allowed more outdoor breaks throughout the day, even to move around in small spaces while taking tests. In recent years there have been severe critiques of schools banning tag, flag football, and dodgeball from recess and PE because the decision would violate "no touching" or "safety" policies. This *Tag Ban* has so far been a mainly American and possibly temporary discussion featuring (anti-)feminist, conservative, and neurobiological arguments. *Where the boys are* or may be, then, is currently as much a complex political question as an important one to the recreation industry.

Further Reading

MacDonald, Robert. *Sons of the Empire: The Frontier and the Boy Scout Movement, 1890–1918.* Toronto: University of Toronto Press, 1993.

Rotundo, E. Anthony. *American Manhood: Transformations in Masculinity from the Revolution to the Modern Era.* New York: Basic Books, 1993.

Diederik F. Janssen

Suicide

Suicide continues to be a problem for our youth, both nationally and globally, resulting in at least 100,000 adolescent deaths by suicide every year in the United States (American Federation of Suicide Prevention (AFSP), 2008). Nationally, at least one suicide is committed every two hours for those aged 15–24, an alarming statistic (American Association of Suicidology (AAS), 2008). From the mid 1950s to the late 1970s, the suicide rates for those aged 15–24 tripled (American Federation of Suicide Prevention, 2008). There was then a decrease in suicides among 15- to 24-year-olds, but for those aged 10–14, the rate has doubled in the last 20 years (AFSP, 2008). According to the AAS (2008), suicide is currently the third leading cause of death for this age group, preceded only by accidents (which are often suicide attempts) and homicides (violent death). Males complete suicide more often than females due to more violent methods used, such as firearms, hanging, and asphyxiation, while females are more likely to overdose or cut themselves. Although females attempt suicide twice as often as males, men complete suicide at a rate four times as much. In 2005, male suicides numbered 25,907 as compared with only 6,730 female suicides (American Federation of Suicide Prevention, 2008).

Given the above figures, it is obvious that we should be concerned about the reasons that males desire to end their lives at such an alarming rate over females. Although it is difficult to determine why any suicide occurs, the following offers a glimpse into what suicide experts currently know about male suicide, specifically in boys aged 15–24.

Although they experience deep sadness and fears, boys have difficulty sharing their feelings and concerns, thus avoiding the stereotype of being "too feminine" or emotional. Wanting to be "regular guys," their vulnerabilities are hidden beneath their bravado. In this, boys are caught in the dichotomous cycle of society's current expectations that they become caring and sensitive men, while fighting against the traditional role of being tough and hardcore.

Because of the cultural stereotype that males do not cry, boys mask their emotions and seek other outlets of release, such as drug and alcohol abuse, sexual promiscuity, reckless driving, cutting, and physical violence (thus the huge number of homicides for this age group). On the more positive side, many boys release tension through sports and other physical activities.

Boys fear bullying and harassment at school and in their communities, resulting in an increased amount of pressure with each passing day. They fear going to school, being at school, and participating in school events and activities. Part of the macho image they feel they must portray is quickly diminished if they are smaller than their peers, are less attractive, or are considered an outsider in terms of academics (geeks and nerds), athletics (chess club instead, for example), or social skills (i.e., shyer or kinder than their counterparts).

Boys who are gay and experiencing difficulty keeping it a secret or in "coming out" often experience many of the characteristics of a suicidal youth. Often without the support, guidance, and compassion of caring adults, the boys' propensity toward suicidal activity increases if they remain silent and alone in their journey. However, this does not mean that the suicide rates are higher among gay and lesbian youth, but only in youth who suffer from the anxiety involved in the situation, which results in more attempts and suicide ideation.

More males are involved in the musical arts (performance) than girls, especially boy bands and rock groups, during their adolescent years. Kurt Cobain's death prompted a revival of interest in the relationship between music and suicide. As a result, research found that a correlation does exist between the individuals' vulnerability toward depression and acting on suicide, regardless of whether they become famous or not.

Due to any or all of the above scenarios, boys can experience intense peer pressure during their adolescent years. They want to fit in and be accepted, yet are torn between acting on their values and beliefs, and participating in at-risk behaviors in order to be in one of the groups.

To conclude, to help our youth, especially boys, we must remain focused on listening carefully, being available and open to having discussions with them, and taking action on their behalf. Suicide does not have to occur.

Further Reading

American Federation for Suicide Prevention (2008). *Facts and Figures.* Retrieved August 10, 2008, from: http://www.afsp.org/index.cfm?fuseaction=home .viewPage&page_id=04EA1254-BD31-1FA3-C549D77E6CA6AA37.

American Association of Suicidology (2008). *Youth and Suicide Fact Sheet,* January 2008. Retrieved August 8, 2008, from: http://www.suicidology.org/web/ guest/stats-and-tools/fact-sheets.

Youth Suicide Prevention Program (2008). *Youth Suicide FAQ.* Retrieved August 10, 2008, from: http://www.yspp.org/aboutSuicide/suicideFAQ.htm.

Teresa Rishel

SECTION 6

"Bad" Boys

Boys and the Adult Justice System

The governments of countries, states, or provinces come up with rules for people to follow in living their lives as citizens, or members, of the country. These rules are called laws. A government enforces these laws by punishing people who break the rules. These punishments are usually decided through courts and judges in the justice system, which is a complicated, interrelated set of laws and procedures. A common misunderstanding about the justice system today is that boys who get in trouble with the law always go to a court that is especially for children, called "juvenile court" or "family court." However, in most U.S. states, children ages 16 and over are dealt with as adults.

When the justice system brings legal action against a person, it is called a prosecution. When people are prosecuted, they may receive a sentence. A sentence is the decision and the punishment that is meted out by the court if someone is found guilty of a crime. Children ages 16 and over in most states can be prosecuted as adults, which means that a 16-year-old boy who gets arrested can be charged with a crime, prosecuted, and potentially sentenced as an adult.

In many urban areas in particular, gone are the days where a boy who is up to mischief is taken to a police precinct and released to his parents with a scolding. Increasingly, boys and young men are targeted by police and are charged with crimes for minor offenses. In the 1960s, states moved to create family courts that would address juvenile crime. Under these courts, emphasis on rehabilitation replaced earlier notions of retribution. *Rehabilitation* and *retribution* are words that are often used when talking about the justice system. Rehabilitation seeks to change behavior through education and counseling, while retribution seeks to strictly punish someone for being bad. Under the family court system, children in their mid-teens who were charged with crimes—including minor drug charges, minor assaults, stealing (called "larceny"), property damage, and other crimes—would be tried in a civil setting. A civil court is a court where going to jail is not the outcome. In these courts, it was hoped that the best interest of the child would be the main concern of the judge. The child in these situations would be given certain basic rights, such as the right to an attorney and the right to be proven guilty beyond a reasonable doubt, which was not the case before the beginning of family courts in the 1960s. Children found guilty in the family courts had a range of outcomes, including therapy, probation, and/or placement away from their homes. The introduction of family courts was considered to be a progressive turning point in the development of the criminal justice system because it was believed that these changes would help the children who were charged with crimes, rather than simply punishing them.

With the increase of drugs and violence in urban areas in the 1970s and 1980s, however, states began to abandon the ideas of rehabilitation in the adult justice system. Under newer, stricter drug-possession laws, adults were sentenced to long prison terms for relatively minor drug charges. This crackdown eventually affected the way in which states viewed children involved in crime as well. In many states, there are cases in which children as young as 14 years old are charged as adults. This presents a serious situation for many boys and young men. Cases in which children are accused of certain robberies and assaults are no longer exclusively filed in family court, but can also be filed in criminal courts, which can impact the sentence as well as the punishment they receive. In many places, a criminal court cannot place a child in foster care if his home situation is not good. These are decisions made by family courts. In fact, in many states, if a child is found to be guilty of a crime, the only options that criminal courts have is either to let the child go back home, send him to jail, or put him on probation.

Today in most states, children 16 years and older are not eligible to be dealt with in family court. Their cases automatically are filed in criminal court with adults. The practical effect of this is that for a large group of boys—an overwhelming majority of whom come from families living in poverty, and most of whom are boys of color—are thrust into a justice system that they do not understand and which is not equipped to understand their developmental stages, or their needs as adolescents. Children 16 years of age may not be able to understand the adult criminal system. They may not understand what is happening to them, and it may be very frightening. Some research indicates that the brain of an adolescent develops well into the late teens and even twenties. Understanding when things are right or wrong and having full comprehension of consequences for actions continue to develop well past the age of 16.

There are many perspectives involved in trying to understand a system that can send a boy to prison. Some people believe that in order to be effective against crime, children must be treated as adults, prosecuted, and imprisoned for the safety of society. Others believe that adolescents should be treated as children (who possibly have done wrong) and provided with support, counseling, guidance, and effective education.

For boys who are charged with serious crimes, this process can be a terrifying and alien experience. Although many states have laws that encourage judges to treat 16, 17, and 18 year olds with a certain degree of leniency or mercy, such treatment is not required, and in many cases is practically discouraged, because of public opinion in favor of "getting tough on crime" and "cleaning up the streets." An example of how serious this issue is, is that if a boy in New York is involved in stealing an iPod, he could go to prison for up to 15 years. This is because, depending on the circumstances, he could be charged with a robbery. He would be treated as an adult in court, and depending on his previous history, he could be sentenced as an adult to prison under a felony sentence. Boys in this situation are often sent to prisons far from where they live. This makes it difficult for family and friends to visit the boy, and in turn the isolation can make it difficult for the boys to be supported when they get released from jail. It can be a hard transition to leave jail and go back to the community, and family support is important to during difficult times. If there is no longer a family closeness, it is harder to get a job or an education and "stay straight" when an incarcerated boy gets out.

There are many factors that contribute to an explosion of boys in the adult justice system. They include administration of schools, the breakdown in foster care, and the increase of gangs in the inner cities. Together they help to create a subculture of boys in jail or on their way to jail. Sometimes the consequences of their actions are not obvious to these boys until it is too late, and they have been arrested and prosecuted. Other times, they are left with few ways out, as one poor choice begins to lead to another, and this continues, as the quality of choices becomes worse and worse.

Foster Care

In the 1980s there was an explosion in the use of crack cocaine in many cities. Crack is a form of cocaine that has been referred to as "the poor man's drug." The increased use of crack cocaine in the mid-1980s coincides with a deterioration of inner city structures and communities. Crime skyrocketed, as did homelessness, and children born to addicted mothers were generally born addicted to cocaine and suffered developmental delays because of it. Often, these children went into foster care, either because their parents were unable to care for them, or they were removed by state social service agencies because they were neglected, abused, or their parents were imprisoned. After the 1980s and early 1990s, there was a large number of children in foster care in urban areas throughout North America. Many of these children had special needs, and as they grew up, they were more likely to be involved in the criminal justice system. This may be because of a complicated set of circumstances, including lack of funding and services in foster care, an often unprepared education system, and lack of community support.

Children in foster care continue to be over-represented in the criminal justice system. These children are more likely to remain in jail while their case is being handled because of their perceived lack of community ties. This is one of the factors that a judge must consider when deciding whether an accused person should be released into the community or kept in jail until their court case is finished. Unfortunately, it is often assumed that children in foster care have no one to care for them and make sure they get to court when they need to be there. In general, people who are in jail while they are awaiting trial are more likely to be convicted of the crime in the long run. This situation has an enormous impact on accused children who are in foster care. As they are often not released on bail, the situation is consequently more likely to have a negative result on their case.

Urban Schools

Urban schools are increasingly reliant on the criminal justice system to solve discipline issues that in the past would have been handled within the schools. Many urban schools have implemented "zero tolerance" policies. Under these policies, school fights are prosecuted as felony assaults, which are very serious. This means that the students involved in certain behaviors can be expelled from school and prosecuted in the criminal justice system. Schools prosecute offenses such as marijuana possession, minor vandalism, and fighting, and put students into courtrooms rather than school-based detention or temporary suspension from school. The disruption in the education of these boys is significant and can lead to other troubles down the road, because these boys often miss many days of school because they are in court, or in jail, and may be transferred out of certain schools because of these criminal charges. Additionally, once they are considered to be a "court-involved youth," many teachers and administrators are no longer interested in helping them succeed in school.

Search and Seizure

The laws of a country provide certain protections to all citizens, including the right not to be searched "unreasonably." Although there are many definitions of what is unreasonable, generally police must have a reason, a "probable cause," in order to search a person. Young men hanging out on streets in urban areas are more likely to be searched and considered suspicious, and even dangerous. Although lawyers may challenge these searches, judges generally support the searches, perhaps because of stereotypes about young men of color being "trouble" and biases in favor of the police.

The Process

An adult criminal defendant has a hard enough time understanding what is going on within a seemingly mysterious system where judges, court reporters, and lawyers each have different roles that may not be obvious to the defendant. In most court hearings, a defendant, or accused, will see two different types of lawyers. There are prosecuting lawyers, whose job is to try to get as many people convicted of crimes as possible, and there are defense lawyers, whose job is to try to defend against the charges that their client is being accused of. District attorneys are prosecutors, and public defenders are defense attorneys. For a boy or a young man, this process can be very confusing and overwhelming.

Assault and robberies are common charges for adolescent boys. Both of these charges can result from something that seems to be minor, such as a fight, but assault and robbery are fairly serious charges that could be considered felonies. A felony is a crime that is punishable by more than a year in jail or state prison, whereas a misdemeanor is a less serious charge that is punishable by up to a year in jail. A 16-year-old boy charged with robbery or an assault is held at the police station until he is transferred to a processing facility at, or near, the courthouse. At the police station, the boy becomes a defendant, which means he is accused of a crime. A police officer or detective will question the boy in an effort to obtain either an explanation or a confession. This process is called an interrogation.

One part of the job of a police officer or detective is to try to get defendants whom the officer believes to be guilty to confess to the crime. These detectives are trained specifically in questioning techniques designed to exploit weaknesses and vulnerabilities of those who they are interrogating, including young defendants, in order to get them to confess. Children under the age of 16 are entitled under the law to have a parent with them during any police interrogation. Police are not permitted to interrogate children without a parent present. Boys 16, 17, and 18 years old are not entitled to have a parent with them during this process. Additionally, in the United States, the Supreme Court has ruled that police are allowed to lie to a defendant in order to extract a confession from him. This leaves a juvenile defendant 16–18 years old particularly vulnerable to being manipulated during interrogation. An interrogation can last indefinitely, and although a detective is not allowed to use "coercive measures," courts have been reluctant to define what coercion is, short of physical coercion. *Coercion* is a word that means someone is being forced to do something, either physically or mentally. Many states do not require a videotaping of interrogations to determine whether or not they are coercive, although there is a movement to require videotaping of all criminal interrogations.

Whether or not a boy confesses, if there is enough evidence, he will be brought to the courthouse where he will wait for many hours in a jail cell with other defendants waiting to see the judge. At this point, very little is explained to any defendant about what is going on, and often they don't even know what charge they are being accused of. This can be an unfamiliar and very scary experience for anyone, especially a child. Boys in this situation may be in unfamiliar surroundings, a situation they have never been in. They often are not able to call anyone to tell them where they are. All their possessions, including their cell phones and wallets, are taken away. They wait in the cell until it is time to meet the judge in what is called an arraignment.

Arraignment is a process where the defendants comes before the judge, are assigned an attorney, and are either released or have bail set for them. Immediately prior to the arraignment, a lawyer, generally a public defender, will interview the defendant and explain what is going on. This generally occurs in a holding cell directly behind the courtroom. A public defender is a lawyer who is assigned by the courts to represent poor defendants, or defendants without money to pay for a lawyer. Generally, many 16- and 17-year-old children are assigned lawyers because they do not have enough money to hire a private lawyer.

At arraignment the prosecutor or district attorney will formally tell the defendant what he is being charged with. His family may or may not be in the courtroom. The defendant will usually plead "not guilty," which is saying that he denies the charges and the case should go to trial. At this point the judge must decide whether the defendant should be released and be free until his next court date, or should be held by the police on what is called bail. Bail is money that must be paid to the court in order to make sure that the defendant comes back to court for his trial. If the defendant or his family pays the bail money and the defendant does not return to court, the defendant does not get the money back.

Once the arraignment is finished, the case gets put over for another date. The case is adjourned, or rescheduled, in order for attorneys to either try and resolve the case or prepare for trial. A trial is a court date when the prosecutor must prove the charges against a defendant. The prosecutor must prove that the defendant committed a crime and must convince a jury that the defendant is guilty. A jury is a group of men and women from the community who listen to witnesses and decide who to believe. Generally, defendants are entitled to a jury of "one's peers," which means people who are like them, who may be able to understand the defendant's situation. However, a boy does not get to have boys on his jury. Only adults over age 18 can be members of juries. If the jury does not believe that the prosecutor has proven the case, then the defendant is acquitted, or determined to be not guilty of the crime, and the case is over. If, however, the jury believes the prosecution's witnesses, then the defendant may be found guilty. A boy who is found guilty, or convicted, can face a range of punishment, from probation to jail time. Probation is a period of time where the defendant is not in jail, but is supervised closely and watched to make sure that he does not violate any laws.

Life on the Inside

In 2007, the United States had more people incarcerated than at any point in her history—more in sheer numbers and more as a percentage of her population. One out of every 31 Americans was either in jail, prison, on parole, or on probation in the United States during 2007 (The Pew Center on the States, 2009). Boys and young men of color are most vulnerable and make up a large portion of this statistic. As the population of incarcerated youth grows, state governments struggle to find money to pay for keeping these prisoners in jail. During harder economic times, programs designed to keep the youth out of trouble are increasingly likely to lose funding.

Once a boy is prosecuted as an adult, he is eligible for the full range of punishments, from the relatively mild community service, to jail, to state prison, to life without the possibility of parole, and, in some states, even the death penalty. The disturbing problem with this type of punishment for a boy who is prosecuted as an adult, there is the possibility that often these children do not understand the full consequences of what is happening to them, what they may have done, and how to deal with it once they are in trouble. There are many examples of cases in which boys are arrested, and confess to crimes, and are later proven innocent after spending many years in jail. This shows the particular vulnerabilities of boys in the adult criminal justice system and the possibilities of their manipulation in moments of high stress and confusion.

Society has always struggled with how to deal with the issues of crime and punishment, and also with how to deal with the young who break the law. In some eras, boys have been dealt with harshly, while in others there have been movements to rehabilitate children to encourage them to become productive members of society. As society struggles, boys in urban areas are often lost in a system designed to punish adults. Only time will tell if this era will move again toward an understanding of the need for rehabilitation and support of children.

Further Reading

Hubner, John. Discarded Lives: Children Sentenced to Life without Parole [Online]. Amnesty International USA Web site <http://www.amnestyusa.org/Spring_2006/Discarded_Lives_Children_Sentenced_to_LifeWithout_Parole/page.do?id=1105357&n1=2&n2=19&n3=392>.

Deskovic, Jeff. Know the Cases [Online]. Innocence Project Web site <http://www.innocenceproject.org/Content/44.php>.

The Pew Center on the States. One in 31: The Long Reach of American Corrections. The Pew Center on the States Web site. Retrieved March 3, 2009, from <http://www.pewtrusts.org/uploadedFiles/wwwpewtrustsorg/Reports/sentencing_and_corrections/PSPP_1in31_report_FINAL_WEB_2-27-09.pdfTimes Topic>. Tankleff, Martin [Online]. *The New York Times* Web site <http://topics.nytimes.com/top/reference/timestopics/people/t/martin_tankleff/index.html>.

Lawrence Siry

Bullying and Masculinity

Over the past four decades, research on bullying has proliferated significantly as researchers have tried to understand, identify, measure, and reduce rates of bullying in schools. Dan Olweus, a researcher from Norway, is widely credited as the first researcher to advance the study of bullying. He published a book based on his research that appeared in the United States in 1978, titled Aggression in the Schools: Bullies and Whipping Boys (the latter being what would now be referred to as victims). Olweus did not include girls in his book, but "presumed that whipping boy/bully problems are more common among boys and have more serious manifestations because of a stronger component of physical violence." Bullies are characterized as those who demonstrate an aggressive personality pattern, indicators for which are physical and verbal aggression, and positive attitude toward violence.

In his subsequent book, *Bullying in Schools: What We Know and What We Can Do*, Olweus describes bullying as being "exposed, repeatedly and over time, to negative actions on the part of one or more other students." Although he focused on boys and bullying in his first book, the definition of bullying in his second book is generic rather than boy-specific. His definition has been highly influential in research on bullying, as well as on policies and programs that attempt to curb it. He is perhaps the most cited researcher in the world on the topic of bullying. A fact sheet on the Web site of Child and Family Canada (2000), for instance, draws from Olweus' definition almost word for word.

Bullying is not the exclusive purview of boys. Olweus asserts that boys tend to attack victims openly and directly, whereas girls are more exposed to subtle and indirect attacks from other girls (1993). Popular films such as *Mean Girls* and *Heathers* make it clear that girls bully, too. Other researchers also claim or imply that boys tend to bully in physically aggressive ways, while girls tend bully in relational ways, such as spreading malicious gossip and exclusion.

Such gendered notions may have some validity, yet it is not unusual for boys to exclude and spread rumors about other boys, and for girls to be physically aggressive with each other. These added complexities of gender are usually excluded from scholarly analysis, even though journalists often sensationalize events labeled as *swarming* among girls. Even if a rigid duality based on gender tends to be overstated, it is nevertheless valid to suggest that gender is socially prescribed and regulated in particular ways that tend to foster cultures wherein bullying can flourish. The normative culture of masculinity is one such venue.

Prior to the early 1970s, bullying was widely minimized as "boys being boys." Especially in the last decade, journalists have cast attention to incidents of bullying that were especially tragic (such as those that resulted in suicide of the victim—called bullycide) or sensational (such as those that resulted in high-profile lawsuits against school districts, administrators, and educators). Other kinds of school violence, such as school shootings, have become linked with everyday, seemingly unremarkable but ongoing cases of bullying. The 1999 massacre at Columbine High School in Littleton, Colorado, in particular, served as a grim reminder that bullying should not be taken lightly, given that the shooters had been routinely bullied by their peers at school.

The sensation of, and conversations about, school shootings obscure the fact that, as Katz and Jhally (1999) argue, it is not kids killing kids as journalists often report, but rather boys killing boys and girls. Kimmel and Mahler (2003) offer two further points. One is that most of the shooters were not only bullied, but they were also all boys who were targeted because they were perceived as not measuring up to dominant norms of masculinity. The other point is that "masculinity is the single greatest risk factor in school violence," yet is often not identified, much less analyzed, in investigations on youth violence and research on bullying. Such oversights are examples of not seeing the trees for the proverbial forest.

Unlike much of the research on bullying, research on masculinity has established that "young men are the most frequent perpetrators of physical violence, and . . . are most at risk of being the victims of violence" (Anderson, 2008). Contemporary masculinity assumes and enacts men's dominance over women, which gives rise to and normalizes sexual harassment and violence against women. Men compete with other men for status and dominance, whereby some men are accorded higher status (specifically white, masculine, heterosexual men) than are those who do not measure up (specifically those deemed as *queers* or *sissies*). Hegemonic masculinity features prominently in popular novels about the cultures of boys and young men, novels such as *Lord of the Flies, Catcher in the Rye,* and *The Outsiders.*

Boys are men in training. As such, most strive to enact and replicate hegemonic masculinity so that they achieve status among male peers, and preemptively guard against accusations or perceptions that their masculinity is deficient. Guided by the norms of hegemonic masculinity, boys strive to prove themselves in the eyes of other boys that they are tough, aggressive, and, without question, heterosexual. Bullying of boys by other boys, which often takes the form of homophobia, includes determining who dominates and who is dominated in accordance with the hierarchy of masculinity. As Mills (2001) points out, boys who do not measure up to dominant prescriptions of masculinity are "likely to be punished by his peers in ways which seek to strip him of his mantle of masculinity."

Boys also bully girls. Prior to the proliferation of bullying discourse, such behaviors were usually and accurately described as *sexual harassment*. However, the label "bullying" is gender neutral.

Given that sexual harassment of women, homophobia toward other men, and general forms of verbal and physical aggression among men are normalized and rewarded in society, it leaves little surprise that boys act in order to be masculine. Media bears much influence on the behaviors and attitudes of boys, as Jhally and Katz demonstrate in their documentary *Wrestling with Manhood: Boys, Bullying and Battering* (2002). Despite the social pressure and media support for boys to adopt masculinity, most approaches to reducing bullying continue to focus on regulating behaviors and promoting healthy relationships. While such approaches are useful, by themselves, they are akin to trying to hold back the tide. Increased critical analysis and education about how masculinity fosters bullying among boys and violence of men is therefore essential to reduce bullying in schools and decrease violence in society.

Further Reading

Anderson, Kristin. 2008. Constructing young masculinity: A case study of heroic discourse on violence. *Discourse & Society*, 19(2): 139–161.

Child and Family Canada. 2000. Fact sheet #15: Bullying [Online June 2008]. <http://www.cfc-efc.ca/docs/vocfc/00000805.htm>.

Katz, Jackson, and Sut Jhally. The national conversation in the wake of Littleton is missing the mark [Online June 2008]. *Boston Globe* Web site <http://www.jacksonkatz.com/pub_missing.html>.

Jhally, S., and Jackson Katz. *Wrestling with manhood: Boys, bullying and battering.* Northampton, MA: Media Education Foundation, 2002.

Kimmel, Michael S., and Matthew Mahler. 2003. Adolescent masculinity, homophobia, and violence: Random school shootings, 1982–2001. *American Behavioral Scientist*, 46(10): 1439–1458.

Mills, Martin. *Challenging violence in schools: An issue of masculinities.* Buckingham, UK: Open University, 2001.

Olweus, Dan. *Aggression in the schools: Bullies and whipping boys.* Washington, DC: Hemisphere, 1978.

Olweus, Dan. *Bullying at school: What we know and what we can do.* Cambridge: Blackwell, 1993.

Gerald Walton

Gangsta Rap

Gangsta rap, or hard core rap as it sometimes called, is the most infamous sub-genre of hip hop music. The influence of gangsta rap on boys is highly debat-able, although it is mostly assumed that it is negative and that boys' exposure to it should be limited. It is very common for those unfamiliar with hip hop music to make the mistake of confusing the subgenre of gangsta rap with all of hip hop music. Though hip hop represents a style of music, within it are a variety of styles, each with its own history, sound, and artists. Unlike con-scious hip hop, underground hip hop, or even mainstream hip hop, gangsta rap is ever present in the media, often being blamed for gang violence, accused of glorifying ghetto thug life, and criticized for its homophobic and sexist lyrics that often refer to women as hos and bitches. Not surprisingly gangsta rap is often also condemned for having a negative influence on boys, especially Black boys as most gangsta rappers—and rappers in general in North America—are Black men. But before we can discuss the debated rela-tionship between gangsta rap and boys, we should take a look at the history of gangsta rap, some of the important artists in this genre, and outline what exactly defines this type of hip hop music and makes it so controversial today.

Hip hop may have started in the Bronx, New York, but most agree that gangsta rap's birthplace is in the West Coast, with rappers such as Ice T and the group NWA being the foremost gangsta rappers in the mid-1980s. How-ever, there is some mention of a Philadelphia rapper named Schoolly D who appeared a few years before the West Coast gangsta rap crews, and was drop-ping lyrics about his gang and their violent acts. Although Schoolly D is not remembered by most hip hop listeners today, he is credited with being a pio-neer in gangsta rap, preceding Ice Cube and Ice T who eventually split from NWA to go on to be among the premier faces of gangsta rap today. These two West Coast artists are known as the O.G.s (or Old Gangstas) of the gangsta rap game and are given much respect because of their contributions to the field and for their ability to keep it real in the hip hop industry and on the streets.

There were of course artists on the East Coast that put out gangsta rap tracks or even albums, but the genre of gangsta rap never really flourished on the East Coast as it did on the West Coast. Some of the first gangsta rap songs are Ice T's "6 in the Morning" from his 1986 record *Rhyme Pays,* which was released with hip hop's parental advisory label and NWA's "Straight Outta Compton," "Fuck tha Police," and "Gangsta Gangsta," all off of their 1988 record *Straight Outta Compton* referring to the West Coast city of Compton. *Straight Outta Compton* was released on rapper Eazy-E's Ruthless Records label and has been re-released twice since 1988, most recently in 2007 with a twentieth anniversary edition. Most of the NWA songs were written and per-formed by Ice Cube who later went on to a prominent solo gangsta rap career. Ice T, Ice Cube, and NWA helped move hip hop's focus from the East Coast to the West Coast and also brought a different style to hip hop both lyrically and musically. Their songs told the story of gangsta life filled with narratives of hustling in the streets, an aggressive in your face attitude toward life, and the materialism of street dreams.

Gangsta rap is known for its ghetto life narratives that depict realities of gang life or life where violence is ever present. The sound is hard hitting, usually with a booming bass, and the lyrics are unapologetically explicit. The rapper is almost always male, which is why gangsta rap is often criticized for perhaps encouraging young boys to lead a life of violence. Some feel that gangsta rap glamorizes street violence; however gangsta rap artists maintain that they are representing the realities that confront young Black men. The two other contentious issues with gangsta rap are its blatant homophobia and sexualizing of women, especially in their videos.

Too often gangsta rap is painted as a one-dimensional musical genre that serves no other purpose than to boost record sales. But gangsta rap is much more complex than just negative stereotypes about young Black men in the streets. Gangsta rappers strive to make social commentary on the state of the streets and the conditions that exist to push young men to take up the kind of gangsta life they are rapping about. Gangsta rappers insist that they rap about violence and other negative aspects because that is what is actually happening in streets across America, and that they are trying to draw attention to the stories of urban youth who would go neglected otherwise. This aspect of social commentary is usually ignored by gangsta rap's critics who choose to focus on the negative lyrics without questioning why it is that these artists are rapping about such a harsh reality. Gangsta rap's most infamous critics include U.S. Senator Bob Dole and television host Oprah Winfrey. In 2001 gangsta rap was one of the targets of a U.S. Senate censorship hearing that took issue with gangsta rap's advertising and explicit lyrics and content. Perhaps the largest criticism of any one gangsta rap song was toward NWA's "Fuck tha Police," which spoke bluntly of the relationship between the Los Angeles Police Department (LAPD) and Black youth. The song received public criticism from the LAPD and many media outlets. The controversial song has since become a protest song beyond Los Angeles' Black youth to youth in any context feeling discriminated against or censored by the authorities.

Tupac Shakur and Snoop Dogg continued in the West Coast gangsta rap tradition, putting their own spin on the genre—Tupac becoming famous for his lyrical, poetic style of writing, and Snoop Dogg for his smooth funked-out sound. Tupac, a respected gangsta rapper, introduced a different element to gangsta rap, with songs such as "Keep Ya Head Up," which spoke to the struggles of the women so frequently ignored or ill-referenced in gangsta rap songs. Tupac's gangsta rap songs showed that the genre does not have to always be hard or put down women; instead, women should be respected by young men and that the women's stories should also be rapped. "Keep Ya Head Up" is regarded as one of the most powerful and influential hip hop songs in history by men and women alike. Other notable gansta rappers are DMX, Scarface, Dr. Dre, Eazy-E, and Mobb Deep. Recent gangsta rappers include 50 Cent and The Game. The 1991 film *Boyz N the Hood* by John Singleton is a good film representation of the zeitgeist of gangsta rap in the late 1980s and early 1990s.

The story of gangsta rap is as complex as its lyrics and the motives behind them. There are songs that offend and songs that inspire, but it seems that the one thing gangsta rap is consistently effective at is getting people talking gangsta rap and its effects on youth, especially young men. Although the gangsta rap industry is mostly Black in North America, young boys regardless of background listen to the music and its diversity of messages. Record sales show that white youth in the United States are the largest consumer of hip hop records, so it would be misleading to state that gangsta rap's influence only applies to young Black men. Because gangsta rap is the most commercially successful of all hip hop genres it is criticized for profiting from the negative images and messages it sends to the youth. Yet it is clear that gangsta rap is speaking to youth, even though what exactly it is speaking to can never be exactly determined. Gangsta rap is many things at the same time: hard-hitting, aggressive, unapologetic, explicit, demeaning to women, violent, homophobic, and inspiring. It is a complex genre of music and its influence on boys and their lives is equally so. In 2008 Ice Cube released a single called "Gangsta Rap Made Me Do It," in which he takes on critics who claim that gangsta rap is the instigator of crimes and violent behavior. It is clear that even after 20 years of gangsta rap, that nothing has been resolved and that everything is just as contentious.

Further Reading

Chang, Jeff. *Can't Stop Won't Stop: A History of the Hip-Hop Generation*. New York: Picador, 2005.
Dyson, Michael Eric. *Between God and Gangsta Rap: Bearing Witness to Black Culture*. New York: Oxford University Press, 1996.
McDermott, Terry. "No One Was Ready for N.W.A's 'Straight Outta Compton.' But It Sold 3 Million Records and Transformed the Music Industry." *LA Times*, April 14, 2002.

Eloise Tan

Guns

Studies have shown that even without prompting or even previous exposure to guns, many boys seem to have an inherent liking for firearms: boys play guns using toy guns, imaginary guns (extended forefinger and raised thumb), and homemade weapons such as elastic guns or even sticks. In a couple of studies, when toddlers were turned loose in a room with a box of toys containing a hidden gun the males quickly found the toy gun and began playing with it. When girls grow up they may discard their dolls for real babies. When boys become adults many of them substitute real guns for their toy weapons. These men are classed as gun collectors, as hunters, or as target shooters, activities for which possession of a weapon (s), or at least access to one, would be mandatory.

The sport of target shooting merits its inclusion in the Olympic Games and it is the only one with competition in both summer and winter games. The summer Olympics features ten shooting events for men and seven for women, with the contestants vying for supremacy in pistol, rifle, and shotgun events, while the winter Olympics has competition in the biathlon. In this latter event, the athletes are required to be both competent skiers and rifle shots as they compete in five races—individual, sprint, pursuit, relay, and mass start. In this combined contest, a missed target adds time to one's race total.

The weapons used in target competition are quite different from those for hunting or other uses of guns such as soldiering or guard duty. Some of the arms are modified substantially and the targets, too, are unusual. In skeet shooting, for example, the targets, which at one time were actual pigeons, are now clay pigeons thrown into the air by a powerful spring mechanism. The shooter stands with a shotgun and hollers when he/she is ready for the clay to be flung into the air. The trajectory of the pigeon may be high or low and the shooter takes turns in order at seven different locations placed in a semi-circle. The skeet (Scandinavian for shoot) or clay pigeon is relatively small. It is a disk 4–5/16 inches by 1/8 inch and travels at high speed about 60 yards, roughly duplicating the flight path of bird flushed from cover. Even with the speed and the unpredictability of the path of the target, the shooters often are perfect, that is, they hit every disk. Not only are the speed and random path of the target a challenge but in some events, such as double trap (similar to skeet shooting), for example, two targets are released simultaneously, one high at ten feet and one low at three feet, and the shooter must break both targets, a great challenge to steadiness, coordination, accuracy, and decision making. Even so it takes a perfect round, no misses, to win a medal, and even a perfect round may only put the shooter in a tie—so accomplished are the best competitors.

In North American society there is no shortage of opportunities for boys to see guns in operation and there are ample models to choose from when the time comes. From toy guns to BB guns, a young person can graduate to a .22 caliber rifle for target or vermin shooting (rats at a dump, ground hogs, or prairie dogs). For many youth, the first real gun they possess is a .22 rifle for plinking—that is, shooting vermin or pests. True hunting, though, usually requires a heavier gun, and deer hunting is a common first experience. A standard gun for deer hunting is a bolt-action 30-06 rifle.

Paint ball warfare is another acceptable use of guns in society. The popularity of paint ball shooting has even been co-opted by certain corporations as a means of encouraging company solidarity, loyalty, and team work. This new sport involves competition between two teams or even individuals who hunt one another in what is often a refurbished warehouse. A person who is shot is distinctly marked with a splotch of paint and is eliminated from the game. Those who have been in a paintball competition are enthusiastic about the merits and excitement of the sport. Incidentally, great care is taken to limit injury in this game by having the players wear protective goggles and outer wear.

Guns, however, do represent a danger. As is obvious from their lethal nature, care must be taken in handling firearms. Sadly, statistics show that young people are at risk in startling numbers: in 2005, almost 90 percent of the children and teens killed by firearms were boys (Children's Defense Fund, 2008). Gun safety, including safe storage and handling, is of paramount importance and every household with a firearm of any sort must follow the rules of gun safety or suffer the consequences.

Despite the continued discussions and emphasis on the handling of firearms the tragedies continue, with people being killed each year partly because weapons are so easily available and anyone with a grudge or mental imbalance can readily obtain a gun. Firearms are here to stay and the only way to prevent the shooting tragedies we have seen in the past is better control of access to weapons and better education in the handling of them.

Further Reading

Children's Defense Fund. Protect Children, Not Guns [Online February 2008]. <http://www.childrensdefense.org/child-research-data-publications/data/protect-children-not-guns-report-2008.pdf>.

Flanagan, Jane. Boys Attraction to Soldiers, Guns, War [Online November 2003]. Downtown Express Web site <http://www.downtownexpress.com/de_30/boysattraction.html>.

Rowland, Rhona. Boys Play With Found Guns [Online February 2008]. CNN Transcript.

White, Julia. Boys and Guns [Online March 2008]. A. C. People's Media Company Web site <www.chiff.com/olympics-olympics-shooting.htm>.

Glynn A. Leyshon

Images of Violent Boys

Teachers and parents are concerned that boys are at risk for violence, and their play, talk, drawing, reading, and writing contribute to this concern. A seven-year-old boy in the United States was suspended from school in October 2007 for drawing a stick figure who was shooting another smiling stick figure with a gun. The school had a policy of zero tolerance for guns, and in this case it included the drawing of stick guns. The boy had given the drawing to another boy on the school bus. When asked, the boy said it was the drawing of a water gun, not a firearm. In March 2000 four kindergarten boys at another American elementary school were suspended after playing cops and robbers and using their fingers as guns. Are these acts of violence, and should they be censored?

The images that children portray in their drawings give us a view of their personal, social, and imagined world. Given the opportunity to write and draw anything of their choice, boys will draw guns. For the most part they know the school rules about this and that teachers do not always understand some of their illustrations; in fact, some illustrations are not allowed. They know that in school they need to be careful, and, indeed, to avoid their teachers' disapproval, they often self-censor their work, which is problematic for them. One boy reported, "I had this idea for a story, but I had to think of something else to write because we are not allowed to write about that."

One grade 5 rural Canadian boy was asked to write about what he had done on the weekend. He had been out shooting gophers, but he realized that that would be perceived as writing about violence, so he had to think of something else. He commented, "The teacher just wants us to write about sunny days and stuff like that" (Kendrick & McKay, 2003, p. 52). In this case the boy was invited to bring his experience, ideas, and thoughts on this task into the classroom, but he knew that if he brought his life experience into his writing, he would meet with disapproval and sometimes be reprimanded by the teacher. These mixed messages are confusing and frustrating for boys and can at times have several effects on them. They might take the texts underground and show them privately to their friends, after school, they might morph their texts into something more palatable to their teachers, or they might shut down when they are asked to write and become what teachers call reluctant writers. These hardly seem the best scenarios for boys who want to write and could very well become novelists of some fame given the right opportunity.

When boys find themselves in conflict with school-based literacy expectations, they sometimes try to make sense of and manipulate the school assignments in ways that are meaningful for them. This may include turning something into humor, rough play, or violence. Others resign themselves to completing what they see as boring schoolwork. When one parent of twins observed her boys, who were avid writers, she realized that what she first saw as violence was in fact a literary tool; the action and violence actually contributed to the plot development (Williams, 2004). Violence in boys' stories, as in this case, are not just random acts; rather, they are planned to contribute to the plot and to move the story along.

Teachers understand that there is a lot of violence in movies or in the serials and cartoons that boys watch on TV. The question arises: just because this is a part of their viewing world, does it mean that boys are at risk for acting out the violence? Teachers are very uncomfortable with violent images and topics in the classroom, and, given that they have the power in the classroom, they censor boys' voices. One grade 1 teacher found a drawing of a character holding what looked like a gun, with dots leading from the gun to a Superman character with a cape. It seemed that the first character was shooting at Superman. Above the picture were these notations and illustrations: "To: C," "From: T," two hearts, and a star. The teacher was disturbed by it and concerned about the violence in the picture, but when she asked the boy, he said that he (T) had drawn this picture for his best friend (C), who was moving away, and he thought that his friend would like it. The boy's explanation was not at all what the teacher expected. The boy's drawing was a gift to show his friend that he would miss him.

Boys will say that they can tell the difference between fictional violence and real violence and that just playing a point-and-shoot video game doesn't mean that they are going to run out and look for a fight with another child or shoot a gun. Just because they write about and illustrate action and battles doesn't mean that they are mean or prone to violence. In fact, to them it is funny to see others downed in a kind of slapstick humor. For the most part, boys don't see the violence in their work as real; they see it as fiction. Boys tend to like to read science fiction, fantasy, and action books; and when they are asked to write fiction at school, they write in the genres that they have read. This is also true of girls. It makes complete sense that their choices in writing and drawing would align with their choices in viewing and reading.

All people write and draw to represent ideas. In doing so, it is important to think about the audience and boys' purpose for writing or drawing. They seldom write and draw for themselves; it is usually for their teacher or their parents. They write many of their pieces for the teacher's assessment. If their self-censoring is restricting their imagination, creativity, and story development, then adults need to open up to the idea that these illustrations and writings are not threats and talk to the boys about their renditions. There are better ways than zero tolerance.

Not all boys draw guns throughout their boyhood. The phenomenon is more common with younger boys, and they seem to move beyond it by the middle years. This may also be the case for descriptions of violent acts in stories. We must also recognize that all writers draw on the world around them when they write, and boys are drawing on a great range of experiences, real, imagined, and digital, and much of this comes from the popular culture, which tends to be the culture of youth. Whether boys' representations of violence indicate engagement with fantasy or social competence, they may also reveal children who are struggling to make sense of their world. Teachers and parents need to realize that boys are not inventing violence; their literacy practices may have nothing to do with real violence, and they are merely reflecting back what they see in a world riddled with conflicts.

Further Reading

Kendrick, Maureen, and Roberta McKay. 2002. Uncovering literacy narratives through children's drawings. *Canadian Journal of Education*, 27(1), 45–60.

Newkirk, Thomas. 2002. Misreading masculinities: Speculations on the great gender gap in writing. *Language Arts*, 77(4), 294–300.

Williams, Bronwyn. 2004. Boys may be boys, but do they have to read and write that way? *Journal of Adolescent and Adult Literacy*, 47(6), 510–515.

Heather Blair and Brenda Kelly

Sexual Violence

Sexual violence can be defined as a nonconsensual violation of an individual's sexual integrity. It can be in the form of sexual harassment, incest, or sexual abuse. There are other terms that are often used in the place of sexual violence, such as sexual assault and rape. The term "sexual assault" is used within the legal system to define all attacks that are of a sexual nature, ranging from inappropriate touching to aggravated assault. Rape, a specific form of sexual assault, is defined as nonconsensual sexual intercourse. The term "sexual violence" is used most often, as it captures a range of experiences and levels of violence.

Historically, acts of sexual violence were not seen as forms of aggression. Instead, they were considered to be types of seduction. Forced intercourse, or rape, from this perspective was seen as sex. The shift toward seeing nonconsensual sexual acts as violent was pivotal in sexual violence becoming a recognized concern of the criminal justice system and within academic research.

The vast majority of academic research on sexual violence focuses on women's experiences as survivors. As some academics have suggested, this emphasis is a result of the feminist literature from the 1970s, which sought to highlight the victimization of women at the hands of men. As a result, there has been little research done on male perpetrators and male survivors of sexual violence. However, some research on these two topics has begun to appear more recently.

How to best refer to those who have experienced sexual violence is by no means clear. As many researchers have found, there are many terms that are commonly used. Within the legal and medical institutions, the term "victim" is always employed, whereas within rape crisis centers, as well as within the majority of academic literature, the term "survivor" is most common. Between those who have experienced an incident of sexual violence, the use of the terms "victim" or "survivor" is often contingent on they way in which individuals understands their own experience.

Rates of male or female sexual violence are difficult to calculate. This difficulty stems from the extremely low numbers of sexually violent acts that are reported to police. Many women do not report crimes of sexual violence because of embarrassment, self-blame, and fear. However, sexual violence against women, perpetrated by men, is one of the most common crimes committed in Canada.

Sexual violence has been shown to occur most commonly between acquaintances, friends, spouses, and family members. Often it is not the strange man who poses the greatest threat to women, but instead men who are close to the victim. Along these lines, the term "date rape" has been coined to highlight rape that occurs between individuals who are dating.

Although it is difficult to suggest the causes of sexual violence, some researchers have identified certain life circumstances and experiences that are correlated with male sexual aggression. "Correlated" here refers to a connection not a cause. Findings such as the ones mentioned challenge the image of the male perpetrators as abnormal and/or insane.

There is a difference between potential explanations for sexual violence that is perpetrated by boys and sexual violence that is perpetrated by men. For boys, being involved in various forms of delinquent behavior and experiencing peer pressure to have sex are two factors correlated with perpetration of sexual violence against women. For men, committing acts of sexual violence in adolescence and being involved in illegal and delinquent behavior are suggested to be connected with acts of adult male sexual aggression.

Other scholars have examined possible cultural explanations of male-perpetrated sexual violence. The predominance of sexual, and sometimes violent, imagery of women in the media has been suggested to play a role in heightening rates of sexual violence perpetrated by men. Furthermore, the prevalence of representations of male aggression and female sexuality in the media has also been seen as other causes of male sexual violence.

Sexual violence has been considered by many to be a "gendered" crime, in that it is characterized and influenced by the effects of gender. It has been theorized to be the result and enactment of unequal levels of power between males and females. This view is somewhat challenged by the evidence of male experiences of sexual violence.

Despite the trend of focusing on women's experience of sexual violence, research has begun to turn to the experiences of male survivors of sexual aggression. As with male-perpetrated violence, there are many myths about a male's experiences of sexual violence that have been shown through scholarly research to be false. It is often assumed that the perpetrators of sexual aggression against boys and men are male. However, as some research suggests, this is not always the case. Females can and do rape. Another common myth about male survivors of sexual violence is that they are homosexual. However, it has been shown that straight men and boys are just as likely to experience sexualized violence as homosexual males.

As with male-perpetrated violence, the rates of sexual violence experienced by males are difficult to determine. It has been shown that males, compared to females, are far less likely to report their experiences of sexual violence to the police. Although these difficulties in understanding sexual aggression do exist, there is a growing interest in comprehending and addressing sexual violence.

Further Reading

Anderson, Irina. *Accounting for Rape: Psychology, Feminism, and Discourse Analysis in the Study of Sexual Violence*. New York: Routledge, 2008.

Domitrz, Michael. *May I Kiss You: A Candid Look at Dating, Communication, Respect and Sexual Assault Awareness*. Greenfield, WI: Awareness Publications, 2003.

Gavey, Nicola. *Just Sex? The Cultural Scaffolding of Rape*. New York: Routledge, 2005.

Katz, Jackson. *The Macho Paradox: Why Some Men Hurt Women and How All Men Can Help*. Naperville IL: Sourcebooks Inc, 2006.

Tarrant, Shira. *Men Speak Out: Views of Gender, Sex and Power*. New York: Routledge, 2008.

Andrea Quinlan

Skateboarding and Rebellion

Though skateboarding has been an element in and marker of white boys' culture since the first commercial skateboard was released in 1959, it was in 1995, with the introduction of The Extreme Games (later dubbed The X Games), that skateboarding became media makers' go-to symbol for adolescent boys and youthful rebellion. Skateboarding's strength as a symbol coincided with its growth in participation: between 1999 and 2000 the number of skateboarders increased 49 percent, to 12 million participants (Yin, 2001). By 2004, professional skateboarder Tony Hawk, spokesman for Bagel Bites and Doritos and the name behind Activision's Tony Hawk line of videogames, was earning approximately $9 million a year, and his brand pulled in $300 million in sales of apparel, skateboards, tours, and videogames. Skateboarders have been central to MTV's contemporary lineup, in Jackass, Viva La Bam, Wildboyz, Rob and Big, and Scarred (Goldman, 2004). They are also the focus of many advertisements, including those for Doritos, Hot Pockets, McDonald's, Coca-Cola, Right Guard deodorant, and Mountain Dew.

In each of these representations, skateboarders are portrayed as either hypercompetitive daredevils or trouble-causing pranksters. Attendant to these images is a sense that skateboarders are dangerous, and American communities have spent considerable time debating the legality of skateboarding in public space and the necessity of establishing public skate parks for community use. City councils and citizens routinely voice concerns about skateboarders' safety, pedestrians' safety in the path of skateboarders, and skateboarders' destruction of public space and disruption of civil society (e.g., the use of vulgar language, loud and rowdy behavior, the destruction of property via both the practice of skateboarding and graffiti, and general disrespect toward elders). Some adults, concerned with the criminalization of this youth activity, come to skateboarders' defense in city meetings, noting that skaters are simply looking for a place to practice their sport. Many American cities have developed public skate parks in order to give skateboarders an alternative to skating on streets and sidewalks. In 2005, there were approximately 2,000 parks in the United States, with about 1,000 more in development (Cave, 2005).

Clearly a significant element of both popular culture and everyday life, skateboarders' ever-shifting location within mainstream youth culture—celebrated yet debated, popular but edgy—suggests that they strike a chord with Americans (parents, advertisers, youth more generally) working to define the boundaries of boys' identities. Though mainstream culture has managed to paint skateboarders as an aggressive, highly competitive group of adrenaline junkies or as slacker-stoners, skaters are far more passionate about the value their culture places on freedom, individuality, and self-expression. For skateboarders, skate culture is a location of difference, an alternative to dominant demands that adolescent boys, as exemplified by "jocks," should overvalue competition, physical dominance, and emotional repression. Though this mostly white, mostly middle-class, mostly heterosexual group of young boys occupy a clear position of social power, they nonetheless feel limited by society's expectations of their identity. Through their participation in skate culture, white adolescent boys both voice critiques of dominant ideas about masculinity and maintain the cultural dominance granted to white males by society.

Alternative Masculinities in Skate Culture

In discussions of their identity as skateboarders and their devotion to skateboarding culture, skaters reveal that masculinity poses a problem for them. In reverent descriptions of the experience of skateboarding, they disclose a yearning for the opportunity to express themselves and a space in which to feel a sense of freedom or transcendence. Though at first glance it may seem as though white middle-class boyhood is entirely focused on freedom and self-expression, in the minds of the skateboarders, male adolescence—and even adulthood—are characterized by institutions that serve to stifle such individualized joy. Work, school, family, and most importantly, organized team sports, all operate as personifications or institutions of patriarchy that place limitations on the type of transcendent, inspirational, and boundless sensation imparted by skateboarding. Skate culture, then, is a space in which boys can escape the demands of mainstream masculinity.

Despite its expansive presence in advertising appeals and youth media and its general importance to such mainstream behemoths as ABC/ESPN/Disney, skateboarding has been used primarily for its rebellious or subcultural image. Many skateboarders argue that these representations are inaccurate, but they also cling to skateboarding's outsider status, frequently reminding one another and themselves of the numerous run-ins they have had with police, business owners, parents, and teachers disapproving of their activity of choice. As such, though the mainstream amplification of skateboarding's extreme, risk-taking nature mischaracterizes, in most skaters' judgment, their culture, skateboarding's illegality, and general aura of rebellion is appealing.

Skateboarders' attachment to skateboarding's association with rebellion, however, pales in comparison to their firm insistence that it offers an alternative to other teen-boy activities, most notably, mainstream sports. Skaters argue that skateboarding is an artistic pursuit rather than a sport, noting its lack of rules, coaches, official playing fields, and teams. Skateboarding has, indeed, been a participant-led activity; skaters continuously invent new tricks, introduce new modes of dress, and discover new places to practice. In this relatively disorganized sphere, skaters believe they have room to be cooperative and expressive, rather than competitive and aggressive. For them, these qualities place skating in stark contrast to traditional—and school-sanctioned—sports, such as football and baseball.

In the noncompetitive and open space of skateboarding, adolescent boys can express themselves and assert their individuality through their style. Although, to an outsider, skateboarding may appear to be the pursuit of expertise in performing skateboarding "tricks" or "moves," to skaters, the practice is about the development of a personal style. Skateboarding can be aggressive or artistic, athletically daring or technically precise. Skateboarders do not wear one uniform: they may don clothing associated with a variety of youth cultures, from punk to hip hop to hippy. For skaters, the choice and development of such styles is more than superficial—it is an individualistic expression of one's "true self."

More than self-expression, skateboarding offers a sense of transcendence, escape, meditation, or fulfillment seemingly unavailable in the boys' other domains. School, work, families, and relationships all produce stress in the skaters' lives; the practice of skating relieves that stress. Skaters describe skateboarding as relaxing, rejuvenating, liberating, and even spiritual. Their reflective and passionate tones contradict dominant images of surly white male teens as well as notions that males are not and cannot be expressive, emotive, or introspective. Furthermore, their discussions of stress and problems belie suggestions that young men are unable to reflect on or talk about what's troubling them. Both the practice of skateboarding and skateboarders' discussions of it provide skaters an opportunity to engage in activities contradictory to dominant norms of masculinity, and as their passionately stated descriptions reveal, they place a high value on this opportunity.

The Preservation of Power in Skateboarding Culture

Although skateboarders see their culture as a place of difference in which they can experiment with alternative masculinities, it can also operate as a regressive and exclusive community that excludes people of color, women, gay men, and the working class from its ranks. In other words, skateboarding is a space in which white adolescent boys can enact difference within dominance—they can operate outside of mainstream norms while maintaining their societal dominance. Although skaters argue that their culture is all-inclusive, that anyone can skateboard as long as they are doing so for the love of the practice, skateboarders' everyday actions and mediated representations of skate culture set up barriers for all but white, middle-class, and straight adolescent males.

Though skateboarding is largely an activity dominated by white boys, skateboarding videos created for the niche skateboarding market do portray the practice as racially diverse. These videos showcase professional skateboarding teams made up of an international group of young men. In addition to the images of skaters traversing various urban spaces throughout the industrialized world, these videos portray skateboarding as an artistic and open-minded culture. Nonetheless, women are almost totally excluded from the world of professional skateboarding, and many of the videos use vulgar jokes about women's bodies that serve to both broadcast the skateboarders' heterosexuality and relegate women to the margins of the culture.

Still, skateboarders suggest that their own experiences of oppression have translated into a general acceptance of all people regardless of race, gender, class, or sexuality. Explaining that police, teachers, shop owners, and parents assume them to be dangerous and citing the tickets they have received for skateboarding in forbidden spaces, skateboarders claim to be profiled, oppressed, and policed. Consequently, they argue, they can empathize with other oppressed groups. In fact, however, by suggesting that they are a truly subjugated group, skateboarders downplay long histories of violent oppression of minority groups.

Skaters contend that their culture is inclusive, and to illustrate the assertion, they note that the culture welcomes and promotes a variety of youth cultures. Talking about race by referring to racially coded styles or music, such as hip hop, rasta, heavy metal, punk, or jazz, they earnestly claim that all individuals are welcome to skateboard, despite their race, class, sexuality, or gender. Despite their claims of acceptance, however, skateboarders make frequent use of epithets based on, especially, class and sexuality—putting others down as "white trash" or "fags." The use of these epithets is obviously exclusionary and places clear boundaries around the culture. Even without the epithets, white masculinity is the unstated norm in skate culture. That is, skateboarding is dominated by white boys, but their whiteness and maleness are rarely discussed explicitly—they are taken to be normal. Such invisibility hides the specific ways in which whiteness and masculinity are dominant and contributes to their power.

White male dominance is most notably upheld in mainstream representations of skate culture, particularly the group of television shows produced by Jeff Tremaine's Dickhouse Productions and released on MTV. These shows include *Jackass* (2000–2002), *Viva La Bam* (2003–2005), *Wildboyz* (2003–2006), and *Rob and Big* (2006–present). Descended from the niche skateboarding magazine *Big Brother* and niche skateboarding videos distributed by the magazine, Tremaine's shows do not always focus on skateboarding as a practice. They are, however, an important aspect of skate culture and its mainstream incarnations.

Each of these shows displays young white men reveling in adolescent humor, taking pleasure in pain and mocking dominant norms of masculinity, all the while maintaining their power at the expense of women, people of color, and working-class whites. As such, they carry on skate culture's not-quite-anti-patriarchal critique of patriarchy. The humor in each of these shows depends upon its simultaneous scorn for conventional male-proving rituals and its derision of all those who are not white, straight, middle-class, young, and male. By making fun of the ways that men typically establish their masculinity, these shows challenge traditional modes of masculinity. For example, in one episode of *Wildboyz*, cast members Steve-O and Chris Pontius participate in the Amazon Mee-Mee Indians' male-proving ritual, in which they place their hand in a glove full of stinging ants. Even though Steve-O and Pontius demonstrate their physical prowess by participating, they also make fun of the ritual: Steve-O snickers, "Why is it the things that make you a man tend to be such dumb things to do?" In another episode set in Jaipur, India, Steve-O and Pontius continually make fun of street performers as "creepy and crazy freaks." Constantly mocking dominant modes of masculinity while maintaining their power over everyone else, Steve-O and Pontius exemplify skate culture's "difference within dominance"—its remarkable ability to provide an alternative place for young white men while excluding all others.

Like many subcultures, skateboarding has been co-opted and commodified by mainstream culture, morphed into a hyper-rebellious, hypermasculine version of its former self in order to sell products from bagels to videogames. Skateboarders disparage this image, arguing that skate culture has been a place in which they can experiment with gentler, more expressive, and cooperative modes of masculinity that fly in the face of traditional images of young men. The feelings of transcendence, self-expression, and creativity that skaters experience are undoubtedly a crucial part of the practice's appeal and suggest that young men are dissatisfied with patriarchal norms of masculinity. Even so, this dissatisfaction does not necessarily translate into a broader critique of the ways in which power is distributed in mainstream culture. In fact, the mostly white, mostly boys culture of skateboarding actively excludes females, people of color, and homosexuals. Maintaining their difference-within-dominance, skateboarders represent a nascent critique of patriarchy that keeps white men firmly in power.

Further Reading

Borden, Iain. *Skateboarding, Space, and the City: Architecture and the Body*. New York: Berg, 2001.

Cave, Damien. Dogtown, U.S.A. *The New York Times*, June 12, 2005, n.p.

Dyer, Richard. *White*. London; New York: Routledge, 1997.

Goldman, Lea. From Ramps to Riches. *Forbes*, 174, no.1 (2004): 98.

Savran, David. *Taking It Like a Man: White Masculinity, Masochism, and Contemporary American Culture*. Princeton: Princeton University Press, 1998.

Yin, Sandra. Going to Extremes. *American Demographics* 6 (June 2001): 26.

Emily Chivers Yochim

Skinhead Culture

"If you have a racist friend, now is the time now is the time, for that friendship to end." The Specials

The heavily male, heavily youth-oriented culture of skinheads is often compared to or equated with Nazis. The audio stimulus of the word skinhead entering the ear provokes the cognitive picture of a swastika. The historical misrepresentation of all skinheads as fascists erases the complex and dynamic cultural history of skins worldwide. There is a substantial number of skinheads who reject racism entirely.

The birth of skinheads begins with post-war British youth heavily influenced by the migration boom of Jamaicans in the mid 1960s, close to the dawn of their independence. In the working-class neighborhoods where Jamaican Rudeboys came into contact with British youth, something new was in the air. For the next few decades British society was taken by a storm of youth creating their own cultures.

MODs, Skinheads, Greasers, Hippies, Teddy Boys, Rudeboys are just some of the most famous of these cultures. The mix of Rudeboys and MODs spawned the Skinhead. What did a skinhead in that time and culture look like? Street-loving youth dressed with impeccable style. Fredd Perry polo shirts, Wrangler Jeans, Doc. Martins Boots, clean-shaven head and face, and an occasional stylish side burn. Working-class youth wanted to look sharp and so they did. Nonetheless, their apparent sophisticated fashion clashed with their street way of life. British youth and society in the late 1960s, as in the rest of the world, was the scenario of serious violent clashes between all segments of society.

Culturally, skins adopted much from the Jamaican Rudeboys—for instance, how they carried themselves. They had a fearsome pack mentality, juxtaposed with their love for rocksteady, skinhead reggae, ska, soul, and they had fun dancing and drinking the night away. The mellow grooves of rocksteady, skinhead reggae, and Rudeboy Jamaican culture give an undeniably Afro-Caribbean root to the culture of skinheads. So, how can skinhead be synonymous with Nazism? With this basic understanding of the history behind the emergence of skinhead culture, it is safe to conclude that skinhead culture does not adhere to an inherent Nazi ideology. In fact, within skinhead culture, the subgroup of Nazi skins are popularly referred to by the term *boneheads*.

Many *skins* are fed up with media stereotypes, misconceptions, and misrepresentations, which often reflect ignorance. Originally a youth culture, skinheads in time became a way of life where boys became grown men, many of whom are now fathers and even grandfathers. Youth as an object of study became salient in British post-war (WWII) youth. The excess of population without work created troublesome social instability that needed to be addressed. The vast spectrum of British post-war youth became the fertile ground that spawned what we know today as skinheads. An analysis of skinhead culture, based not only on documented history but lived experiences is crucial in the process of demystifying old stigmas that have demonized skinheads since the emergence of the British National Front. There is no denial that within the culture of skinheads there are indeed right wing or fascist, but to automatically assume that all skins are bad is basically inaccurate.

Skinhead Culture in Puerto Rico

Skinheads and boy culture go hand in hand, not only in the UK but in every country where the youth culture of skinheads exist. The skinhead culture in Puerto Rico is an example of how this culture grew and multiplied globally.

To write about skinheads is to write about the Caribbean. To write about skinheads is to write about colony/metropolis relationships. To write about skinheads is to write about patterns of migrations. To write about skinheads is to write about youth as agents of social change and creators of their own cultures. To write about skinheads is to write about a 40-year-old culture. To write about skinheads is to write how boys became men and skinhead girls became women as they established their own ways of life.

Under the backdrop of the Spanish colonial city of old San Juan, under a clear blue sky and flirtatious waves pounding the shores of Puerto Rico's capitol building, something happened that changed the lives of hundreds of youth. In the late 1980s, close to 100,000 people demanded Puerto Rico's independence. In the middle of the crowd some members appeared out of the ordinary. There were shiny heads (none due to baldness). Fragmented bands of skinheads from all over the island slowly gravitated to one another. Fragmented groups of skinheads met, they talked, but above all shared a youthful euphoria that they were not the only skinheads on the island. On that day, skinheads in Puerto Rico grew in numbers and were ready to take on the world. Over the next few months, a network of skinheads grew. In an instant, skinheads in Puerto Rico found out about Puerto Rican skins in New York City and other skins throughout the United States and Latin America, who had come to Puerto Rico to learn about the skinhead presence in the Caribbean. Skinheads in Puerto Rico metamorphosed into a self-forged identity. As such they became more coherent, more articulate as they created their own distinct name *Cabeza de Piel de Puerto Rico* (CPPR), or Skinheads of Puerto Rico.

Over time, these teenage boys made sense of their world with a do-it-yourself philosophy that quickly became a way of life. From show to show, hang-out session to hang-out session, knowledge of self, pride of self, and love of self were ever pervasive in the skinhead culture in Puerto Rico. There is something about Puerto Rico where somehow whatever culture gets introduced, quickly mutates into something different. This applies to everything—music, aesthetics, mannerisms, and self-identity. The skinhead scene in Puerto Rico is very different from skinhead scenes from other areas, and does not have clear-cut boundaries that evolve around only aesthetics or music. Typically the skinhead identity goes hand and hand with a unique aesthetic and musical taste. The Puerto Rican Skinhead (CPPR) does not ascribe to just one musical genre or aesthetic. Skinheads in Puerto Rico listen to rocksteady, salsa, punk, ska, hip hop, oi!, hardcore, metal, and they may dress like a punker, hip hopper, traditional skinhead, surfer, or none of the above. Such phenomena attest to anthropologist Nestor Canclini's notion of hybrid cultures.

For example, a historical vignette within the skinhead culture in Puerto Rico made skinheads in Puerto Rico aware of how different and unique they are from traditional or original skinhead culture. In one memorable instance in 1992, when the government was celebrating 500 years of the "discovery" of Puerto Rico, two original skins from the UK came into contact with some eager CPPRs at a local bar. What many wanted to become a festive encounter quickly became a slap in the face. As both parties started to share skinhead bonds, it all came into a grinding halt when the two UK skins made it clear that musical genres determined the type of skin you were. For the CPPRs, this was quite a paradox as music does play a role in who they are and how they identify with each other, but CPPRs also recognize that music is music and nobody owns it. Furthermore, being a skinhead is a lot more than the type of music that one listens to, but, at the same time, it is also the music that one does listen to. To the CPPR's surprise, other skins quickly created a taxonomy of the type of skin one was based the music one listened to. The CPPR identity is not necessarily based on a specific music or aesthetic but rather by the attitude the person conveys. Anybody can say he listens to "skinhead" music and dress like a skinhead, but in Puerto Rico that does not make the person a skinhead. As with many cultures, there is a right of passage, a scrutiny where extant members of that culture determine whether or not an outsider becomes a member of that community. The hybrid nature of cultural identities presents CPPRs with a prudent breaking point to establish the origins of skinhead culture in the UK. For skinhead culture, it also spawned from hybrid cultural identities and manifestations.

"All you kids out there, always keep the faith." Warzone

Twenty years and counting, and the culture started by the teenage boys and girls—now full-grown men and women, who are teachers, fathers, mothers, chefs, musicians, tattoo artists, university professors, film makers, beauticians, and entrepreneurs—still meet at an occasional ska, hard core, or punk show.

They now see the younger generations take the scene into new places never dreamed possible.

In Puerto Rico, there exists a unique flavor and style of skinhead scene known as CPPR who are part of a bigger family known as *La Escena* (the scene). As such punks, skinheads, and others have coexisted in ways that are mind boggling to other punks and skins worldwide. Punk bands that come from Spain or Argentina cannot comprehend how it is possible that skins dance and sing punk music. Skins from the States and other parts of the world cannot understand how Puerto Rican skinheads can talk about oi! and hard-core while listening to rumba, salsa, reggae, rockabilly, and countless other musical genres. CPPRs are a rare fusion of styles and modalities. They embrace music from other parts of the world, while simultaneously never forgetting their heritage or their roots. They do not adhere to one way of seeing or doing things, much less being wedded to a musical genre.

To Be a Skin

What is it about being a skin that appeals to boys 20 years after the first ones coined the term? There is something about it that young boys want to be a part of it. It gives them a sense of community, purpose, and identity that can be best described by the following: To be a skin is to walk the darkest alleys in the city with no fear. To be a skin is to beat the pulp out of anyone who is abusing someone weaker. To be a skin is all about pride and respect of self. To be a skin is to seek refuge in friends that give the comfort and space needed to find yourself when you are lost. To be a skin is to celebrate life when the whole world comes to an end. To be a skin is to rage against all forms of oppression. To be a skin is to have the freedom to be who you are. To be a skin is to listen to the music you like. To be a skin is to have fun as you hang out with friends and family. To be a skin is to celebrate 40 years of your history in the world. To be a skin in Puerto Rico is to be proud of Afro-Caribbean roots. To be a skin is to endure. To be a skin is to persevere. To be a skin is to overcome. To be a skin is to become wise with age. To be a skin is to survive in a system driven by genocide. To be a skin is to live, for it is a way of life. OI! y punto.

Further Reading

Hebdige, D. *Subculture: The Meaning of Style*. New York: Methuen and Co., 1979.
Marshal, G. *Spirit of '69: A Skinhead Bible*. UK: ST Publishing, 1994.
Meadows, S. *This Is England*. DVD Film, 2007.

Joseph Carroll-Miranda and Ernesto Rentas-Robles

Street Gangs

The term gang can be used to describe a group of individuals that share common goals and identities. This could mean a gang of soccer fans, a gang of snowboarders, or a gang of students who meet each week to study algebra. The term does, however, tend to hold a negative connotation; that is, it is perceived negatively in most social contexts. The term street gang holds even stronger negative connotations as it typically refers to street-orientated groups of teens whose identity is formed through the perpetration of various illegal activities.

Collecting data on street gangs is difficult for a number of reasons. First, street gangs are not organized in a manner where they keep a record of who belongs to the gang. Second, teens would likely not admit to police officers or researchers that they are part of a gang. Third, street gangs might not be as organized as people believe, suggesting that certain groups may not consider themselves a gang, or some individuals may not identify with a particular gang. And finally, some individuals might lie and claim to be in a gang or exaggerate their activities to gain street credibility.

Teens are believed to enter street gangs for a variety of reasons, including monetary gain, a sense of belonging, status/power, and physical protection. Many individuals that join street gangs come from impoverished social conditions where turning to illegal activities can be perceived as an opportunity to make money through various petty crimes. Gangs also appear to be more prevalent among minority populations that experience blocked social mobility due to prejudice, racism and discrimination. Turning to crime becomes a way to reach one's needs and wants, in a society that does not provide legitimate means of attaining those things.

Street gangs also provide a sense of belonging. Many teens are believed to enter street gangs because they are bored and want to be part of something that is bigger than themselves. Many of these teens live in communities that do not have the economic resources to run sports programs or develop local libraries. Out of boredom, these teens might turn to crime as something exciting to do. Joining a gang gives them something to do, a sense of belonging, and an identity.

In certain social locations, being in a street gang can also be a means to achieving status and power. The concern of many street youths is credibility and/or reputation. In street cultures, reputation is not determined by how many books one reads or what scholastic award one wins but rather, by how tough one is and how many crimes one has successfully committed.

Credibility and reputation are also determined by street smarts. Being street smart means not getting caught for crimes, and not getting violently assaulted or retaliated against by other street youths. Entering a street gang can be a form of street smarts because there is safety in numbers. Gangs offer a sense of protection from other violent gangs, and they protect each other from criminal prosecution. For example, if one gang member is caught, he will not rat out his fellow gang members as accomplices.

Street gangs can be organized along many lines. There are ethnic gangs defined by nationality or race such as white-supremacist gangs or Latino gangs. In the case of white-supremacist gangs, they are defined less by their own ethnicity and more by their lack of tolerance for other ethnicities. Turf gangs define themselves by the geographical locations that they control. This can often lead to turf wars between rival street gangs competing for control over certain territory. There are also prison gangs, as individuals do not relinquish their street gang memberships in prison, continuing to feud with other rival gangs behind prison walls.

Street gangs also engage in a variety of activities such as tagging/graffiti, violence and intimidation, criminal mischief, and drug use. Street gangs engage in graffiti, also termed *tagging*, for a few reasons: first, to mark their territory; second, to develop a symbol that unites gang members; third, to communicate with other gang members; and finally, to warn, threaten, or intimidate rival gangs.

Street gangs also use violence or the threat of violence to intimidate rival gangs. Much of street gang life is predicated on holding one's turf and maintaining a reputation or street credibility. One way to gain credibility is to gain turf or to take down someone who has a reputation. Likewise, reputation is lost when turf or a fight is lost, particularly if it is to someone with less credibility. This leads to violent struggles between street gangs to gain and maintain turf, which accounts for much of the crime committed by street gangs against one another.

Through criminal mischief, street gangs do, however, commit crimes against individuals without gang affiliation. Criminal mischief generally suggests the damaging of property. It does not tend to be done for monetary gain but rather, simply to be destructive. Graffiti could be considered a form of criminal mischief, but street gangs engage in many other forms such as damaging cars, throwing rocks through building windows, and other acts of vandalism.

Drugs are also a major activity of street gangs. Although street gangs generally make little monetary gain, the money they do generate comes primarily from the distribution of drugs. Gangs are able to profit off of the drug trade because the demand for illicit drugs such as marijuana and cocaine is high, and yet there is no legitimate or legal means to purchase these drugs. Street gangs provide this illicit service. The use of illicit drugs is also believed to be a common activity of street gangs.

Further Reading

Covey, Herbert. *Street Gangs Throughout the World*. Springfield, IL: Charles C. Thomas Publisher, 2003.

Chettleburgh, Michael. *Young Thugs: Inside the Dangerous World of Canadian Street Gangs*. Toronto: HarperCollins, 2007.

Delaney, Tim. *American Street Gangs*. Upper Saddle River, NJ: Pearson Prentice Hall, 2006.

Kontos, Louis, and David Brotherton (eds.). *Encyclopedia of Gangs*. Westport, CT: Greenwood Press, 2008.

Mullins, Chris. *Holding Your Square: Masculinities, Streetlife and Violence*. Portland, OR: Willan Publishing, 2007.

Curtis Fogel

Warfare and Boys

The Beat of War Drums and the Collective Imagination

The physical, mental, moral, and spiritual marks that warfare produces and their impact on the children who survive it have no comparison because warfare not only affects individuals; it also affects generations. Consequently, the drama is not only each suffering child. That would be, in fact, just its atrocious starting point. The pedagogical challenge comes with the understanding of the historical process warfare triggers and especially with the efforts to comprehend its effects in its multiple levels of complexity.

In an educated society, warfare always finds an educational rationale. In this sense, regardless of its content, this rationale has the potential to acquire a life of its own, and soon, if it is not systematically challenged, may also acquire a symbolic value that will permeate the collective memory of any given historical community.

War, as an annihilating phenomenon, is an expression of cultural and social disconnectedness. Educators know that dissonance inevitably precedes the emergence of a new cognitive paradigm. But when we deal with war, what often emerges from that dissonance is not a new cognitive paradigm, but a commodified version of knowledge dressed up as a ritual. It is like the warp on which the tapestry of culture will be woven, thereby creating an artificial world that serves as an agency of socialization.

It is important to be reminded that rituals hide discrepancies and conflicts between social principles and social organizations. So, as long as we as individuals are not explicitly conscious of the ritual character of the process through which we are initiated to the forces that shape our world, we cannot break the spell and shape a new one. Many educators believe that if we do not challenge those rituals and the commodified knowledge that carry them, then our schools and societies will continue to be dominated by oppressive custodians of intelligence.

A careful review of U.S. history textbooks reveals the unquestioned and keen presence of a figure that played an important strategic role in the warfare communications system: the drummer boy. It was a common practice for armies, well into the nineteenth century, to recruit young boys for service as drummers. Through various rolls, the drummers signaled different commands that soldiers would immediately follow. They were not only instrumental to the development of warfare routines, but their strategically designed mediation was certainly critical to the overall outcome.

It is interesting to verify that it was commonly assumed that drummers did not carry weapons, nor did they have any military duties to perform. The position, in direct contrast with reality, was portrayed as highly desirable, provoking many boys to try to get enlisted, sometimes as an attempt at an early emancipation from home. But drummer boys were, in fact, in the battlefield. Some of them were recognized and decorated. But, most of the times, they became casualties, and their violent deaths were romanticized. Completely out of the realm of moral deliberation, the death of children became folklore, and was forbidden.

The beat of war drums and the collective imaginary have, since then, evolved into more sophisticated but not less harmful forms. The concept of boyhood, sometimes strongly mediated by corporate interests who have transformed violence into entertainment, has become highly ritualized and exhibits a playful and unabashed militaristic component in a context of a society where boys and young men are incarcerated in juvenile detention centers, prisons, and psychiatric hospitals in greater numbers than in any other country in the world.

To make things more dramatic, the growth of boyhood industry is only paralleled by a fast-paced legislative trend toward criminalizing wrong-doing in boyhood itself. Children younger than 14 can be tried in adult courts in half the Union. Furthermore, in 13 states, there is no minimum age at which a child can be tried as an adult and, in some cases, boys as young as 11 years old have in fact been tried as adults.

Boyhood rituals play an important role in this contradictory situation. They silence the pain boys might be experiencing, exacerbate their confusion, and perpetuate their moral fragility. The notion that boys don't cry is just one of the multiple examples of silencing what is just human nature. This sort of emotional numbing is possible simply because some of them have not developed a sense of control of their basic impulses, some others have not developed a sense of consciousness, some are still learning how to articulate right and wrong, and some others simply lack a sense of empathy. However, emotional numbing is mostly the result of the blame targeted at youth when their self image does not conform to the traditional gender identity.

More than ever, it is clear today that boys want to break free from their parents earlier than their parents wish to, or are legally able to. In this context, popular culture becomes, again, an affective and effective vehicle for this transition. Like a drummer boy, they see popular culture as a means to define their identity and establish a relationship to their peers. And it all begins like a game.

Play, as is commonly understood and that most of us accept, is disassociated from real life. It happens in the realm of fantasy, where the actions of our everyday life are stripped from their meanings and consequences. Its intensity can even enable a release of tension that—as a valued byproduct—may allow children to cope more effectively with their more mundane frustrations. But this cathartic element, enhanced by a technology that does not differentiate between reality and fantasy but rather creates a strangely empowering new space, a virtual one, needs to be carefully observed because of its ambiguity.

Rituals cruise very easily through those ambivalences to serve normative functions. Such is the case of notions such as patriotism and national pride. They are governed by beliefs rooted in psychic structures established through a continuous process of socialization that starts very early in school. For example, as part of a strategically increasing military presence in the form of recruitment propaganda in all high school campuses, an instructive brochure made available to all students is entitled "Marines. The Few. The Proud." Its direct text and distinct imagery mutually reinforce each other, and in a sublime and unambiguous manner, they promise warfare as the optimal experience. Making use of powerful marketing techniques, and inserting itself in the trend that life must be lived to its full potential and in as fully stimulating way as possible, the instructive brochure effectively conveys the core of a militaristic philosophy of life making it sound attractive. The text says: "Time and time again, the Marines have been called into service to protect our nation's interests. We operate around the world as America's quick strike expeditionary force, ready at the moment's notice to effectively insert our warriors into any situation that calls for it. We are proud to be America's shining tip of the spear, and we are ready for the next victory. Maybe you can be one of us."

The brochure is disconcerting. Its forthright language unabashedly describes a curriculum and the philosophy of education that supports it: "No one simply joins the Marines, because the title must be earned. Marine Corps Recruit Training is where the separation begins: the weak from the strong, the child from the adult, the civilian from the Marine. The 13 weeks will break away all the things that bind you to the excesses of the past. And in the end, you will become a confident member of the finest warrior force in the world. You'll be a United States Marine."

In a few words, it is warfare as pedagogy—a philosophy that assumes that we are all enmeshed in a commonality of interests and that those interests need to be protected against everyone and everything. It assumes that those interests admit no limits and that its supposed protection does not recognize any sovereign barrier in the world. It assumes that warfare has its own logic, and that it can be imposed anywhere at the moment needed. It assumes that war is a cultural trait and that only warriors express the fullness of its human condition. It assumes military supremacy as a lead and structuring value. And finally, and most important it assumes that education is a natural selection process. If the drummer boy remains untouched as a romantic image of history, the U.S. Marine portrayed in this brochure becomes its more sophisticated updated version.

The drummer boy can't buy alcohol, but he, or the commodified patriotic expression of him, will kill or die following orders. If he survives he will get more public education, but once inserted in a world where his actions are disassociated from real life, he seems to have all the things he needs to irremediably remain bound by a logic of new excesses. The most dramatic thing is that this doesn't happen in the realm of fantasy, but like in real life, his actions will be stripped from their meaning and consequences and, like in the drummer boy's case, his humanity will be disallowed and interdicted.

Many educators believe that they must create a space to recycle the experience of boyhood and ponder how we should insert that experience in a more general educational project where the capacity to think critically about our culture, its products, and byproducts is an essential component. Education, after all, is a quest for lives of meaning, and boys need to participate in this process. What is at stake is not, then, an academic result that can be estimated, predicted, or measured, but the consciousness, the awareness, and the moral commitment of those whose lives have been entrusted to educators, parents, and other concerned citizens.

Further Reading

Giroux, Henry A. *Schooling and the Struggle for Public Life. Democracy's Promise and Education's Challenge.* Boulder, CO: Paradigm Publishers. 2005.

Shapiro, H. Svi. *Losing Heart: The Moral and Spiritual Miseducation of America's Children.* Mahwah, NJ: Lawrence Erlbaum Associates, 2006.

Steinberg, R. Shirley, and Joe L. Kincheloe, eds. *Kinderculture: The Corporate Construction of Childhood*. Boulder, CO: Westview Press. 1998.

Eric D. Torres

White Supremacy

White supremacy is the idea that white people, typically those who have European Protestant backgrounds, are better than and should have dominance over people of color. A similar term, white separatism, describes a devotion to keeping the races separate both socially and physically. Several groups use these ideas as a basis for their existence. These groups can be cataloged under four major categories: the Ku Klux Klan, Neo-Nazism, Christian Identity, and some who identify as skinheads, but are not aligned with the music movement. Young men are a common factor for all racist organizations: recruitment depends heavily on young white males to maintain the groups' ranks.

White supremacy can trace its beginnings in America to the Ku Klux Klan. In 1865, shortly after the Civil War, a group of former Confederate soldiers founded the Klan in Pulaski, Tennessee. Relying on fear tactics and violence, the Klan carried out an on-again/off-again domestic terrorism campaign against Black America and anyone sympathetic to it, a campaign that lasted more than a century. The all-male group shrouded itself in secrecy, donned robes and hoods, and created rituals and symbols not unlike a traditional fraternal organization. In fact, some argue the group was created simply as a diversion for bored young men. Although the Klan is a shadow of itself today, young men still find their way into the fold. The Southern Poverty Law Center, a nonprofit anti-racism organization based in Montgomery, Alabama, reports that as of 2007 there were 155 Klan chapters across the nation.

Neo-Nazis adopted the anti-Semitic propaganda of Adolph Hitler, Nazi Germany's dictator, shortly after World War II. Groups, such as the National Renaissance Party, the American Nazi Party, and the National Alliance, have frequently held militant rallies throughout the United States with young men dressed in Nazi uniforms in an effort to espouse and spread their hatred of the Jewish religion and people. Christian Identity looks to Judeo-Christian scripture to justify its beliefs that white people are God's true chosen people. These beliefs are propagated through Christian Identity churches, such as Aryan Nations, and the men those churches deem as their leaders. Racist skinheads have their roots in 1960s Great Britain, where disaffected working-class youth adopted a uniform as an effort in solidarity. Members are predominantly males who sport Doc Martens boots, suspenders, and sheared heads. Caution: not all skinheads are racists, this is referring to those who appropriate the look of skinheads, not the musical taste and lifestyle. Those who are, typically share beliefs similar to those of Neo-Nazis, with strong anti-Semitic and xenophobic sentiments. The Hammerskins is one of the most prominent groups of racist skinheads.

Of course, young men do not have to join a racist organization to participate in hate-related crimes or speech. Boys may decide to scrawl racist graffiti on a wall or even beat up a minority out of boredom and frustration. The deed is an exercise in thrill-seeking and gives the perpetrators something to boast about. Other troubles in their lives, such as family problems, social rejection, or lack of direction, often help to spur their asocial behavior. Such alienation is exactly what racist groups use to convince recruits to join.

Racist organizations provide a place where young men can find acceptance, purpose, and strength in numbers. Racist ideals are reinforced via group activities, such as rallies, and lifestyle trappings, such as racist music. Raucous concerts featuring hard-driving white power punk bands from the racist Resistance Records label are a particularly common sight in the racist skinhead community. Typically, these concerts are accompanied by violent male-dominated mosh pits. And now white supremacy is simply a click away. The Internet has become a hotbed of activity for racist organizations and a great recruitment tool. Groups that seem scattered and unorganized offline seem unified and organized online. Racist organizations have complete control over their Web site's content and direct access to an unlimited number of prospective members, which by definition would include any white Protestant male with a computer and Internet access.

Further Reading

Dobratz, Betty A., and Stephanie L. Shanks-Meile. *"White Power, White Pride!" The White Separatist Movement in the United States.* New York: Twayne Publishers, 1997.

Holthouse, David, and Mark Potok. Intelligence Report: The Year in Hate [Online March 2008]. Southern Poverty Law Center <http://www.splcenter.org/intel/intelreport/intrep.jsp?iid=44>.

Levin, Jack, and Gordana Rabrenovic. *Why We Hate.* Amherst, NY: Prometheus Books, 2004.

Robert Andrew Dunn

Youth Incarceration

When compared to juveniles of other developed countries, American youth commit higher rates of crime (Nation's Health, 1997). In fact, in a given year, over two million American youth become entangled with the juvenile justice system, and over 100,000 are detained in facilities every day (National Mental Health Association, 2007). Statistics on boys involved in the juvenile justice system are more revealing. They are overrepresented in correctional facilities, are taken into custody more often than girls, and are most often the perpetrators and victims of crime and violence.

American social worker Jane Addams founded the first juvenile court in 1899 in Chicago, Illinois. She, along with the progressive women of Hull House, a community center for the poor, were set with many other social reforms to redirect boys and girls out of a life of crime. They planned for a juvenile court that would act as a "kind and just parent." In many ways the juvenile court was a substitute for parents and acted as a conscientious guardian for wayward boys. In the early twentieth century the number of juvenile courts grew and by 1950 every state had one. Early juvenile court practices were different than the adult courts. They were more informal and flexible, with a judge acting as the offender's advocate who offered no or few procedural protections such as the right to an attorney. In those days, young crime offenders were considered victims of societal problems (such as poverty, broken homes, and so forth). So instead of punishment, boy offenders received warnings or rehabilitation of sorts in an institution, and sometimes to their detriment they were given harsher sentences than what was handed to adults.

The juvenile courts today are more sophisticated and offer boys constitutional protections such as the notice of charges against the offender, right to a lawyer, right to remain silent, and so forth. The juvenile courts now serve to protect and rehabilitate status offenders (i.e., those who commit acts considered illegal for minors such as truancy and curfew violations) and delinquents (i.e., those who commit acts that are crimes for adults), and attend to serious, chronic delinquents who may be violent. Juvenile courts offer intervention, prevention, and youth programs to status offenders and delinquents to lead them away from a life of crime.

Unlike the adult court counterparts, juveniles are *taken into custody* (rather than *arrested*); the prosecutors *petition the court* (instead of *charge with a crime*); the charge is *violation of juvenile/family code* (rather than *crime under a penal code*); the minors go through *adjudication hearings* (whereas adults have a *trial*); delinquents are found with *delinquent conduct* and *adjudicated* (rather than found *guilty*); and instead of *sentencing,* juveniles can expect *disposition.* Thereafter, they can be *committed to a state facility for juveniles,* whereas adults are sent to *jail* or *prison.* Nearly half of juvenile justice cases are informal and most of these are dismissed (Juvenile Justice FYI, 2007). But when a boy is adjudicated, a judge imposes an informal disposition. At that point, the youngster agrees to meet the court requirements outlined in a consent degree. These requirements can range from restitution to mandatory curfew. The boy is then released on a probationary period to fulfill the obligations. The most severe penalty is to spend time in an institution, which can run the gamut from a boot camp style facility to a more secure residential placement. About 28 percent of all adjudications require institutionalization (del Carmen and Trulson, 2006).

Most state laws define juveniles as persons under 18 years old; however, any boy over the age of 15 in Connecticut, New York, and North Carolina is considered an adult and is tried in the respective adult courts when they commit a crime. Ten states define the upper age of jurisdiction at 16, and 37 states and the District of Columbia define that age at 17. Juveniles are taken into custody for crimes that range from curfew violations to aggravated assault and murder, although typical violations are minor; nearly 2.3 million juveniles were arrested in 2003 (U.S. Department of Juvenile Justice, 2004). Data shows that the juvenile crime rate increased steadily from the 1960s and peaked in the mid-1990s, but has since declined (Snyder, 2004). In 1997, for example, 1,700 youth were arrested for murder. In 2003, the figure was nearly half that at 783. Moreover, arrests for rape in 1997 was 3,800, but 2,966 in 2003 (Siegel, Welsh, and Senna, 2006). Federal figures indicate that the number of boys taken into custody decreased 22 percent from 1994 to 2004, and the number of boys arrested for serious violent crimes decreased a welcoming 33 percent (Siegel, Welsh, and Senna, 2006).

According to 2003 federal data, about 484,000 juveniles (under 18) were taken into custody for serious crimes (e.g., homicide, forcible rape, robbery, larceny, and so forth). About 16 percent of these were for violent crimes, and 29 percent for property crimes (Siegel, Welsh, and Senna, 2006). Another 1.2 million were taken into custody for less serious crimes: 87,000 were taken in for running away from home, 137,000 for disorderly conduct, 138,000 for drug abuse, and 95,000 for violating curfew. With numbers associated with juvenile crimes, it is important to note that these often do not represent actual crimes for three reasons: first, some offenders are never caught; second, those that are caught could have committed several offenses, but the most serious crime is the only one recorded; third, some offenders are taken into custody multiple times.

Boys are more delinquent than girls. Adolescent boys are four times more likely to commit a serious violent crime than girls, and they are two times more likely to commit a property crime. Studies of self-reported delinquent acts also show that boys tend to shoplift and hurt others (to the point of needing medical attention) more often than girls. Other studies have found that between 30 to 40 percent of adolescent boys report having committed a serious violent offense by the age of 17 (Elliot, Hatot, and Sirovatka, 2001). In all, about three-quarters of juveniles arrested for illegal behavior are boys (largely from minority groups). Additionally, boys are also more likely to be the victims of juvenile offenses in all categories except sex offenses and kidnapping.

Noteworthy of the juvenile justice system is the issue of racial bias. Perpetual federal data suggest that race may play a factor in how boys are treated in some jurisdictions. As of late, for instance, nearly 28 percent of the juvenile court population is comprised of African American youth despite the fact that African Americans make up only 15 percent of the national population (Siegel, Welsh, and Senna, 2006). Such data impelled Congress in 1992 to amend the Juvenile Justice and Delinquency Prevention Act of 1974, which set forth that nondelinquent boys (i.e., dependent youth victim of neglect) cannot be treated like delinquent boys and that juveniles cannot be detained or confined in facilities that accommodate adult inmates; it also required states to investigate the matter of minority overrepresentation and to ensure that all stages of the system are equitable for all youth. In fact, states that have disproportionate numbers of youth of color in their system must design and institute a plan to reduce it.

Though the disparity represented between youth of color and their white counterparts in the juvenile justice system has significantly declined since the 1980s (e.g., from a six-to-one disparity in 1980 to four-to-one in 2003), youth of color are overrepresented at most stages of the system. The Office of Juvenile Justice and Delinquency Prevention (OJJDP) statistics indicate that the majority (67 percent) of the 2002 delinquency cases involved white youth (1,068,700), while 29 percent was attributed to African American juveniles (473,000). Seemingly these numbers are not prominent, but considering that white youth comprise 78 percent of youth population and African Americans 16 percent, those figures represent a disproportionate number of African American youngsters in the system. To emphasize the matter, statistics indicate that nearly half of all juvenile violence arrests are of African American youth (mostly boys) despite the white youth (about 40 million living in the United States) outnumbering the African American youth (nine million) by 4.5 to 1 (Siegel, Welsh, and Senna, 2006).

As a matter of clarity, local jurisdictions may not witness overrepresentation because state data often reflect the activities in urban and nonurban areas. Consequently, metropolitan cities, which are often comprised of large youth of color populations, may experience such overrepresentation while rural areas may not. That said, OJJDP research suggests that racial/ethnic disparities are more evident at arrest than any other stage of the process, and when such disparities exist in a system, they become more pronounced as the youth pass through it. For instance, African American youth are overrepresented in juvenile arrests for violent crime (nearly 3.5 times that of white youth) and property crime (nearly double). African American youth are also arrested more often for murder, robbery, rape, and assault than their white counterparts, while white youth are arrested more often for arson and alcohol-related violations.

African American youth are more likely to be formally processed, face trial, be detained, and convicted than white youth. Evidence suggests that African American youth are frequently treated more harshly by the justice system than their white counterparts who commit similar offenses. (That white youth are twice as likely to be represented by a private attorney may be of influence because youth with private counsel are less likely to be convicted (Hubner, 2005).) In 2002, African American youth faced detention more often for all offenses (except public order) than the youth of other races, and 1999 data found that youth of color—African American (39 percent), Hispanic (18 percent), Native American (2 percent), and Asian (2 percent) youth—were more likely to be held in custody than their white counterparts (38 percent) (Sickmund, 2004). Despite the numbers, Hispanics are barely overrepresented in the juvenile justice system because of their general population size; the rates of the Hispanic youth becoming entangled in the juvenile justice system are notable. Federal data indicate that the number of Hispanic youth in confinement increased sharply in a 20-year span: in 1977, Hispanic juveniles made up 8 percent of the youth confined, 11 percent in 1985, and 18 percent in 1997. As a whole, they too are subject to racial bias. A Michigan State University study found that Hispanic youth charged with: (a) violent offenses were more than five times as likely as their white counterparts to be incarcerated, and (b) property offenses were nearly twice as likely to be incarcerated. Hispanic youth also tended to stay in custody longer (305 days) than their white (193 days) and African American (254) counterparts.

Clearly, overrepresentation of youth of color in the juvenile justice systems exists. However, amid all of this data on racial bias lies a contentious debate: does racial discrimination exist or do youth of color engage in criminal activity more often than white youth? Some may be inclined to favor one position over the other; however, this delicate issue cannot be easily resolved, considering a myriad of complex factors—such as the decision-makers' perceptions of youth of color, the influence of stereotypes, the number of police officers patrolling a specific geographic areas, and so forth—that meet at the cross-roads of crime and justice.

A variety of reasons explain why boys engage in delinquent behaviors. For some boys, behaving illegally can make them feel important and respected and gives them a false sense of status. Other boys may not have effective problem-solving skills, so they resort to crime to seemingly escape or resolve the conflict in their lives. Many boys may not have positive role models, and the ones they do have use crime to make themselves powerful. The boys see this as an advantage in life and imitate the behaviors of those role models. Some boys simply do not have good families that expose them to civil values or supervise their behaviors, or they live in neighborhoods that reward them for criminal activities. Researchers have noted that violent boys younger than 13 who engage in delinquent behaviors are more likely to commit more crimes, more serious ones, and for longer time periods. Often times they continue their delinquent behavior well into adulthood.

Researchers have identified numerous risk factors during boyhood that can predict violent criminal behavior. These risk factors are established as authentic determinants that work collectively. In other words, not one risk factor can account for a boy becoming a violent delinquent. Instead, multiple risk factors shape their behavior, and the more risk factors in a boy's life, the greater the likelihood that he will later become seriously violent. Conversely, there are protective factors that counter the risk factors. They moderate the risks, which affect the behaviors. Risk and protective factors can be found in four divisions: family, individual, community, and environmental.

In family, risk factors include a lack of parental involvement, a victim of abuse and neglect, and a history of witnessed violence. The protective factors in family would be: strong parental involvement, just discipline, and nurturing parenting. In the individual division, the risk factors might be hyperactivity and restlessness or aggressive behaviors in early boyhood. The protective factors would be giving the boy proper medication, specialized counseling services, and structured, consistent discipline. For the community category, the risk factors might include living in areas where drugs and firearms are readily available; the crime rate is high; and so forth. To moderate those risks, a community might open a police precinct, demolish a crack house to open a public park and playground, and open a boys and girls club to offer the neighborhood youth a place to play and receive positive mentorship. Last, with environment, a risk factor might be exposure to considerable violence by way of TV and video games. The protective factors would be to monitor the amount of TV youth watch and violent video games they play, and/or discuss why violence does not resolve conflict nor is it the way to function in society.

Further Reading

Del Carmen, Rolando, and Trulson, Chad. *Juvenile Justice: The System, Process, and Law*. Belmont, CA: Thomson Wadsworth, 2006.

Hubner, John. *Last Chance in Texas: The Redemption of Criminal Youth*. New York: Random House, 2005.

Elliot, Delbert, Hatot, Deborah, and Sirovatka, Paul. *Youth Violence: A Report of the Surgeon General*. Washington, DC: U.S. Department of Health and Human Services, 2001.

Juvenile Justice FYI. A Typical Juvenile Delinquency Case. Retrieved August 18, 2007, from http://www.lawyershop.com/practice-areas/criminal-law/juvenile-law/cases/.

Hess, Karen, and Drowns, Robert. *Juvenile Justice* (4th ed.). Belmont, CA: Thomson Wadsworth, 2004.

Liss, Steve. *No Place for Children: Voices from Juvenile Detention*. Austin: University of Texas Press, 2005.

Nakaya, Andrea, ed. *Juvenile Crime: Opposing Viewpoints*. Detroit: Thomson Gale, 2005.

Nation's Health. *U.S. Has the Highest Rate of Youth Violence Among Developed Countries, CDC Reports*. Retrieved July 25, 2007, from http://web109.epnet.com/DeliveryPrintSave.asp?tb=1&_ug=sid+FA4EA60E-C91B-4360.

National Mental Health Association. Children with Emotional Disorders in the Juvenile Justice System. Retrieved August 18, 2007, from http://www.nmha.org/children/justjuv/index.cfm.

Prothrow-Stith, Deborah, and Spivak, Howard. *Murder Is No Accident: Understanding and Preventing Youth Violence in America*. San Francisco: Jossey-Bass, 2004.

Sickmund, Melissa. *Juveniles in Corrections. Juvenile Offenders and Victims National Report Series*. Washington, DC: Office of Justice Programs, 2004.

Siegel, Larry, Welsh, Brandon, and Senna, Joseph. *Juvenile Delinquency: Theory, Practice, and Law* (9th ed.). Belmont, CA: Thomson Wadsworth, 2006.

Snyder, Howard. *Juvenile Arrests* 2002. Washington, DC: U.S. Department of Justice, 2004.

David Campos